Natsume's BOOK of FRIENDS

Shojo Beat

Natsume's BOOK of FRIENDS

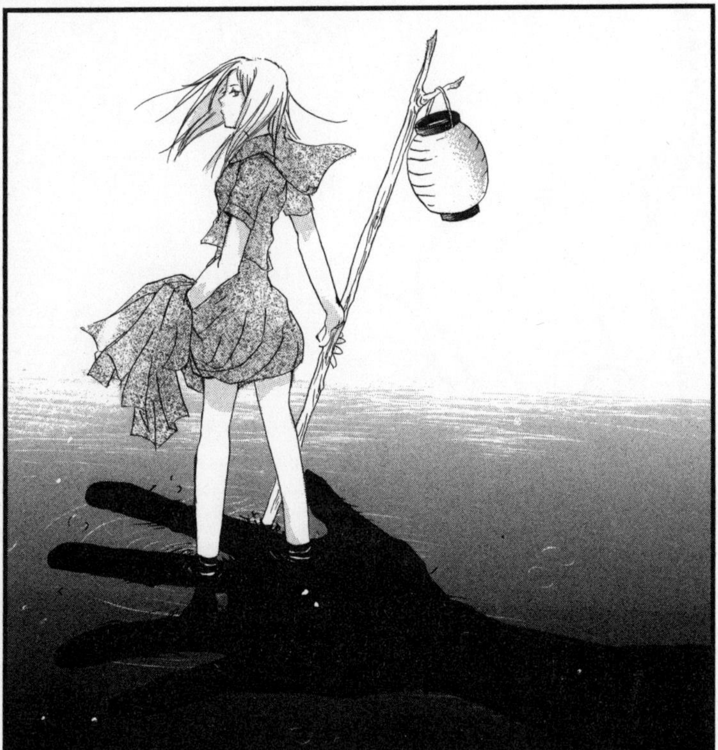

STORY and ART by
Yuki Midorikawa

VOLUME 4

Natsume's BOOK of FRIENDS

VOLUME 4 CONTENTS

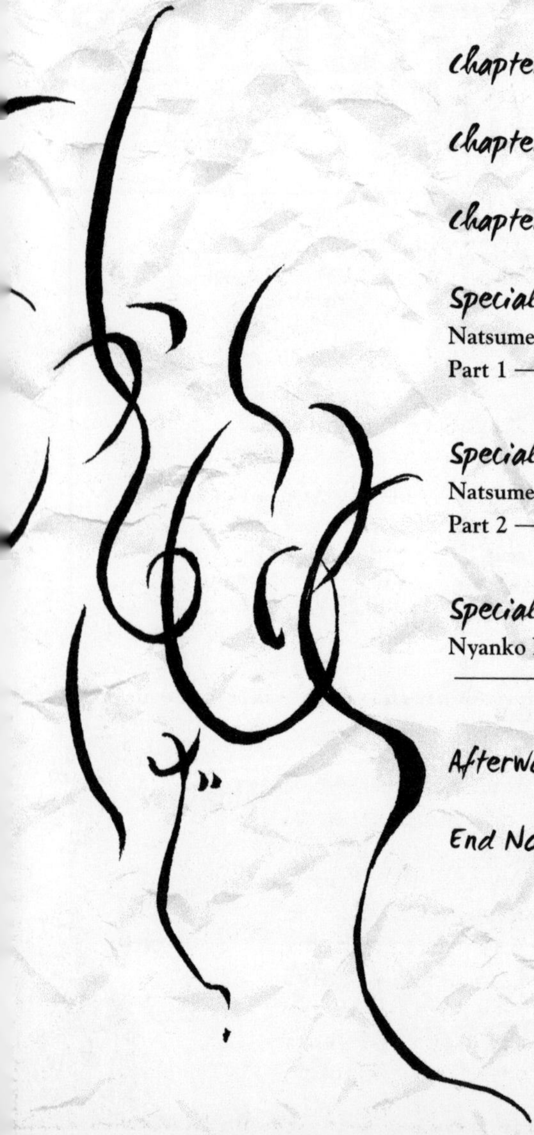

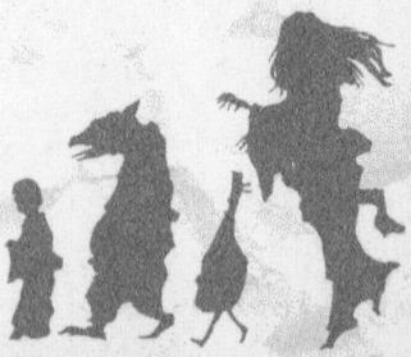

Natsume's BOOK of FRIENDS
CHARACTER GUIDE

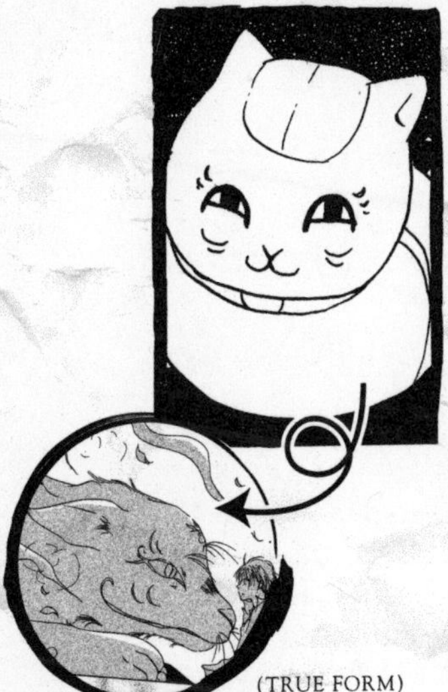
(TRUE FORM)

Nyanko Sensei

Natsume's bodyguard, posing as a cat. His yokai name is Madara. He saves Natsume when danger strikes, but he has a noninterference policy and is thus usually out drinking.

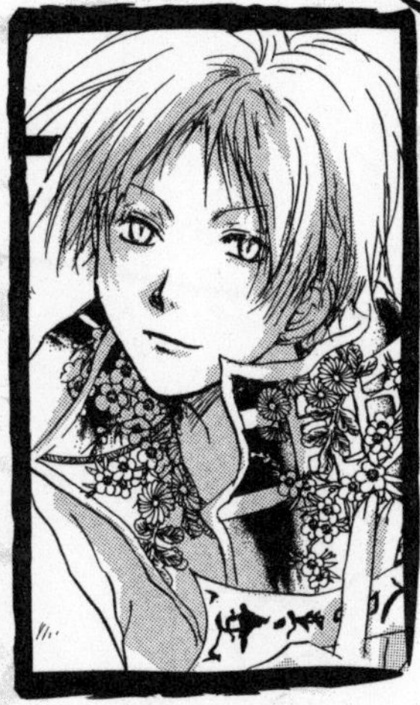

Takashi Natsume

A lonely orphan with the ability to see the supernatural. He inherited the *Book of Friends* from his grandmother and currently lives with the Fujiwaras, to whom he is distantly related. His powers enable him to fend off yokai with his bare hands, just like his grandmother.

THE STORY

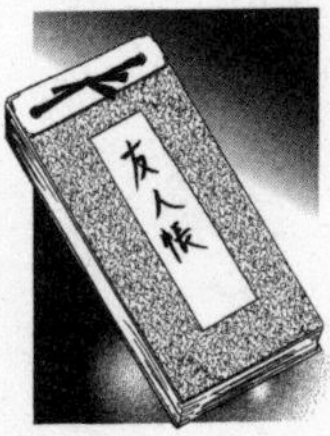
友人帳

Takashi Natsume has a secret sixth sense—he can see supernatural creatures called yokai. And ever since he inherited the *Book of Friends* from his grandmother, the local yokai have been coming after him. Takashi frees Nyanko Sensei from imprisonment and promises he will get the *Book* when Takashi dies. With his new bodyguard, Takashi leads a busy life returning names to yokai.

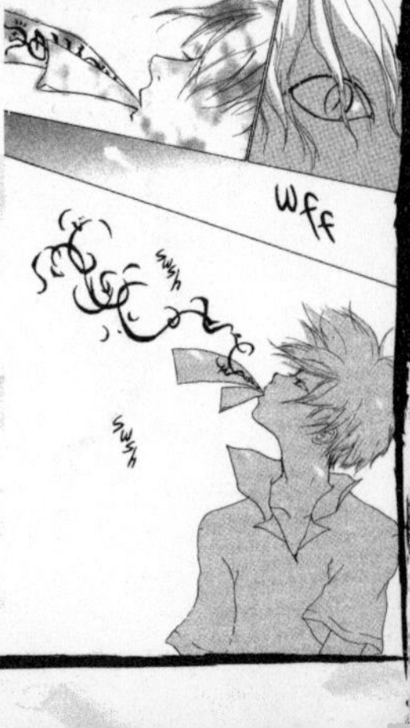
wff
swsh
swsh

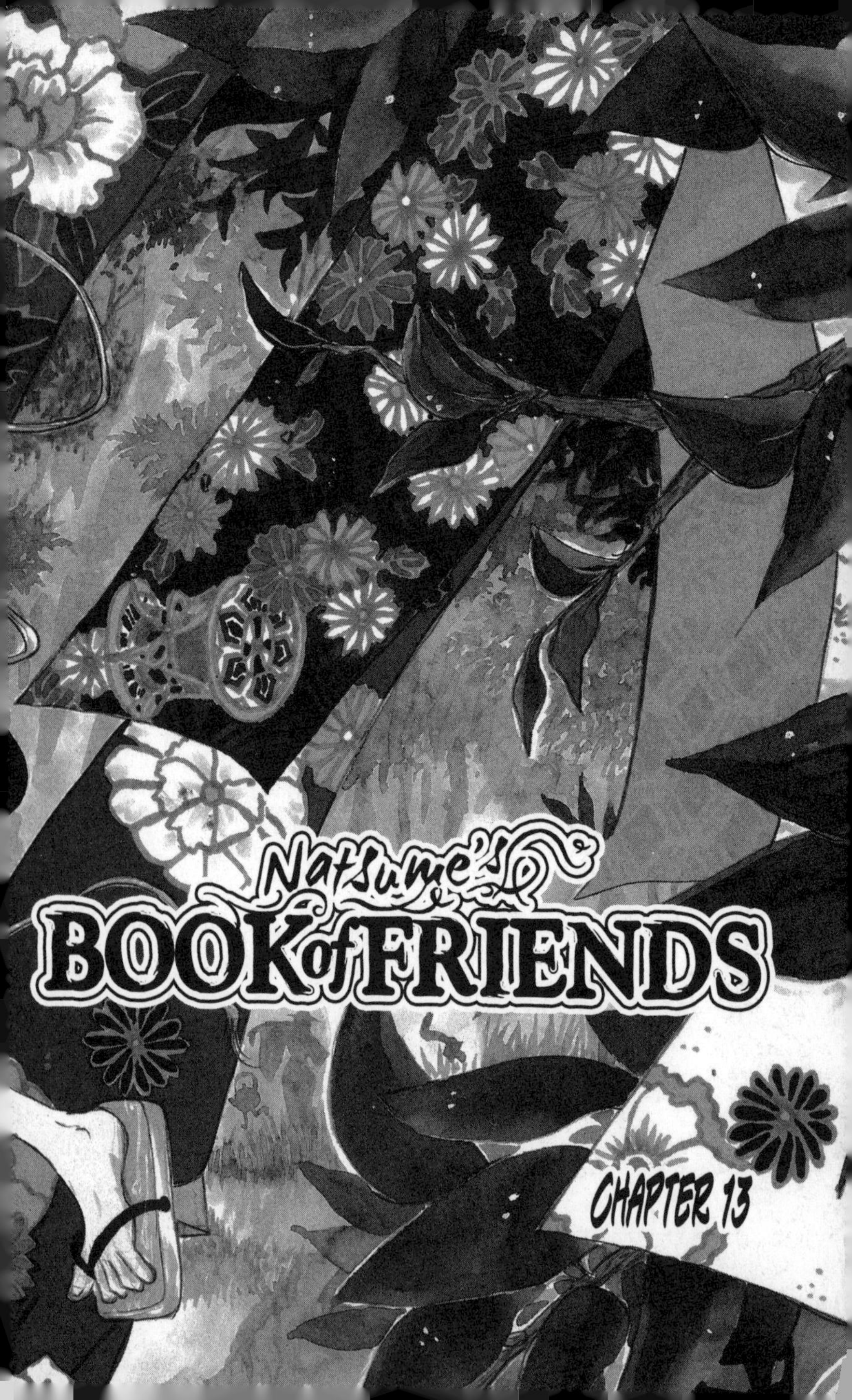
Natsume's
BOOK of FRIENDS
CHAPTER 13

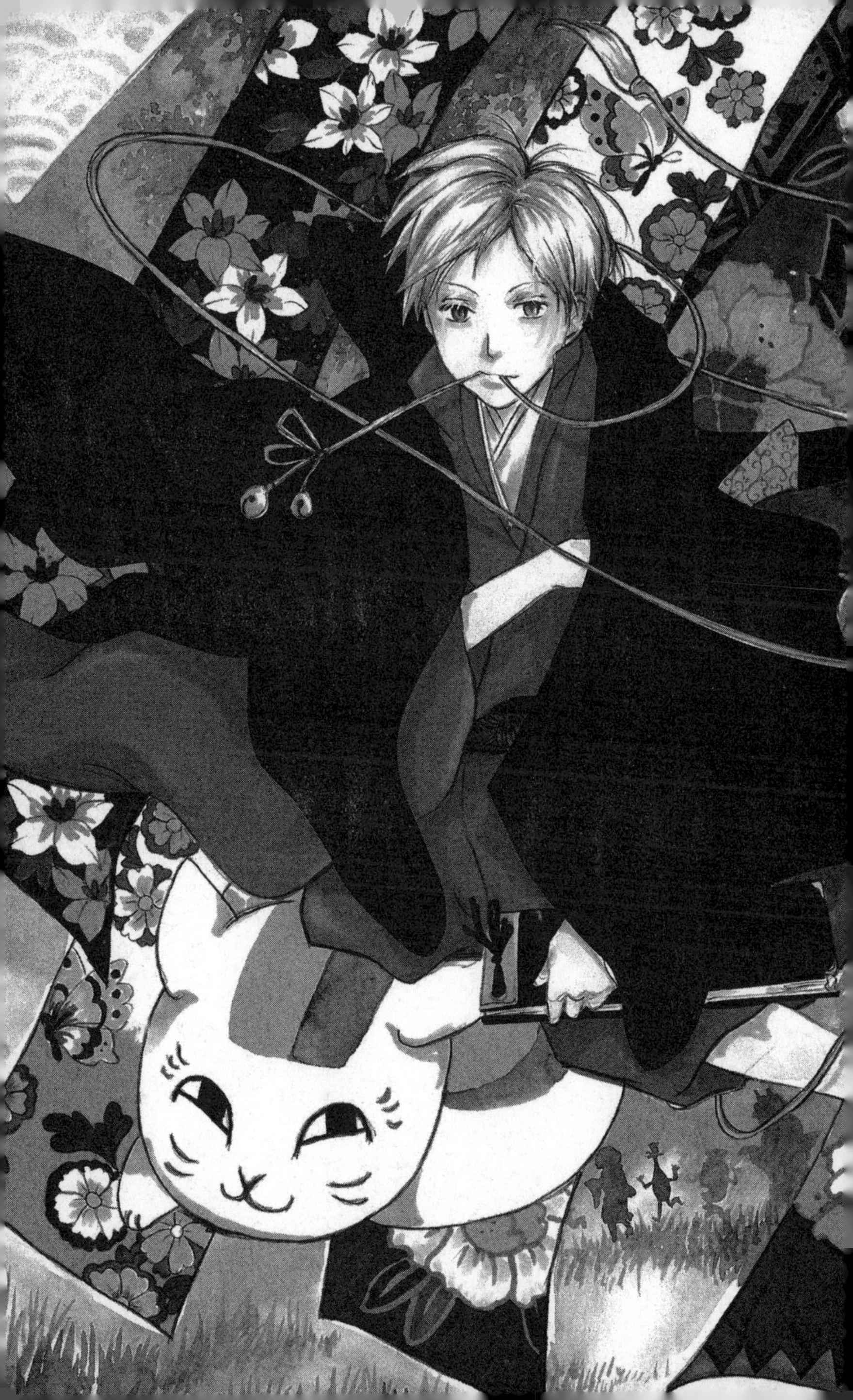

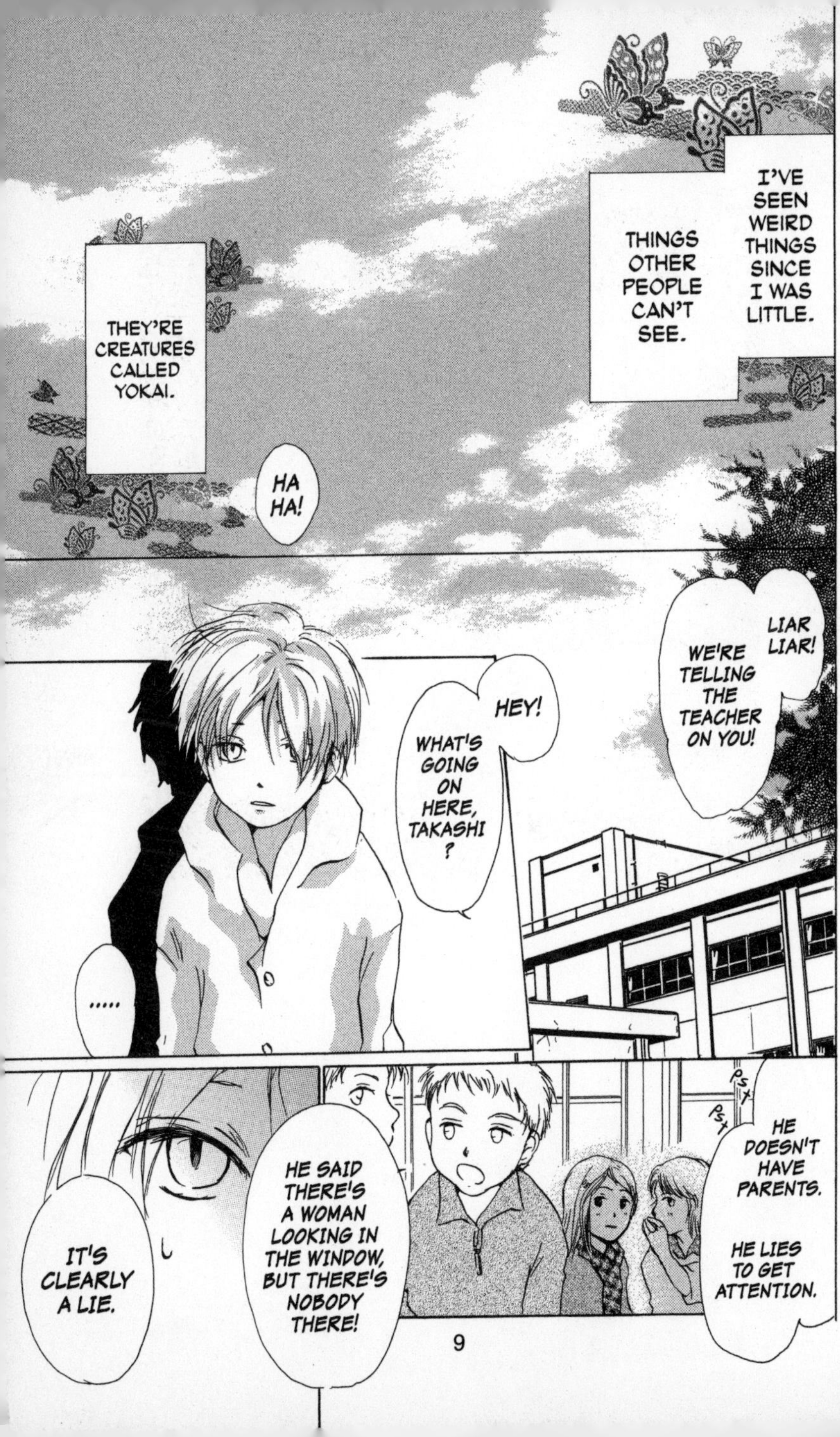
I'VE SEEN WEIRD THINGS SINCE I WAS LITTLE.
THINGS OTHER PEOPLE CAN'T SEE.
THEY'RE CREATURES CALLED YOKAI.
HA HA!
LIAR LIAR!
WE'RE TELLING THE TEACHER ON YOU!
HEY!
WHAT'S GOING ON HERE, TAKASHI?
.....
PST
PST
HE DOESN'T HAVE PARENTS.
HE LIES TO GET ATTENTION.
HE SAID THERE'S A WOMAN LOOKING IN THE WINDOW, BUT THERE'S NOBODY THERE!
IT'S CLEARLY A LIE.

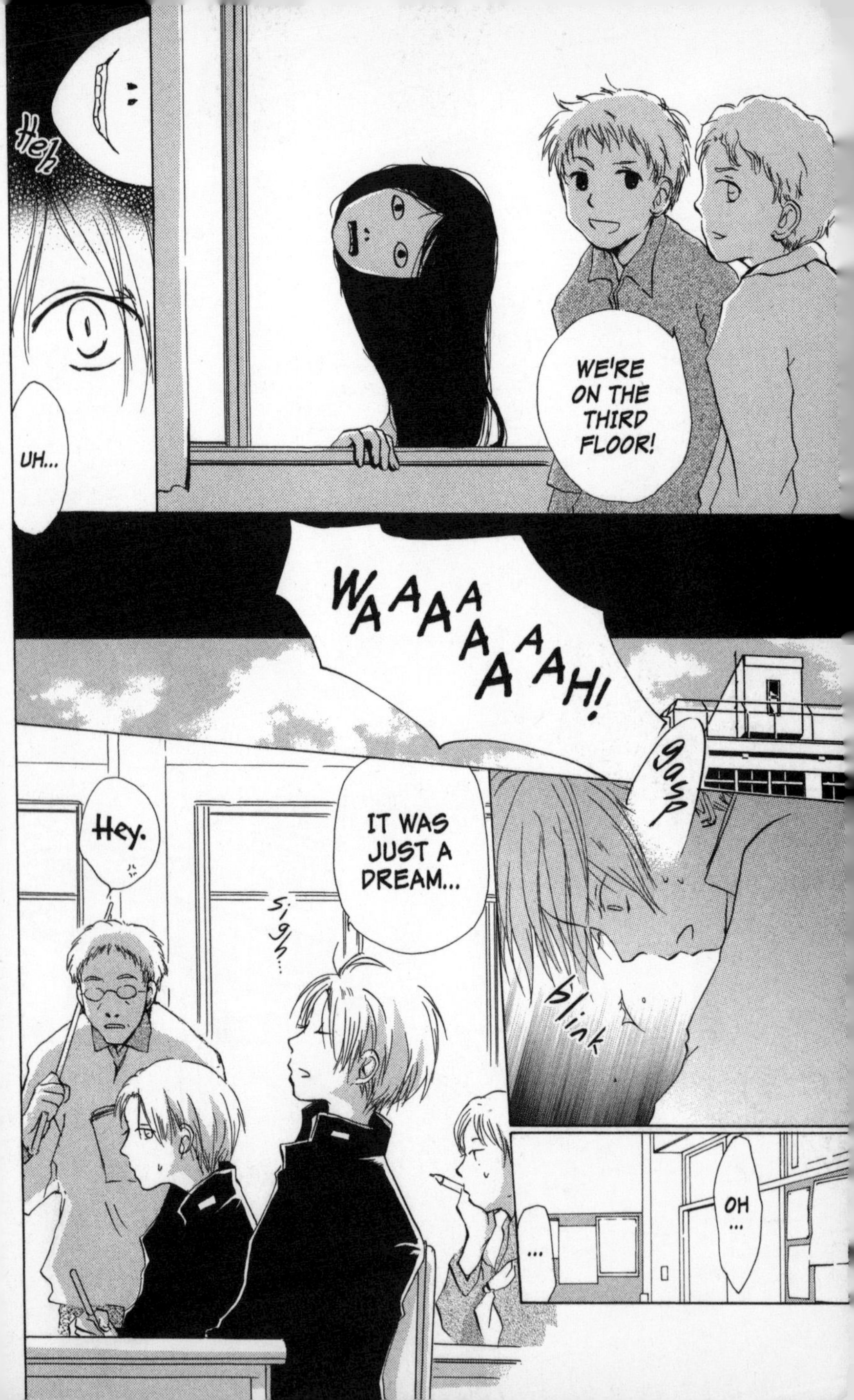
WE'RE ON THE THIRD FLOOR!
Heh
UH...
WAAAAAAAAH!
gasp
blink
OH ...
...
IT WAS JUST A DREAM...
sigh...
Hey.

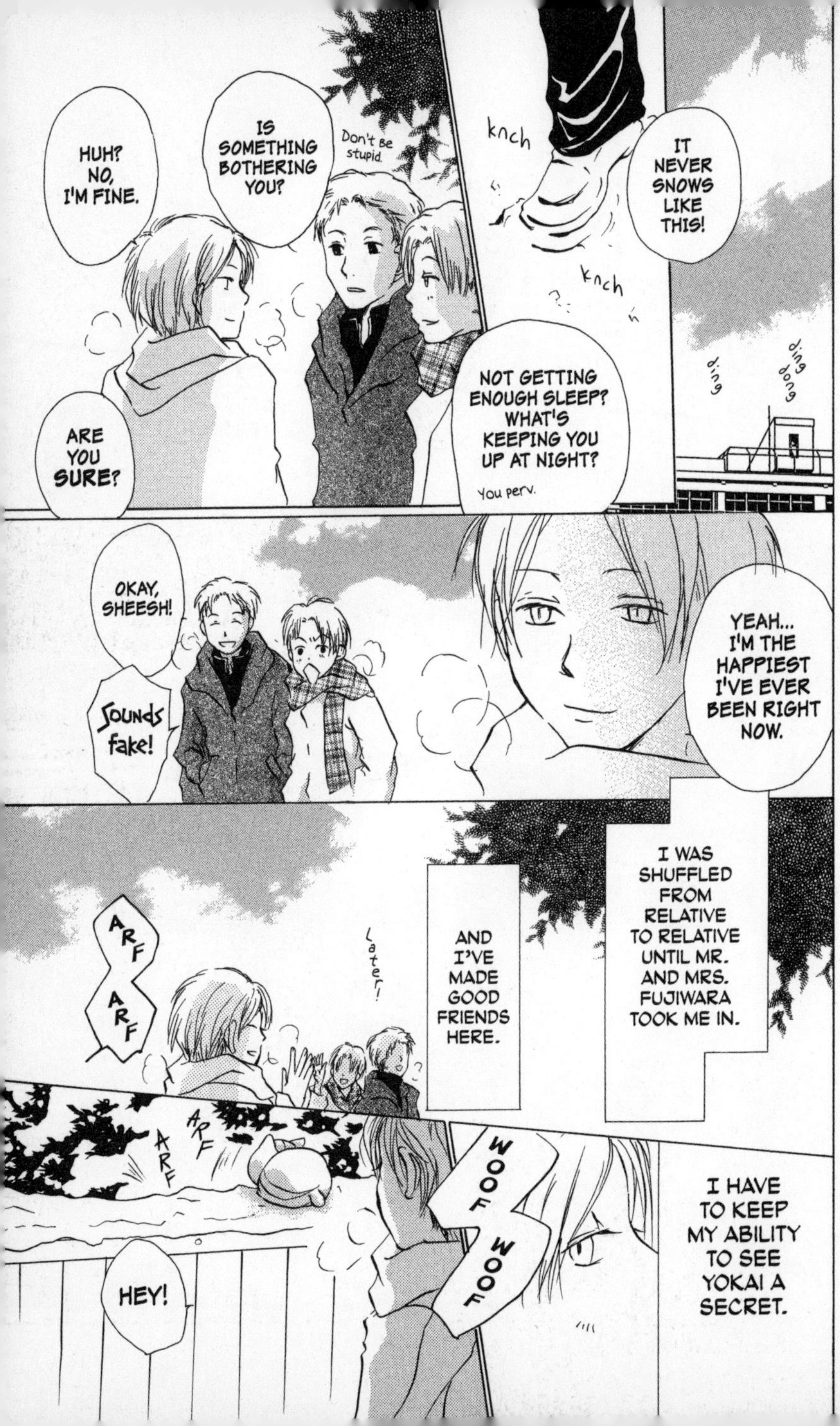
knch
IT NEVER SNOWS LIKE THIS!
knch
ding dong
ding
IS SOMETHING BOTHERING YOU?
Don't be stupid.
HUH? NO, I'M FINE.
NOT GETTING ENOUGH SLEEP? WHAT'S KEEPING YOU UP AT NIGHT?
You perv.
ARE YOU SURE?
YEAH... I'M THE HAPPIEST I'VE EVER BEEN RIGHT NOW.
OKAY, SHEESH!
Sounds fake!
I WAS SHUFFLED FROM RELATIVE TO RELATIVE UNTIL MR. AND MRS. FUJIWARA TOOK ME IN.
AND I'VE MADE GOOD FRIENDS HERE.
Later!
ARF ARF
I HAVE TO KEEP MY ABILITY TO SEE YOKAI A SECRET.
WOOF WOOF
ARF ARF
HEY!

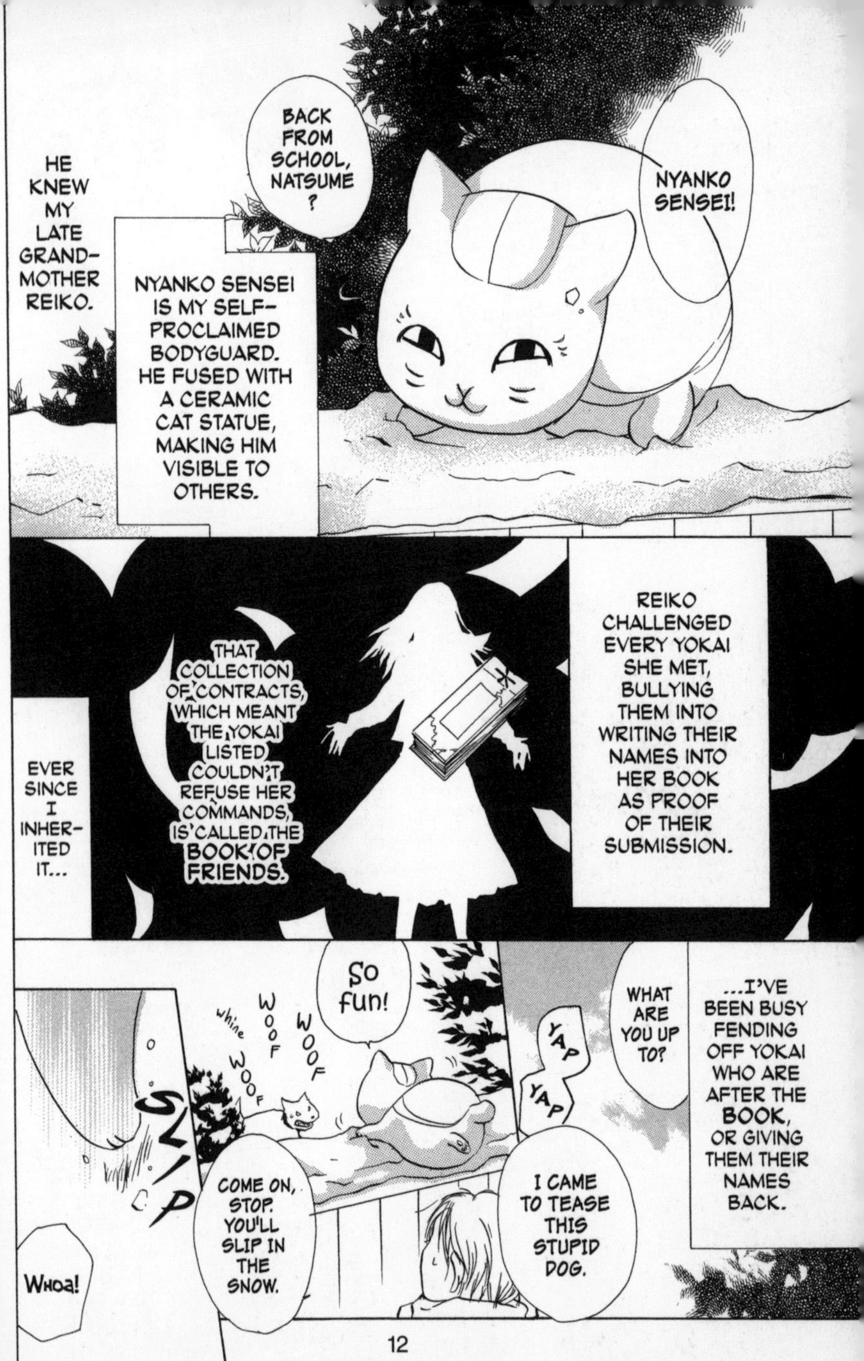
NYANKO SENSEI!
BACK FROM SCHOOL, NATSUME?
NYANKO SENSEI IS MY SELF-PROCLAIMED BODYGUARD. HE FUSED WITH A CERAMIC CAT STATUE, MAKING HIM VISIBLE TO OTHERS.
HE KNEW MY LATE GRANDMOTHER REIKO.
REIKO CHALLENGED EVERY YOKAI SHE MET, BULLYING THEM INTO WRITING THEIR NAMES INTO HER BOOK AS PROOF OF THEIR SUBMISSION.
THAT COLLECTION OF CONTRACTS, WHICH MEANT THE YOKAI LISTED COULDN'T REFUSE HER COMMANDS, IS CALLED THE BOOK OF FRIENDS.
EVER SINCE I INHERITED IT...
...I'VE BEEN BUSY FENDING OFF YOKAI WHO ARE AFTER THE BOOK, OR GIVING THEM THEIR NAMES BACK.
WHAT ARE YOU UP TO?
YAP
YAP
So fun!
WOOF
WOOF
whine
WOOF
I CAME TO TEASE THIS STUPID DOG.
COME ON, STOP. YOU'LL SLIP IN THE SNOW.
SLIP
Whoa!

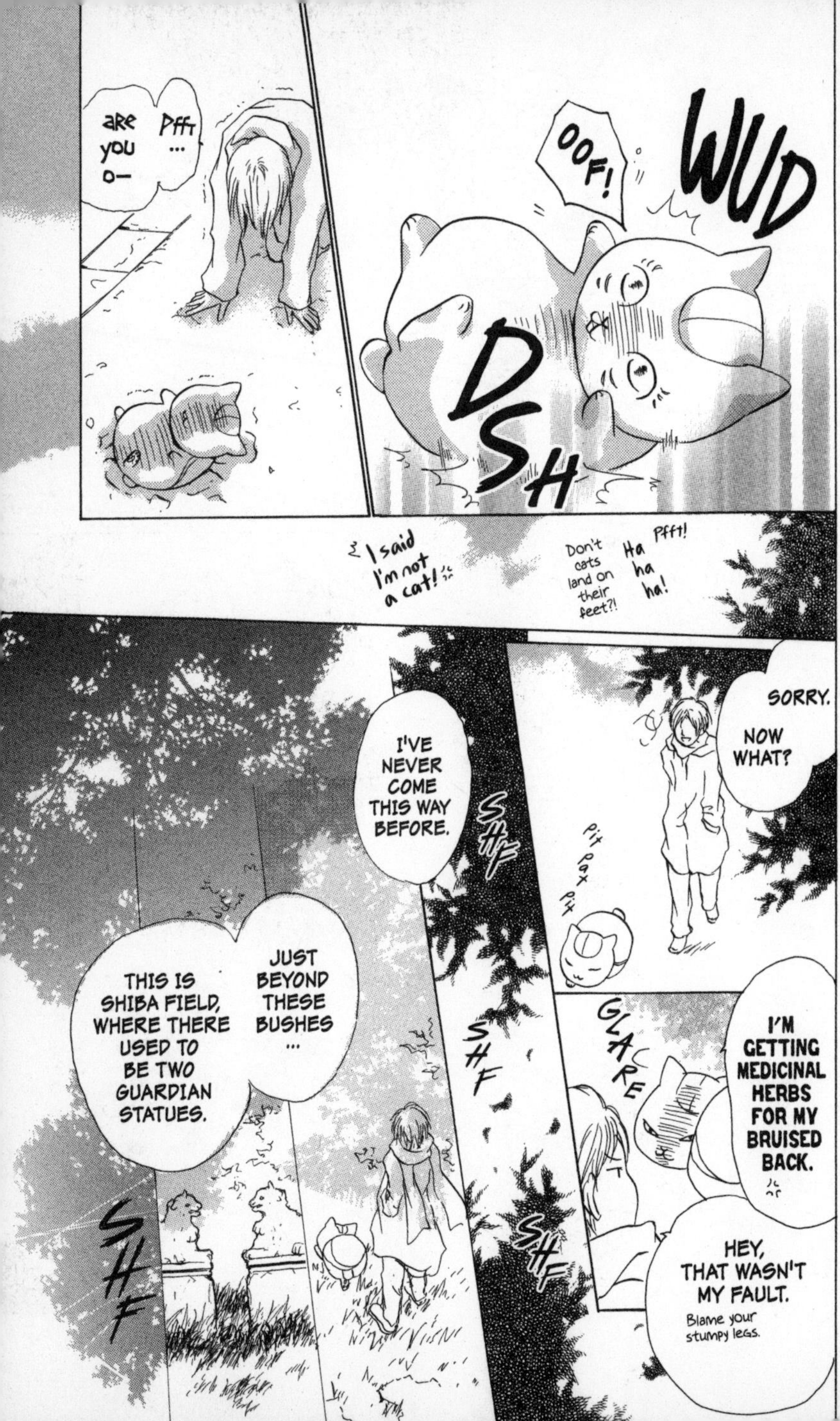
WUD
OOF!
DSH
Pfft...
are you o—
Pfft! Ha ha ha!
Don't cats land on their feet?!
I said I'm not a cat!
SORRY.
NOW WHAT?
Pit pat pit
GLARE
I'M GETTING MEDICINAL HERBS FOR MY BRUISED BACK.
HEY, THAT WASN'T MY FAULT.
Blame your stumpy legs.
SHF
I'VE NEVER COME THIS WAY BEFORE.
SHF
SHF
JUST BEYOND THESE BUSHES...
THIS IS SHIBA FIELD, WHERE THERE USED TO BE TWO GUARDIAN STATUES.
SHF

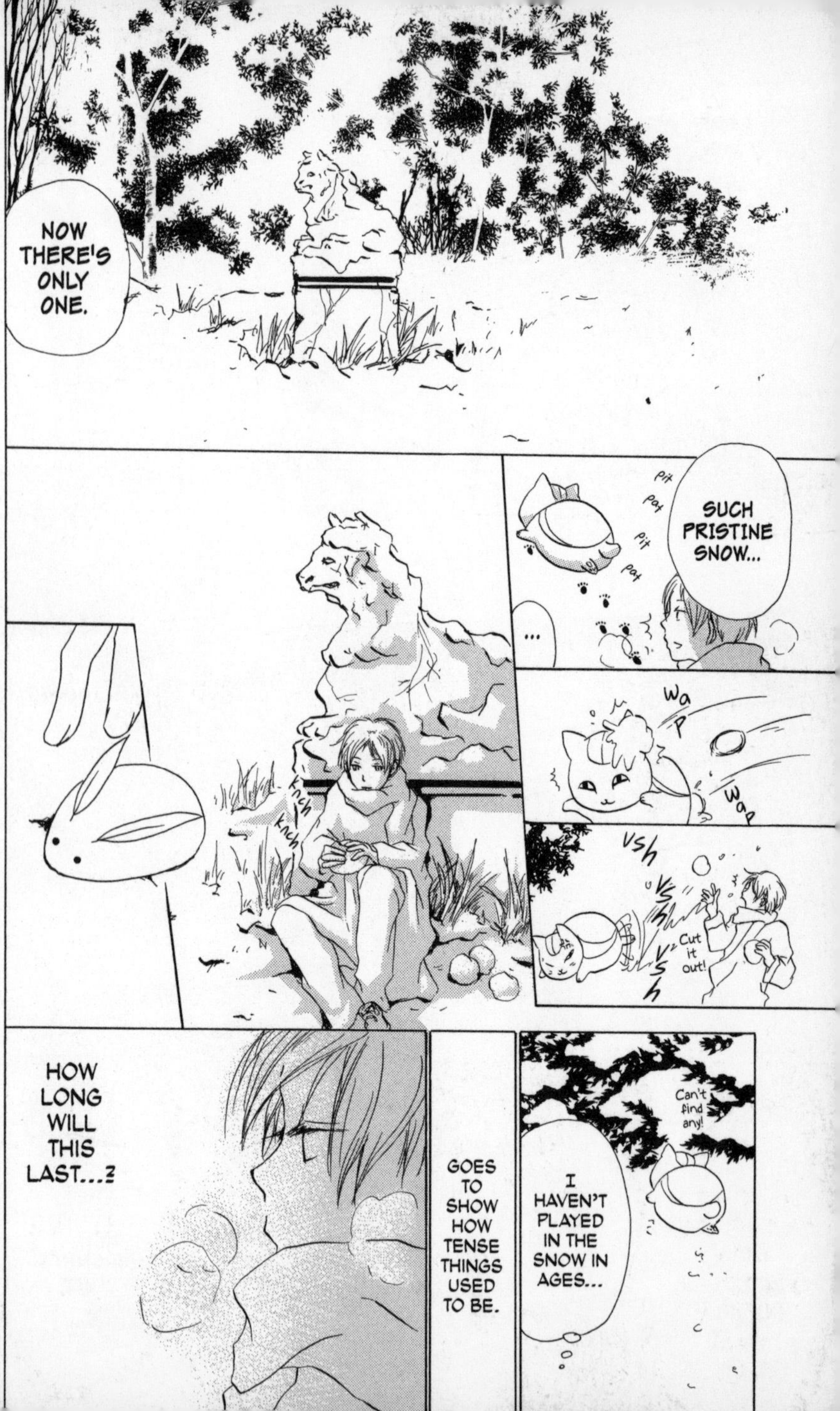
NOW THERE'S ONLY ONE.
pit pat pit pat
SUCH PRISTINE SNOW...
...
wap
wap
vsh vsh vsh
Cut it out!
knch knch
Can't find any!
I HAVEN'T PLAYED IN THE SNOW IN AGES...
GOES TO SHOW HOW TENSE THINGS USED TO BE.
HOW LONG WILL THIS LAST...?

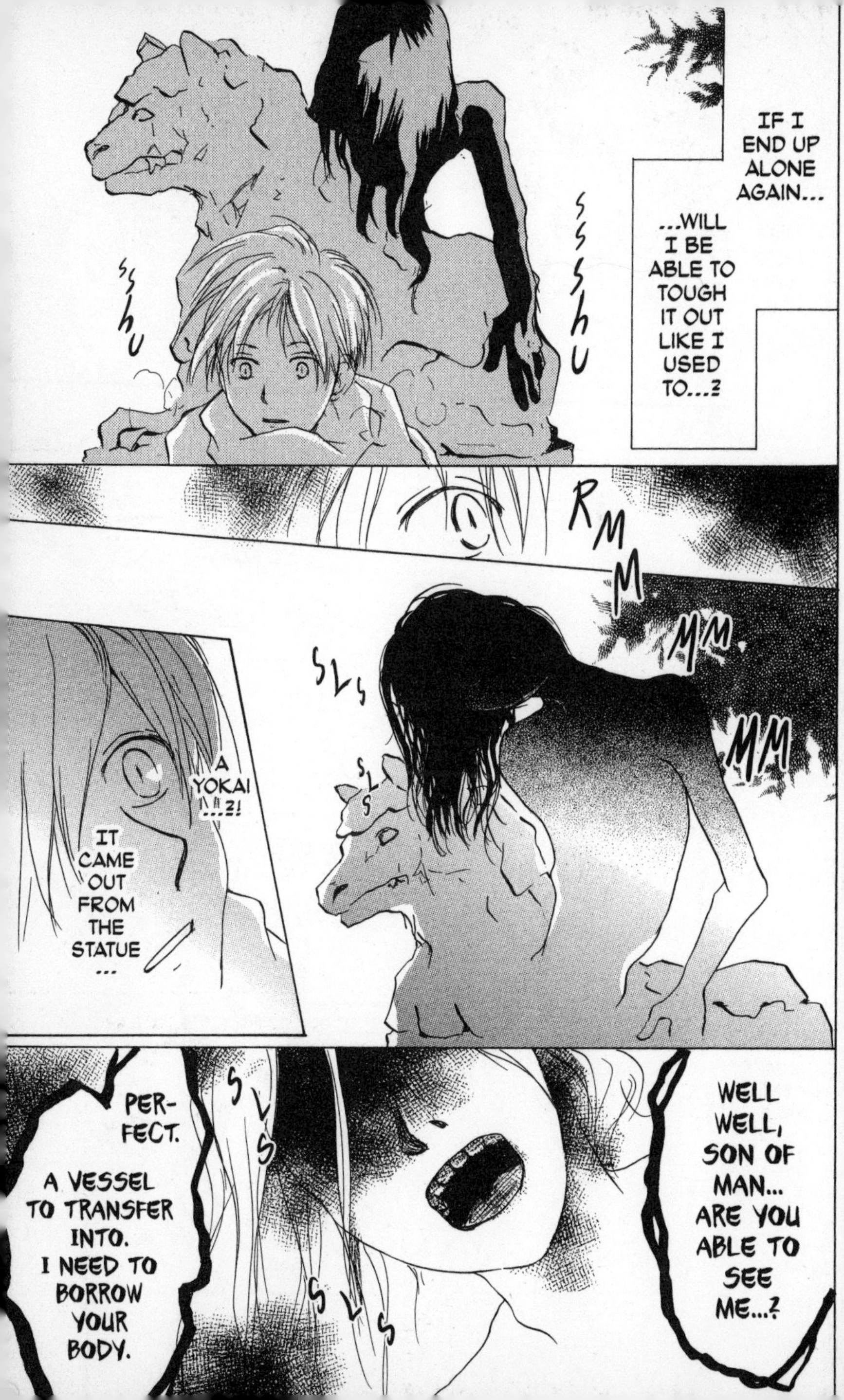
IF I END UP ALONE AGAIN...
...WILL I BE ABLE TO TOUGH IT OUT LIKE I USED TO...?
SSSHU
SSHU
RMMMMMMM
SLS
SLS
A YOKAI...?!
IT CAME OUT FROM THE STATUE...
WELL WELL, SON OF MAN... ARE YOU ABLE TO SEE ME...?
PER-FECT.
A VESSEL TO TRANSFER INTO. I NEED TO BORROW YOUR BODY.
SLS
SLS

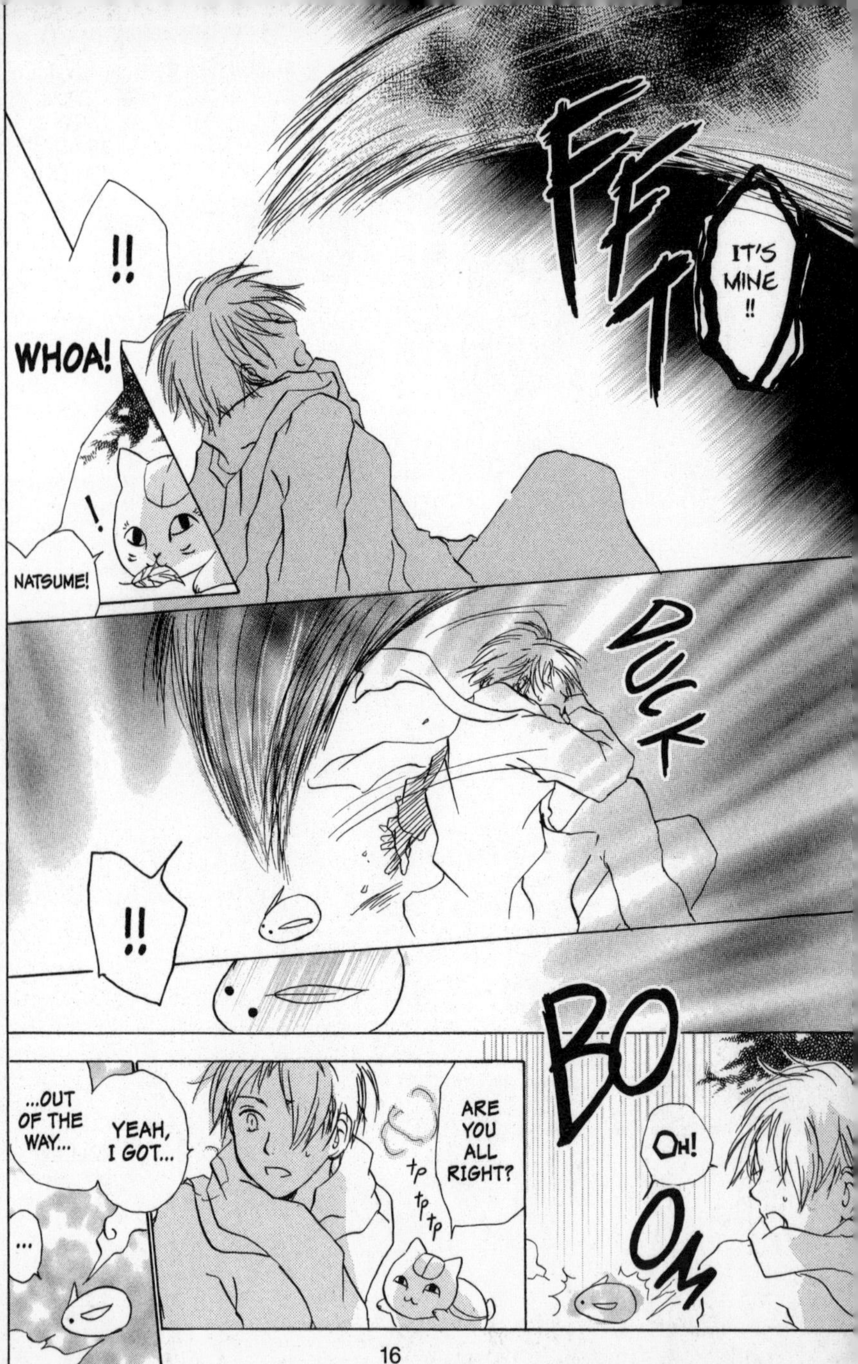
FFT
IT'S MINE!!
!!
WHOA!
!
NATSUME!
DUCK
!!
BOOM
OH!
ARE YOU ALL RIGHT?
tp tp tp tp
YEAH, I GOT...
...OUT OF THE WAY...
...

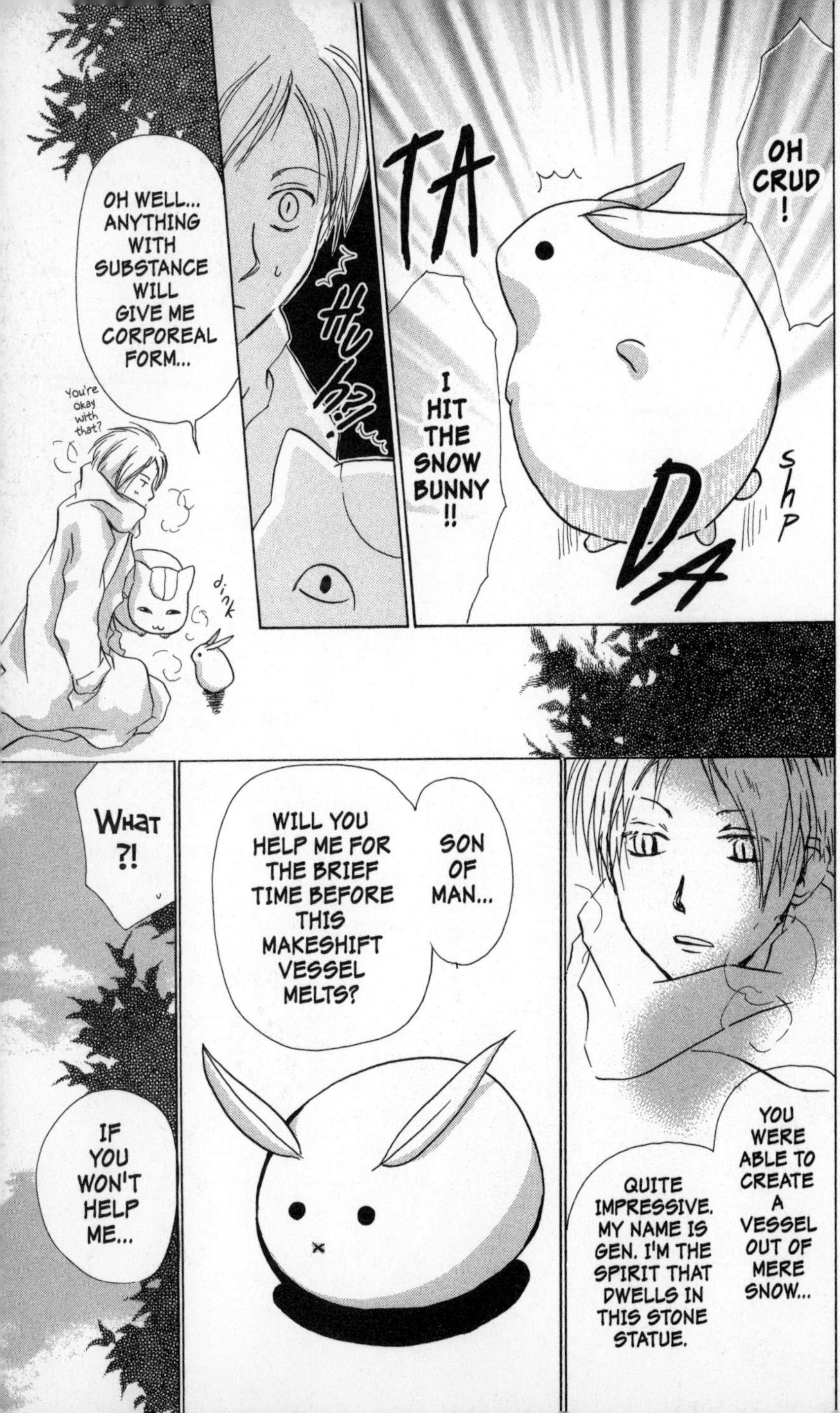

OH CRUD!
TA
I HIT THE SNOW BUNNY!!
shp
DA
HUH?!
OH WELL... ANYTHING WITH SUBSTANCE WILL GIVE ME CORPOREAL FORM...
You're okay with that?
dink
YOU WERE ABLE TO CREATE A VESSEL OUT OF MERE SNOW...
QUITE IMPRESSIVE. MY NAME IS GEN. I'M THE SPIRIT THAT DWELLS IN THIS STONE STATUE.
SON OF MAN...
WILL YOU HELP ME FOR THE BRIEF TIME BEFORE THIS MAKESHIFT VESSEL MELTS?
WHAT?!
IF YOU WON'T HELP ME...

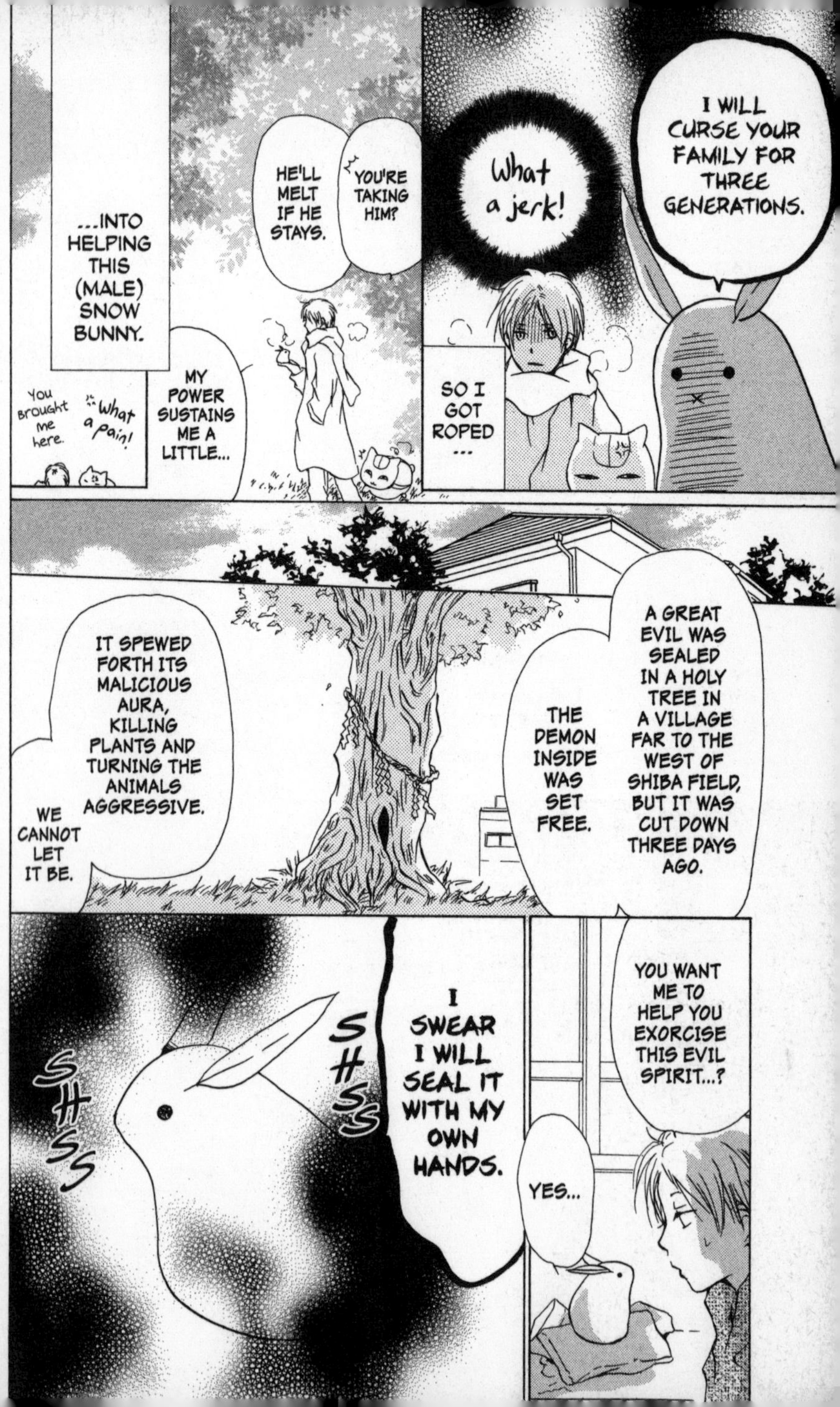
I WILL CURSE YOUR FAMILY FOR THREE GENERATIONS.
What a jerk!
SO I GOT ROPED...
YOU'RE TAKING HIM?
HE'LL MELT IF HE STAYS.
MY POWER SUSTAINS ME A LITTLE...
...INTO HELPING THIS (MALE) SNOW BUNNY.
What a pain!
You brought me here.
A GREAT EVIL WAS SEALED IN A HOLY TREE IN A VILLAGE FAR TO THE WEST OF SHIBA FIELD, BUT IT WAS CUT DOWN THREE DAYS AGO.
THE DEMON INSIDE WAS SET FREE.
IT SPEWED FORTH ITS MALICIOUS AURA, KILLING PLANTS AND TURNING THE ANIMALS AGGRESSIVE.
WE CANNOT LET IT BE.
YOU WANT ME TO HELP YOU EXORCISE THIS EVIL SPIRIT...?
YES...
I SWEAR I WILL SEAL IT WITH MY OWN HANDS.
SHSS
SHSS

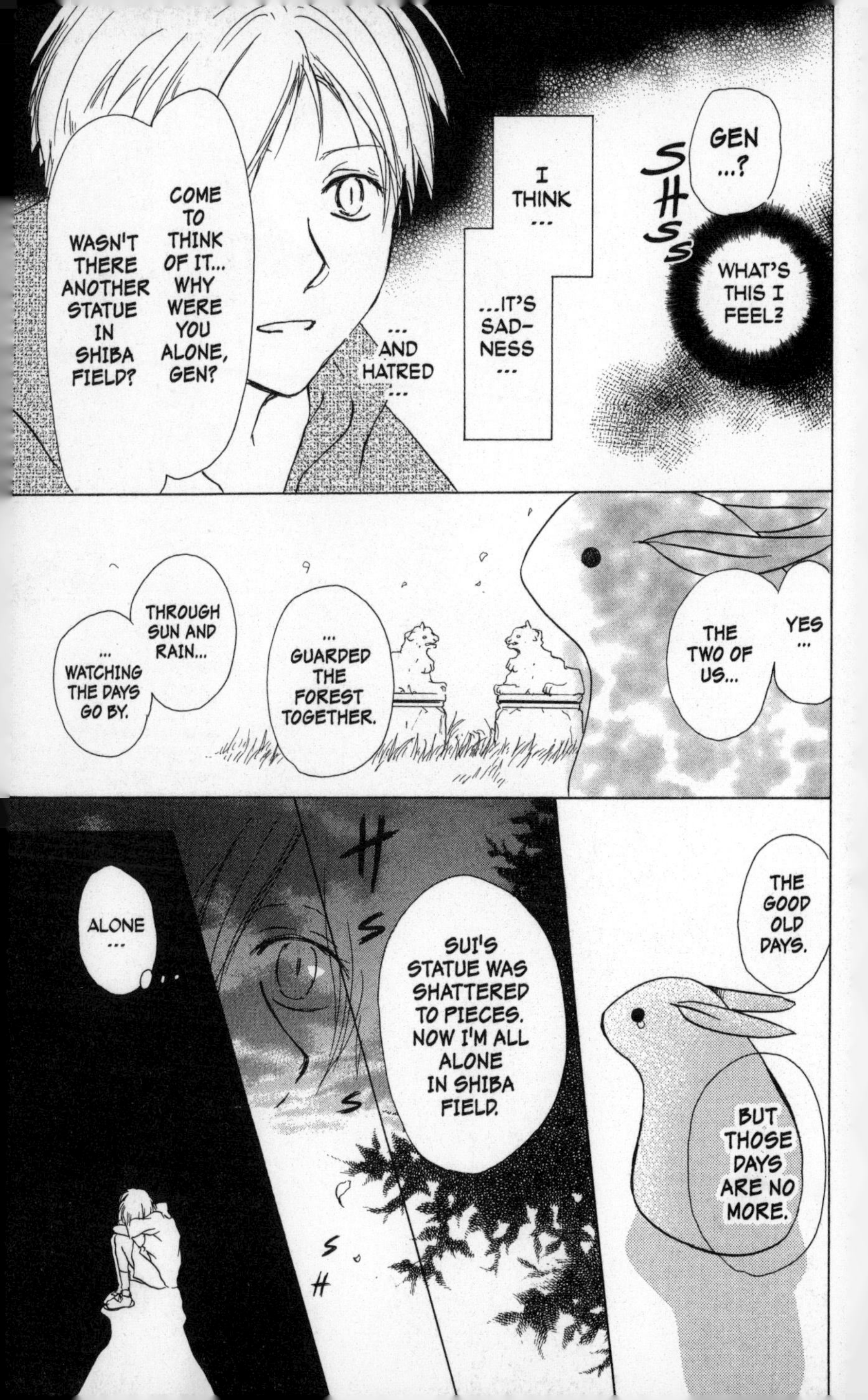
GEN ...?
SHSS
WHAT'S THIS I FEEL?
I THINK ...
...IT'S SADNESS ...
... AND HATRED ...
COME TO THINK OF IT... WHY WERE YOU ALONE, GEN?
WASN'T THERE ANOTHER STATUE IN SHIBA FIELD?
YES ...
THE TWO OF US...
... GUARDED THE FOREST TOGETHER.
THROUGH SUN AND RAIN...
... WATCHING THE DAYS GO BY.
THE GOOD OLD DAYS.
BUT THOSE DAYS ARE NO MORE.
SUI'S STATUE WAS SHATTERED TO PIECES. NOW I'M ALL ALONE IN SHIBA FIELD.
ALONE ...
...

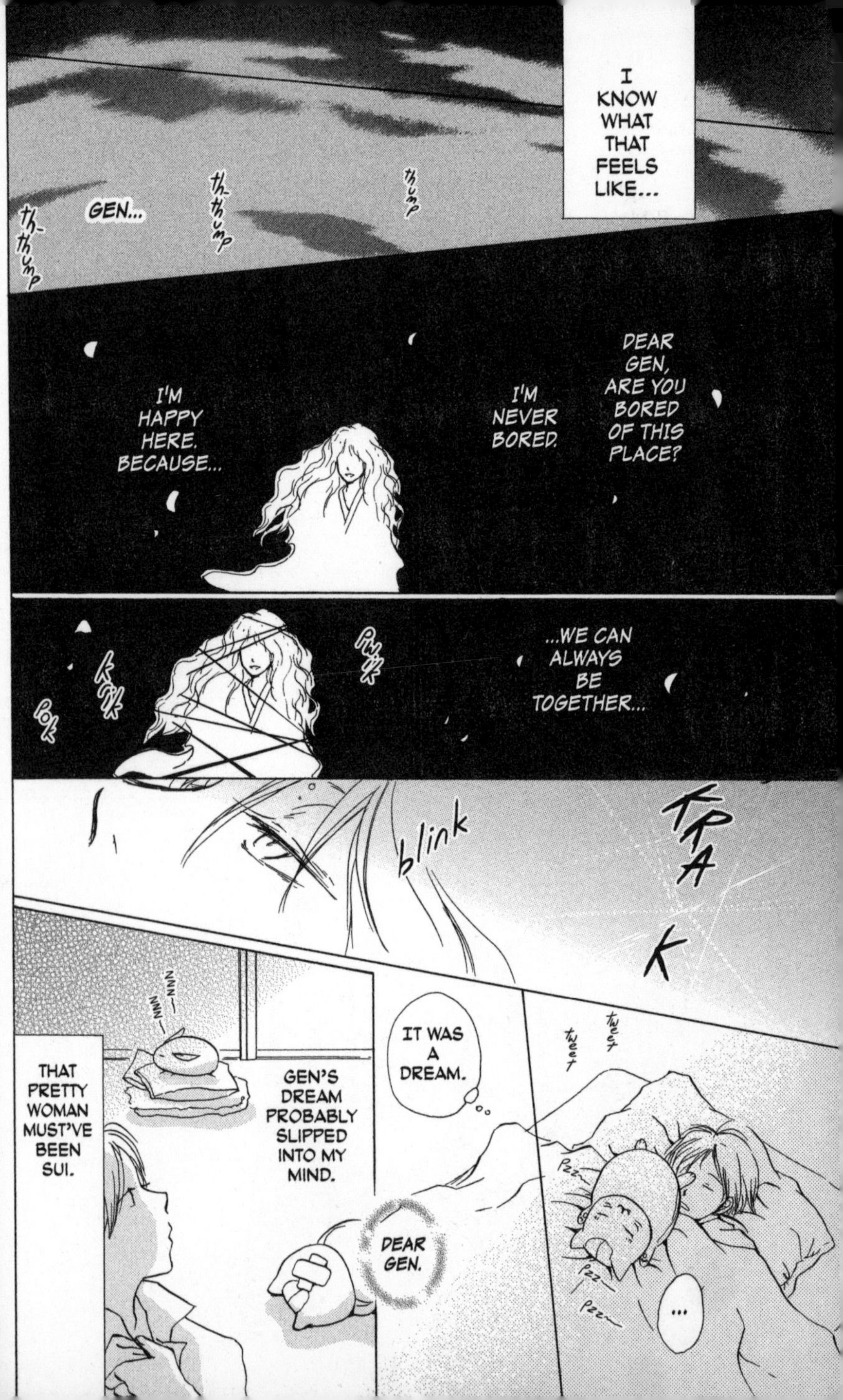
I KNOW WHAT THAT FEELS LIKE...
thump
th-thump
GEN...
th-thump
DEAR GEN, ARE YOU BORED OF THIS PLACE?
I'M NEVER BORED.
I'M HAPPY HERE. BECAUSE...
...WE CAN ALWAYS BE TOGETHER...
Pwik
krik
Pok
KRAK
blink
tweet
tweet
Pzz
Pzz
Pzz
...
IT WAS A DREAM.
GEN'S DREAM PROBABLY SLIPPED INTO MY MIND.
DEAR GEN.
THAT PRETTY WOMAN MUST'VE BEEN SUI.

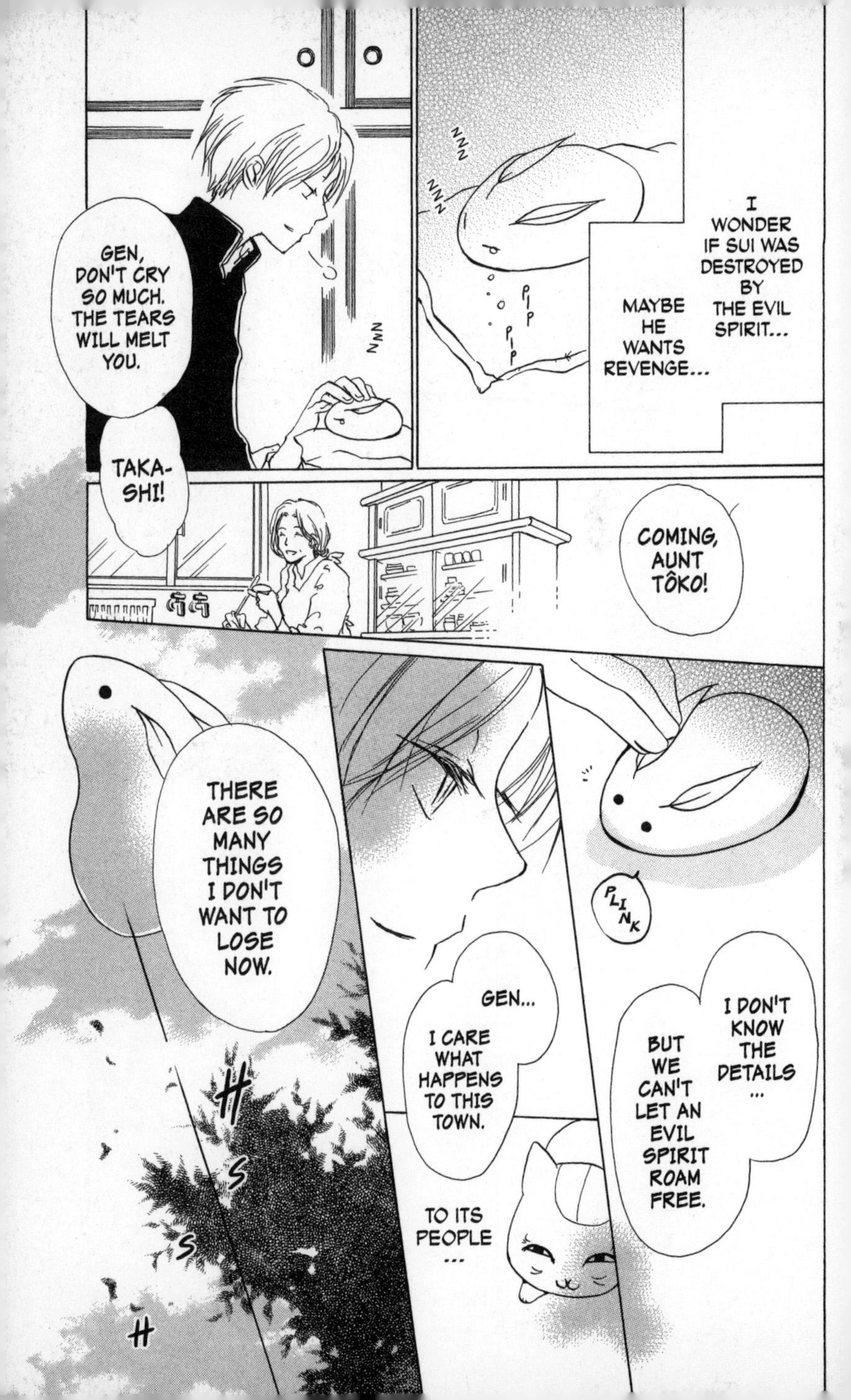
ZZZ
ZZZ
PIP PIP
I WONDER IF SUI WAS DESTROYED BY THE EVIL SPIRIT...
MAYBE HE WANTS REVENGE...
GEN, DON'T CRY SO MUCH. THE TEARS WILL MELT YOU.
ZZZ
TAKA-SHI!
COMING, AUNT TÔKO!
PLINK
I DON'T KNOW THE DETAILS...
BUT WE CAN'T LET AN EVIL SPIRIT ROAM FREE.
GEN...
I CARE WHAT HAPPENS TO THIS TOWN.
TO ITS PEOPLE...
THERE ARE SO MANY THINGS I DON'T WANT TO LOSE NOW.
HSSH

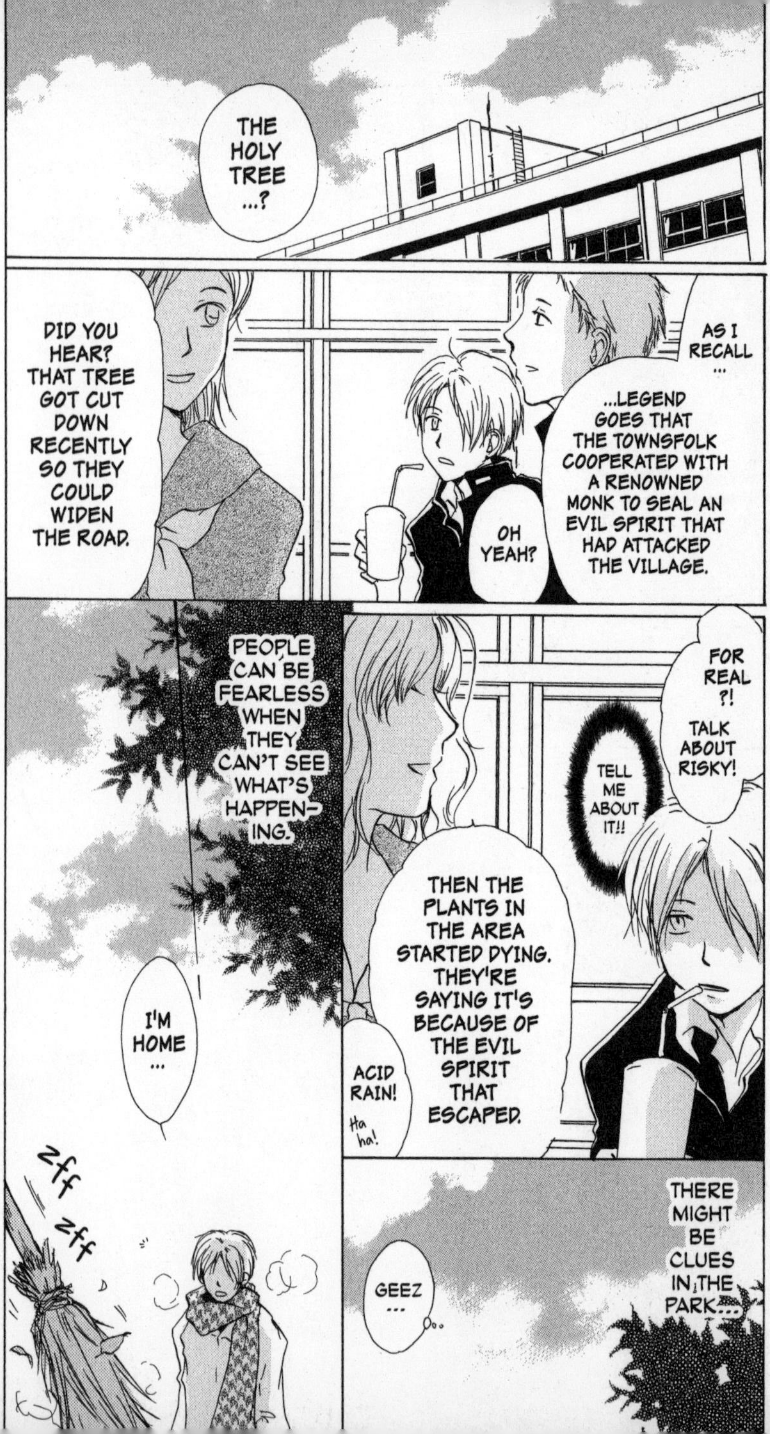
THE HOLY TREE ...?
AS I RECALL ...
...LEGEND GOES THAT THE TOWNSFOLK COOPERATED WITH A RENOWNED MONK TO SEAL AN EVIL SPIRIT THAT HAD ATTACKED THE VILLAGE.
DID YOU HEAR? THAT TREE GOT CUT DOWN RECENTLY SO THEY COULD WIDEN THE ROAD.
OH YEAH?
FOR REAL ?!
TALK ABOUT RISKY!
TELL ME ABOUT IT!!
THEN THE PLANTS IN THE AREA STARTED DYING. THEY'RE SAYING IT'S BECAUSE OF THE EVIL SPIRIT THAT ESCAPED.
ACID RAIN!
Ha ha!
THERE MIGHT BE CLUES IN THE PARK...
GEEZ ...
PEOPLE CAN BE FEARLESS WHEN THEY CAN'T SEE WHAT'S HAPPEN-ING.
I'M HOME ...
zff
zff

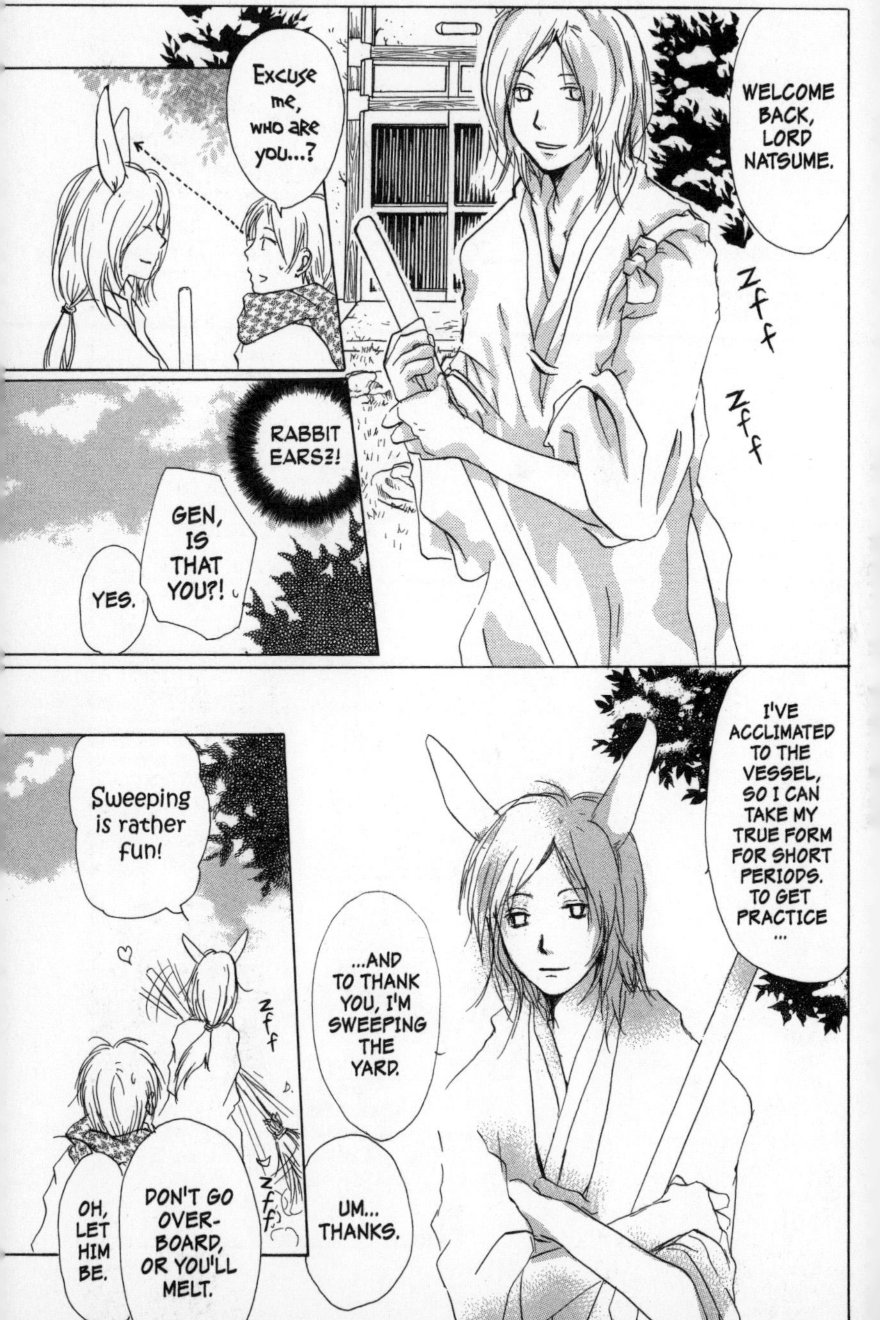
WELCOME BACK, LORD NATSUME.
Zff
Zff
Excuse me, who are you...?
RABBIT EARS?!
GEN, IS THAT YOU?!
YES.
I'VE ACCLIMATED TO THE VESSEL, SO I CAN TAKE MY TRUE FORM FOR SHORT PERIODS. TO GET PRACTICE ...
...AND TO THANK YOU, I'M SWEEPING THE YARD.
UM... THANKS.
Sweeping is rather fun!
Zff
Zff
DON'T GO OVERBOARD, OR YOU'LL MELT.
OH, LET HIM BE.

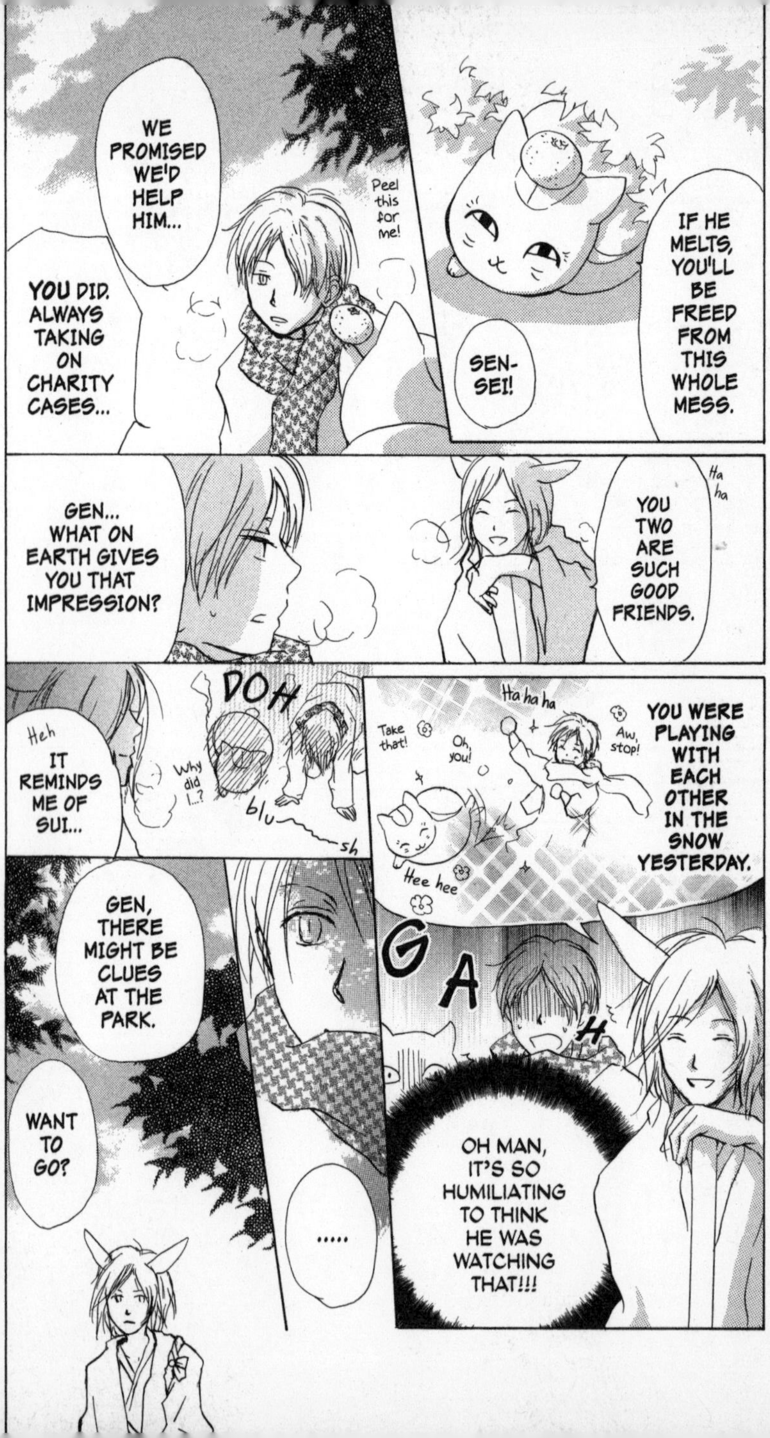
IF HE MELTS, YOU'LL BE FREED FROM THIS WHOLE MESS.
SEN-SEI!
Peel this for me!
WE PROMISED WE'D HELP HIM...
YOU DID. ALWAYS TAKING ON CHARITY CASES...
Ha ha
YOU TWO ARE SUCH GOOD FRIENDS.
GEN... WHAT ON EARTH GIVES YOU THAT IMPRESSION?
YOU WERE PLAYING WITH EACH OTHER IN THE SNOW YESTERDAY.
Aw, stop!
Ha ha ha
Oh, you!
Take that!
Hee hee
DOH
Why did I...?
blush
Heh
IT REMINDS ME OF SUI...
GAH
OH MAN, IT'S SO HUMILIATING TO THINK HE WAS WATCHING THAT!!!
GEN, THERE MIGHT BE CLUES AT THE PARK.
WANT TO GO?
.....

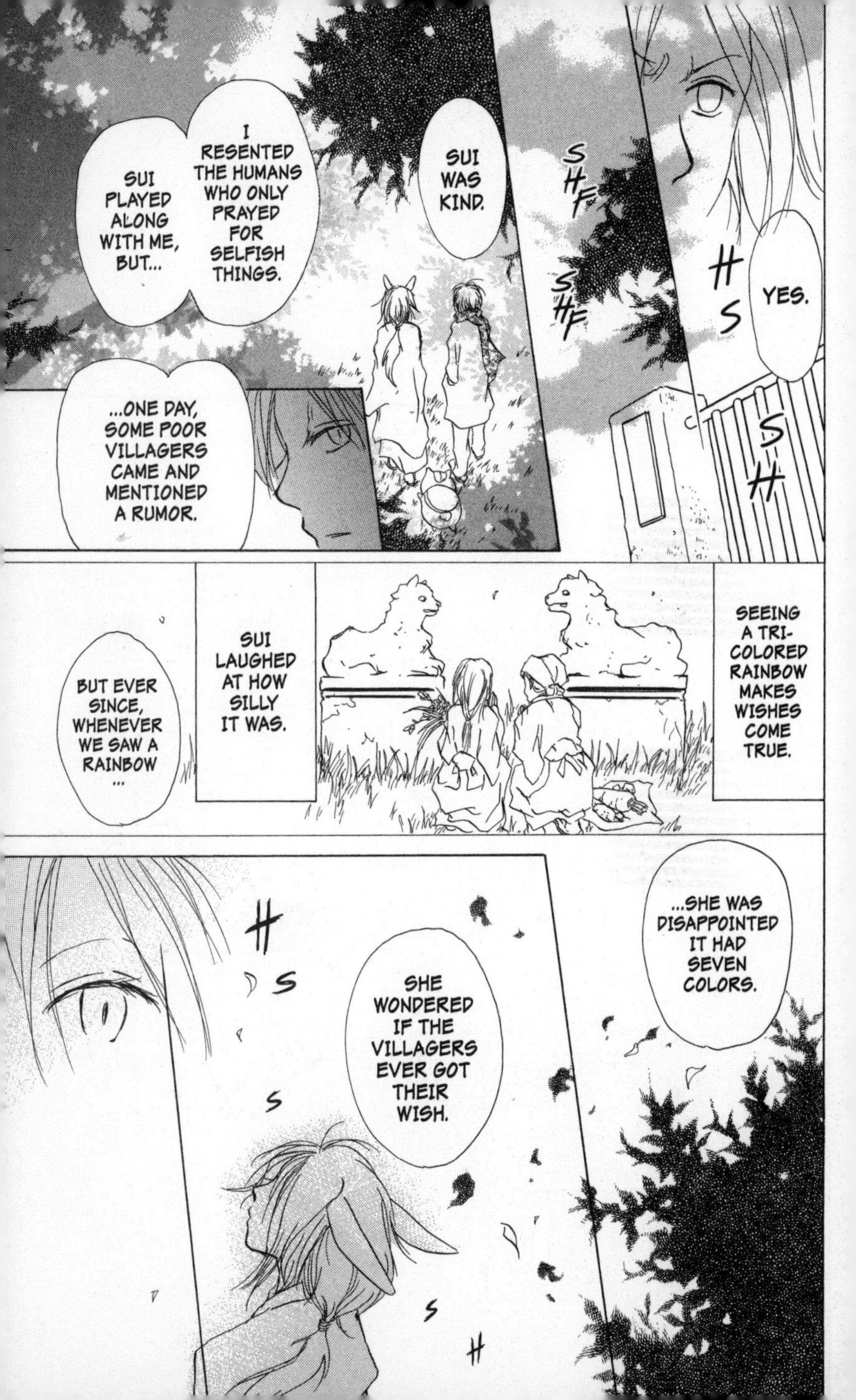
HS
YES.
SH
SHF
SHF
SUI WAS KIND.
I RESENTED THE HUMANS WHO ONLY PRAYED FOR SELFISH THINGS.
SUI PLAYED ALONG WITH ME, BUT...
...ONE DAY, SOME POOR VILLAGERS CAME AND MENTIONED A RUMOR.
SEEING A TRI-COLORED RAINBOW MAKES WISHES COME TRUE.
SUI LAUGHED AT HOW SILLY IT WAS.
BUT EVER SINCE, WHENEVER WE SAW A RAINBOW ...
...SHE WAS DISAPPOINTED IT HAD SEVEN COLORS.
SHE WONDERED IF THE VILLAGERS EVER GOT THEIR WISH.
HS
S
SH

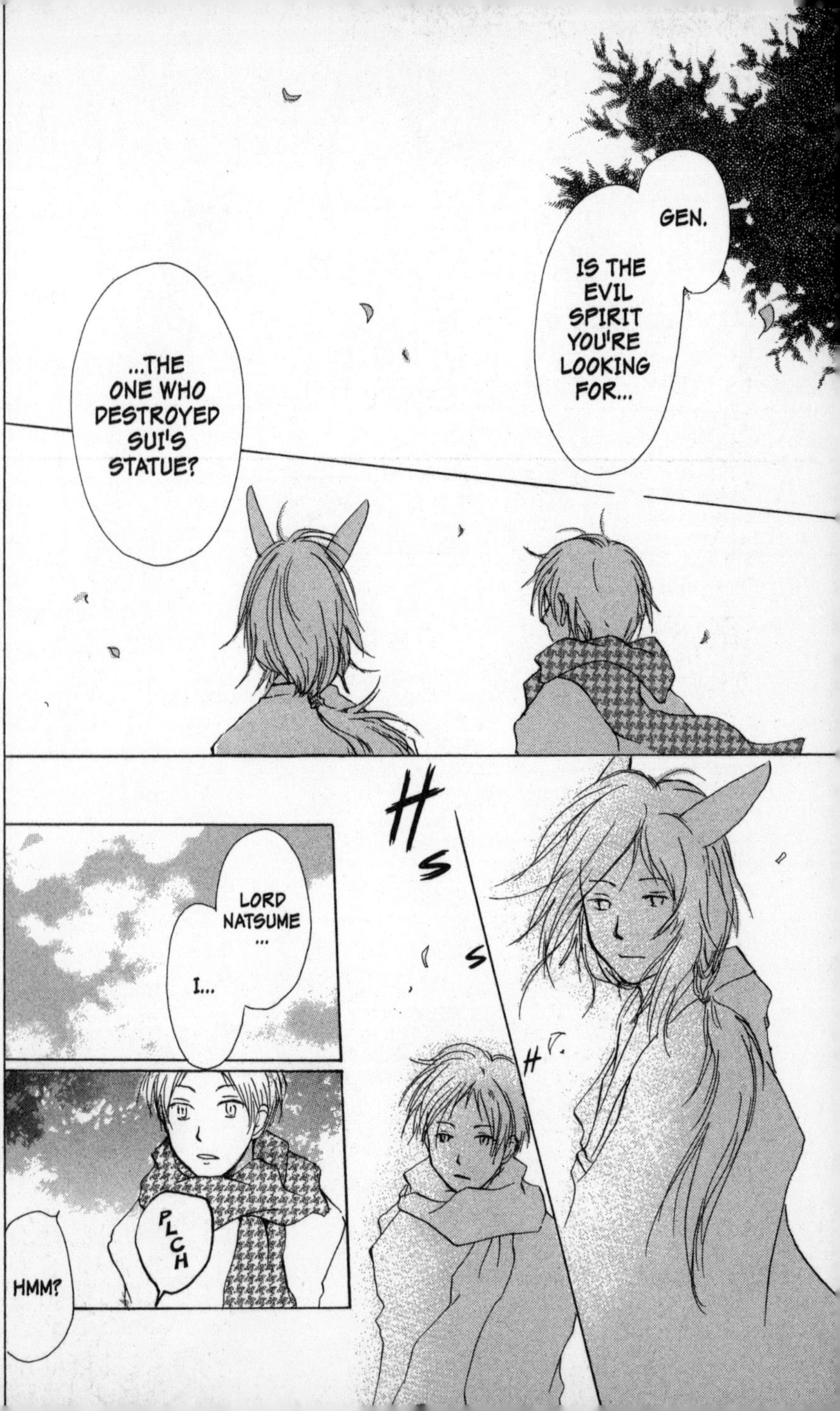
GEN.
IS THE EVIL SPIRIT YOU'RE LOOKING FOR...
...THE ONE WHO DESTROYED SUI'S STATUE?
HSS
H
LORD NATSUME...
I...
PLCH
HMM?

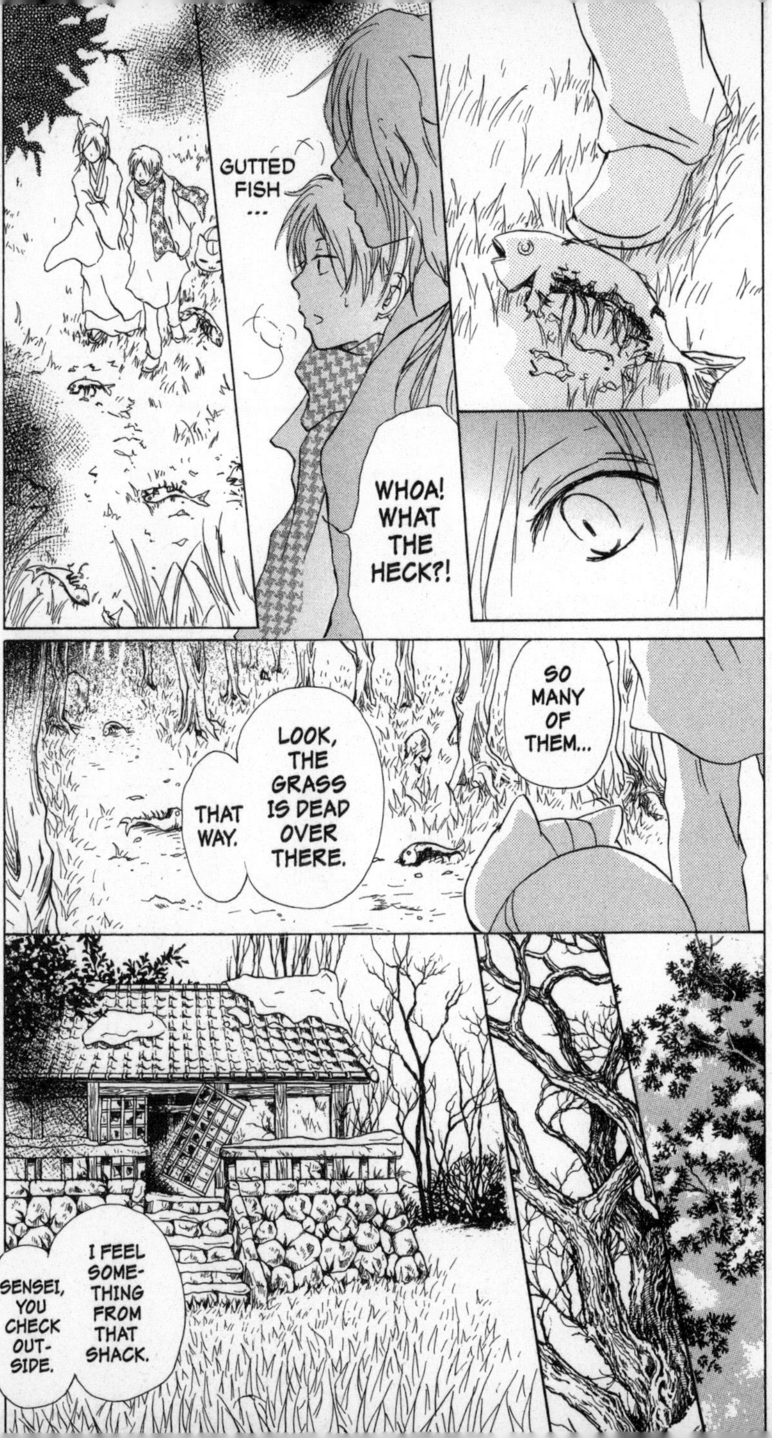
WHOA! WHAT THE HECK?!
GUTTED FISH ...
SO MANY OF THEM...
LOOK, THE GRASS IS DEAD OVER THERE.
THAT WAY.
I FEEL SOME-THING FROM THAT SHACK.
SENSEI, YOU CHECK OUT-SIDE.

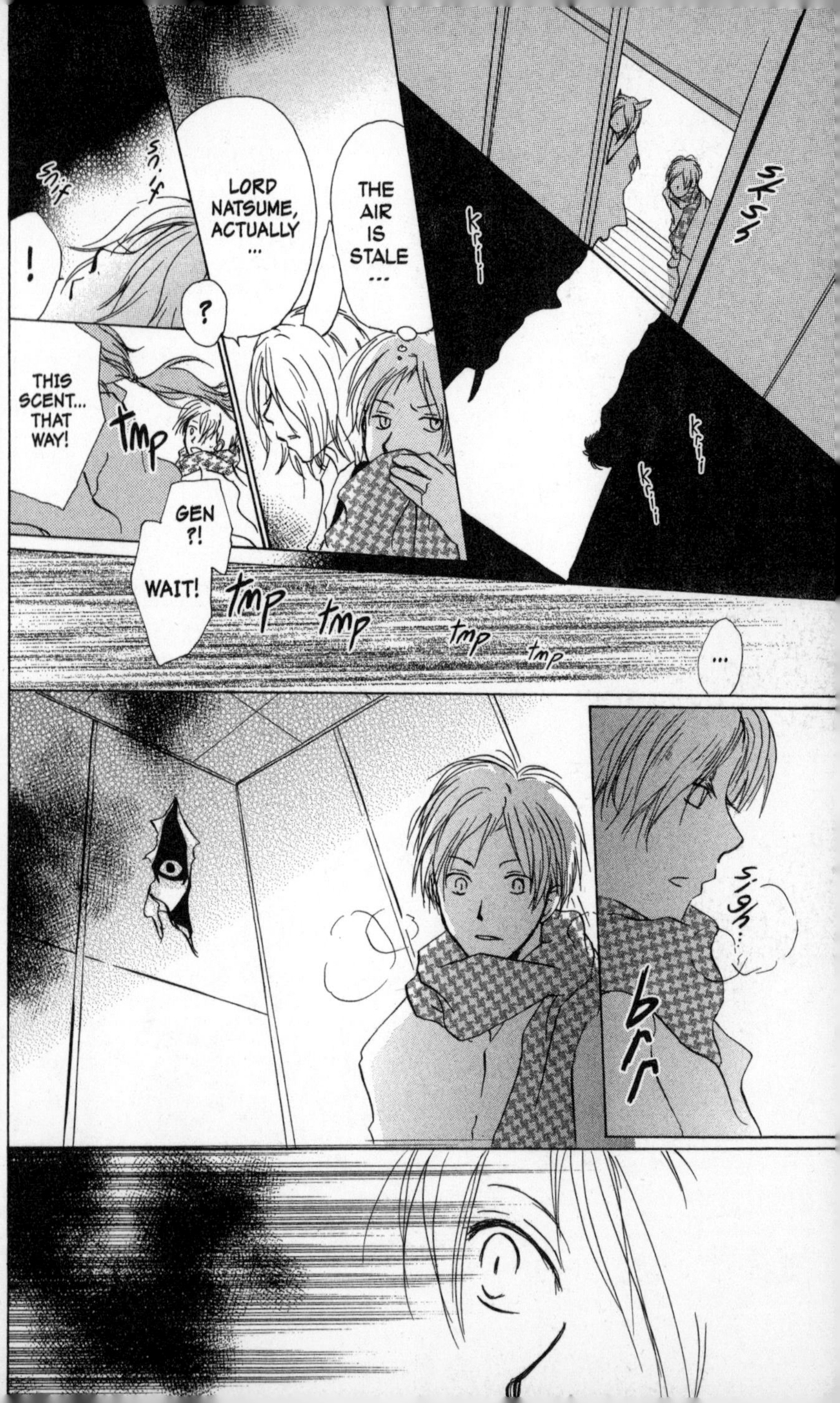
shsh
krii
kri
kri
THE AIR IS STALE...
LORD NATSUME, ACTUALLY...
?
sniff
sniff
!
THIS SCENT... THAT WAY!
tmp
GEN?!
WAIT!
tmp
tmp
tmp
tmp
...
sigh...
brr

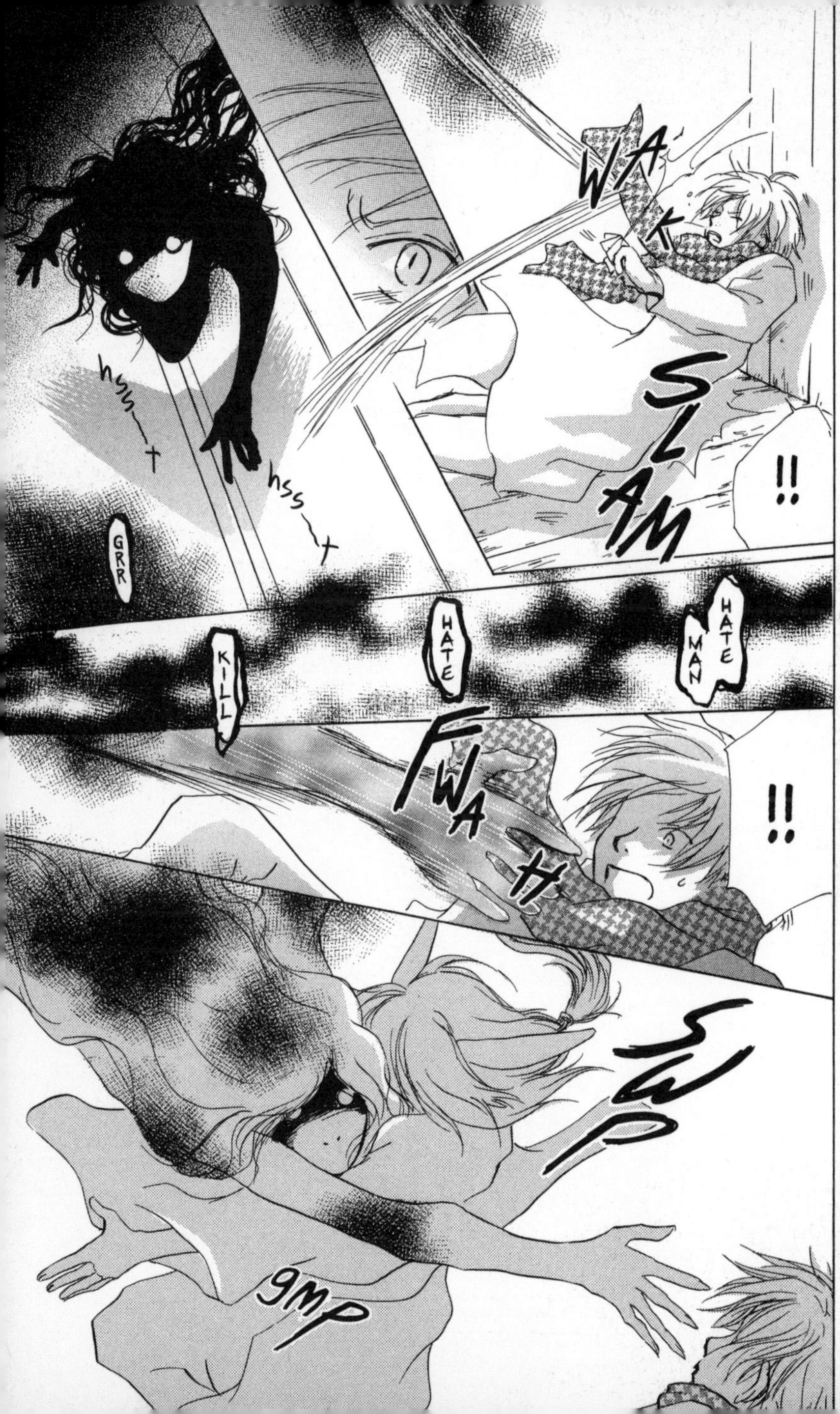

WAK
SLAM
!!
hss—t
hss—t
GRR
HATE MAN
HATE
KILL
!!
FWAH
SWP
gmp

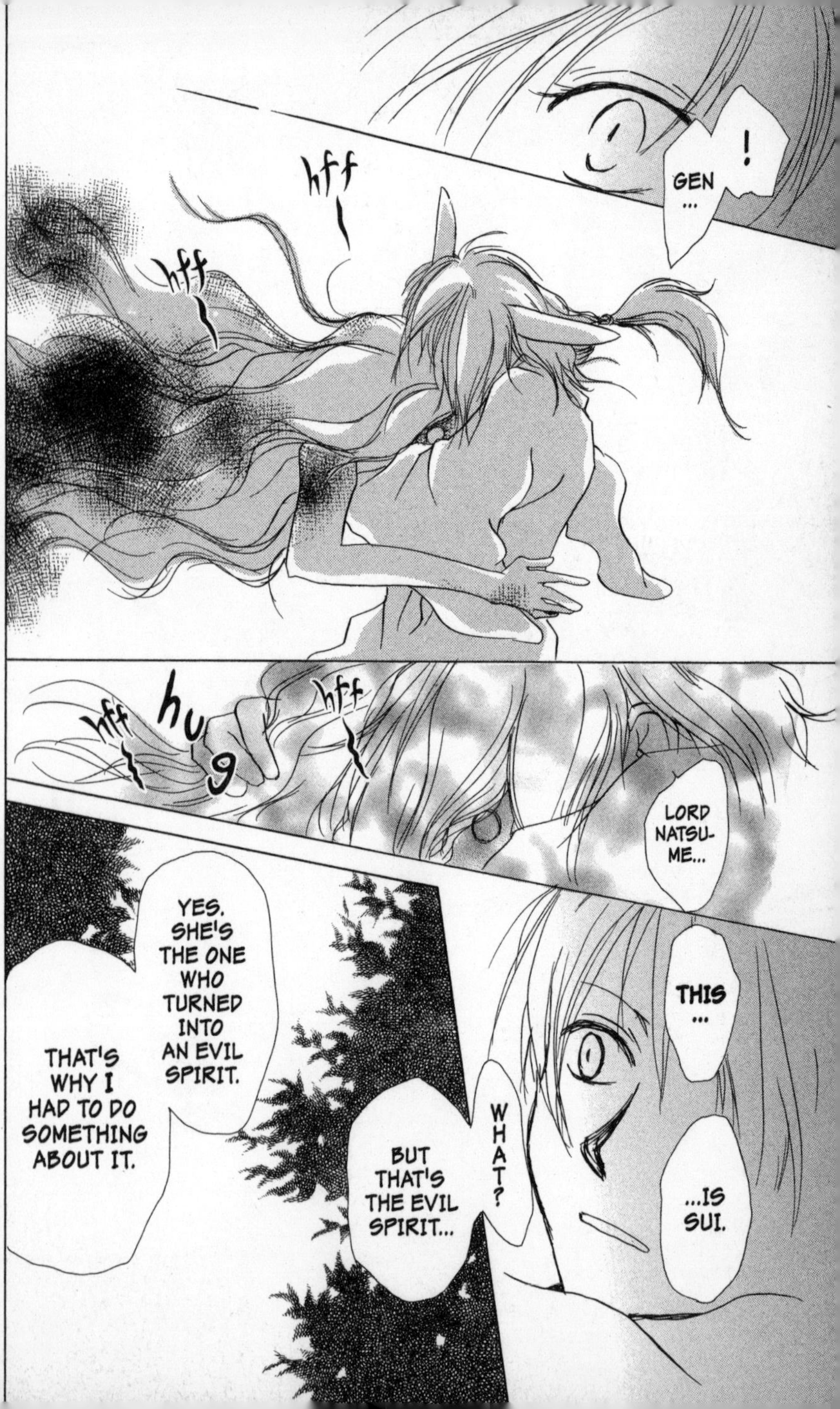
!
GEN...
hff
hff
hff
hug
hff
LORD NATSUME...
THIS...
...IS SUI.
WHAT?
BUT THAT'S THE EVIL SPIRIT...
YES. SHE'S THE ONE WHO TURNED INTO AN EVIL SPIRIT.
THAT'S WHY I HAD TO DO SOMETHING ABOUT IT.

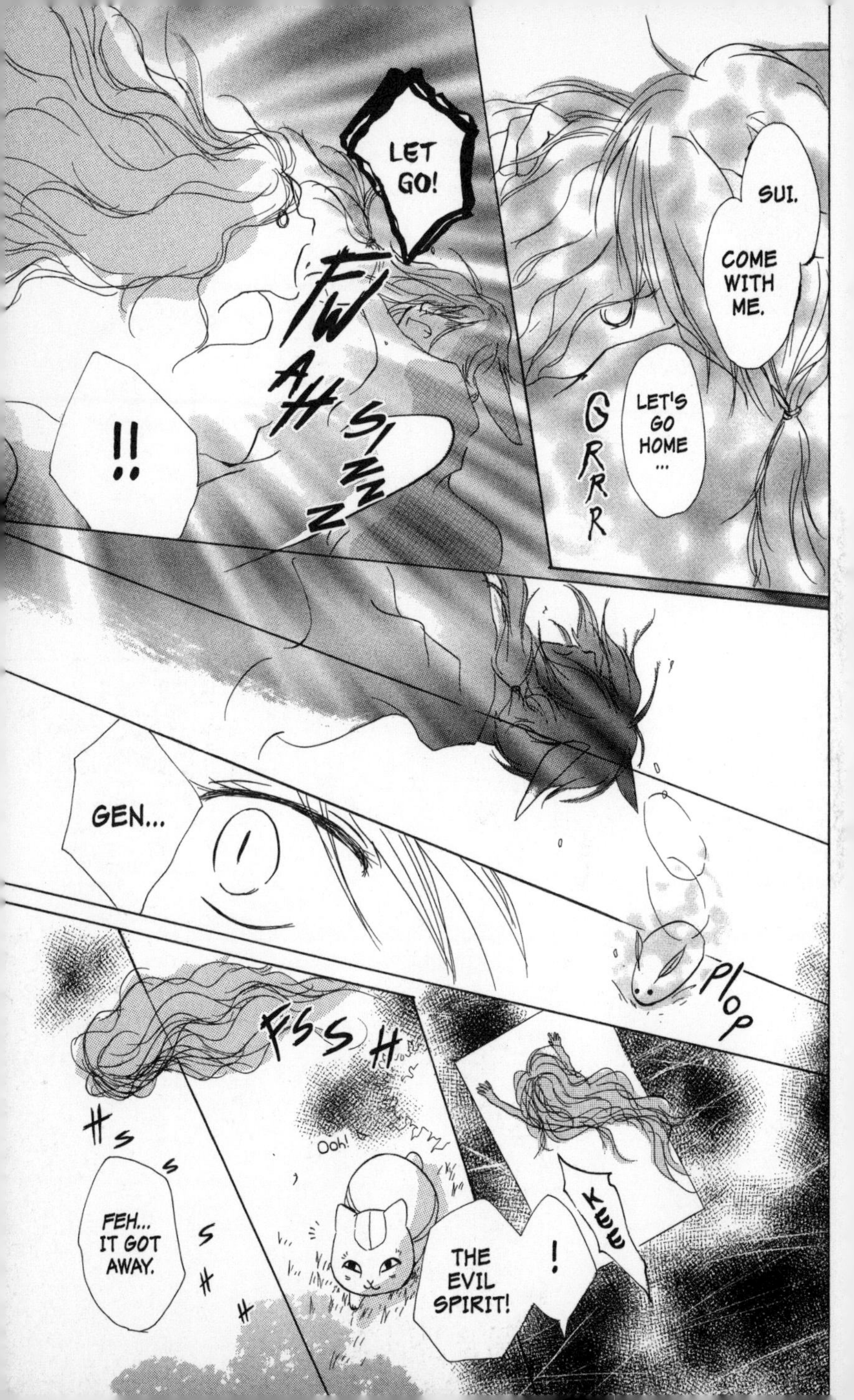

SUI.
COME WITH ME.
LET'S GO HOME...
GRRR
LET GO!
FWAHH
SIZZZZ
!!
GEN...
PLOP
KEEE
!
THE EVIL SPIRIT!
Ooh!
FSSH
HSSSHH
FEH... IT GOT AWAY.

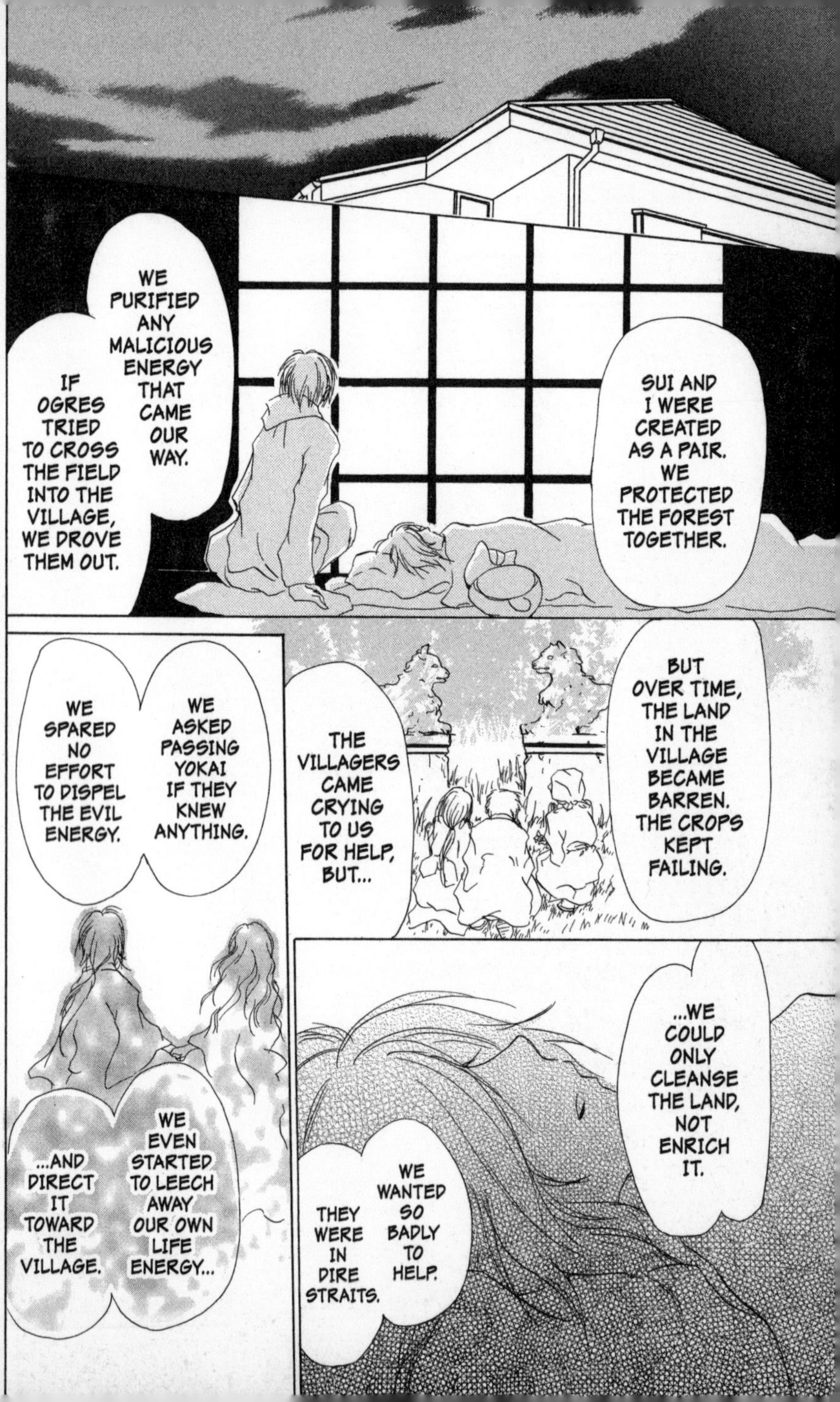
SUI AND I WERE CREATED AS A PAIR. WE PROTECTED THE FOREST TOGETHER.
WE PURIFIED ANY MALICIOUS ENERGY THAT CAME OUR WAY.
IF OGRES TRIED TO CROSS THE FIELD INTO THE VILLAGE, WE DROVE THEM OUT.
BUT OVER TIME, THE LAND IN THE VILLAGE BECAME BARREN. THE CROPS KEPT FAILING.
THE VILLAGERS CAME CRYING TO US FOR HELP, BUT...
WE ASKED PASSING YOKAI IF THEY KNEW ANYTHING.
WE SPARED NO EFFORT TO DISPEL THE EVIL ENERGY.
...WE COULD ONLY CLEANSE THE LAND, NOT ENRICH IT.
WE WANTED SO BADLY TO HELP.
THEY WERE IN DIRE STRAITS.
WE EVEN STARTED TO LEECH AWAY OUR OWN LIFE ENERGY...
...AND DIRECT IT TOWARD THE VILLAGE.

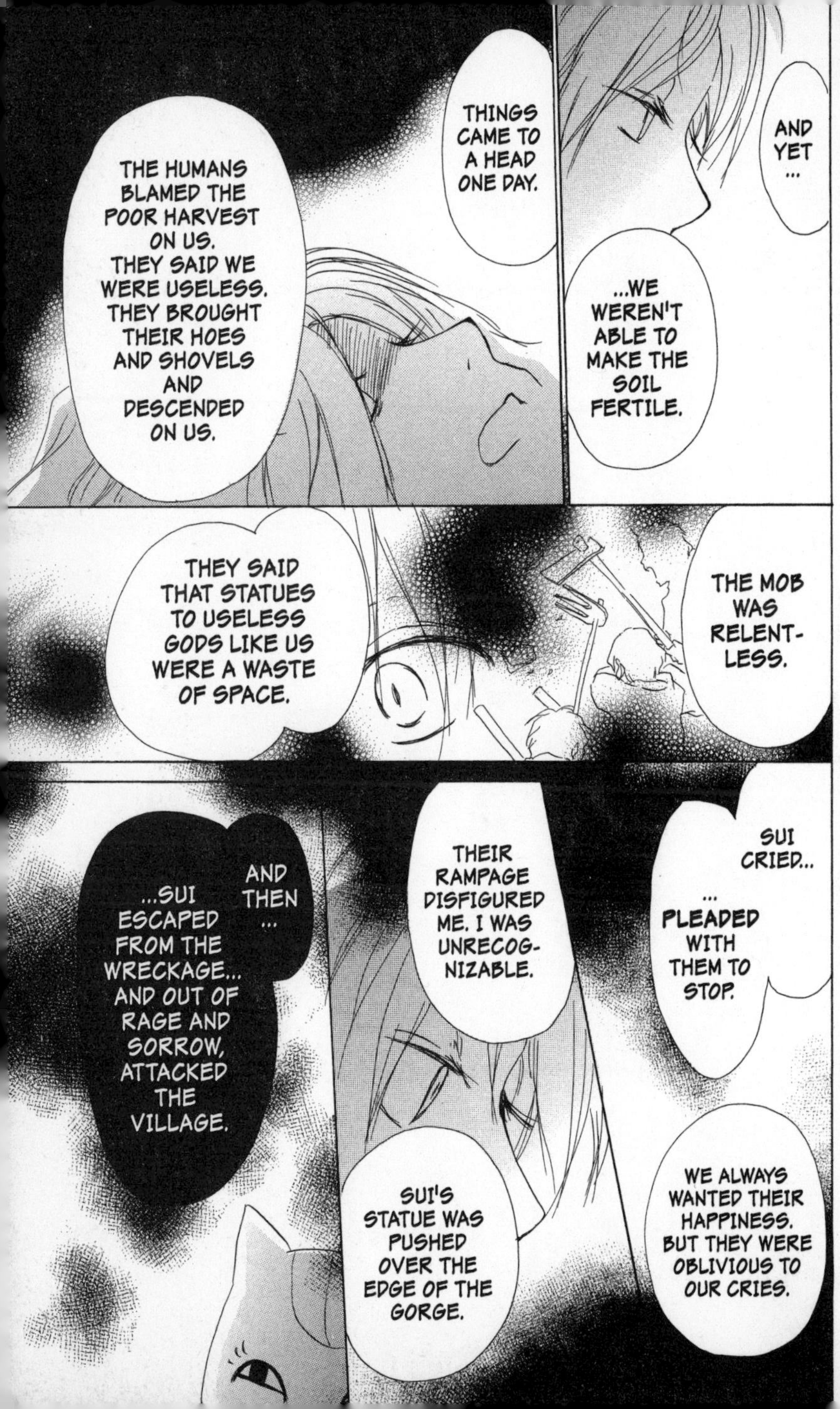
AND YET ...
...WE WEREN'T ABLE TO MAKE THE SOIL FERTILE.
THINGS CAME TO A HEAD ONE DAY.
THE HUMANS BLAMED THE POOR HARVEST ON US. THEY SAID WE WERE USELESS. THEY BROUGHT THEIR HOES AND SHOVELS AND DESCENDED ON US.
THE MOB WAS RELENT- LESS.
THEY SAID THAT STATUES TO USELESS GODS LIKE US WERE A WASTE OF SPACE.
SUI CRIED...
...PLEADED WITH THEM TO STOP.
WE ALWAYS WANTED THEIR HAPPINESS. BUT THEY WERE OBLIVIOUS TO OUR CRIES.
THEIR RAMPAGE DISFIGURED ME. I WAS UNRECOG- NIZABLE.
SUI'S STATUE WAS PUSHED OVER THE EDGE OF THE GORGE.
AND THEN ...
...SUI ESCAPED FROM THE WRECKAGE... AND OUT OF RAGE AND SORROW, ATTACKED THE VILLAGE.

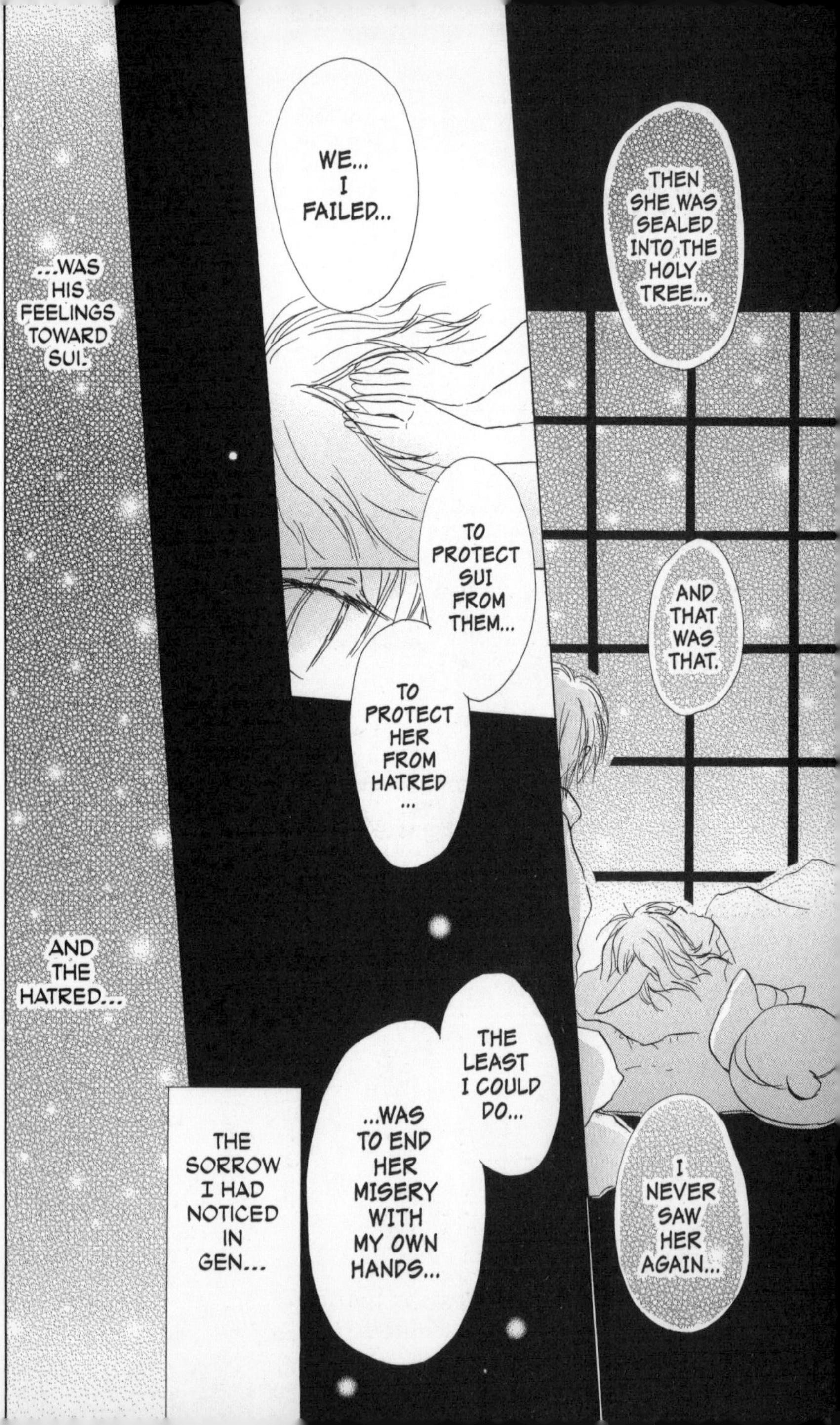
THEN SHE WAS SEALED INTO THE HOLY TREE...
AND THAT WAS THAT.
I NEVER SAW HER AGAIN...
WE... I FAILED...
TO PROTECT SUI FROM THEM...
TO PROTECT HER FROM HATRED...
THE LEAST I COULD DO...
...WAS TO END HER MISERY WITH MY OWN HANDS...
THE SORROW I HAD NOTICED IN GEN...
...WAS HIS FEELINGS TOWARD SUI.
AND THE HATRED...

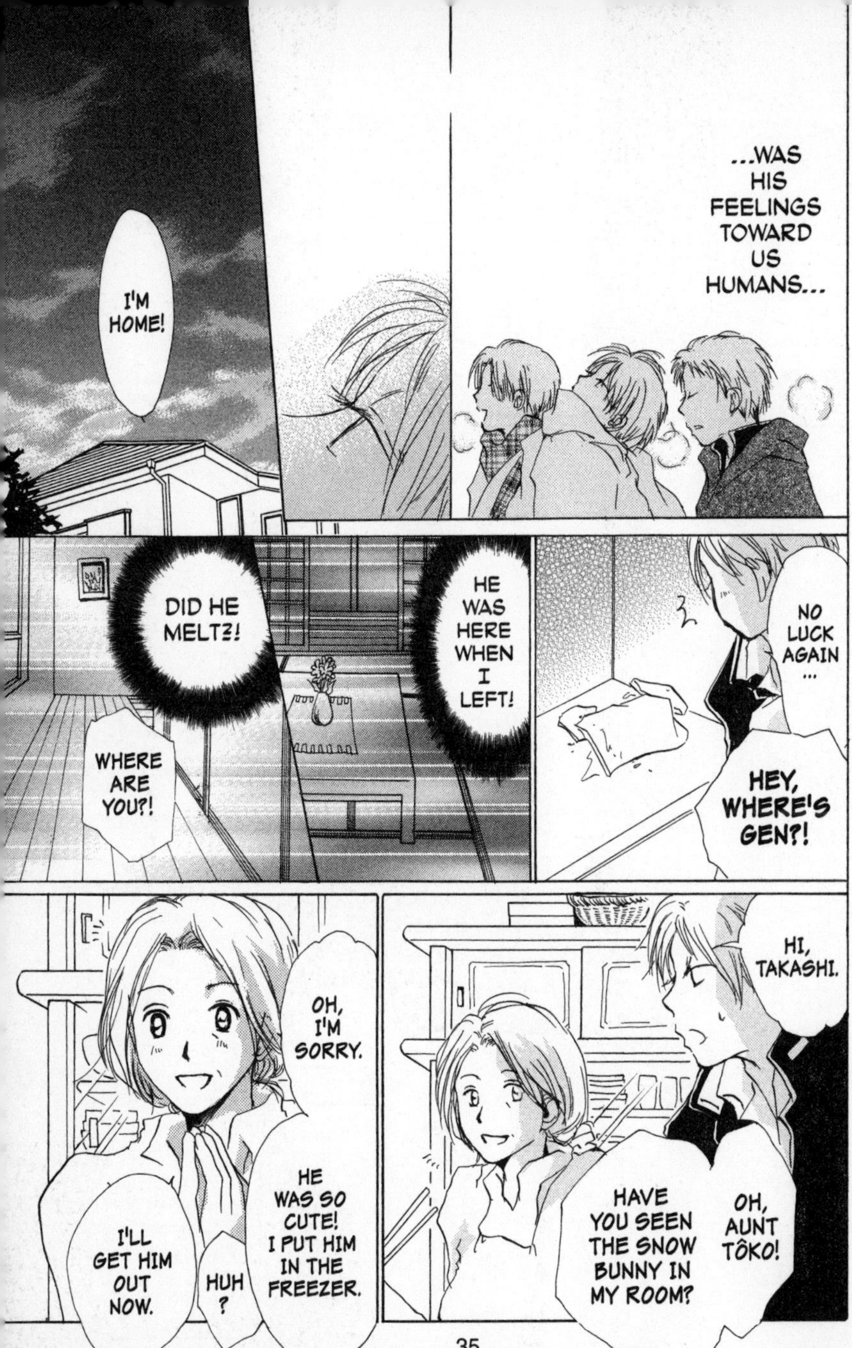
...WAS HIS FEELINGS TOWARD US HUMANS...
I'M HOME!
NO LUCK AGAIN...
HEY, WHERE'S GEN?!
HE WAS HERE WHEN I LEFT!
DID HE MELT?!
WHERE ARE YOU?!
HI, TAKASHI.
OH, AUNT TÔKO!
HAVE YOU SEEN THE SNOW BUNNY IN MY ROOM?
OH, I'M SORRY.
HE WAS SO CUTE! I PUT HIM IN THE FREEZER.
HUH?
I'LL GET HIM OUT NOW.

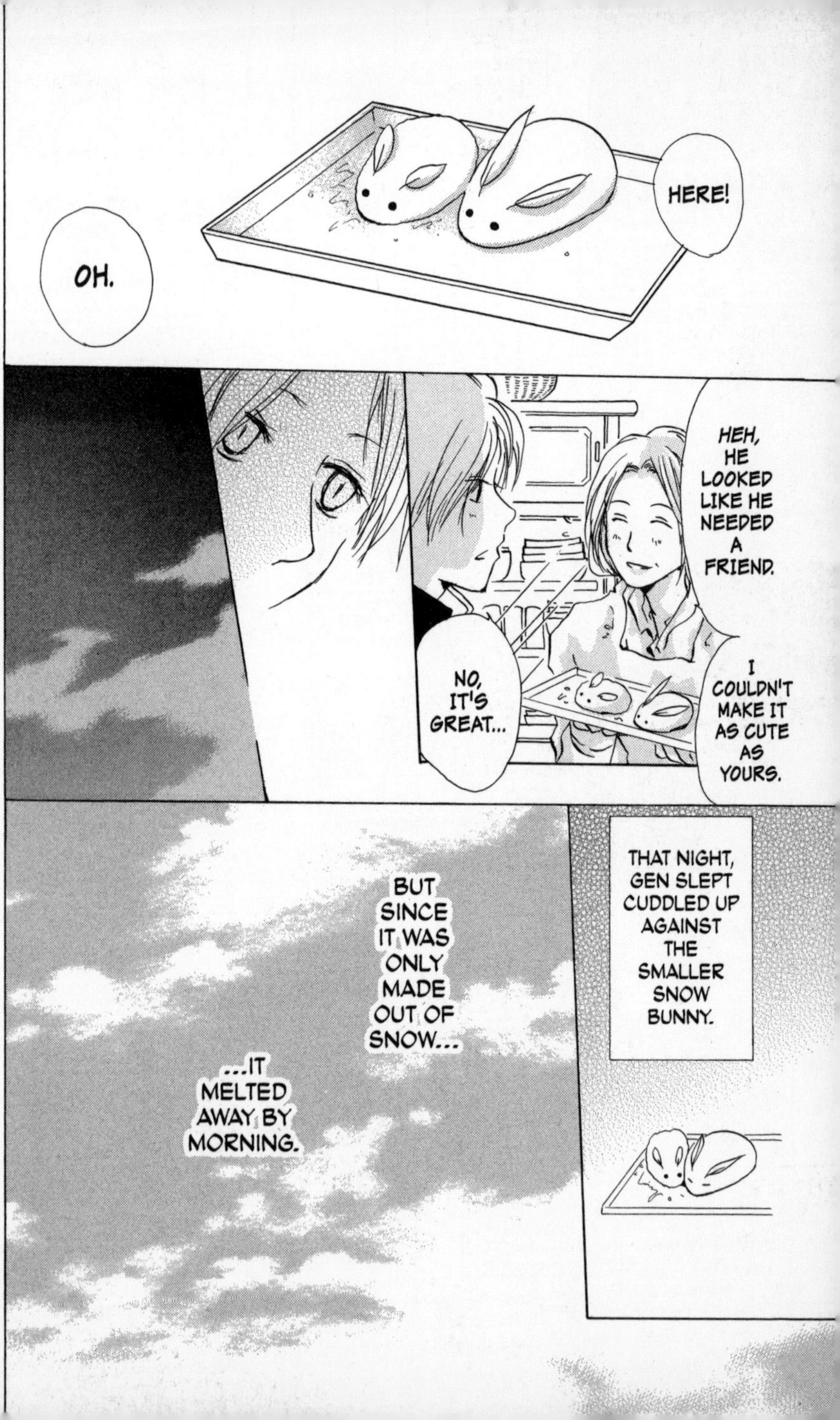
HERE!
OH.
HEH, HE LOOKED LIKE HE NEEDED A FRIEND.
I COULDN'T MAKE IT AS CUTE AS YOURS.
NO, IT'S GREAT...
THAT NIGHT, GEN SLEPT CUDDLED UP AGAINST THE SMALLER SNOW BUNNY.
BUT SINCE IT WAS ONLY MADE OUT OF SNOW...
...IT MELTED AWAY BY MORNING.

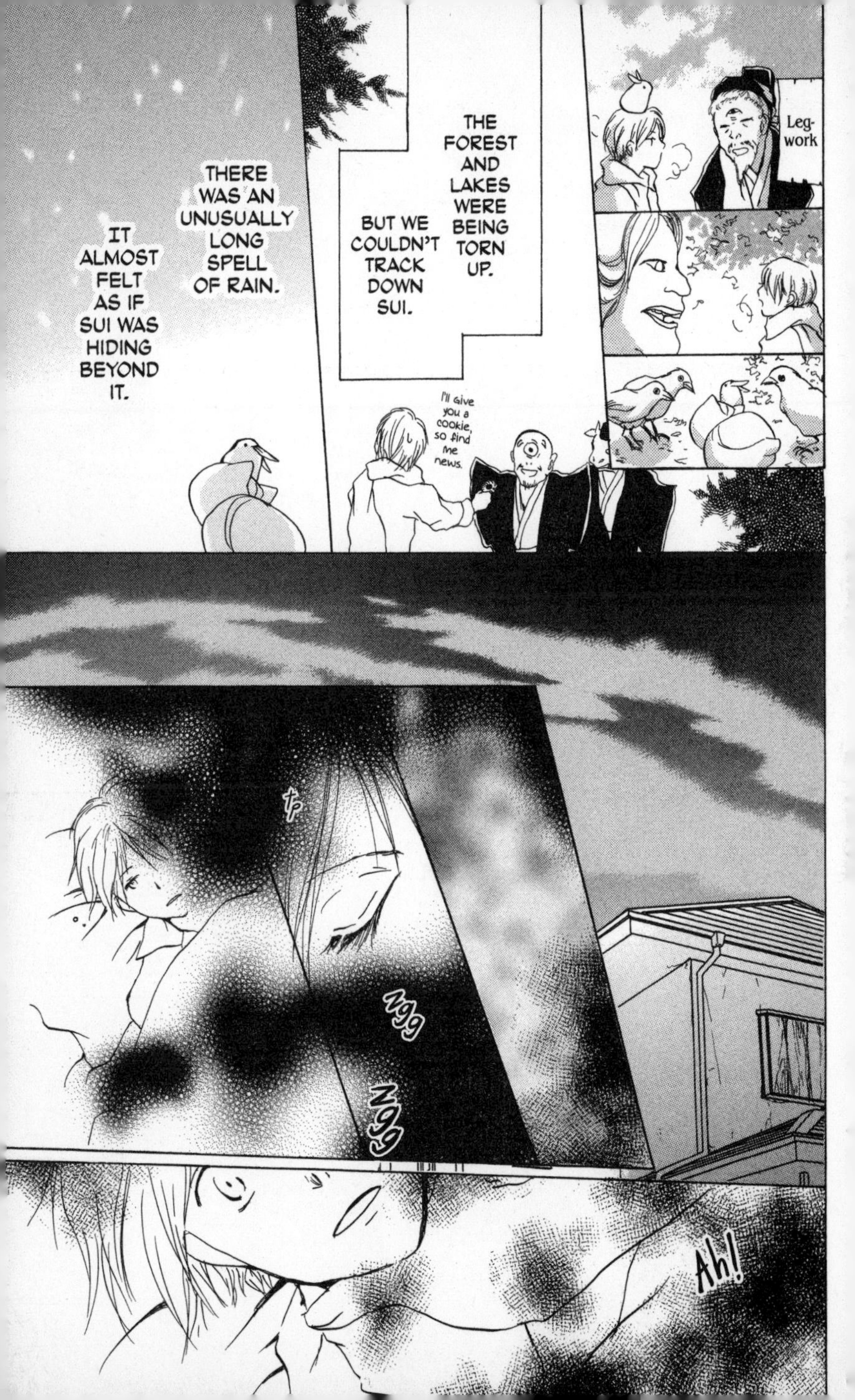
Leg-work
THE FOREST AND LAKES WERE BEING TORN UP.
BUT WE COULDN'T TRACK DOWN SUI.
I'll give you a cookie, so find me news.
THERE WAS AN UNUSUALLY LONG SPELL OF RAIN.
IT ALMOST FELT AS IF SUI WAS HIDING BEYOND IT.
tp
ngg
ngg
Ah!

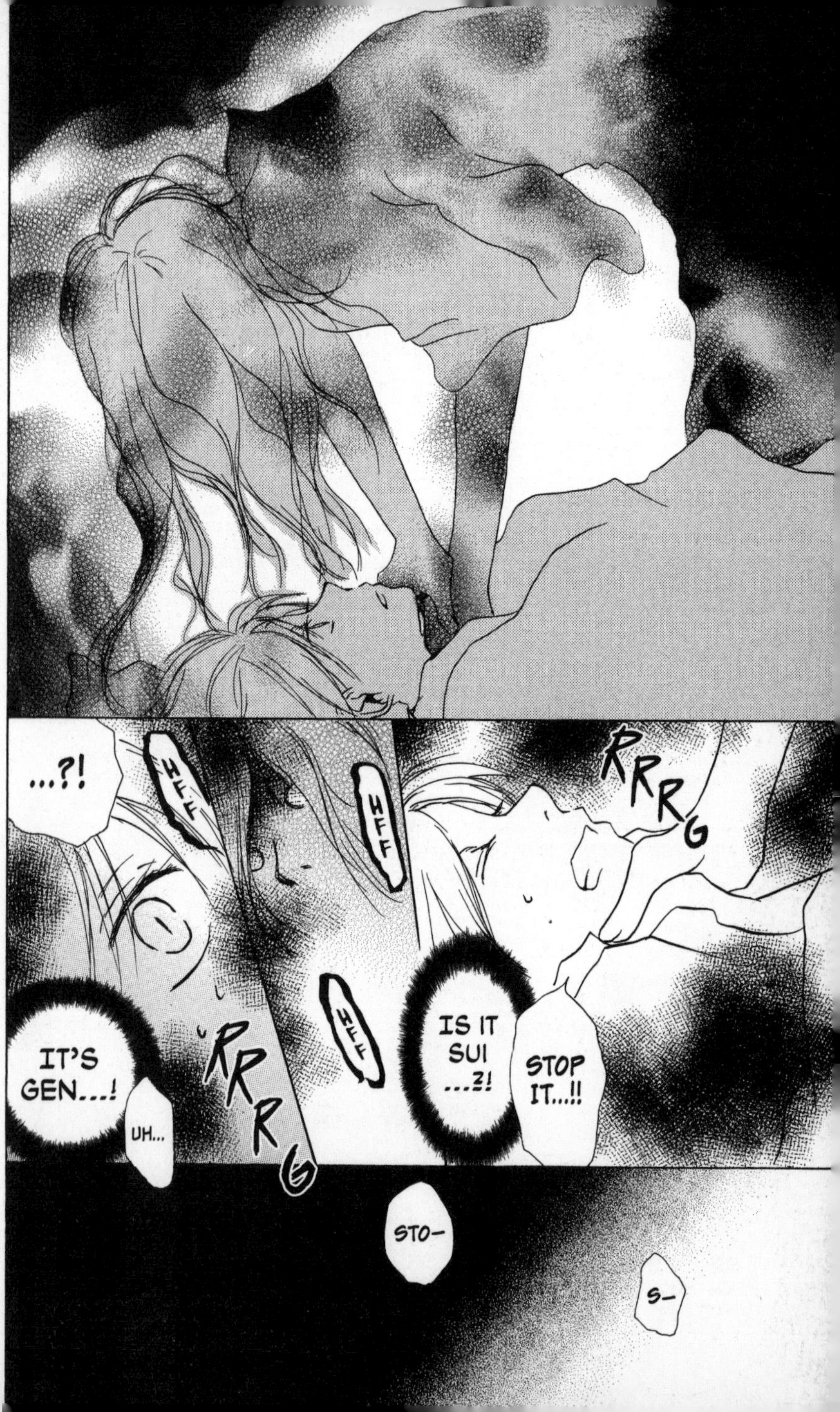
RRRG
STOP IT...!!
IS IT SUI...?!
HFF
HFF
HFF
...?!
IT'S GEN...!
UH...
RRRG
STO-
S-

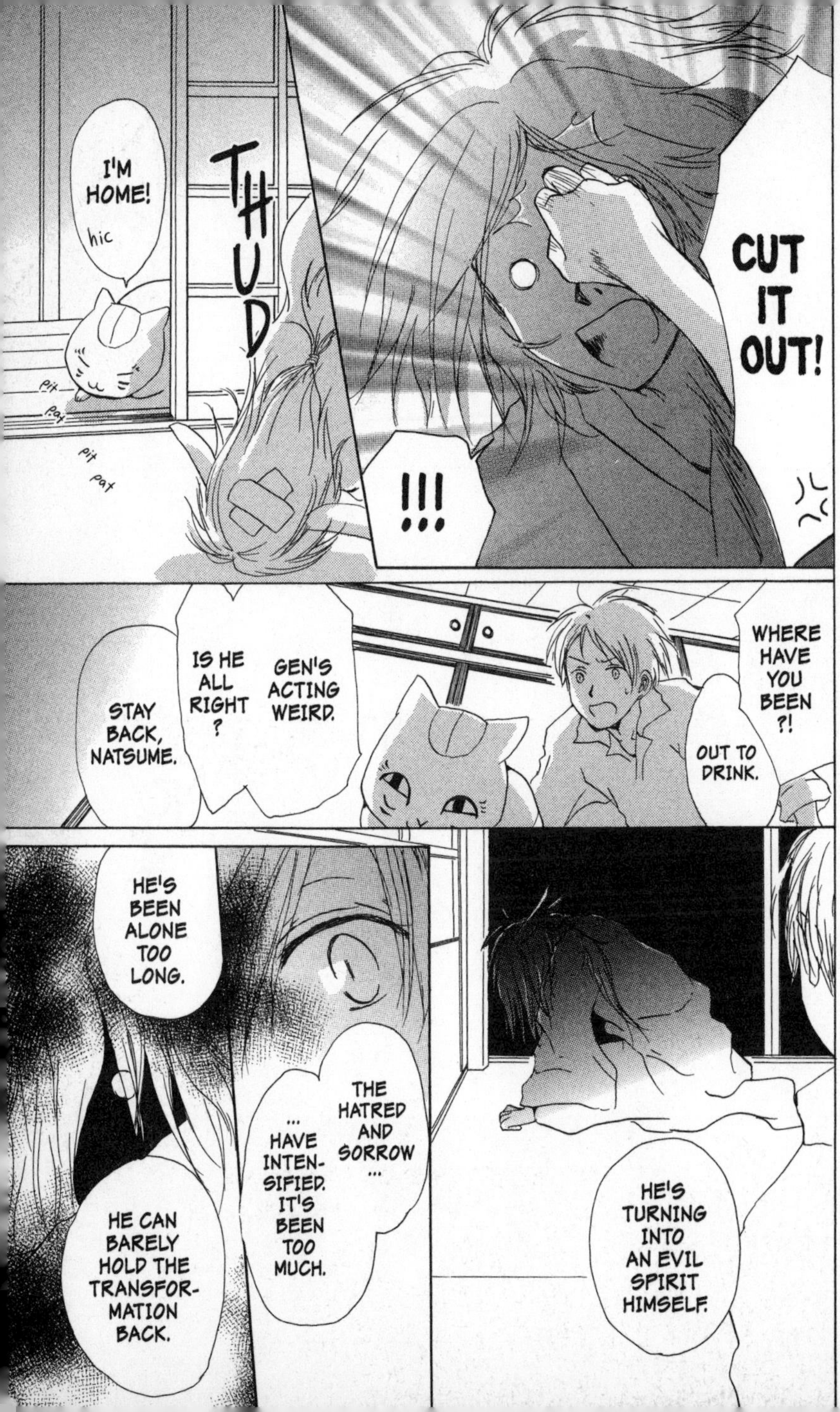
CUT IT OUT!
!!!
THUD
I'M HOME! hic
pit pat pit pat
WHERE HAVE YOU BEEN?!
OUT TO DRINK.
GEN'S ACTING WEIRD.
IS HE ALL RIGHT?
STAY BACK, NATSUME.
HE'S TURNING INTO AN EVIL SPIRIT HIMSELF.
HE'S BEEN ALONE TOO LONG.
THE HATRED AND SORROW...
...HAVE INTEN-SIFIED. IT'S BEEN TOO MUCH.
HE CAN BARELY HOLD THE TRANSFOR-MATION BACK.

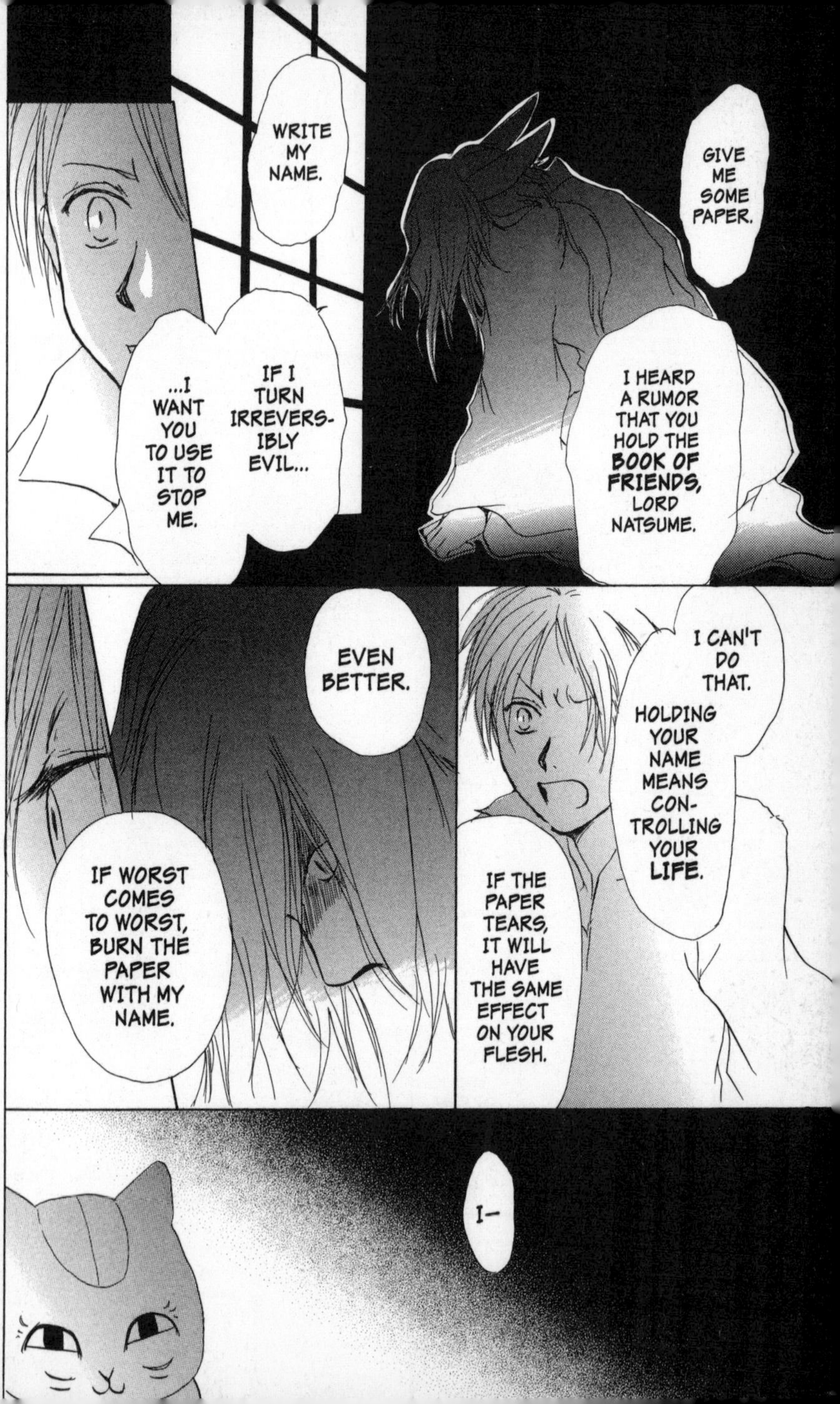
GIVE ME SOME PAPER.
I HEARD A RUMOR THAT YOU HOLD THE **BOOK OF FRIENDS,** LORD NATSUME.
WRITE MY NAME.
IF I TURN IRREVERS-IBLY EVIL...
...I WANT YOU TO USE IT TO STOP ME.
I CAN'T DO THAT.
HOLDING YOUR NAME MEANS CON-TROLLING YOUR **LIFE.**
IF THE PAPER TEARS, IT WILL HAVE THE SAME EFFECT ON YOUR FLESH.
EVEN BETTER.
IF WORST COMES TO WORST, BURN THE PAPER WITH MY NAME.
I–

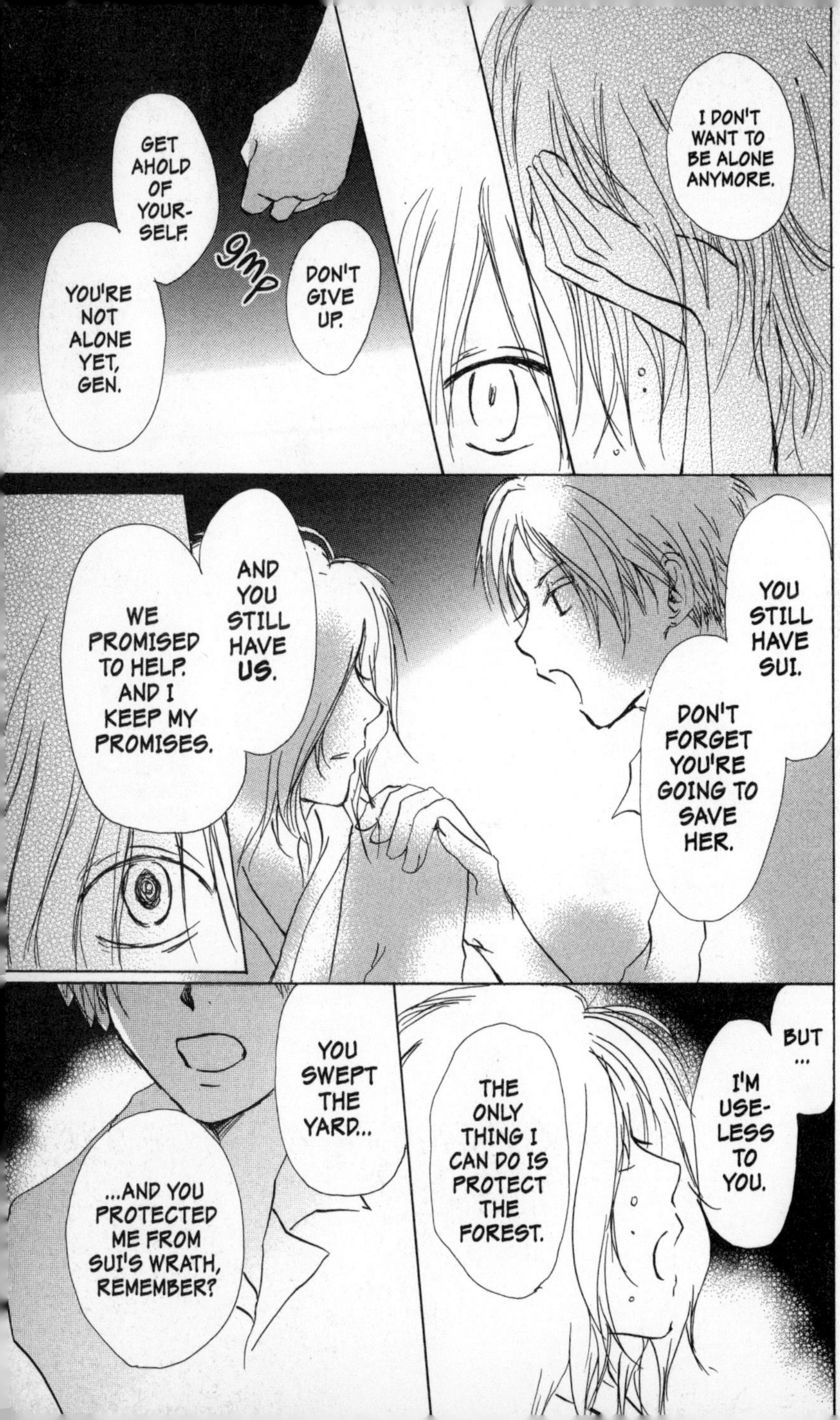
I DON'T WANT TO BE ALONE ANYMORE.
GET AHOLD OF YOURSELF.
DON'T GIVE UP.
gmp
YOU'RE NOT ALONE YET, GEN.
YOU STILL HAVE SUI.
DON'T FORGET YOU'RE GOING TO SAVE HER.
AND YOU STILL HAVE US.
WE PROMISED TO HELP. AND I KEEP MY PROMISES.
BUT...
I'M USELESS TO YOU.
THE ONLY THING I CAN DO IS PROTECT THE FOREST.
YOU SWEPT THE YARD...
...AND YOU PROTECTED ME FROM SUI'S WRATH, REMEMBER?

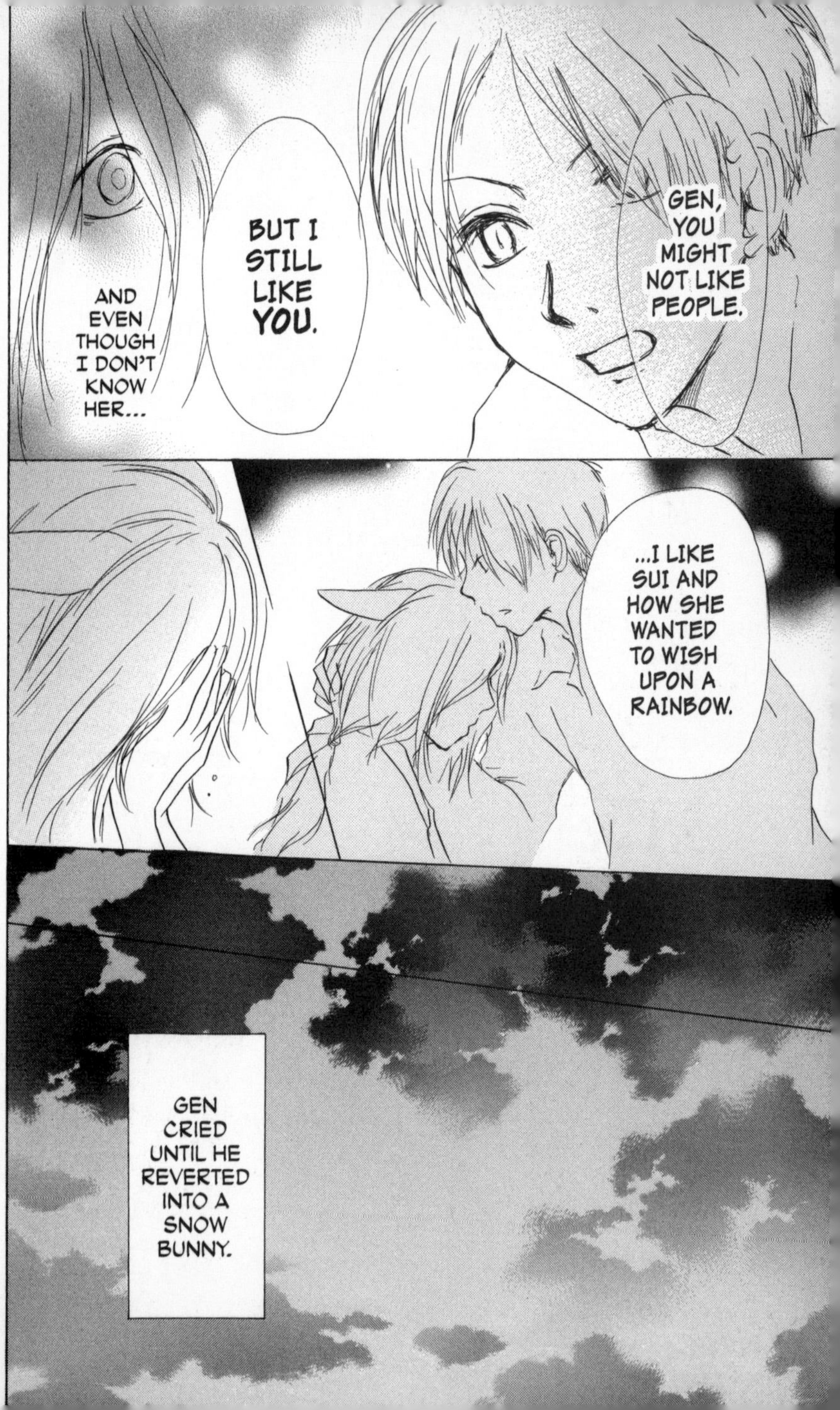
GEN, YOU MIGHT NOT LIKE PEOPLE.
BUT I STILL LIKE YOU.
AND EVEN THOUGH I DON'T KNOW HER...
...I LIKE SUI AND HOW SHE WANTED TO WISH UPON A RAINBOW.
GEN CRIED UNTIL HE REVERTED INTO A SNOW BUNNY.

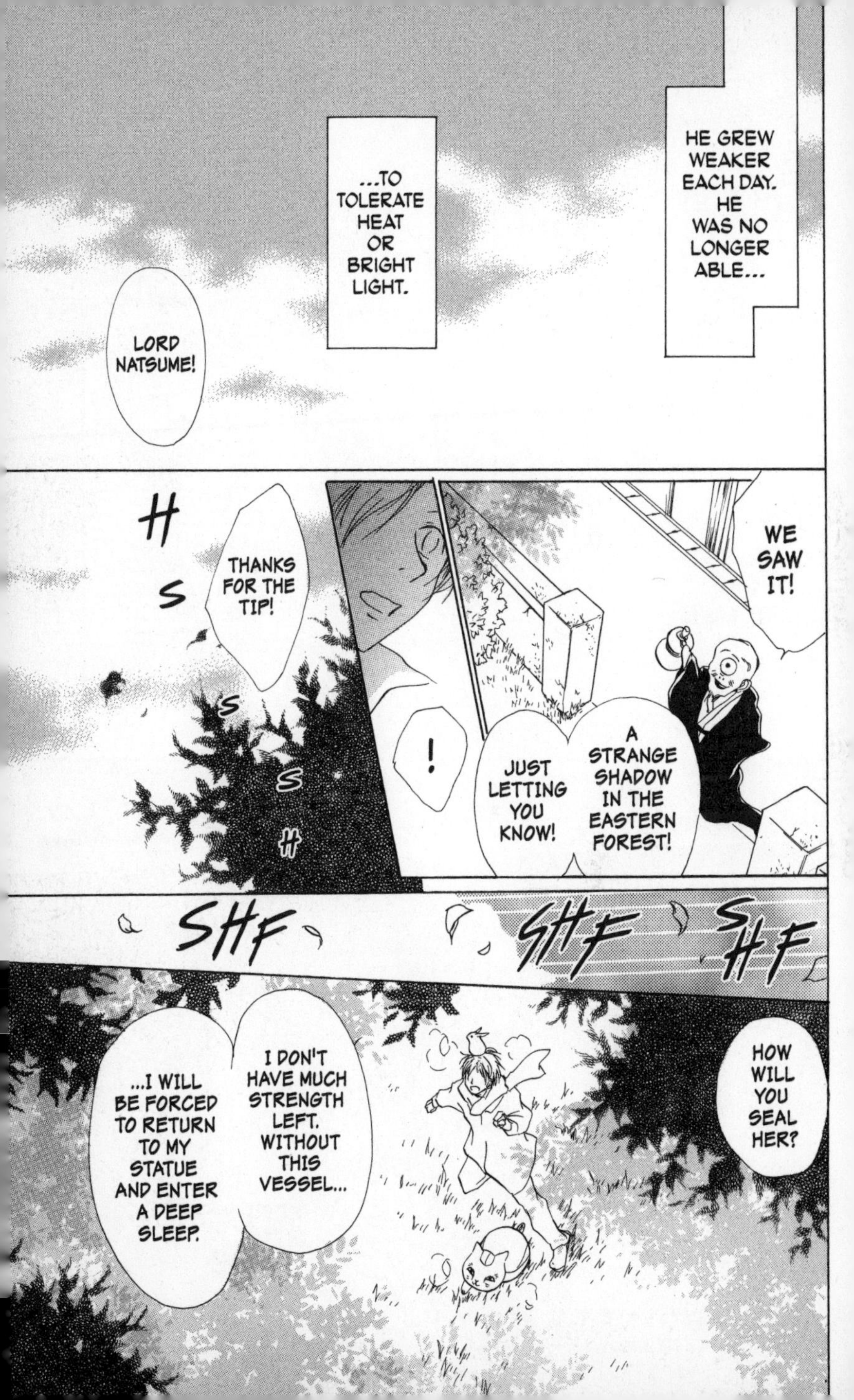
HE GREW WEAKER EACH DAY. HE WAS NO LONGER ABLE...
...TO TOLERATE HEAT OR BRIGHT LIGHT.
LORD NATSUME!
WE SAW IT!
A STRANGE SHADOW IN THE EASTERN FOREST!
JUST LETTING YOU KNOW!
!
THANKS FOR THE TIP!
HSSSH
SHF SHF SHF
HOW WILL YOU SEAL HER?
I DON'T HAVE MUCH STRENGTH LEFT. WITHOUT THIS VESSEL...
...I WILL BE FORCED TO RETURN TO MY STATUE AND ENTER A DEEP SLEEP.

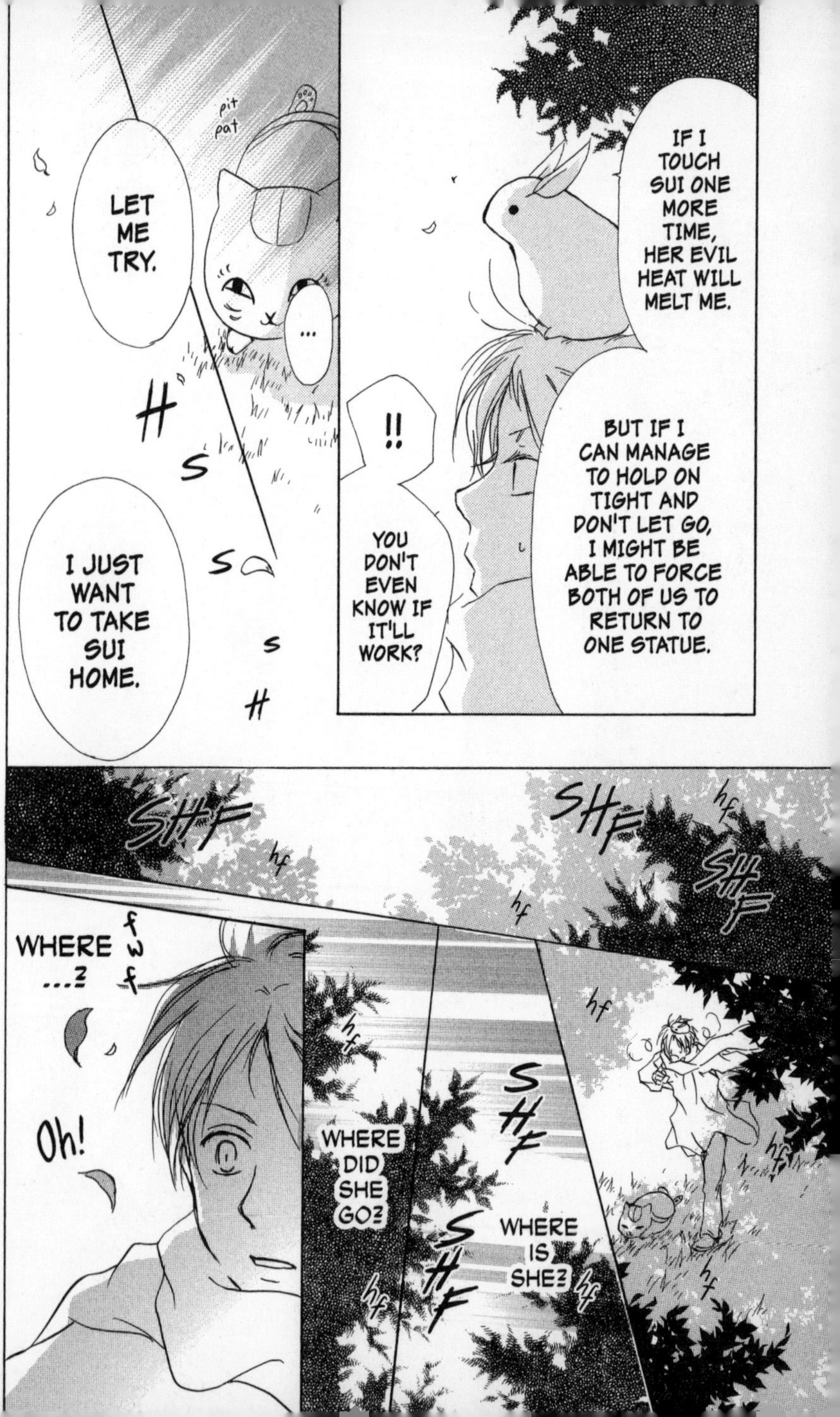
IF I TOUCH SUI ONE MORE TIME, HER EVIL HEAT WILL MELT ME.
BUT IF I CAN MANAGE TO HOLD ON TIGHT AND DON'T LET GO, I MIGHT BE ABLE TO FORCE BOTH OF US TO RETURN TO ONE STATUE.
!!
YOU DON'T EVEN KNOW IF IT'LL WORK?
pit pat
LET ME TRY.
...
I JUST WANT TO TAKE SUI HOME.
SHF
hf
SHF
SHF
hf
hf
hf
hf
SHF
WHERE IS SHE?
WHERE DID SHE GO?
SHF
hf
hf
WHERE ...?
fwf
Oh!

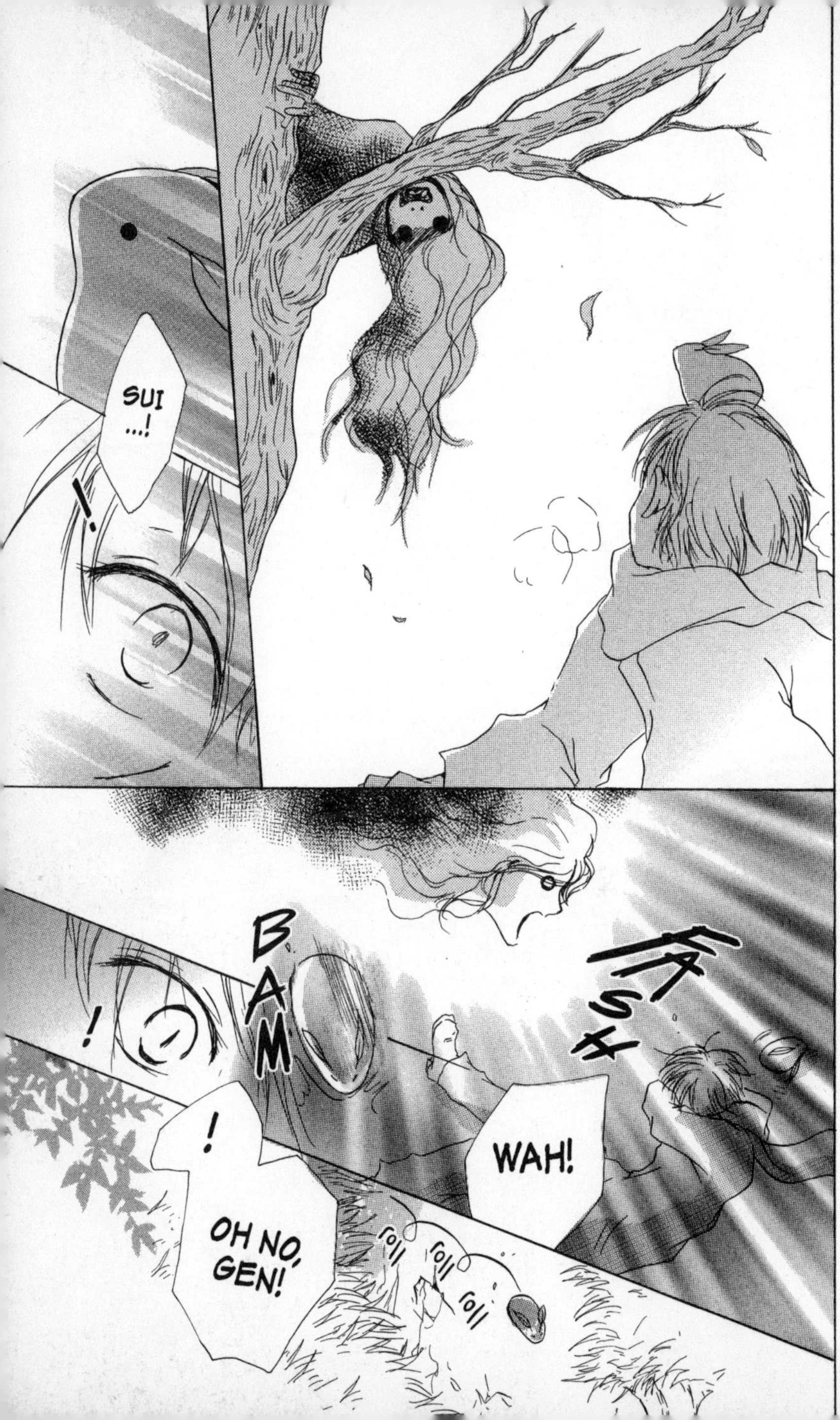
SUI ...!
!
FASH
WAH!
BAM
!
!
OH NO, GEN!
roll roll roll

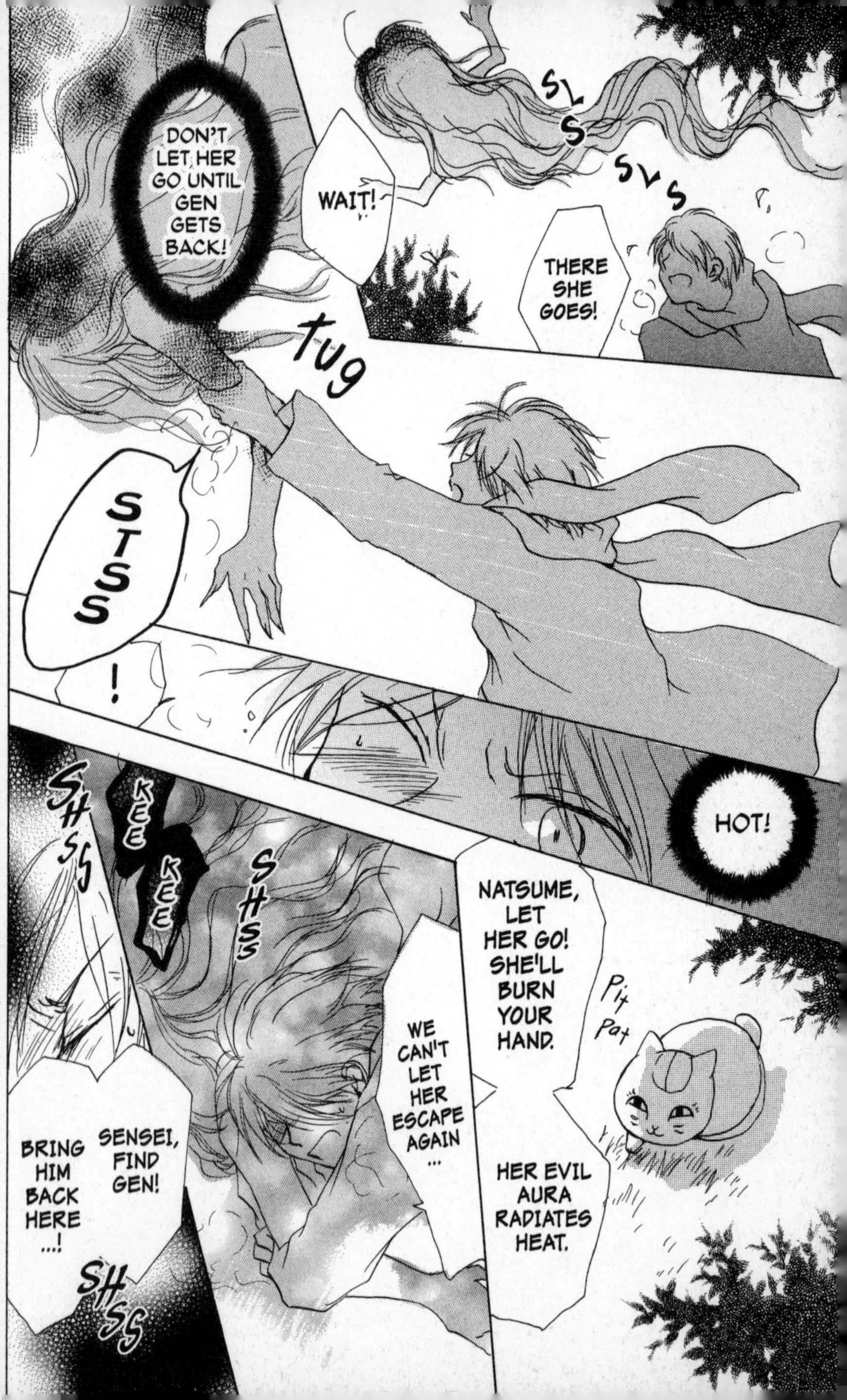
SLS S
SVS
THERE SHE GOES!
WAIT!
DON'T LET HER GO UNTIL GEN GETS BACK!
tug
STSS
!
HOT!
NATSUME, LET HER GO! SHE'LL BURN YOUR HAND.
Pit Pat
HER EVIL AURA RADIATES HEAT.
WE CAN'T LET HER ESCAPE AGAIN ...
SHSS
KEE KEE
SHSS
SENSEI, FIND GEN!
BRING HIM BACK HERE ...!
SHSS

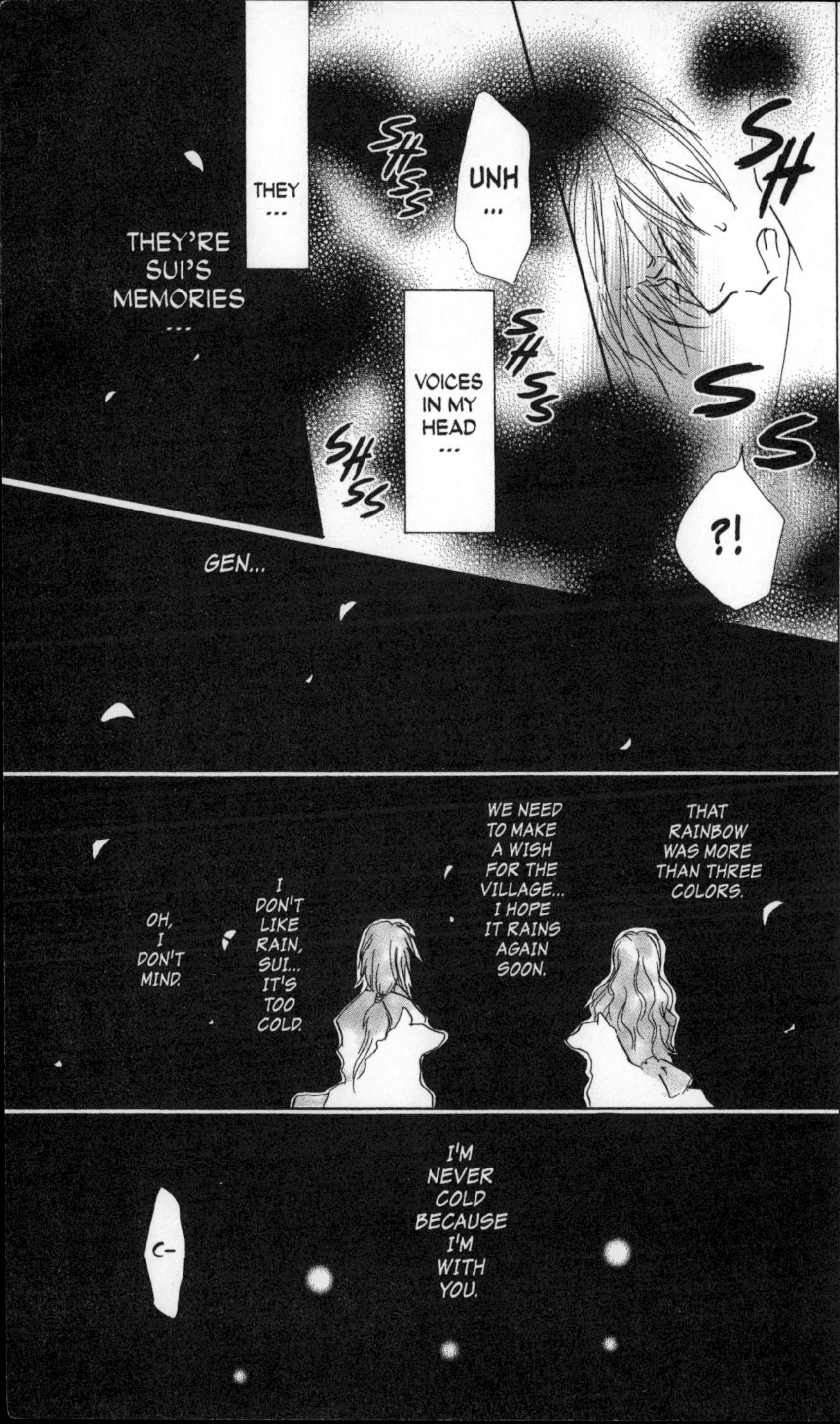
SH
UNH...
SHSS
THEY...
S
S
?!
SHSS
VOICES IN MY HEAD...
SHSS
THEY'RE SUI'S MEMORIES...
GEN...
THAT RAINBOW WAS MORE THAN THREE COLORS.
WE NEED TO MAKE A WISH FOR THE VILLAGE... I HOPE IT RAINS AGAIN SOON.
I DON'T LIKE RAIN, SUI... IT'S TOO COLD.
OH, I DON'T MIND.
I'M NEVER COLD BECAUSE I'M WITH YOU.
C–

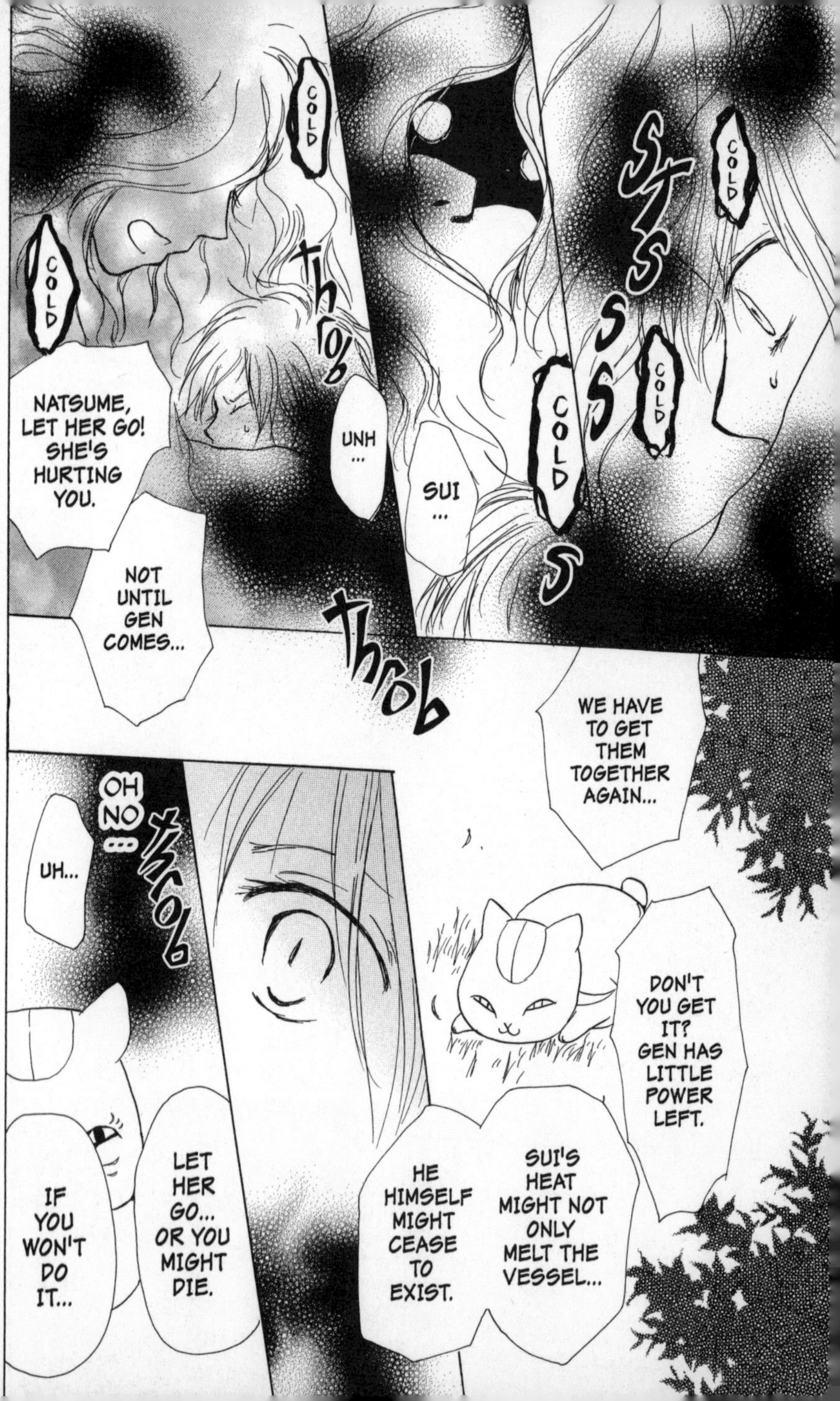
COLD
SSSSS
COLD
COLD
SUI...
UNH...
COLD
throb
COLD
NATSUME, LET HER GO! SHE'S HURTING YOU.
NOT UNTIL GEN COMES...
throb
WE HAVE TO GET THEM TOGETHER AGAIN...
DON'T YOU GET IT? GEN HAS LITTLE POWER LEFT.
SUI'S HEAT MIGHT NOT ONLY MELT THE VESSEL...
HE HIMSELF MIGHT CEASE TO EXIST.
OH NO...
throb
UH...
LET HER GO... OR YOU MIGHT DIE.
IF YOU WON'T DO IT...

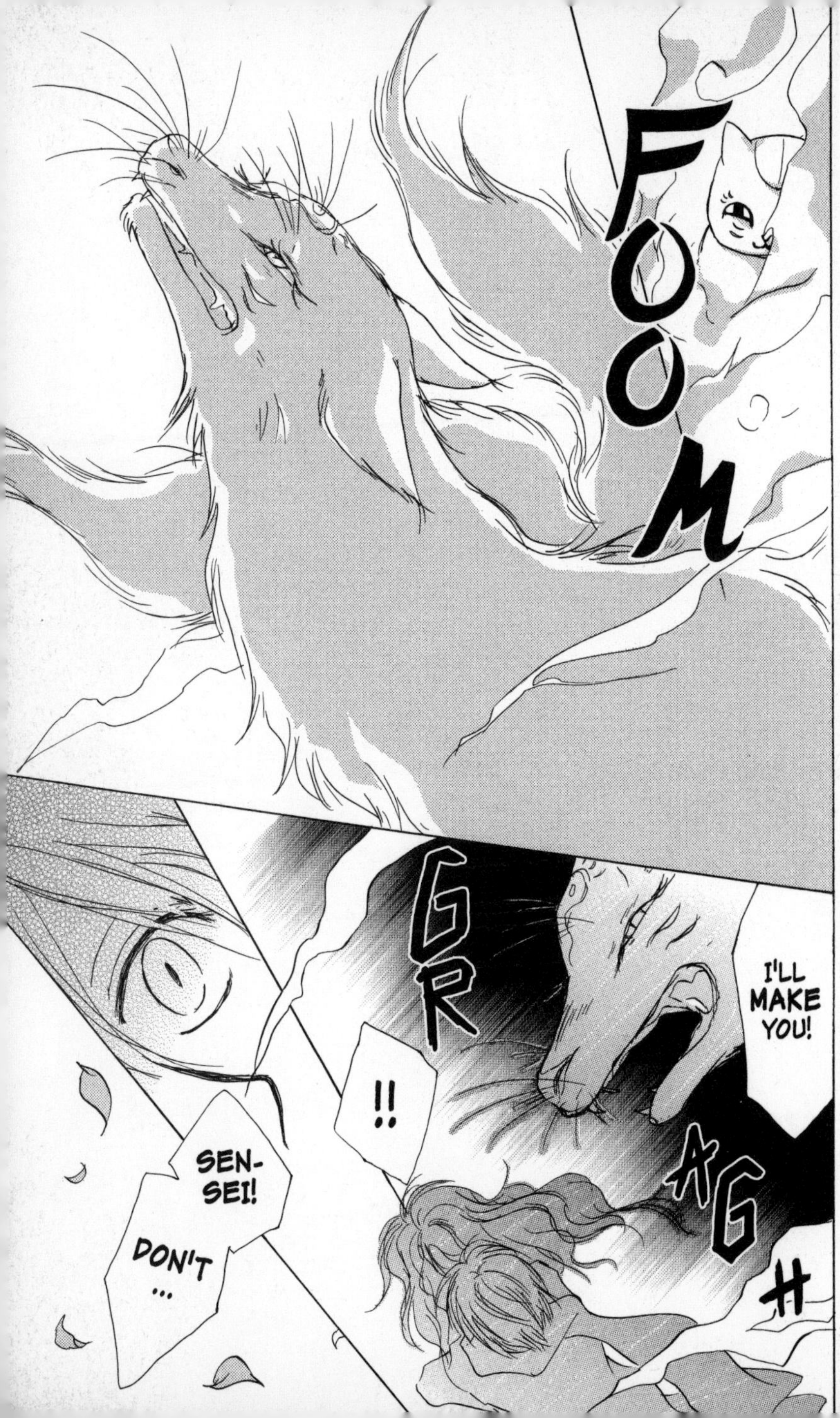
FOOOM
I'LL MAKE YOU!
GRAGH
!!
SEN-SEI!
DON'T ...

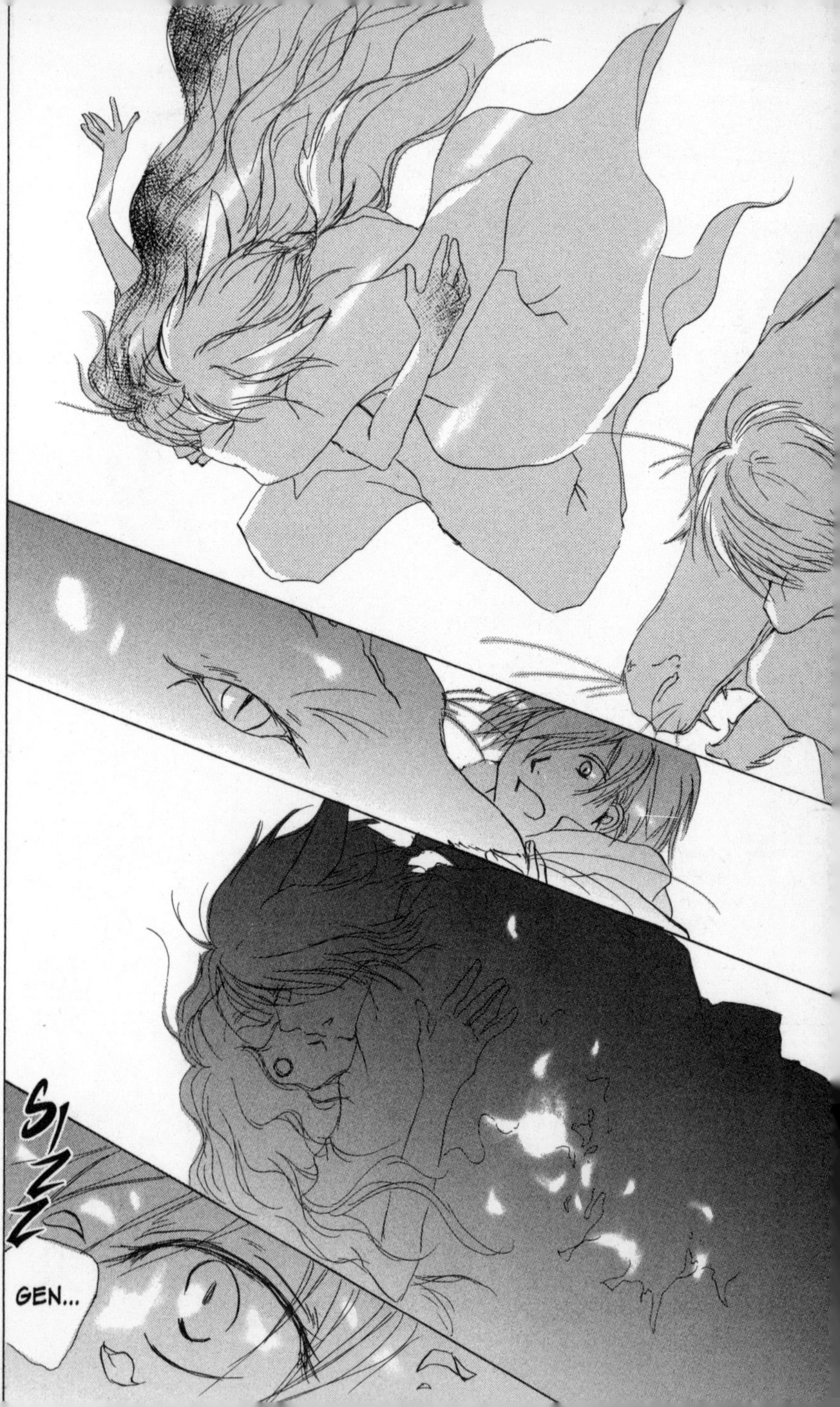
SIZZ
GEN...

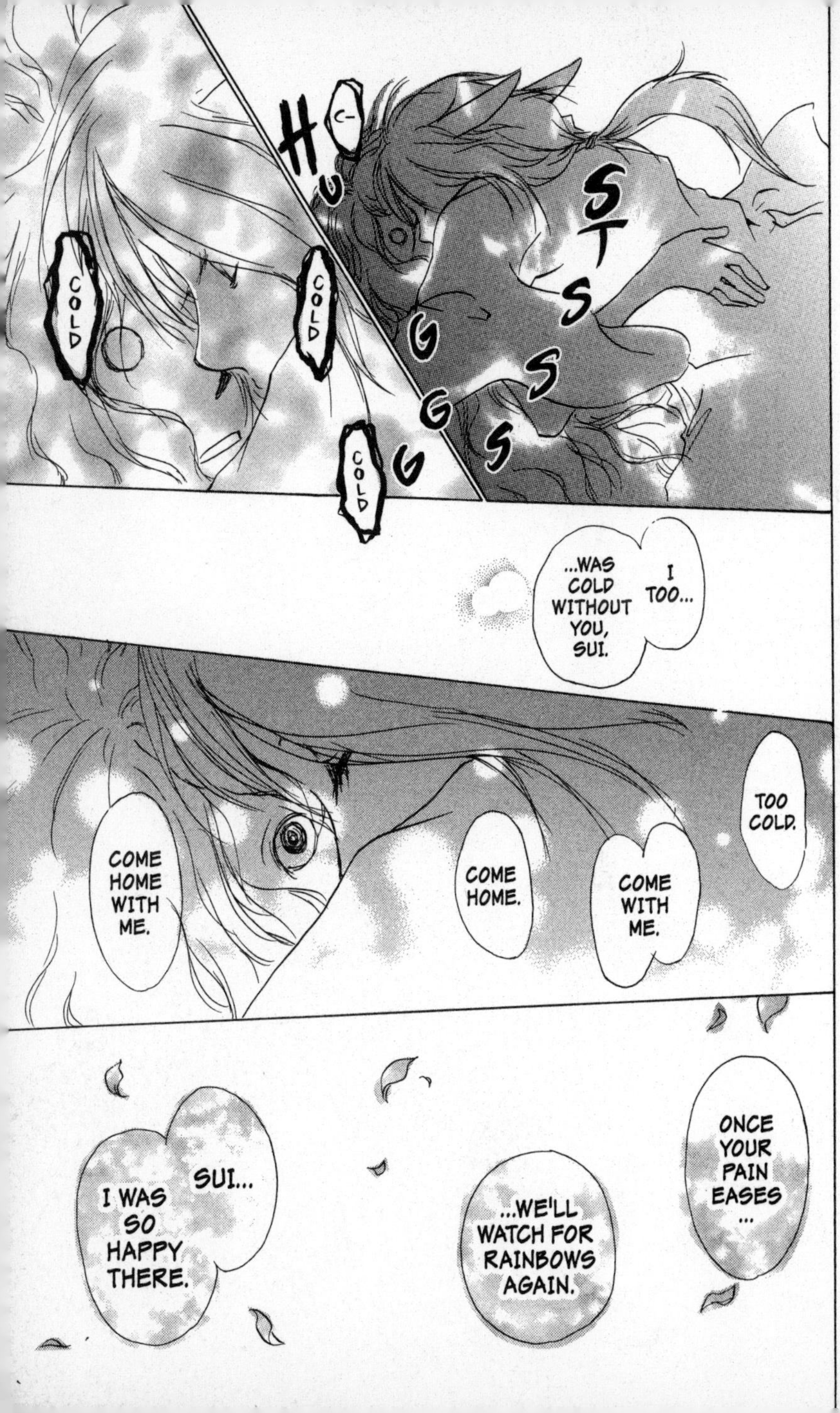
C-
HU
STSSS
GGG
COLD
COLD
COLD
I TOO...
...WAS COLD WITHOUT YOU, SUI.
TOO COLD.
COME WITH ME.
COME HOME.
COME HOME WITH ME.
ONCE YOUR PAIN EASES...
...WE'LL WATCH FOR RAINBOWS AGAIN.
SUI...
I WAS SO HAPPY THERE.

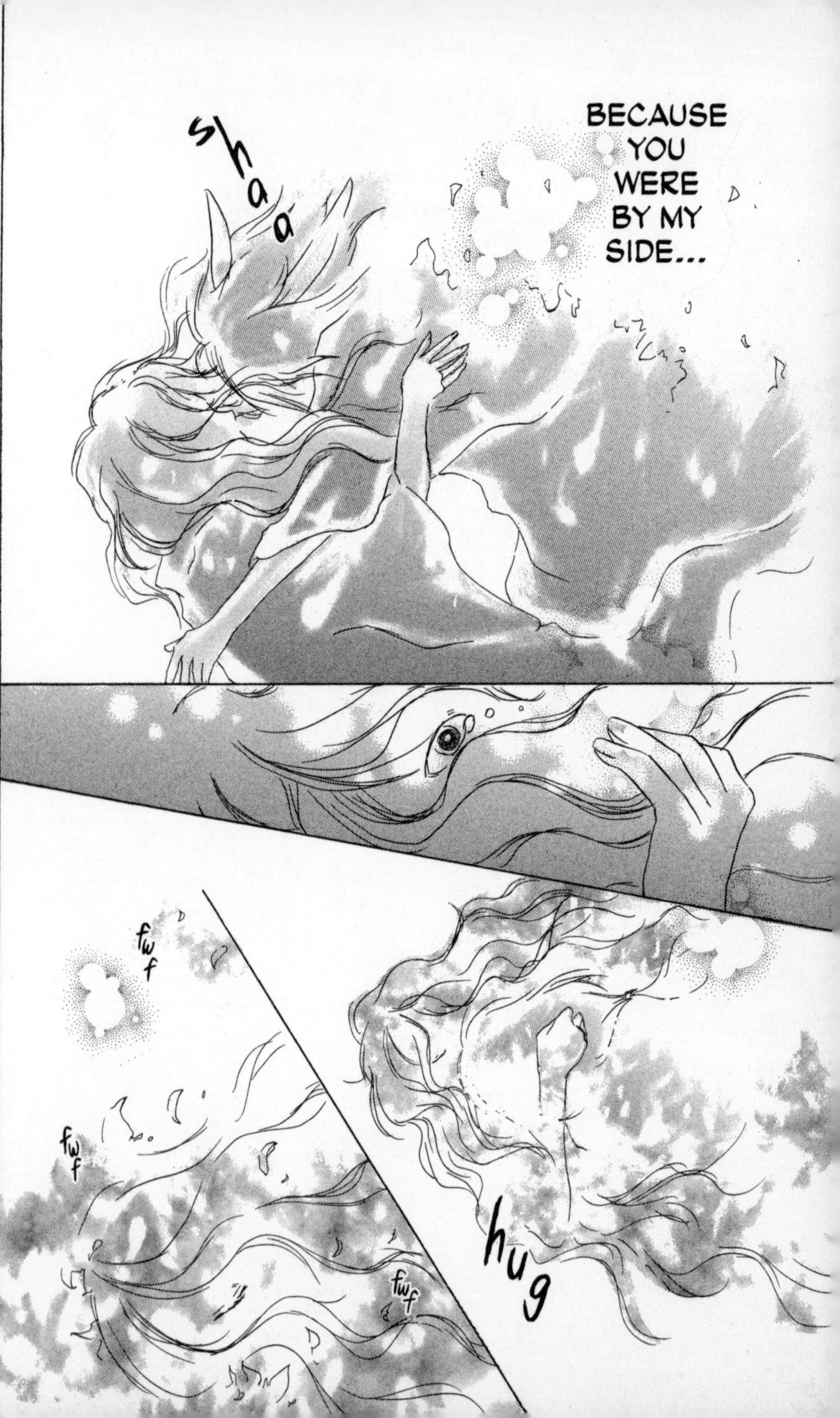
BECAUSE YOU WERE BY MY SIDE...
shaa
hug
fwf
fwf
fwf

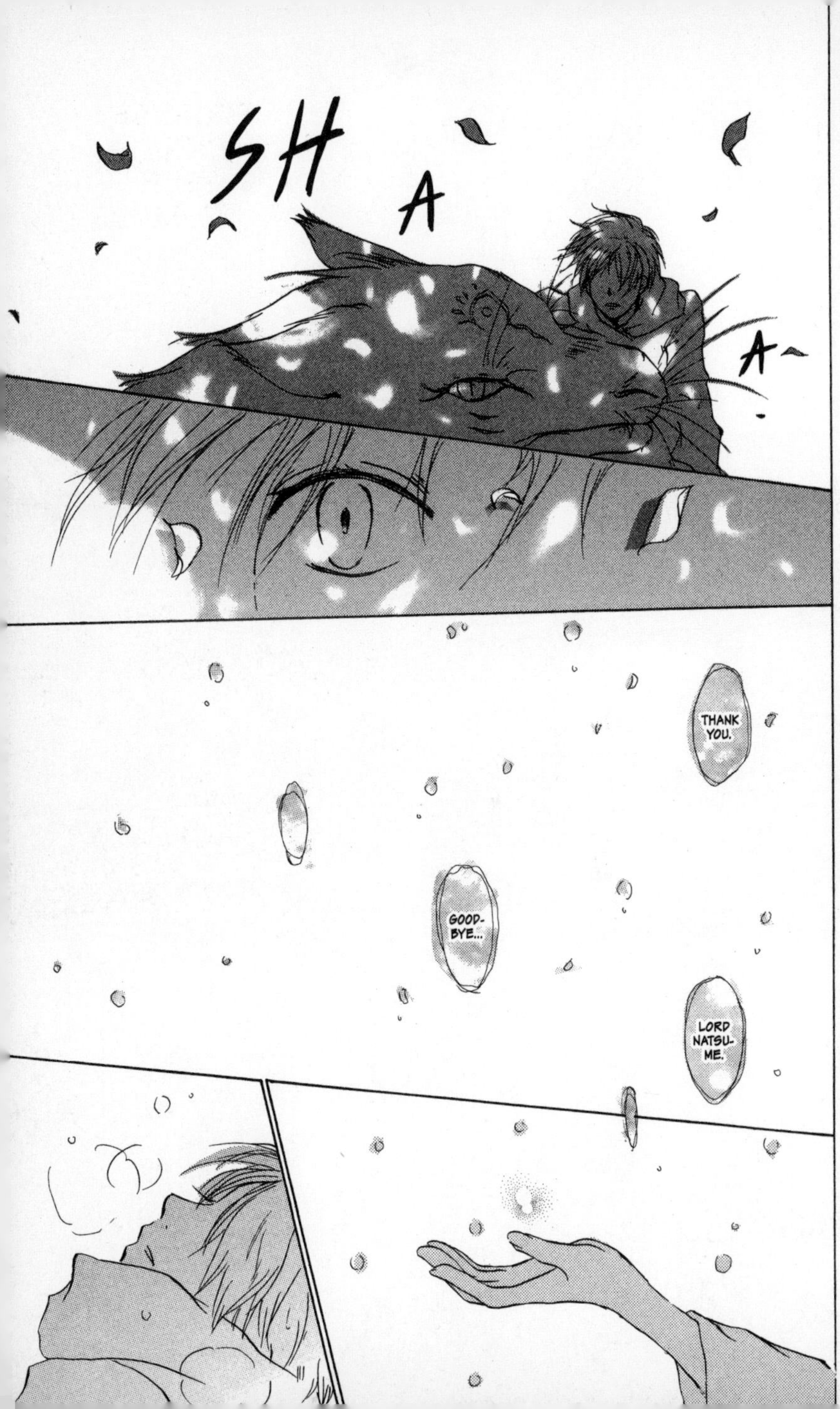
SHA
A-
THANK YOU.
GOOD-BYE...
LORD NATSU-ME.

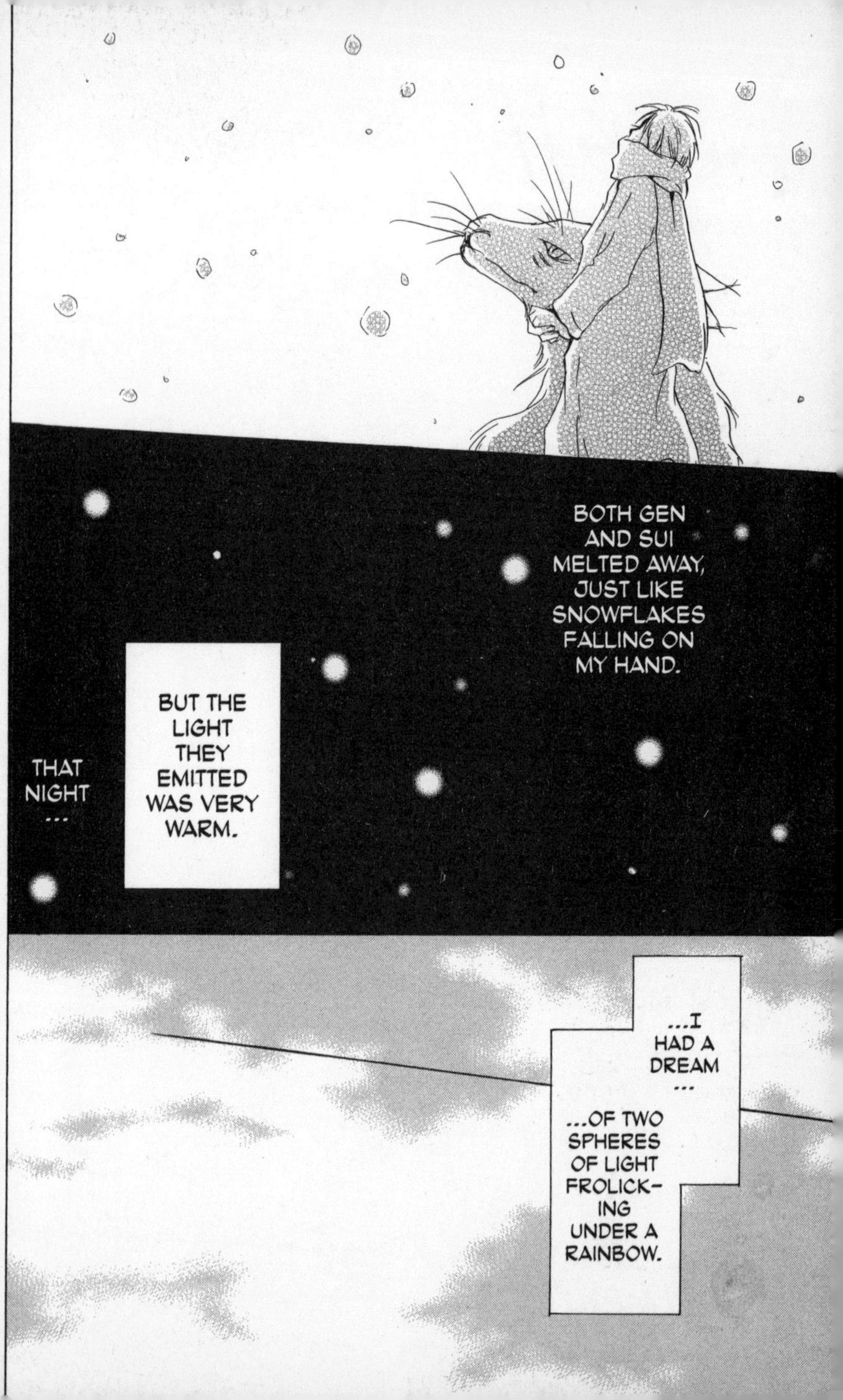
BOTH GEN AND SUI MELTED AWAY, JUST LIKE SNOWFLAKES FALLING ON MY HAND.
BUT THE LIGHT THEY EMITTED WAS VERY WARM.
THAT NIGHT ...
...I HAD A DREAM ...
...OF TWO SPHERES OF LIGHT FROLICK-ING UNDER A RAINBOW.

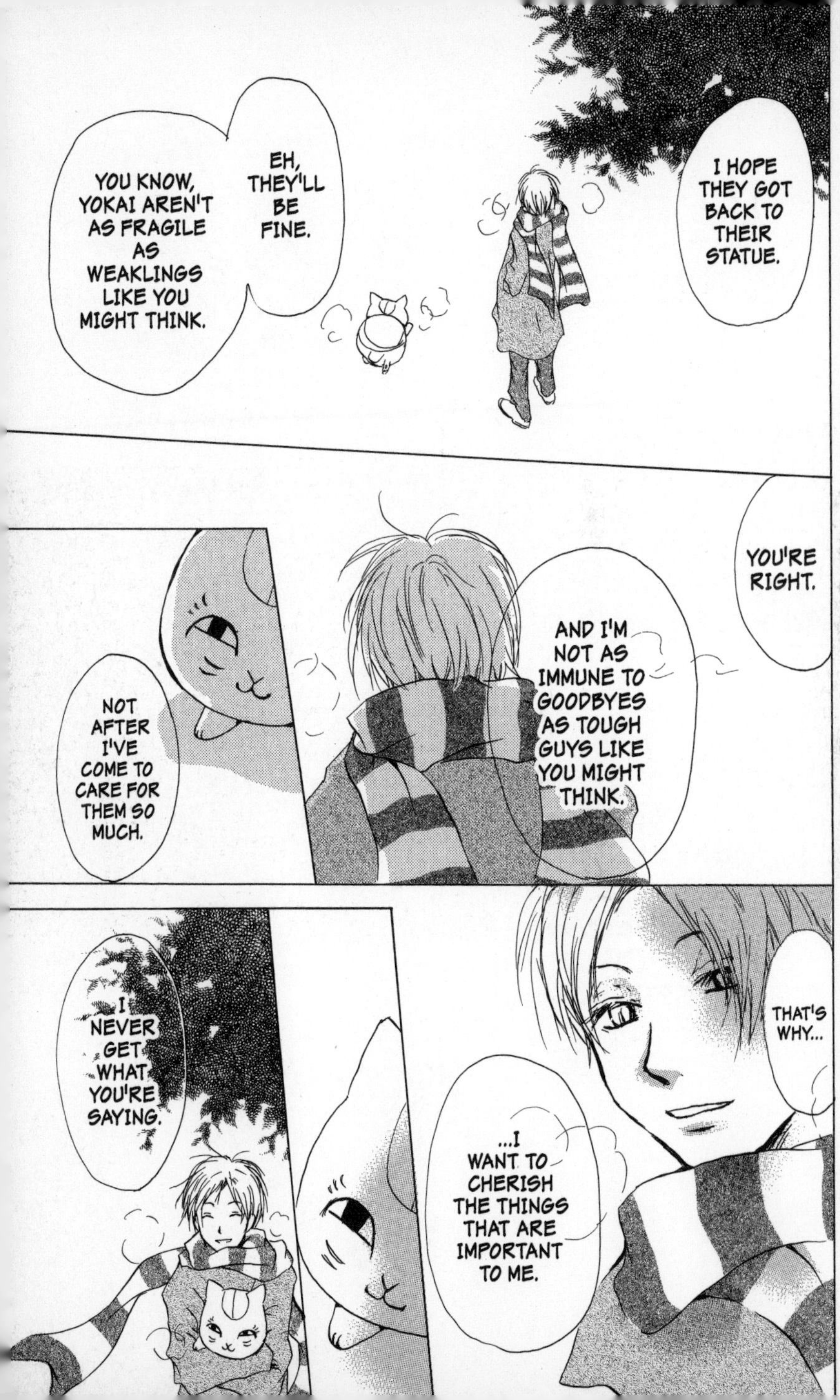
I HOPE THEY GOT BACK TO THEIR STATUE.
EH, THEY'LL BE FINE.
YOU KNOW, YOKAI AREN'T AS FRAGILE AS WEAKLINGS LIKE YOU MIGHT THINK.
YOU'RE RIGHT.
AND I'M NOT AS IMMUNE TO GOODBYES AS TOUGH GUYS LIKE YOU MIGHT THINK.
NOT AFTER I'VE COME TO CARE FOR THEM SO MUCH.
THAT'S WHY...
...I WANT TO CHERISH THE THINGS THAT ARE IMPORTANT TO ME.
I NEVER GET WHAT YOU'RE SAYING.

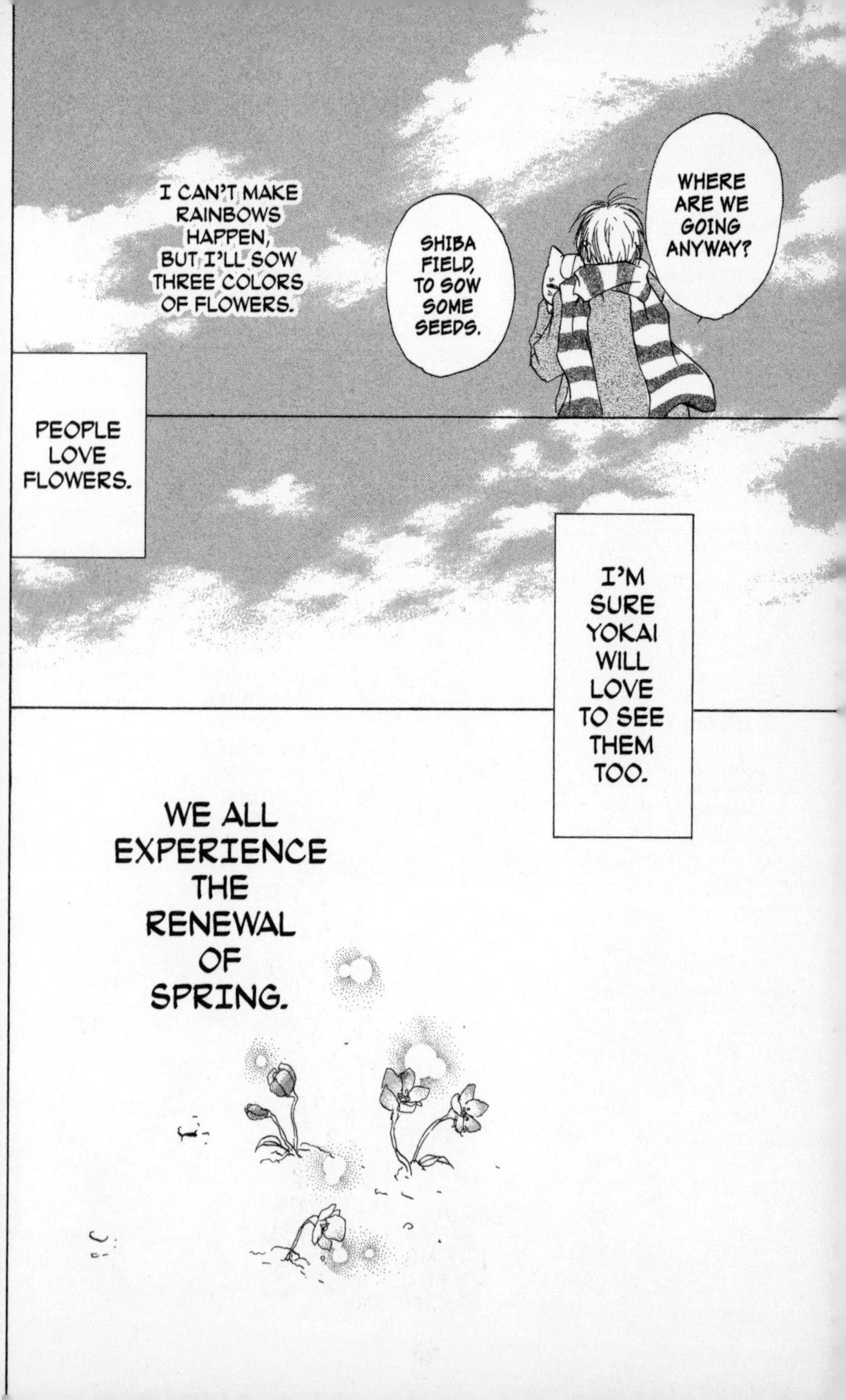
WHERE ARE WE GOING ANYWAY?
SHIBA FIELD, TO SOW SOME SEEDS.
I CAN'T MAKE RAINBOWS HAPPEN, BUT I'LL SOW THREE COLORS OF FLOWERS.
PEOPLE LOVE FLOWERS.
I'M SURE YOKAI WILL LOVE TO SEE THEM TOO.
WE ALL EXPERIENCE THE RENEWAL OF SPRING.

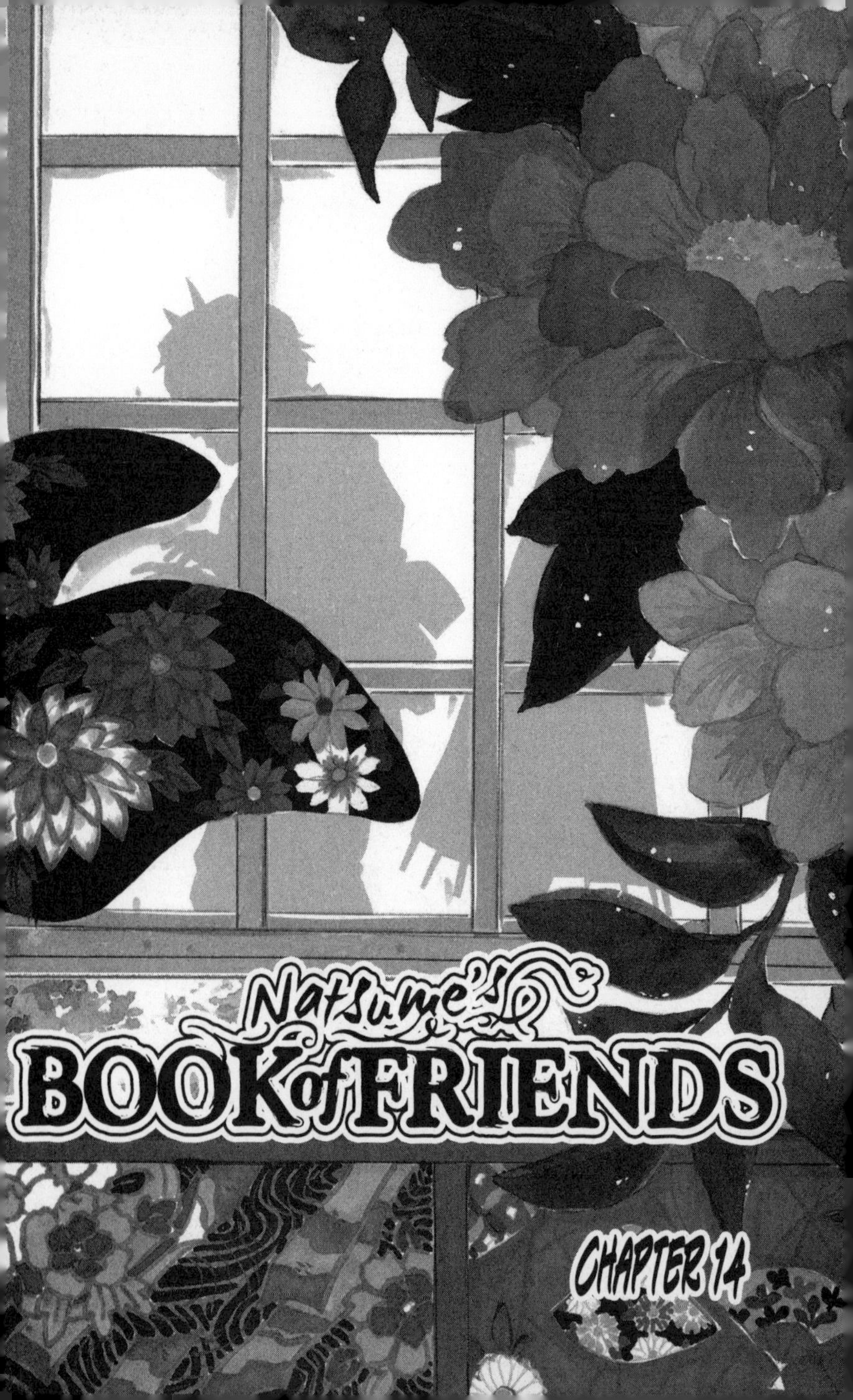
Natsume's
BOOK of FRIENDS
CHAPTER 14

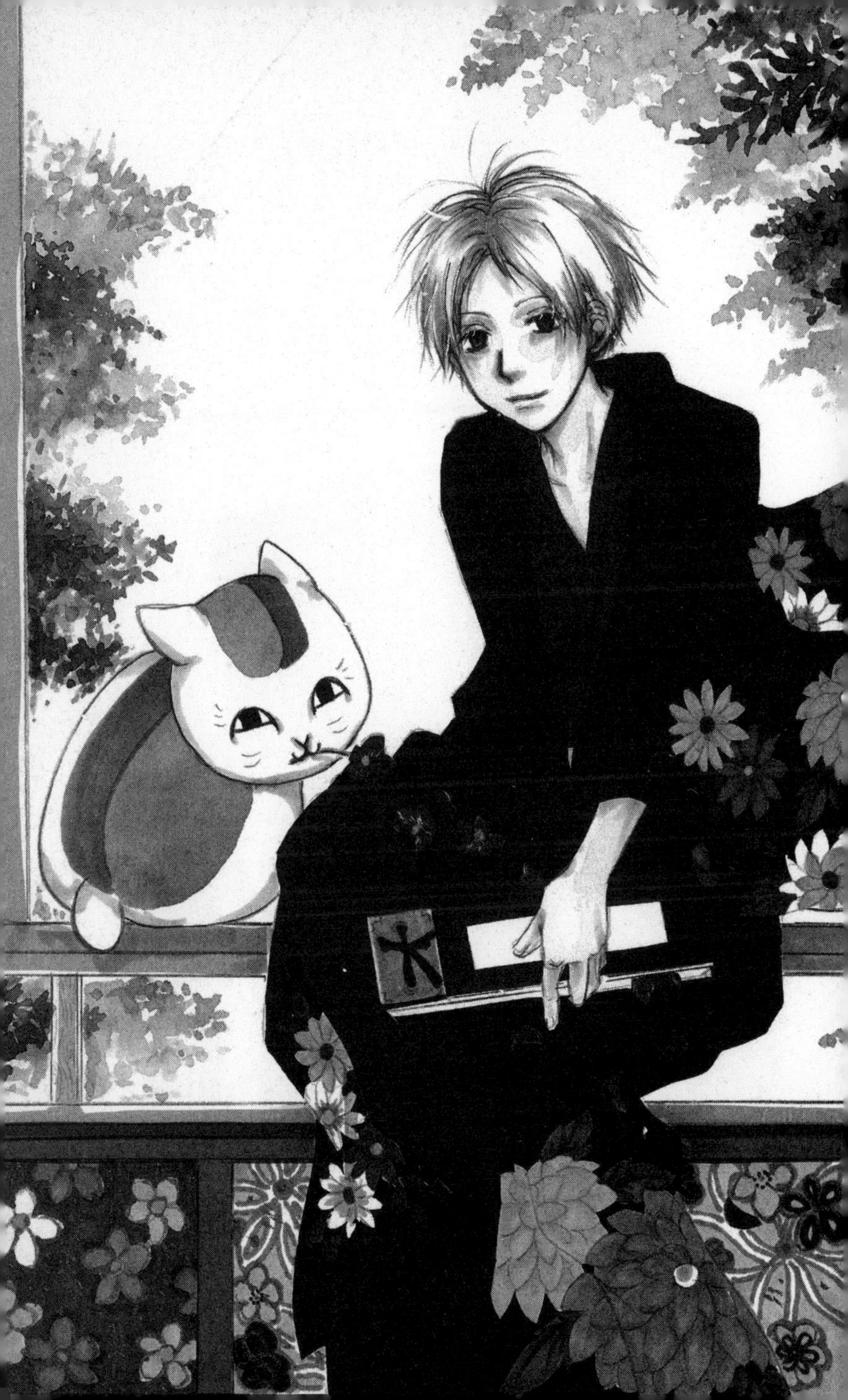

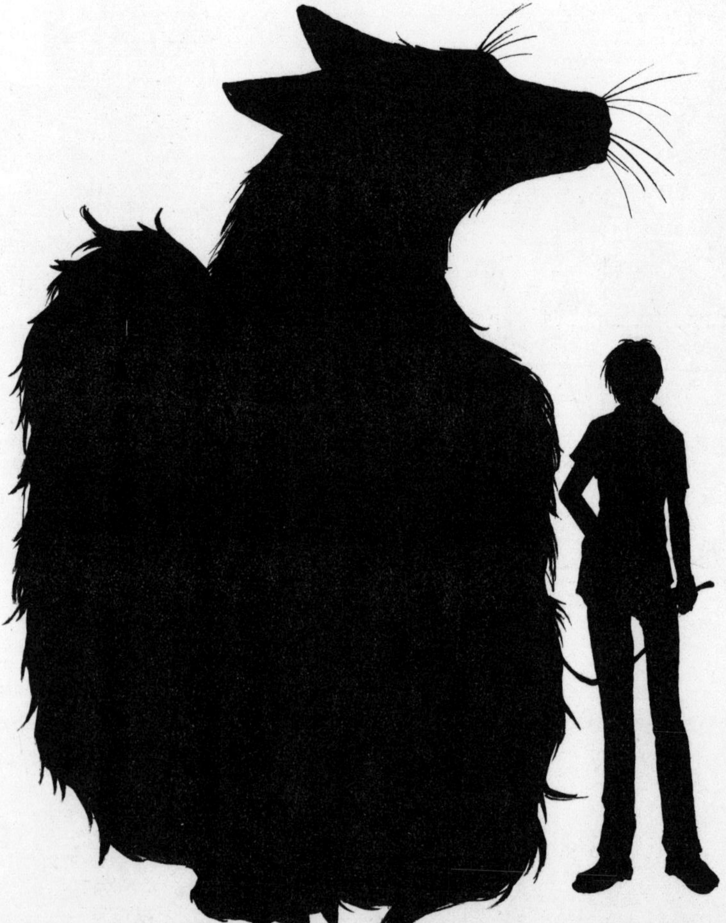

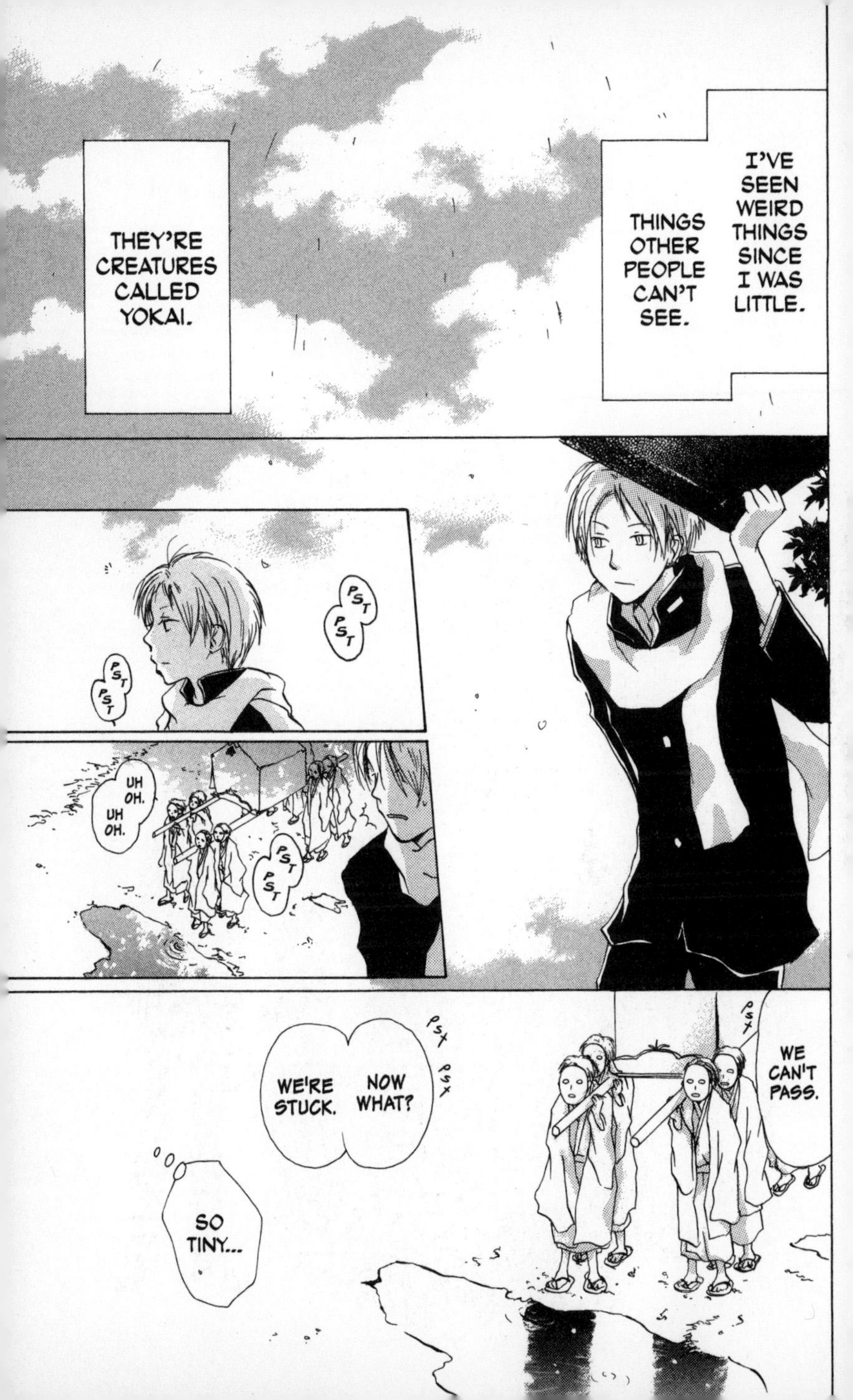

I'VE SEEN WEIRD THINGS SINCE I WAS LITTLE.
THINGS OTHER PEOPLE CAN'T SEE.
THEY'RE CREATURES CALLED YOKAI.
PST PST
PST PST
PST PST
UH OH. UH OH.
PST
WE CAN'T PASS.
PST PST
NOW WHAT?
WE'RE STUCK.
SO TINY...

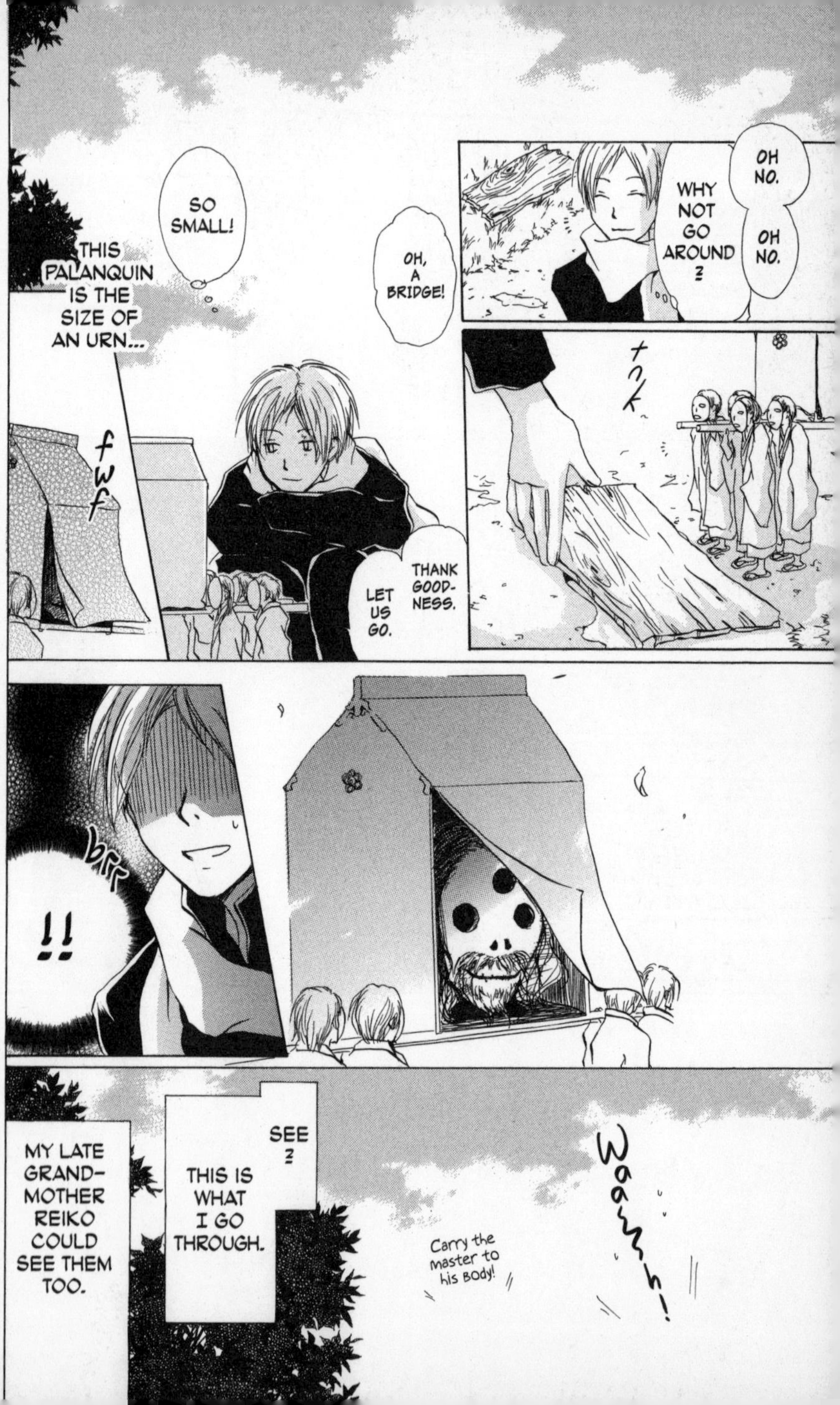
OH NO.
OH NO.
WHY NOT GO AROUND?
tok
OH, A BRIDGE!
SO SMALL!
THIS PALANQUIN IS THE SIZE OF AN URN...
fwf
THANK GOODNESS.
LET US GO.
brr
!!
Waaah!
Carry the master to his Body!
SEE?
THIS IS WHAT I GO THROUGH.
MY LATE GRANDMOTHER REIKO COULD SEE THEM TOO.

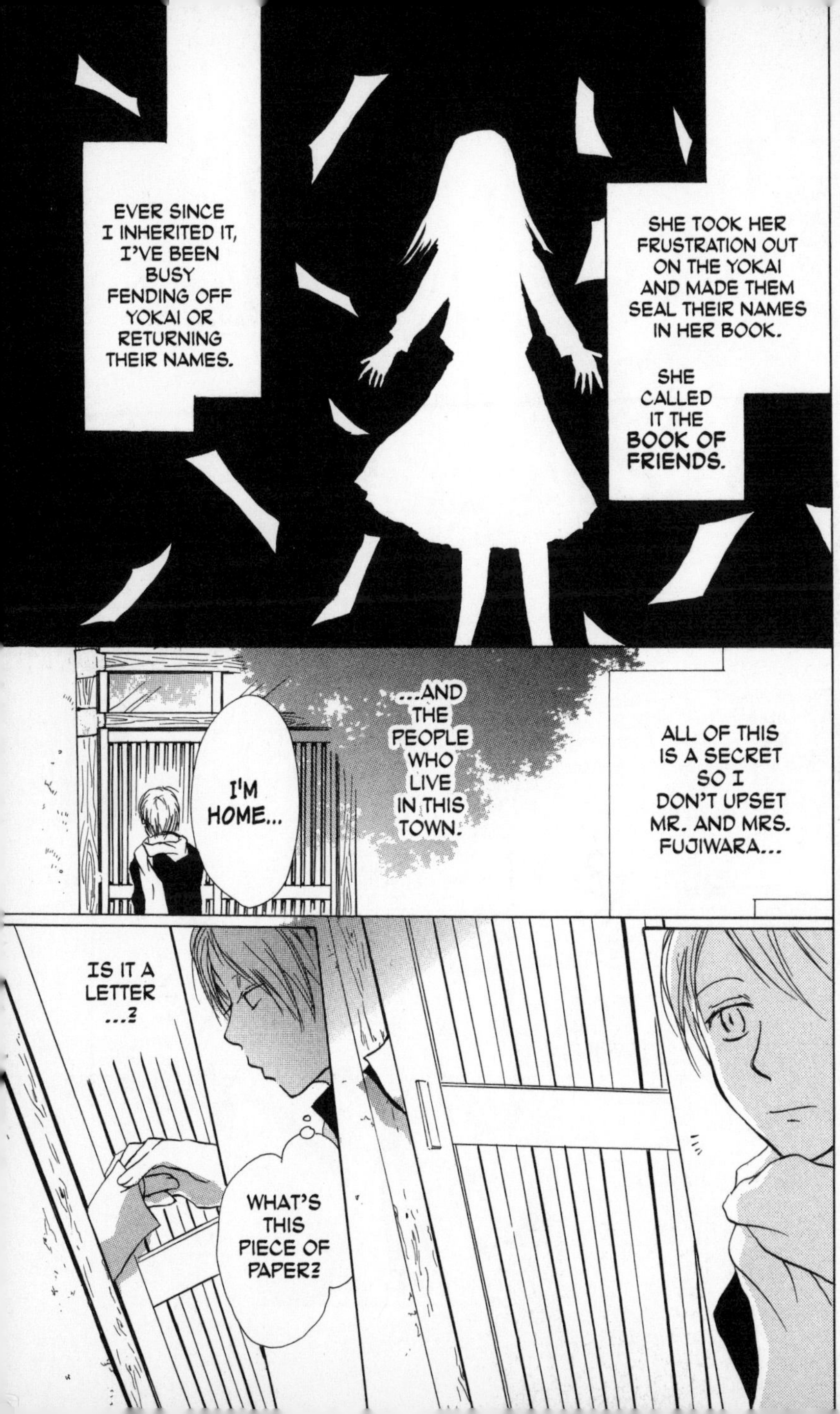
SHE TOOK HER FRUSTRATION OUT ON THE YOKAI AND MADE THEM SEAL THEIR NAMES IN HER BOOK.
SHE CALLED IT THE BOOK OF FRIENDS.
EVER SINCE I INHERITED IT, I'VE BEEN BUSY FENDING OFF YOKAI OR RETURNING THEIR NAMES.
ALL OF THIS IS A SECRET SO I DON'T UPSET MR. AND MRS. FUJIWARA...
...AND THE PEOPLE WHO LIVE IN THIS TOWN.
I'M HOME...
WHAT'S THIS PIECE OF PAPER?
IS IT A LETTER ...?

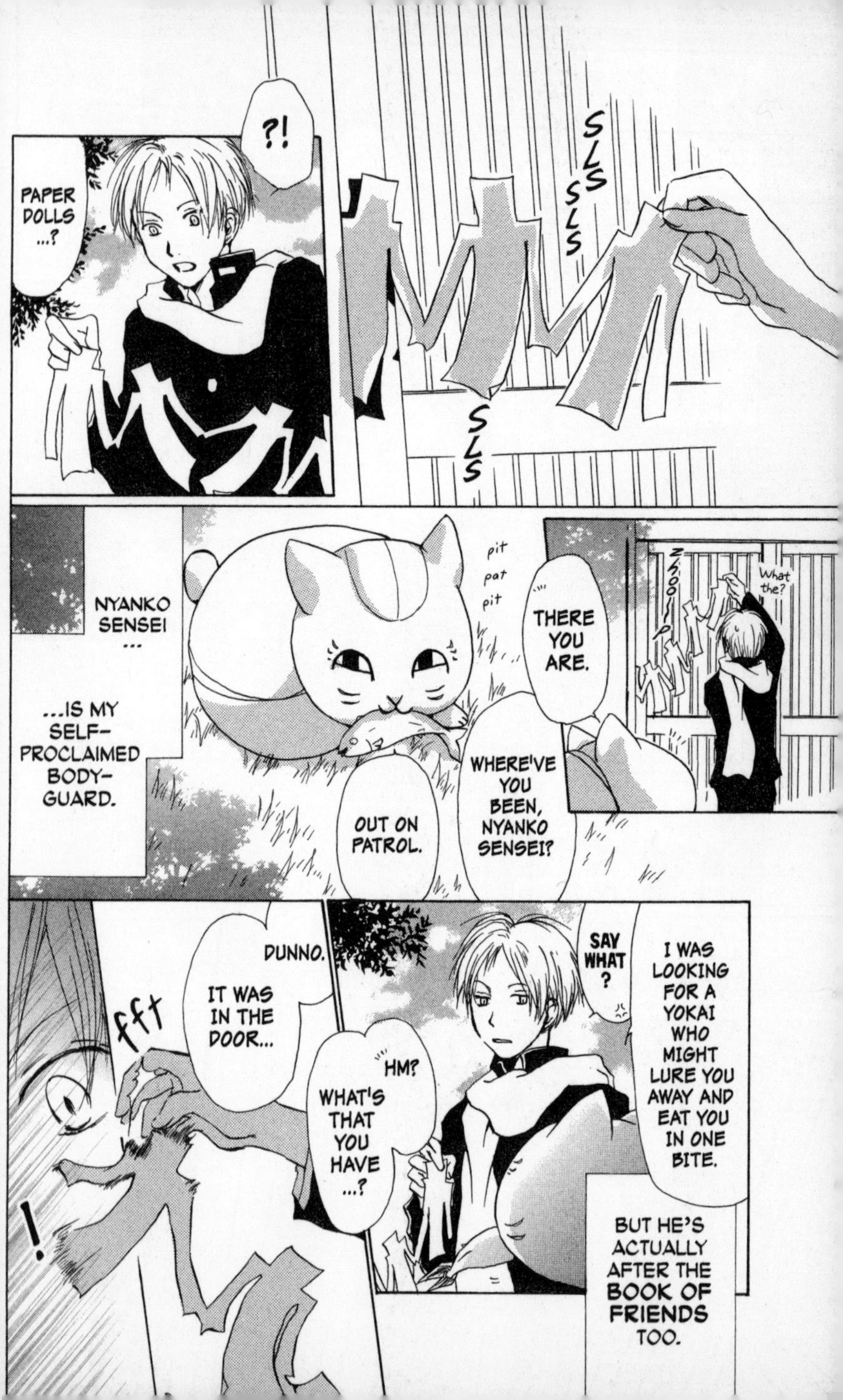
SLS
SLS
SLS
?!
PAPER DOLLS ...?
What the?
pit
pat
pit
THERE YOU ARE.
WHERE'VE YOU BEEN, NYANKO SENSEI?
OUT ON PATROL.
NYANKO SENSEI ...
...IS MY SELF-PROCLAIMED BODY-GUARD.
SAY WHAT?
I WAS LOOKING FOR A YOKAI WHO MIGHT LURE YOU AWAY AND EAT YOU IN ONE BITE.
HM?
WHAT'S THAT YOU HAVE ...?
BUT HE'S ACTUALLY AFTER THE BOOK OF FRIENDS TOO.
DUNNO.
IT WAS IN THE DOOR...
fft
!

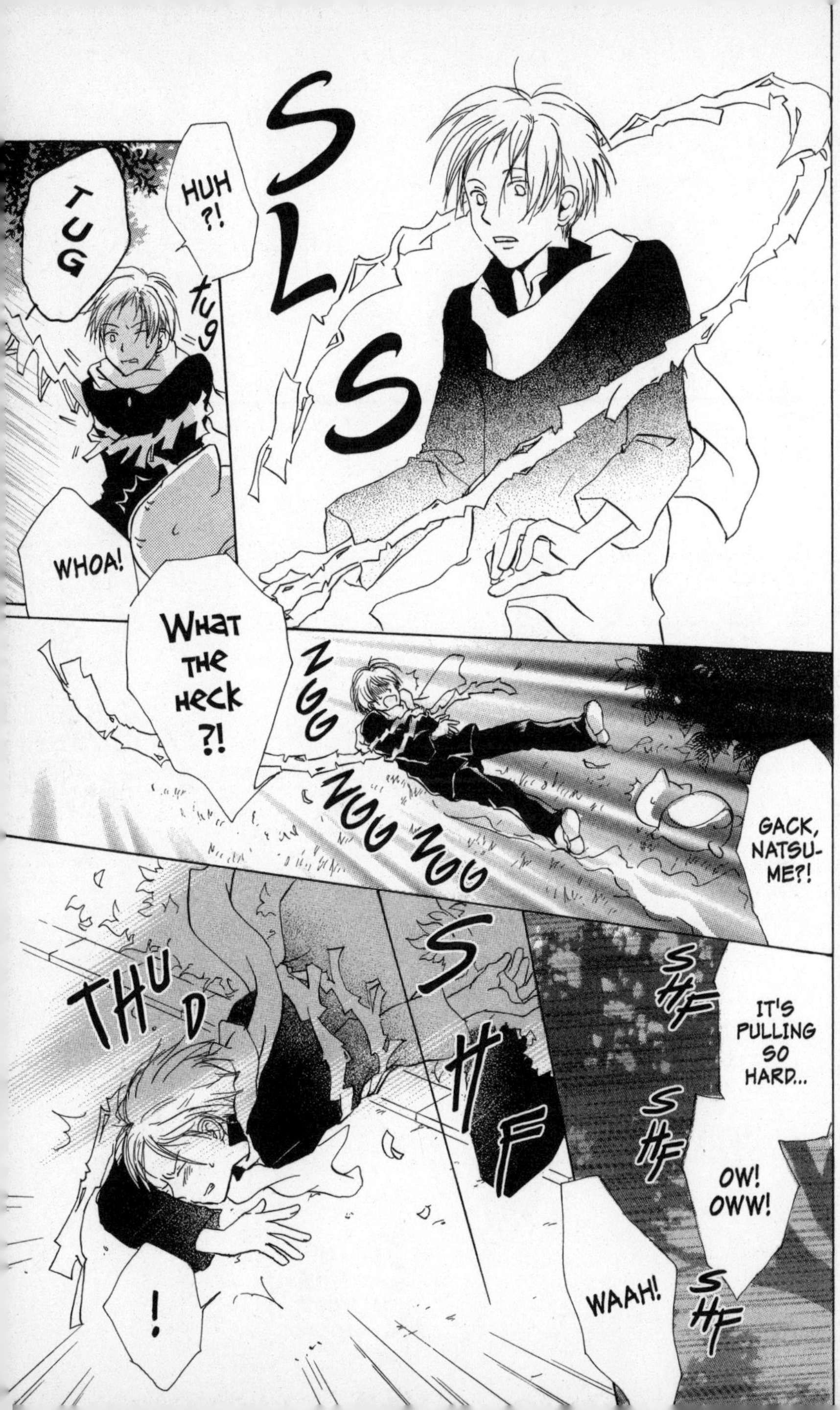
SLS
HUH ?!
TUG
tug
WHOA!
GACK, NATSU-ME?!
ZGG
ZGG ZGG ZGG
What the heck ?!
SHF
IT'S PULLING SO HARD...
SHF
OW! OWW!
SHF
WAAH!
SHF
THUD
!

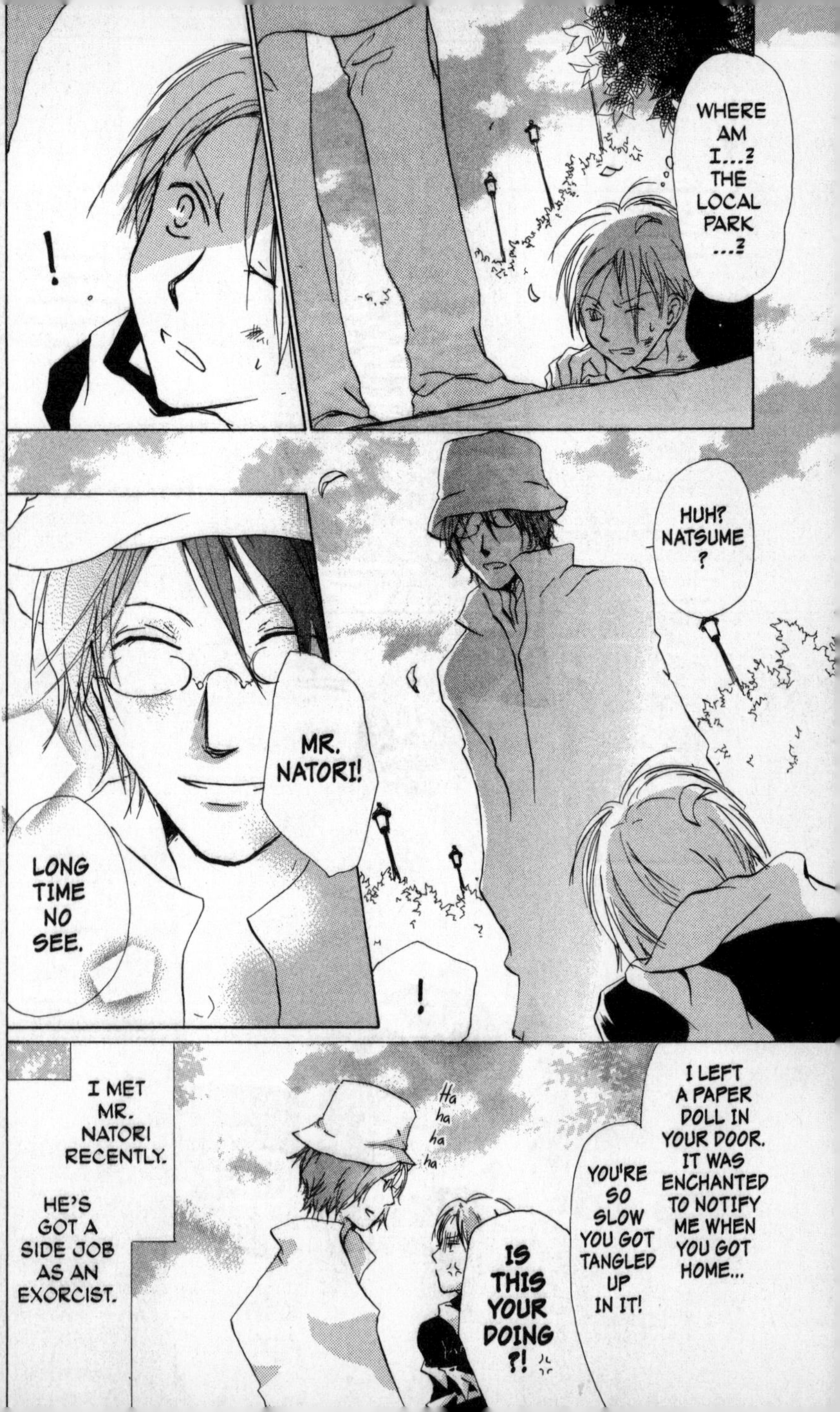
WHERE AM I...? THE LOCAL PARK...?
!
HUH? NATSUME?
!
MR. NATORI!
LONG TIME NO SEE.
I LEFT A PAPER DOLL IN YOUR DOOR. IT WAS ENCHANTED TO NOTIFY ME WHEN YOU GOT HOME...
YOU'RE SO SLOW YOU GOT TANGLED UP IN IT!
IS THIS YOUR DOING?!
Ha ha ha ha
I MET MR. NATORI RECENTLY.
HE'S GOT A SIDE JOB AS AN EXORCIST.

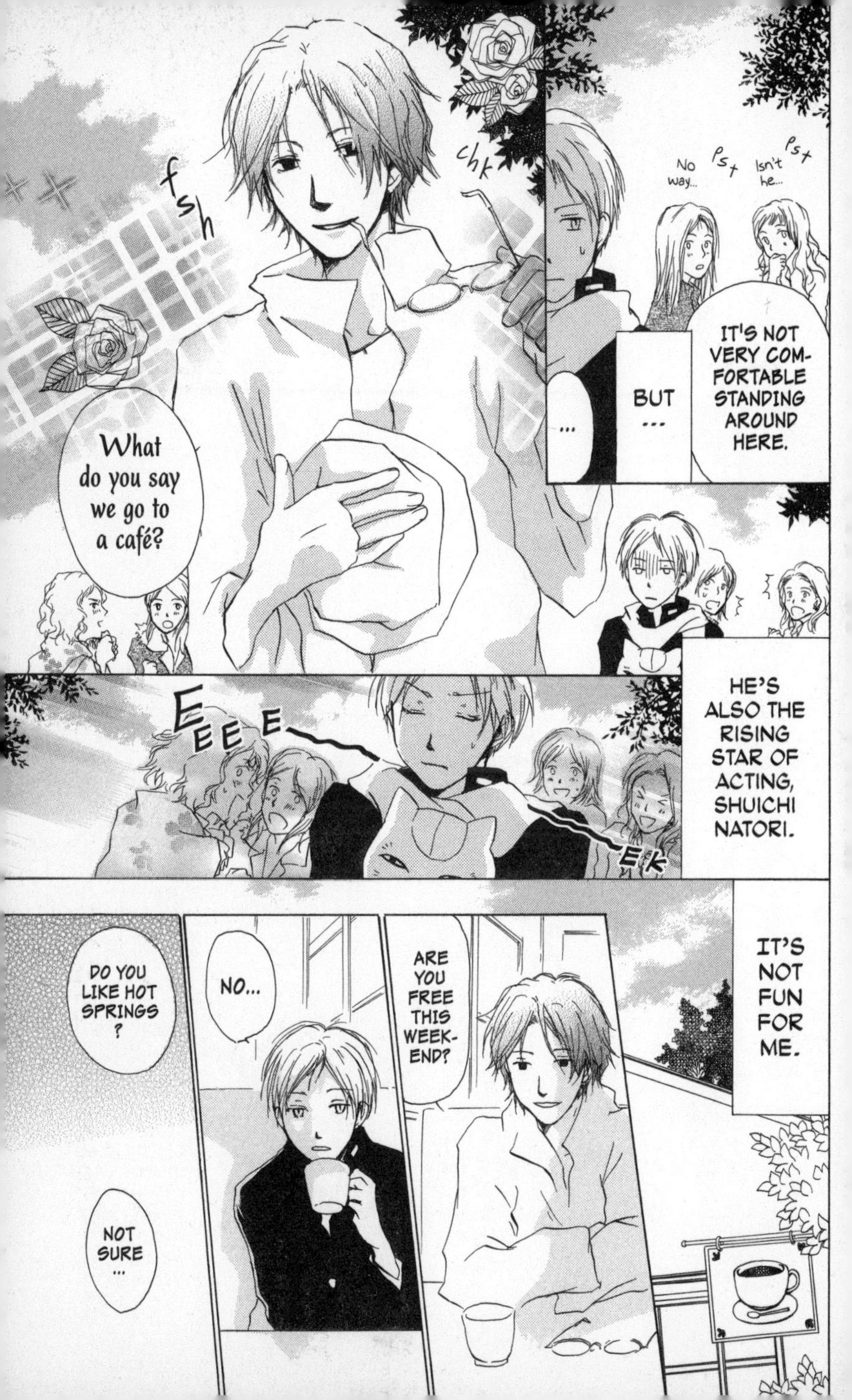
Pst
Isn't he...
Pst
No way...
IT'S NOT VERY COM-FORTABLE STANDING AROUND HERE.
BUT ...
...
chk
fsh
What do you say we go to a café?
HE'S ALSO THE RISING STAR OF ACTING, SHUICHI NATORI.
EEEEE—EK
IT'S NOT FUN FOR ME.
ARE YOU FREE THIS WEEK-END?
NO...
DO YOU LIKE HOT SPRINGS ?
NOT SURE ...

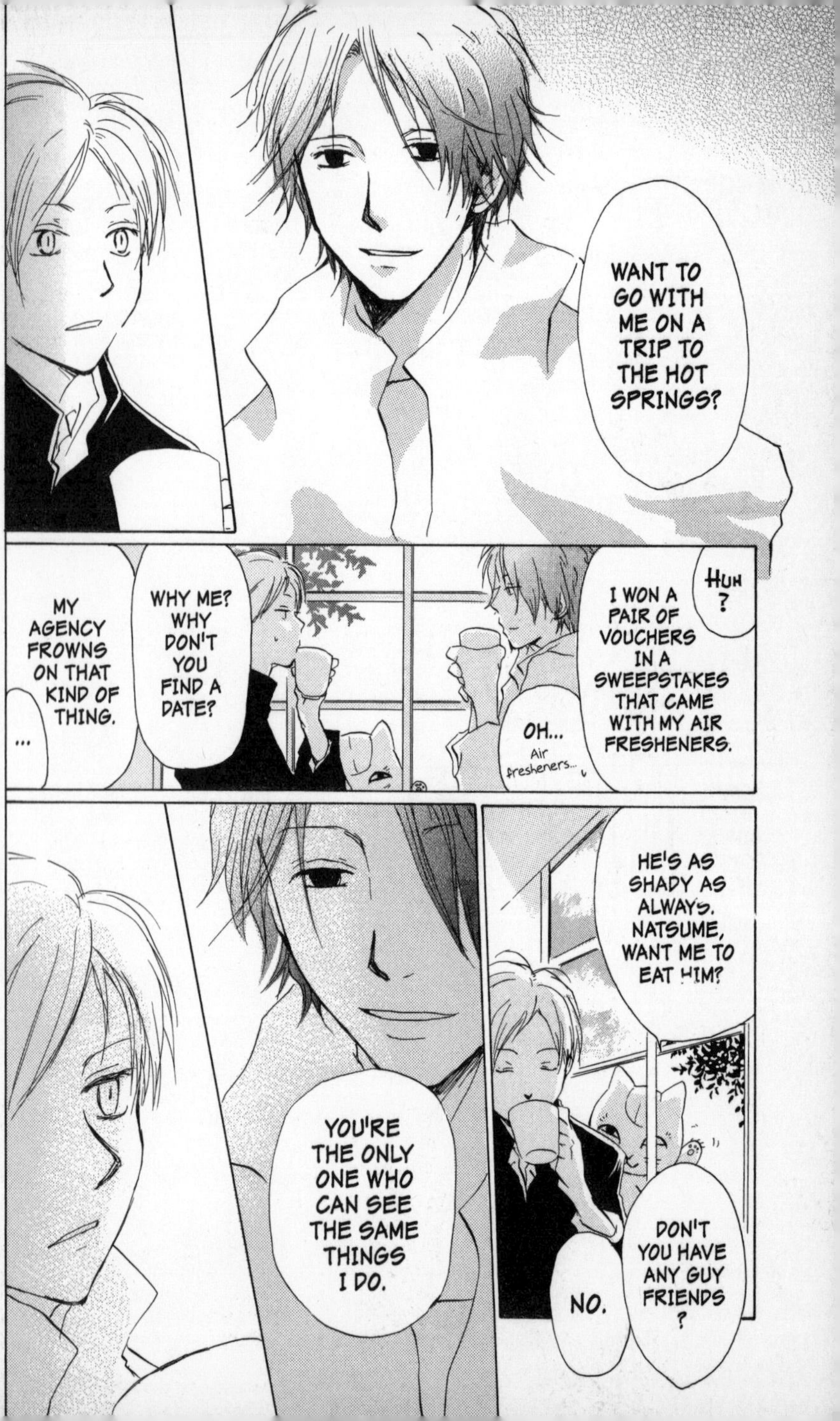
WANT TO GO WITH ME ON A TRIP TO THE HOT SPRINGS?
HUH?
I WON A PAIR OF VOUCHERS IN A SWEEPSTAKES THAT CAME WITH MY AIR FRESHENERS.
OH...
Air fresheners...
WHY ME? WHY DON'T YOU FIND A DATE?
MY AGENCY FROWNS ON THAT KIND OF THING.
...
HE'S AS SHADY AS ALWAYS. NATSUME, WANT ME TO EAT HIM?
DON'T YOU HAVE ANY GUY FRIENDS?
NO.
YOU'RE THE ONLY ONE WHO CAN SEE THE SAME THINGS I DO.

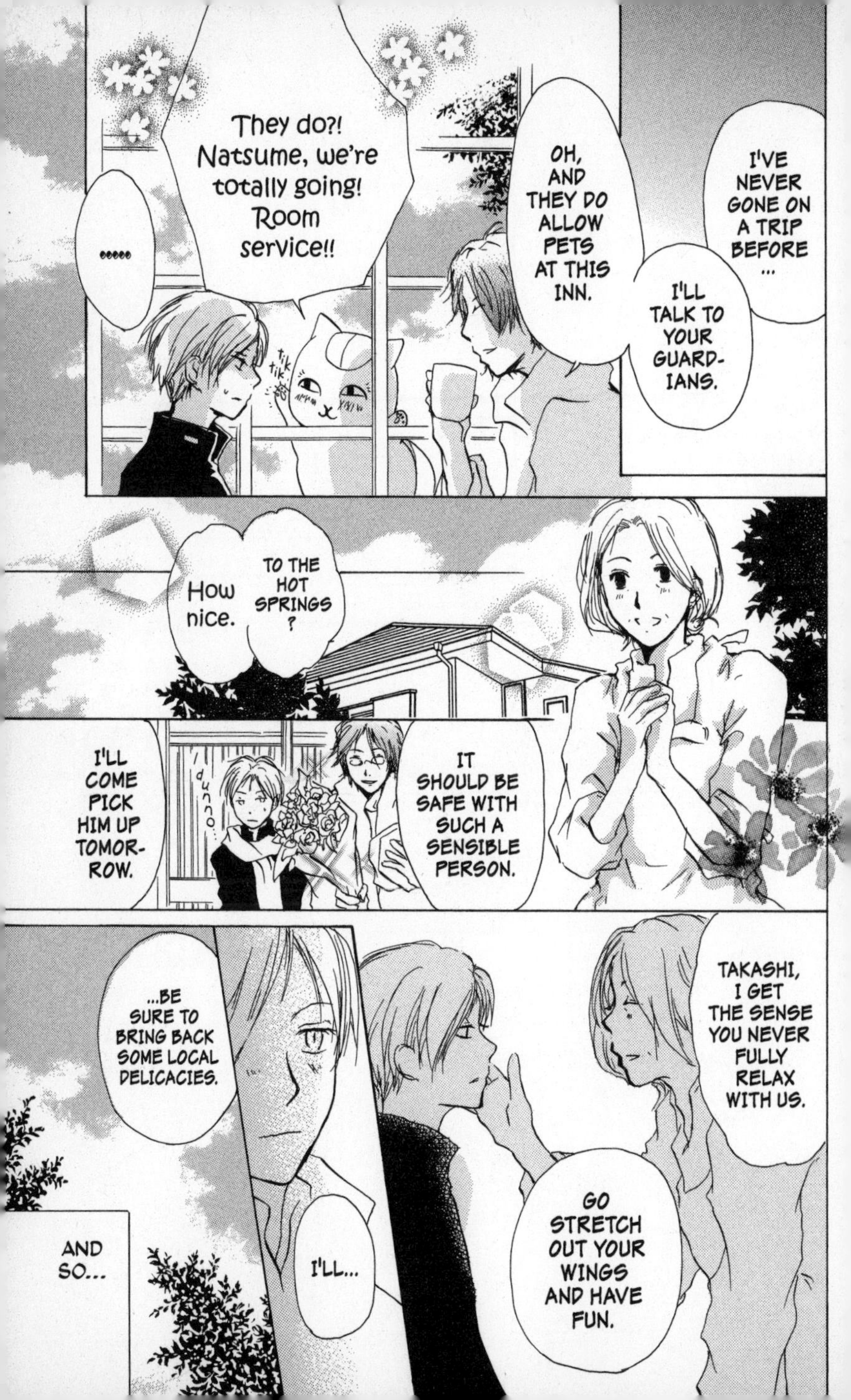
I'VE NEVER GONE ON A TRIP BEFORE ...
I'LL TALK TO YOUR GUARDIANS.
OH, AND THEY DO ALLOW PETS AT THIS INN.
They do?! Natsume, we're totally going! Room service!!
tik tik
•••••
TO THE HOT SPRINGS?
How nice.
IT SHOULD BE SAFE WITH SUCH A SENSIBLE PERSON.
I dunno...
I'LL COME PICK HIM UP TOMORROW.
TAKASHI, I GET THE SENSE YOU NEVER FULLY RELAX WITH US.
GO STRETCH OUT YOUR WINGS AND HAVE FUN.
...BE SURE TO BRING BACK SOME LOCAL DELICACIES.
I'LL...
AND SO...

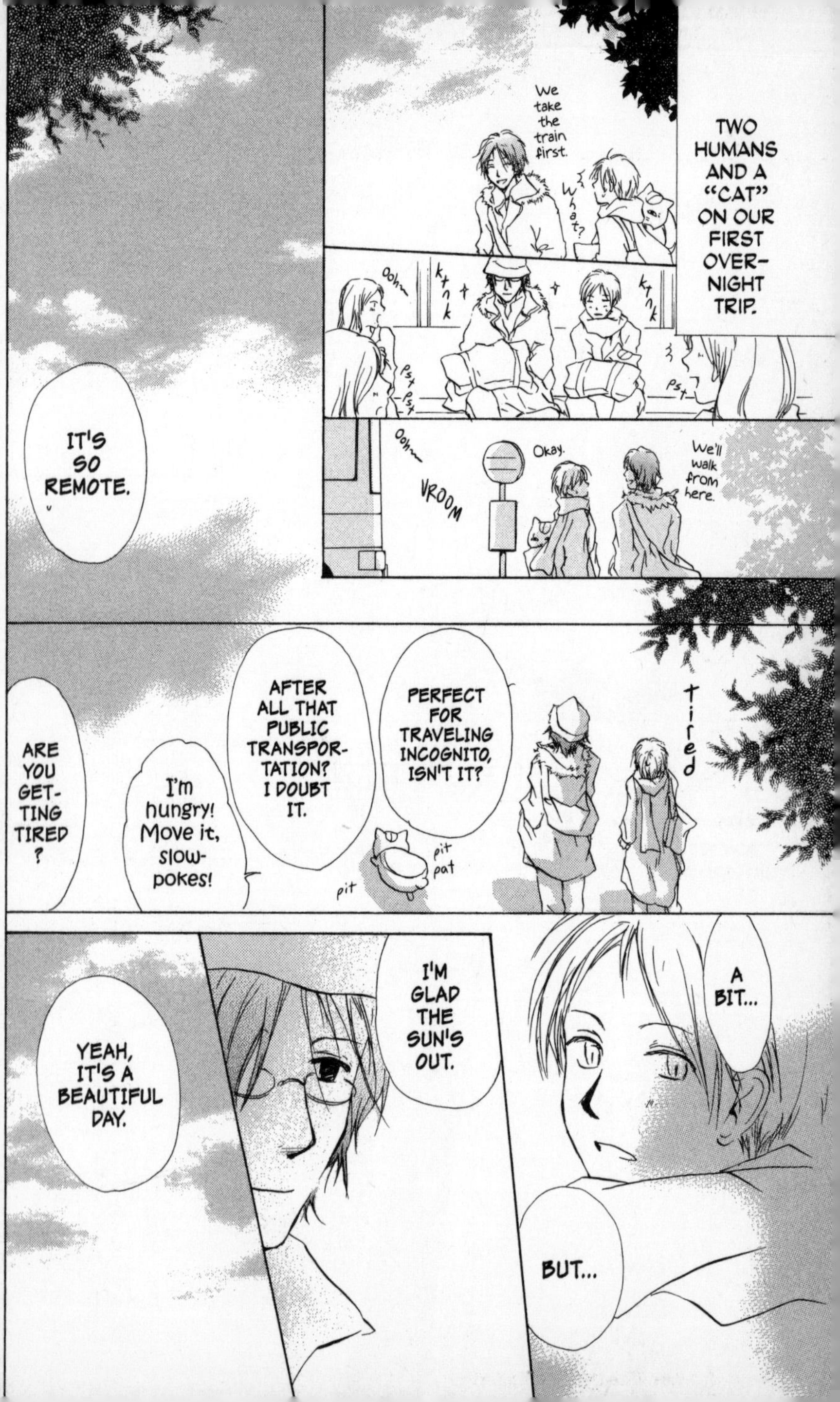
TWO HUMANS AND A "CAT" ON OUR FIRST OVER-NIGHT TRIP.
We take the train first.
What?
Ooh~
ktnk
ktnk
pst
pst pst
pst
We'll walk from here.
Okay.
Ooh~
VROOM
IT'S SO REMOTE.
tired
PERFECT FOR TRAVELING INCOGNITO, ISN'T IT?
AFTER ALL THAT PUBLIC TRANSPOR-TATION? I DOUBT IT.
pit pat
pit
I'm hungry! Move it, slow-pokes!
ARE YOU GET-TING TIRED?
A BIT...
BUT...
I'M GLAD THE SUN'S OUT.
YEAH, IT'S A BEAUTIFUL DAY.

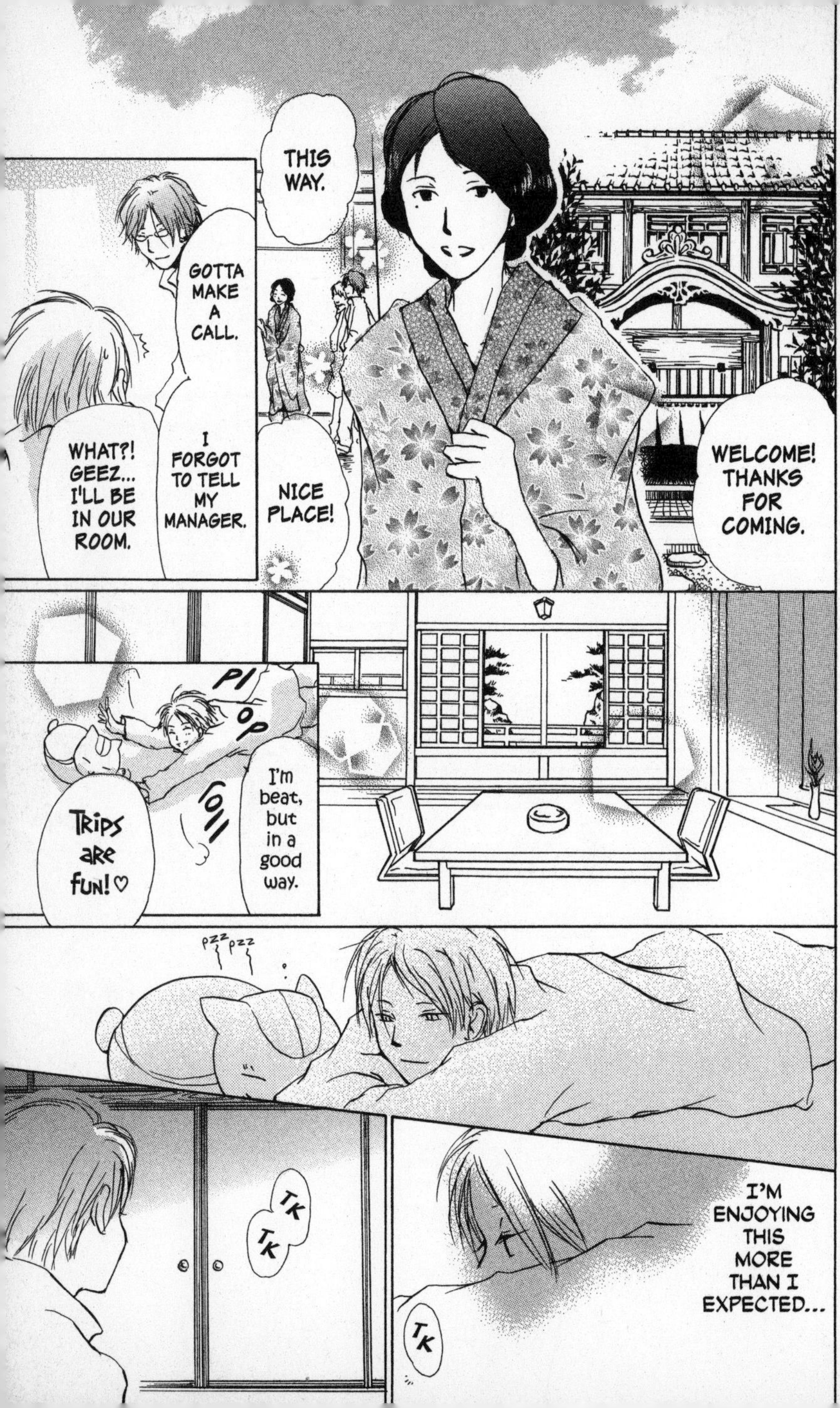
WELCOME! THANKS FOR COMING.
THIS WAY.
NICE PLACE!
GOTTA MAKE A CALL.
I FORGOT TO TELL MY MANAGER.
WHAT?! GEEZ... I'LL BE IN OUR ROOM.
PLOP
I'm beat, but in a good way.
ROLL
Trips are fun!♡
pzz pzz
I'M ENJOYING THIS MORE THAN I EXPECTED...
TK
TK TK

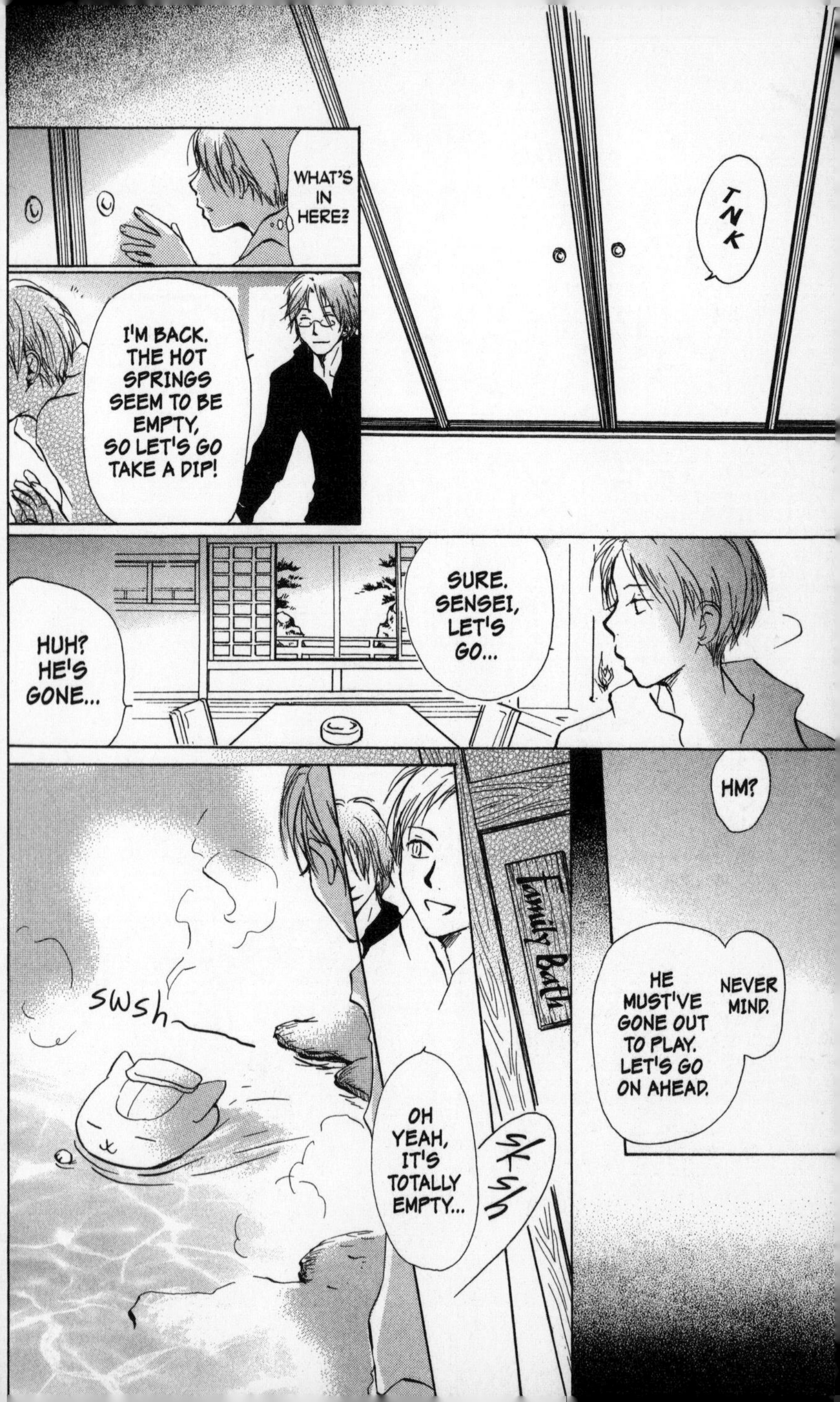
TNK
WHAT'S IN HERE?
I'M BACK. THE HOT SPRINGS SEEM TO BE EMPTY, SO LET'S GO TAKE A DIP!
SURE. SENSEI, LET'S GO...
HUH? HE'S GONE...
HM?
NEVER MIND.
HE MUST'VE GONE OUT TO PLAY. LET'S GO ON AHEAD.
Family Bath
SKSH
OH YEAH, IT'S TOTALLY EMPTY...
SWSH

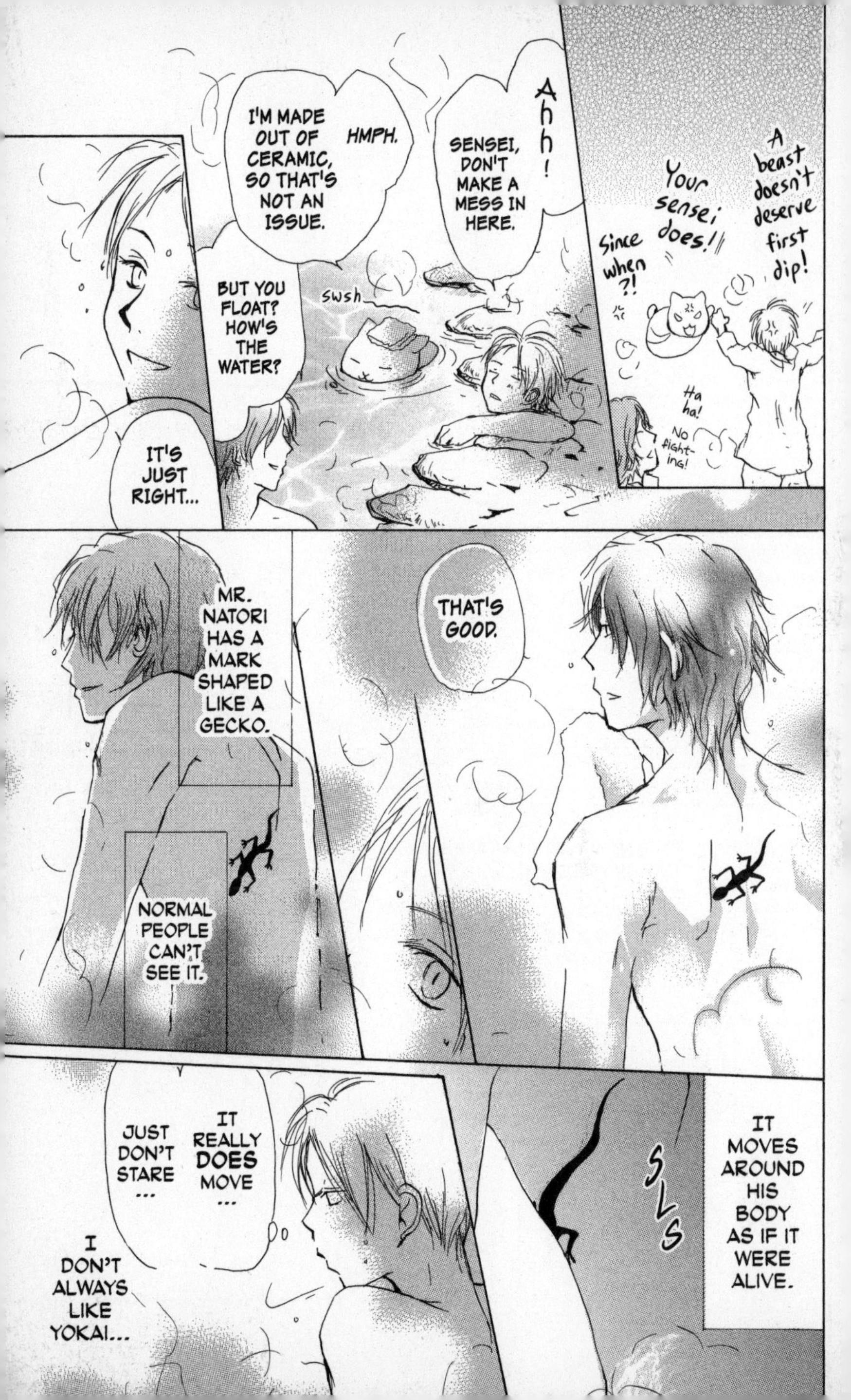
A beast doesn't deserve first dip!
Your sensei does!!
Since when?!
Ha ha!
No fighting!
Ahh!
SENSEI, DON'T MAKE A MESS IN HERE.
HMPH.
I'M MADE OUT OF CERAMIC, SO THAT'S NOT AN ISSUE.
swsh
BUT YOU FLOAT? HOW'S THE WATER?
IT'S JUST RIGHT...
THAT'S GOOD.
MR. NATORI HAS A MARK SHAPED LIKE A GECKO.
NORMAL PEOPLE CAN'T SEE IT.
IT MOVES AROUND HIS BODY AS IF IT WERE ALIVE.
IT REALLY DOES MOVE...
JUST DON'T STARE...
I DON'T ALWAYS LIKE YOKAI...

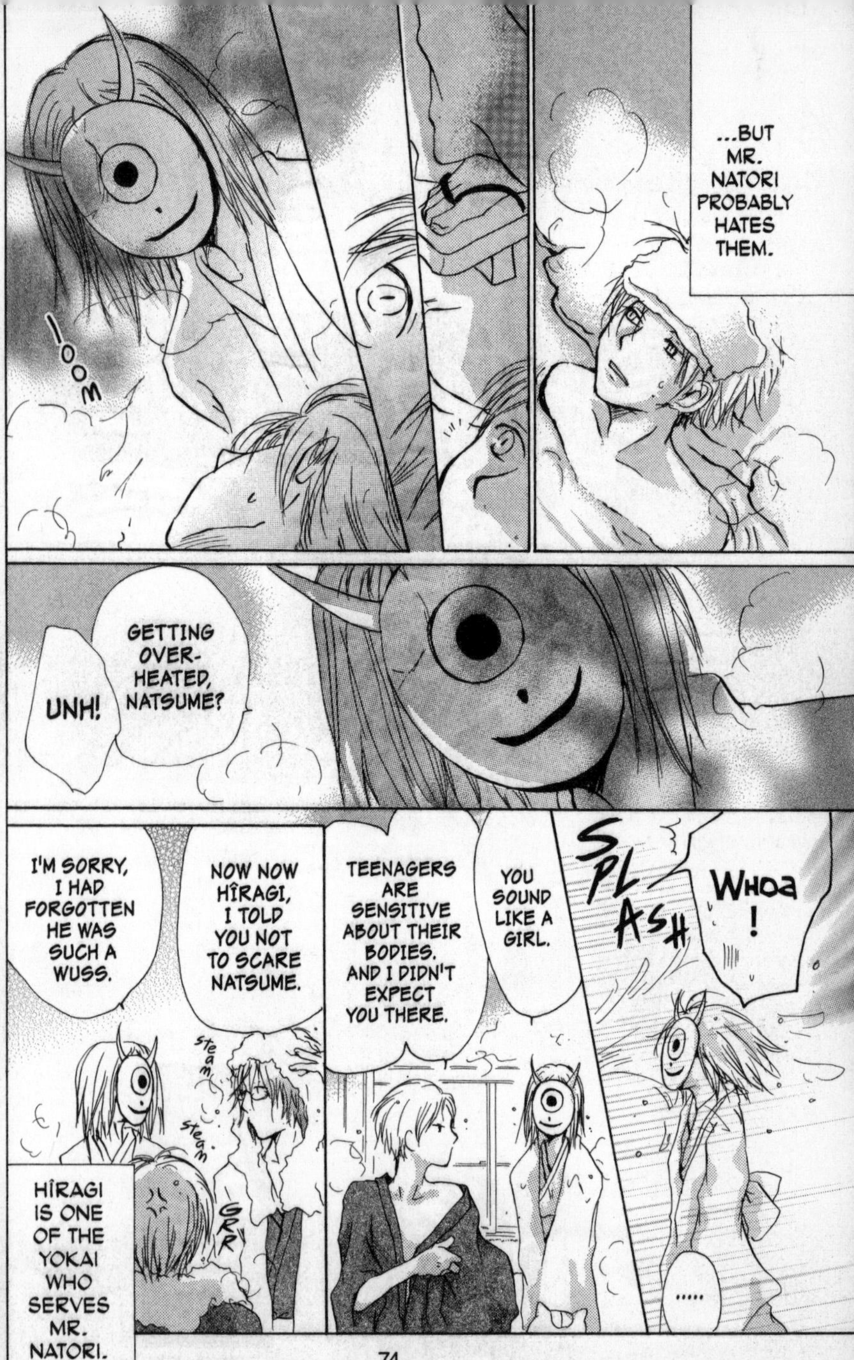
...BUT MR. NATORI PROBABLY HATES THEM.
WOO!
GETTING OVER-HEATED, NATSUME?
UNH!
WHOA!
SPLASH
.....
YOU SOUND LIKE A GIRL.
TEENAGERS ARE SENSITIVE ABOUT THEIR BODIES. AND I DIDN'T EXPECT YOU THERE.
NOW NOW HÎRAGI, I TOLD YOU NOT TO SCARE NATSUME.
I'M SORRY, I HAD FORGOTTEN HE WAS SUCH A WUSS.
steam steam
GRR
HÎRAGI IS ONE OF THE YOKAI WHO SERVES MR. NATORI.

01

Hello, I'm Midorikawa. This is my 12th ever graphic novel. I would like to thank the readers who are picking this up for the first time, as well as those who have been with me from the beginning.

I'm happy to say that with Natsume's Book of Friends I've achieved my goal of having a series longer than three volumes! The goal seemed so far off that I coordinated my short story collections in one color, just in case. I aspired to show my determination to have something that kept going for more than three volumes, even if they were short story collections. Natsume is kind of like a collection of short stories too, but I'm so glad I was able to reach another one of my goals with the help of my fans. I'd like to slowly but surely keep working to make more milestones. Thank you so much.

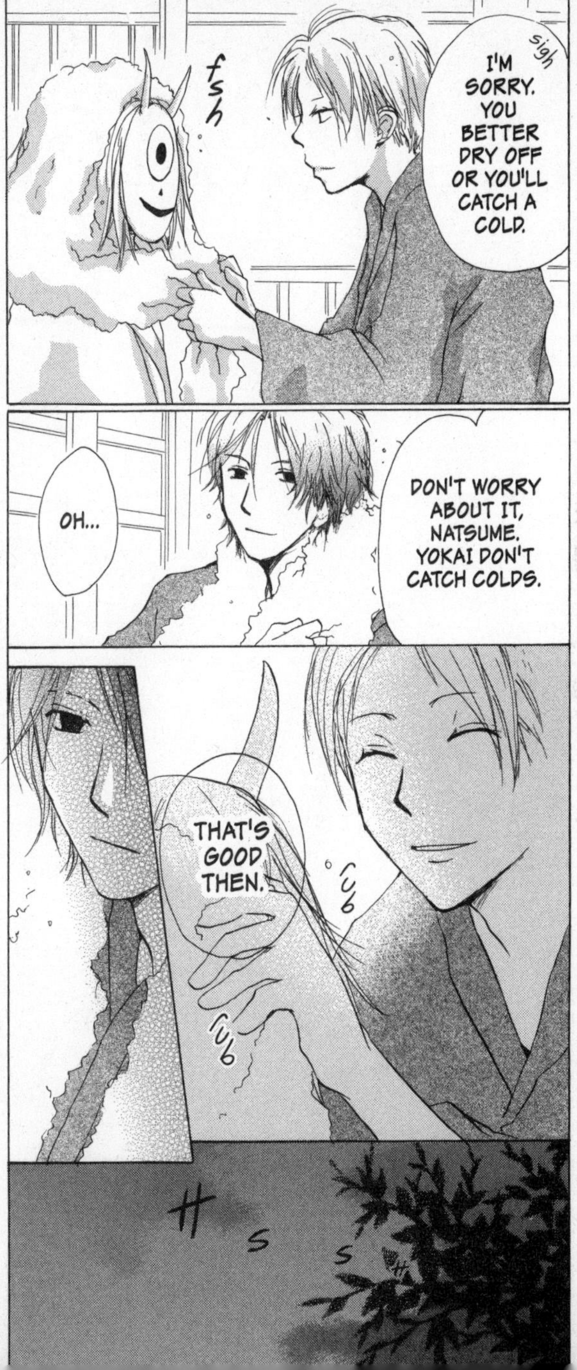
sigh
I'M SORRY. YOU BETTER DRY OFF OR YOU'LL CATCH A COLD.
fsh
DON'T WORRY ABOUT IT, NATSUME. YOKAI DON'T CATCH COLDS.
OH...
rub
THAT'S GOOD THEN.
rub

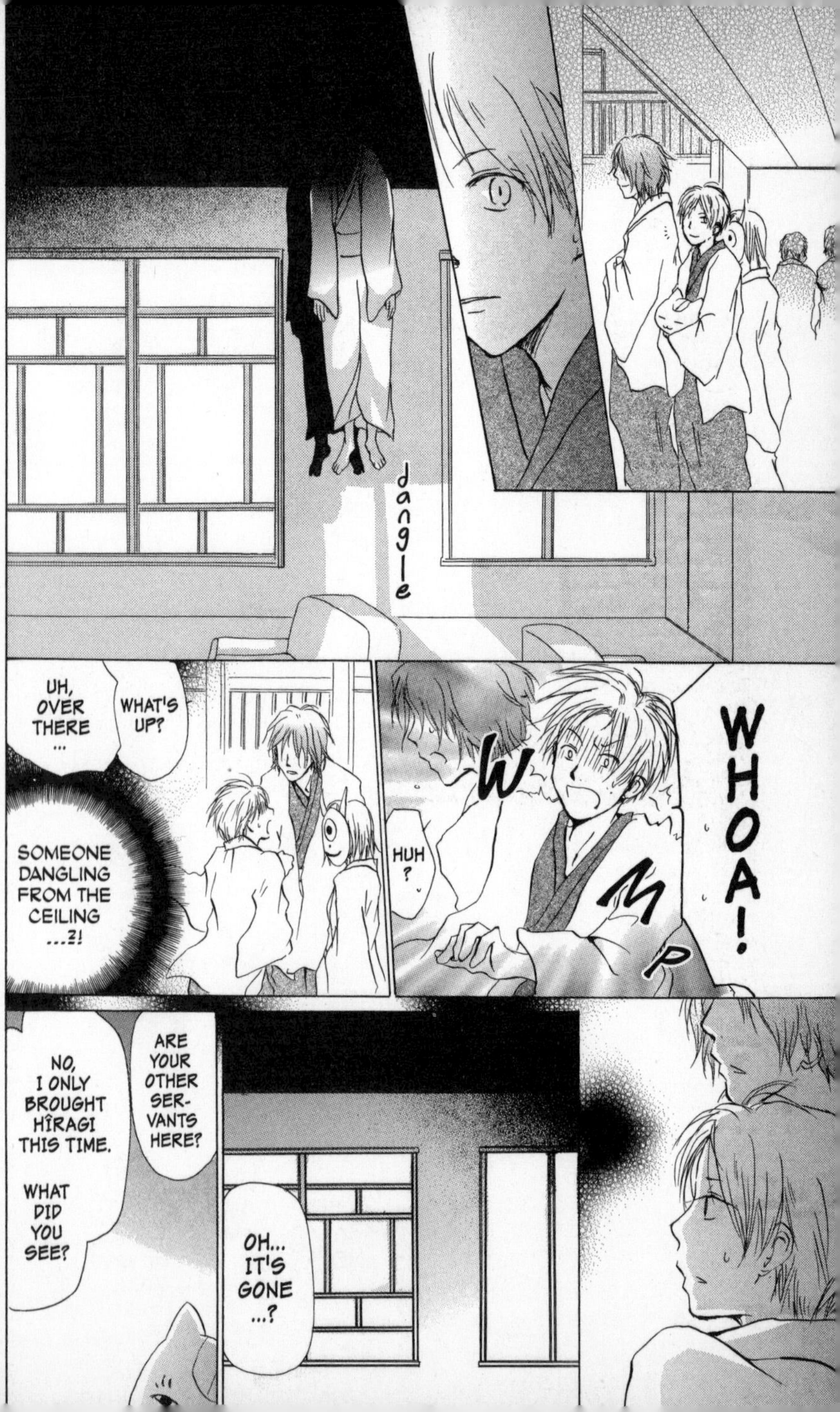
dangle
WHOA!
WMP
HUH?
WHAT'S UP?
UH, OVER THERE ...
SOMEONE DANGLING FROM THE CEILING ...?!
OH... IT'S GONE ...?
ARE YOUR OTHER SER-VANTS HERE?
NO, I ONLY BROUGHT HÎRAGI THIS TIME.
WHAT DID YOU SEE?

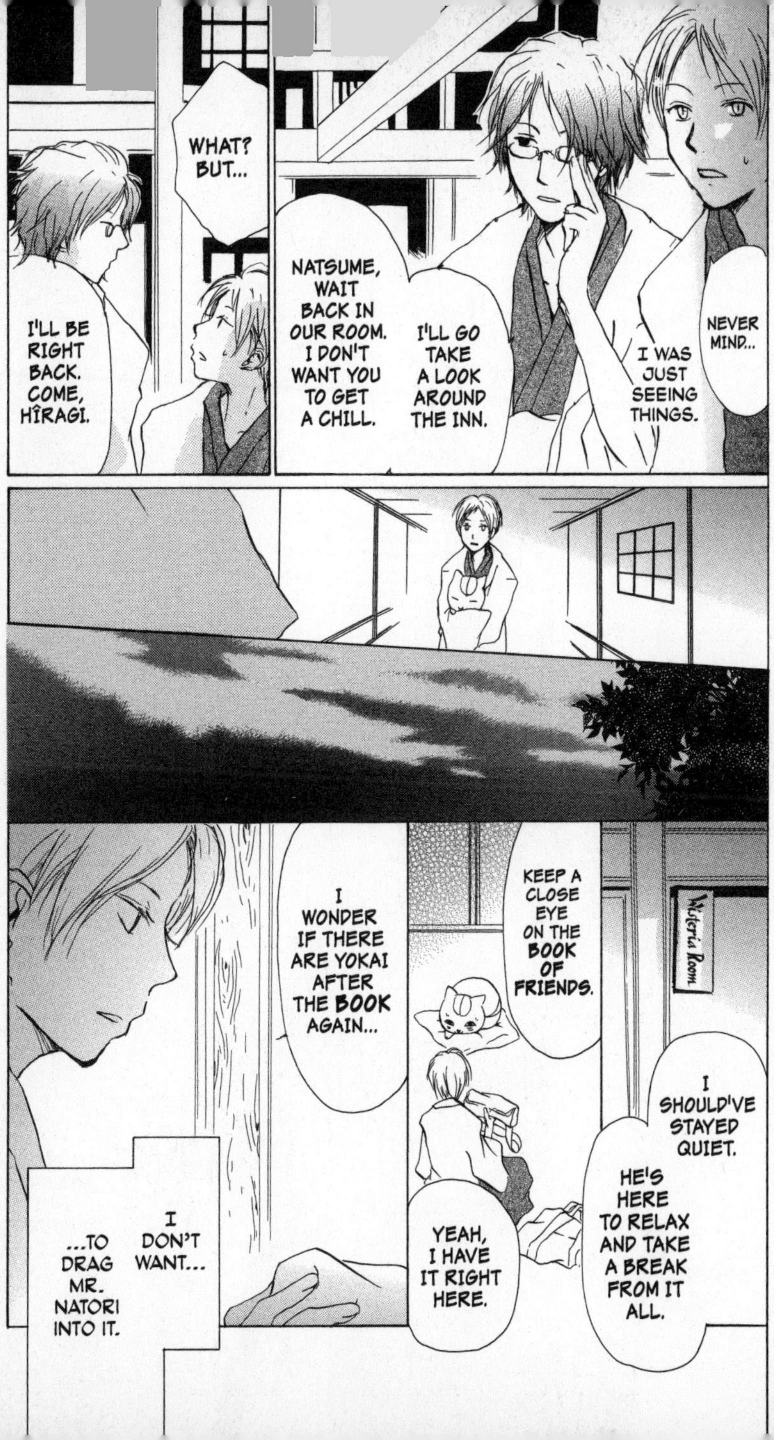
NEVER MIND...
I WAS JUST SEEING THINGS.
I'LL GO TAKE A LOOK AROUND THE INN.
NATSUME, WAIT BACK IN OUR ROOM. I DON'T WANT YOU TO GET A CHILL.
WHAT? BUT...
I'LL BE RIGHT BACK. COME, HÎRAGI.
I SHOULD'VE STAYED QUIET.
HE'S HERE TO RELAX AND TAKE A BREAK FROM IT ALL.
KEEP A CLOSE EYE ON THE BOOK OF FRIENDS.
Wisteria Room
YEAH, I HAVE IT RIGHT HERE.
I WONDER IF THERE ARE YOKAI AFTER THE BOOK AGAIN...
I DON'T WANT...
...TO DRAG MR. NATORI INTO IT.

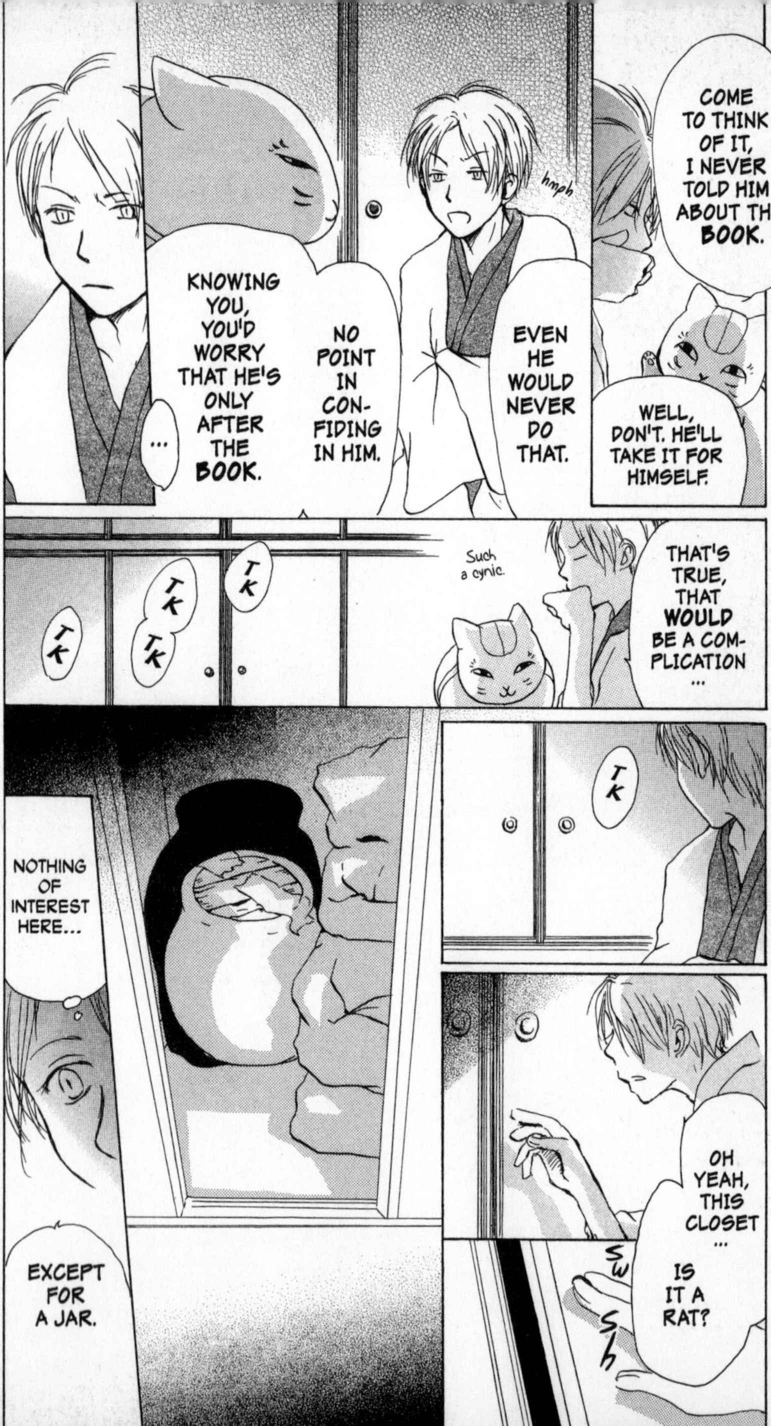
COME TO THINK OF IT, I NEVER TOLD HIM ABOUT THE BOOK.
WELL, DON'T. HE'LL TAKE IT FOR HIMSELF.
hmph
EVEN HE WOULD NEVER DO THAT.
NO POINT IN CON-FIDING IN HIM.
KNOWING YOU, YOU'D WORRY THAT HE'S ONLY AFTER THE BOOK.
...
THAT'S TRUE, THAT WOULD BE A COM-PLICATION...
Such a cynic.
TK
TK
TK
TK
TK
OH YEAH, THIS CLOSET...
IS IT A RAT?
SWSH
NOTHING OF INTEREST HERE...
EXCEPT FOR A JAR.

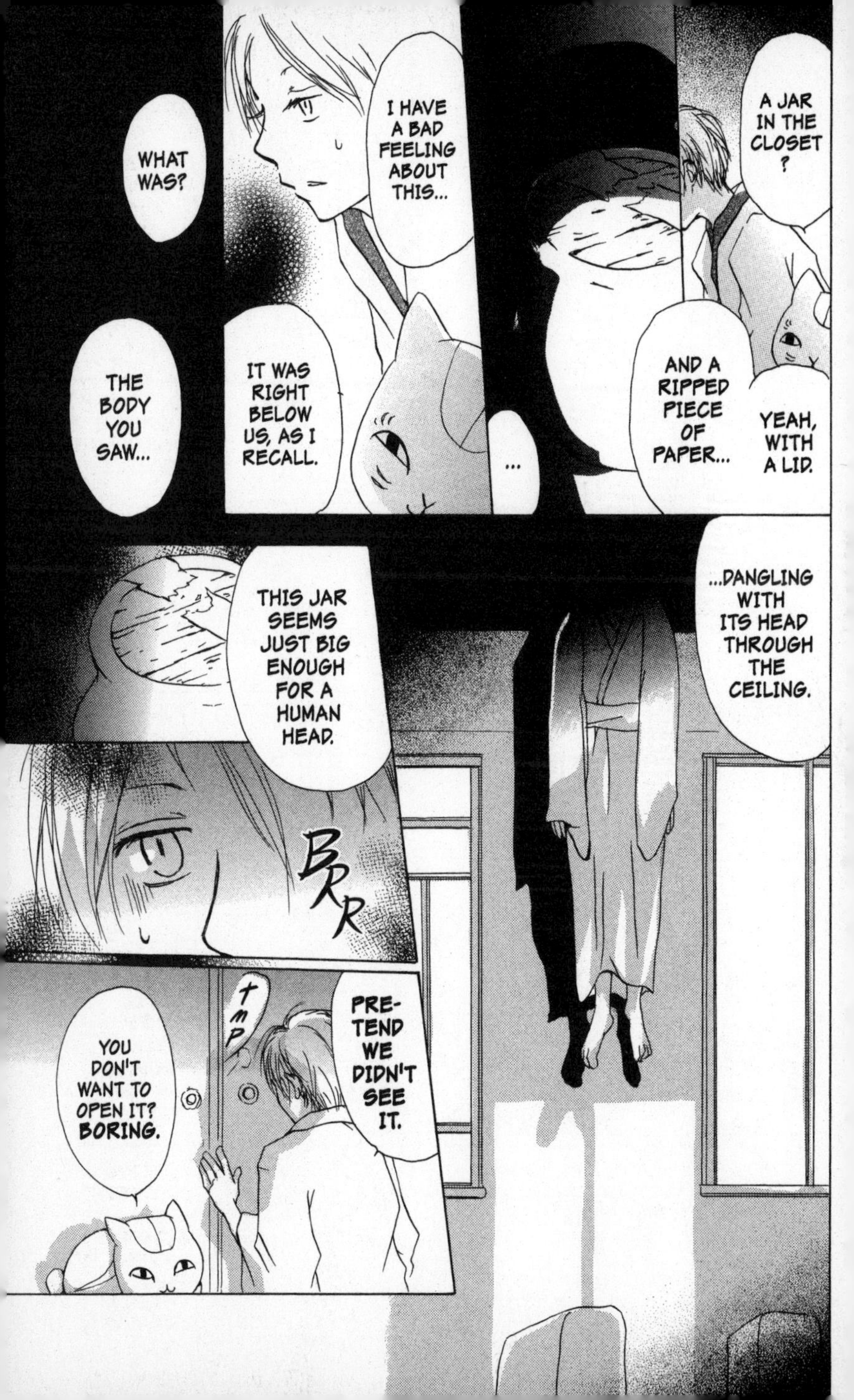
A JAR IN THE CLOSET?
YEAH, WITH A LID.
AND A RIPPED PIECE OF PAPER...
...
I HAVE A BAD FEELING ABOUT THIS...
IT WAS RIGHT BELOW US, AS I RECALL.
WHAT WAS?
THE BODY YOU SAW...
...DANGLING WITH ITS HEAD THROUGH THE CEILING.
THIS JAR SEEMS JUST BIG ENOUGH FOR A HUMAN HEAD.
BRR
PRE-TEND WE DIDN'T SEE IT.
TMP
YOU DON'T WANT TO OPEN IT? BORING.

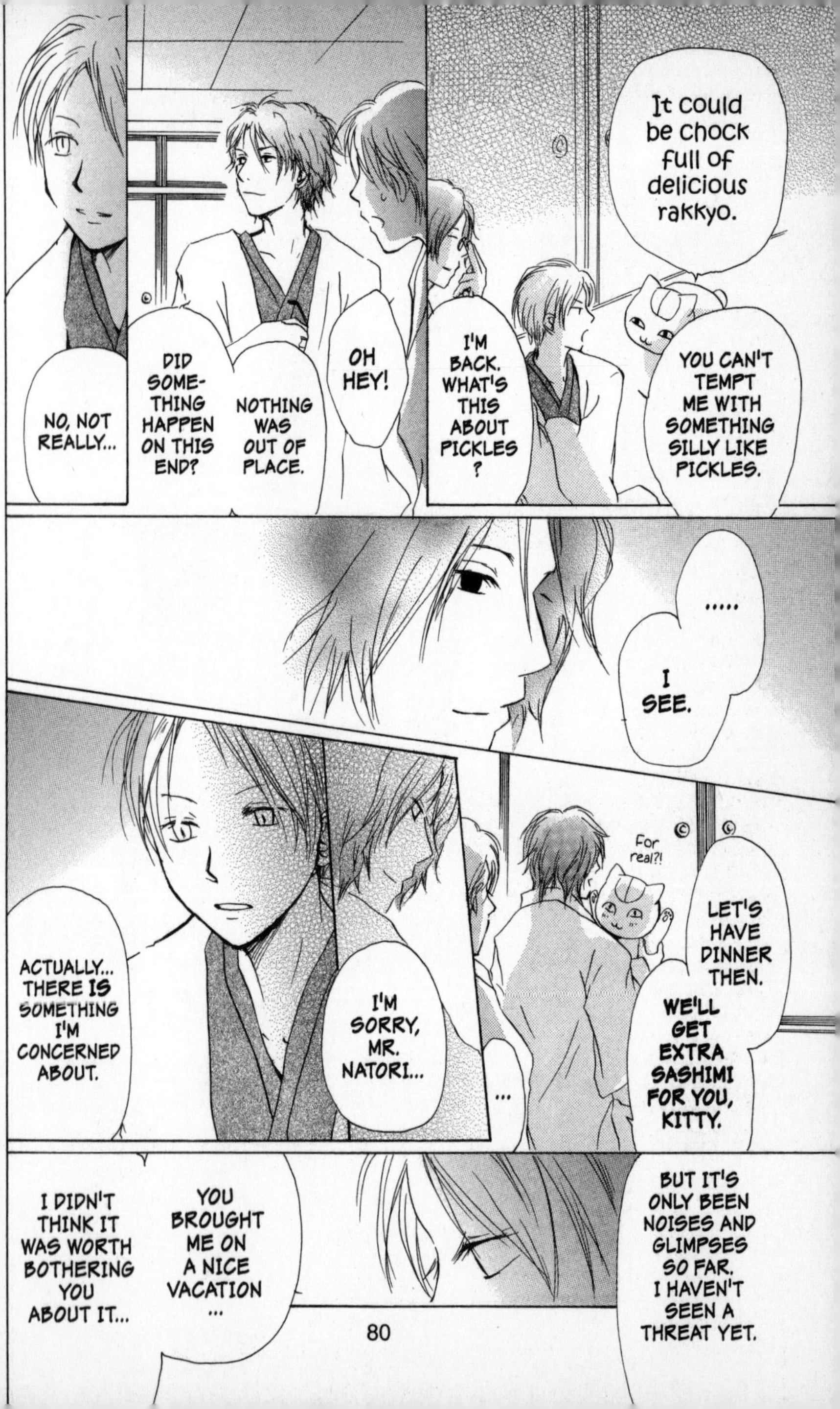

It could be chock full of delicious rakkyo.
YOU CAN'T TEMPT ME WITH SOMETHING SILLY LIKE PICKLES.
I'M BACK. WHAT'S THIS ABOUT PICKLES?
OH HEY!
NOTHING WAS OUT OF PLACE.
DID SOMETHING HAPPEN ON THIS END?
NO, NOT REALLY...
.....
I SEE.
LET'S HAVE DINNER THEN.
For real?!
WE'LL GET EXTRA SASHIMI FOR YOU, KITTY.
...
I'M SORRY, MR. NATORI...
ACTUALLY... THERE **IS** SOMETHING I'M CONCERNED ABOUT.
BUT IT'S ONLY BEEN NOISES AND GLIMPSES SO FAR. I HAVEN'T SEEN A THREAT YET.
YOU BROUGHT ME ON A NICE VACATION...
I DIDN'T THINK IT WAS WORTH BOTHERING YOU ABOUT IT...

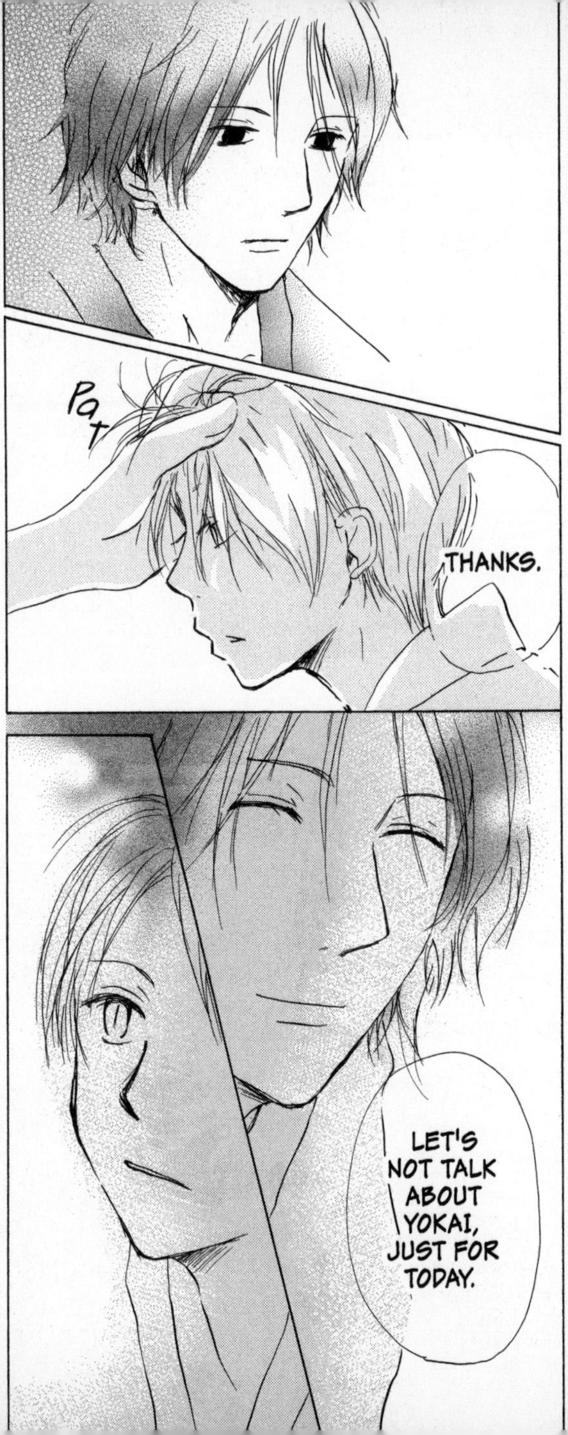
Pat
THANKS.
LET'S NOT TALK ABOUT YOKAI, JUST FOR TODAY.

02

❋Interviews

Thanks to this series, I've been invited to do things I'd never experienced before (like illustrating the cover of the magazine and an autograph session), so there are more things I get giddy and excited about. Now I've been asked to do an interview for a magazine called *S Quarterly*. I saw that they crafted the questions after a careful reading of *Natsume*. I never imagined that it would feel so delightful to have questions asked about my work. So I was entranced with joy, when I read the instructions "please handwrite your answers if possible." I wondered if that was to prevent someone else answering in my place, and I was fascinated by the professionalism (I was so stupid). So I wrote out the answers with great enthusiasm.

← Continued in part 03.

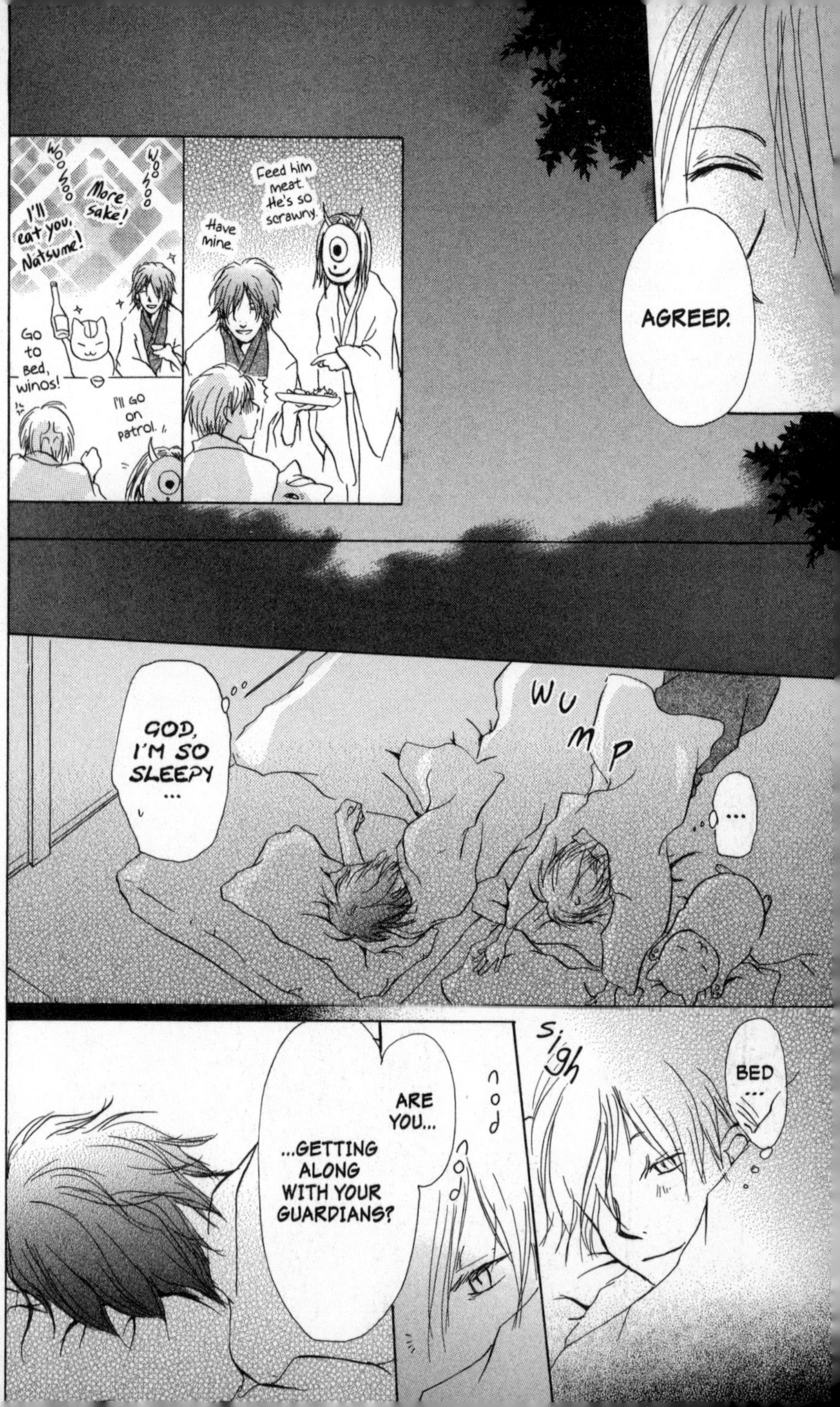
AGREED.
Feed him meat. He's so scrawny.
Have mine.
Woo hoo
Woo hoo
More sake!
I'll eat you, Natsume!
Go to bed, winos!
I'll go on patrol.
...
WUMP
GOD, I'M SO SLEEPY...
BED...
sigh
nod nod
ARE YOU...
...GETTING ALONG WITH YOUR GUARDIANS?

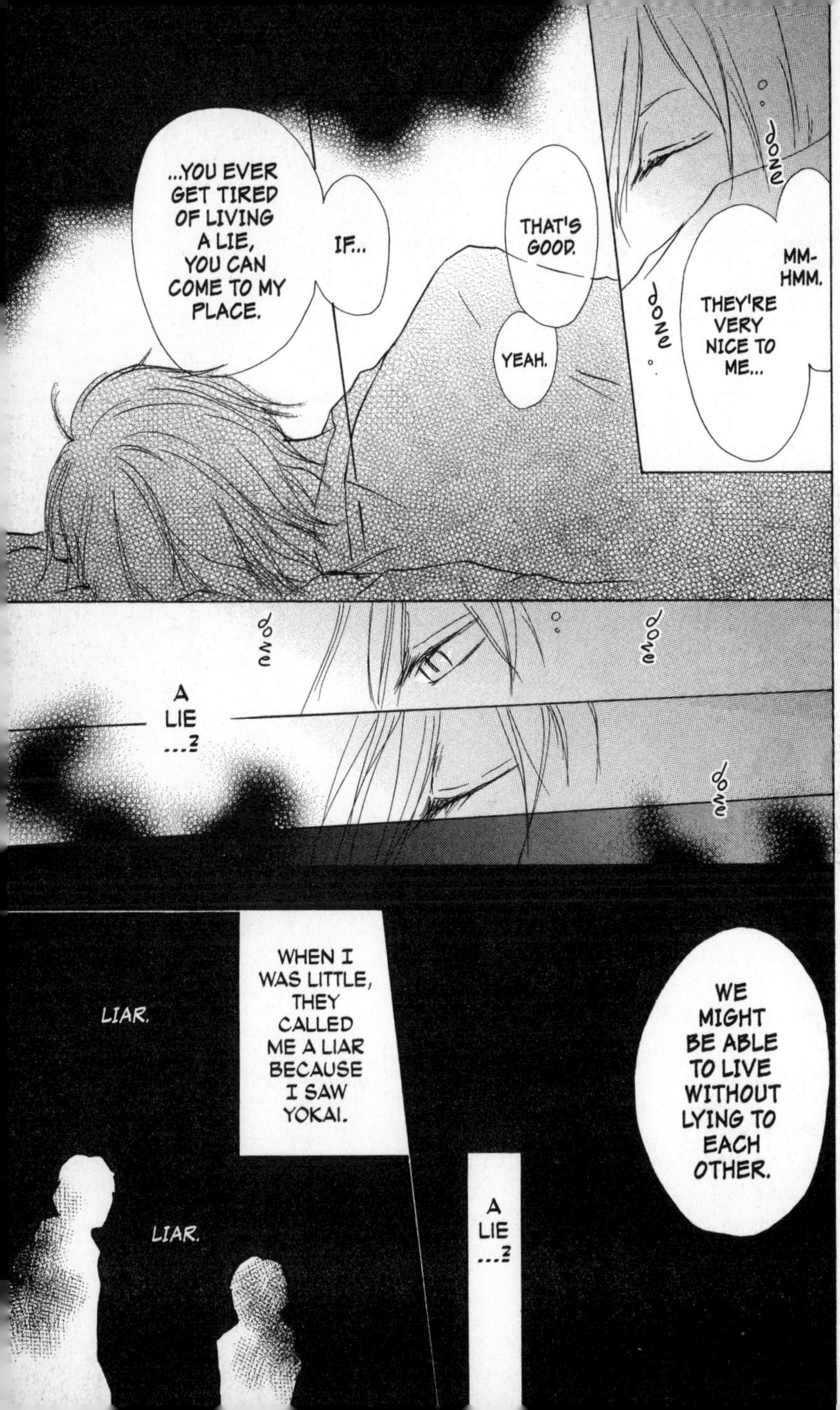

doze
doze
MM-HMM.
THEY'RE VERY NICE TO ME...
THAT'S GOOD.
YEAH.
IF...
...YOU EVER GET TIRED OF LIVING A LIE, YOU CAN COME TO MY PLACE.
doze
doze
A LIE ...?
doze
WE MIGHT BE ABLE TO LIVE WITHOUT LYING TO EACH OTHER.
A LIE ...?
WHEN I WAS LITTLE, THEY CALLED ME A LIAR BECAUSE I SAW YOKAI.
LIAR.
LIAR.

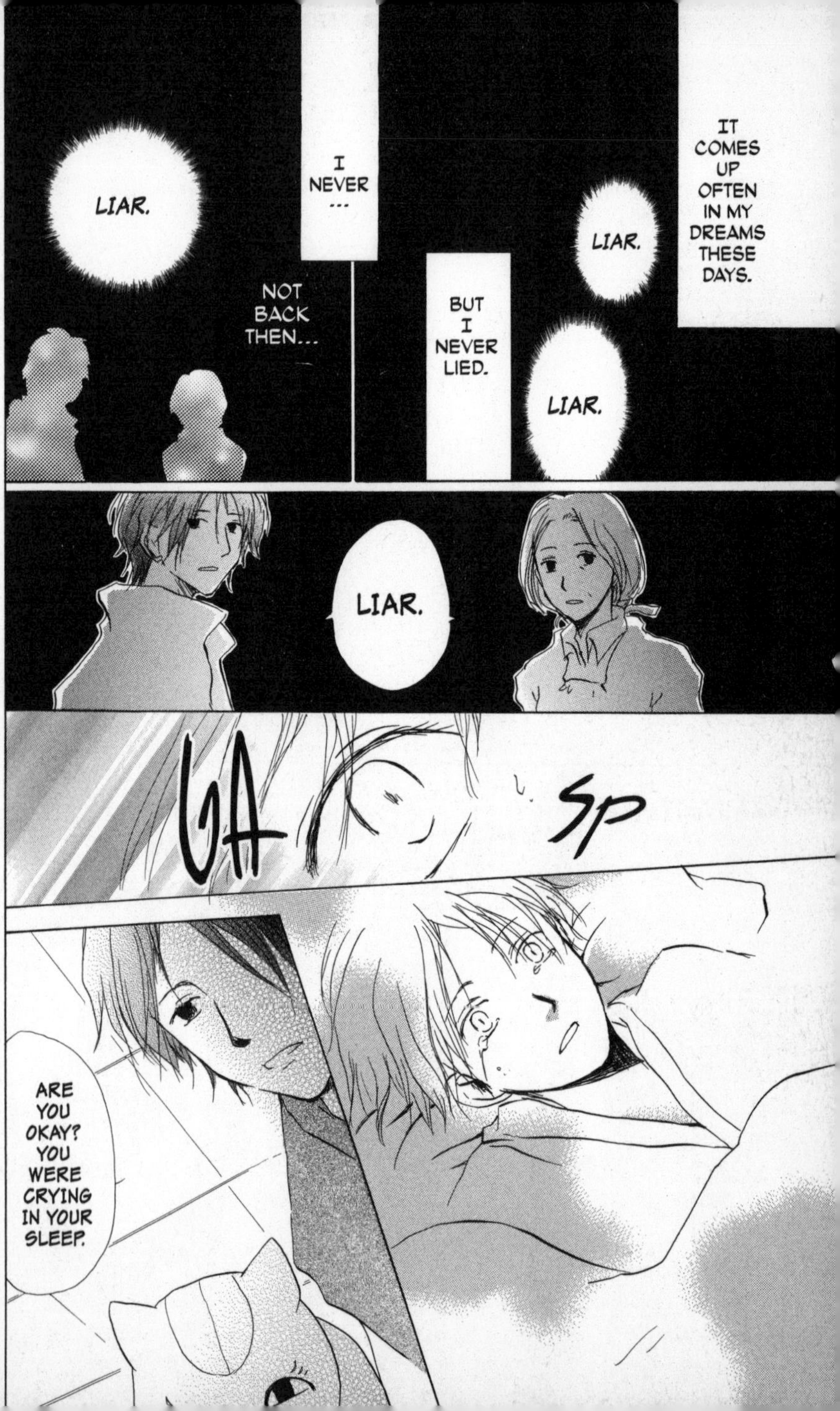

IT COMES UP OFTEN IN MY DREAMS THESE DAYS.
LIAR.
BUT I NEVER LIED.
LIAR.
I NEVER ...
LIAR.
NOT BACK THEN...
LIAR.
GASP
ARE YOU OKAY? YOU WERE CRYING IN YOUR SLEEP.

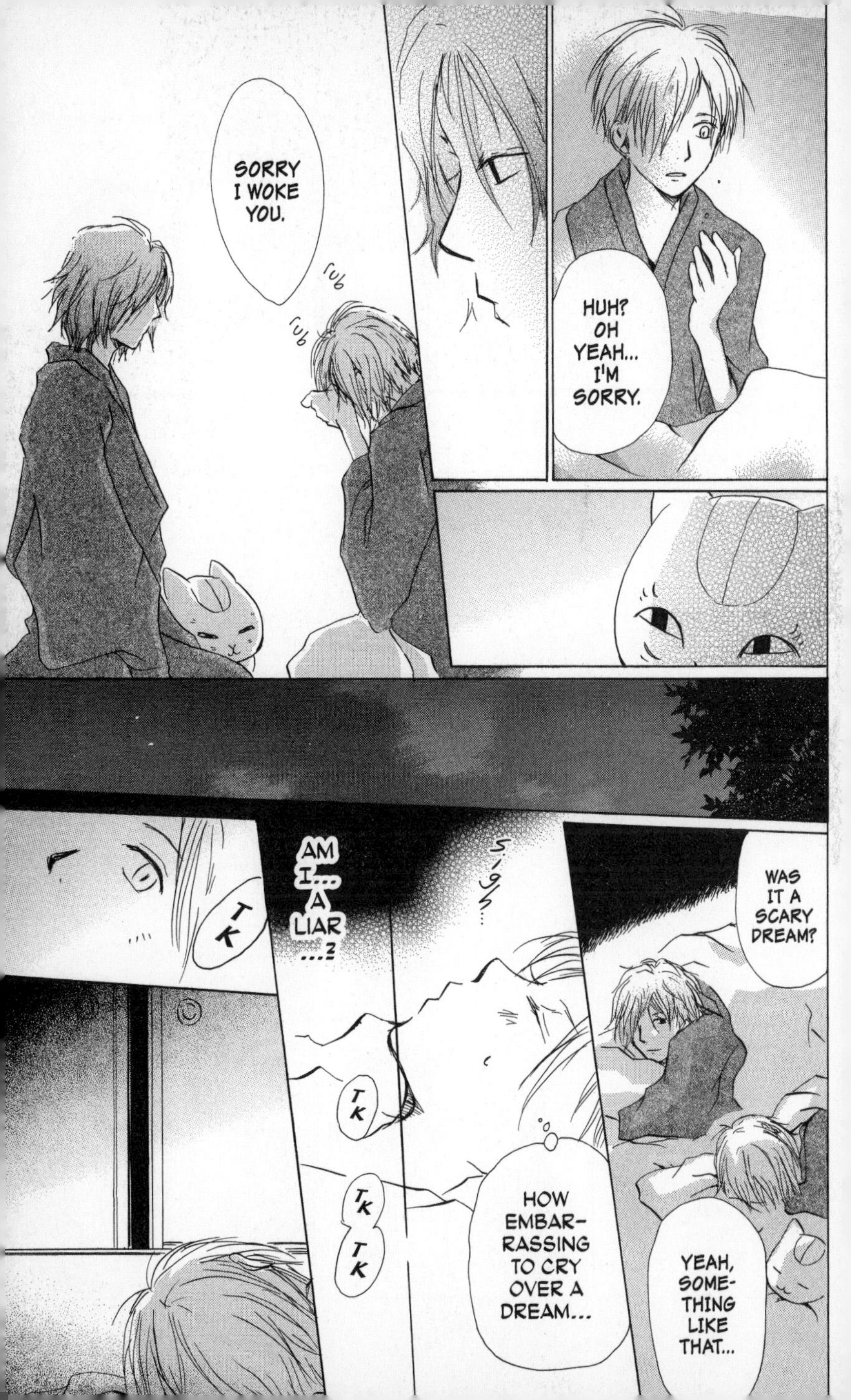
HUH? OH YEAH... I'M SORRY.
SORRY I WOKE YOU.
rub
rub
WAS IT A SCARY DREAM?
YEAH, SOMETHING LIKE THAT...
sigh...
HOW EMBARRASSING TO CRY OVER A DREAM...
TK
TK
TK
AM I... A LIAR...?
TK

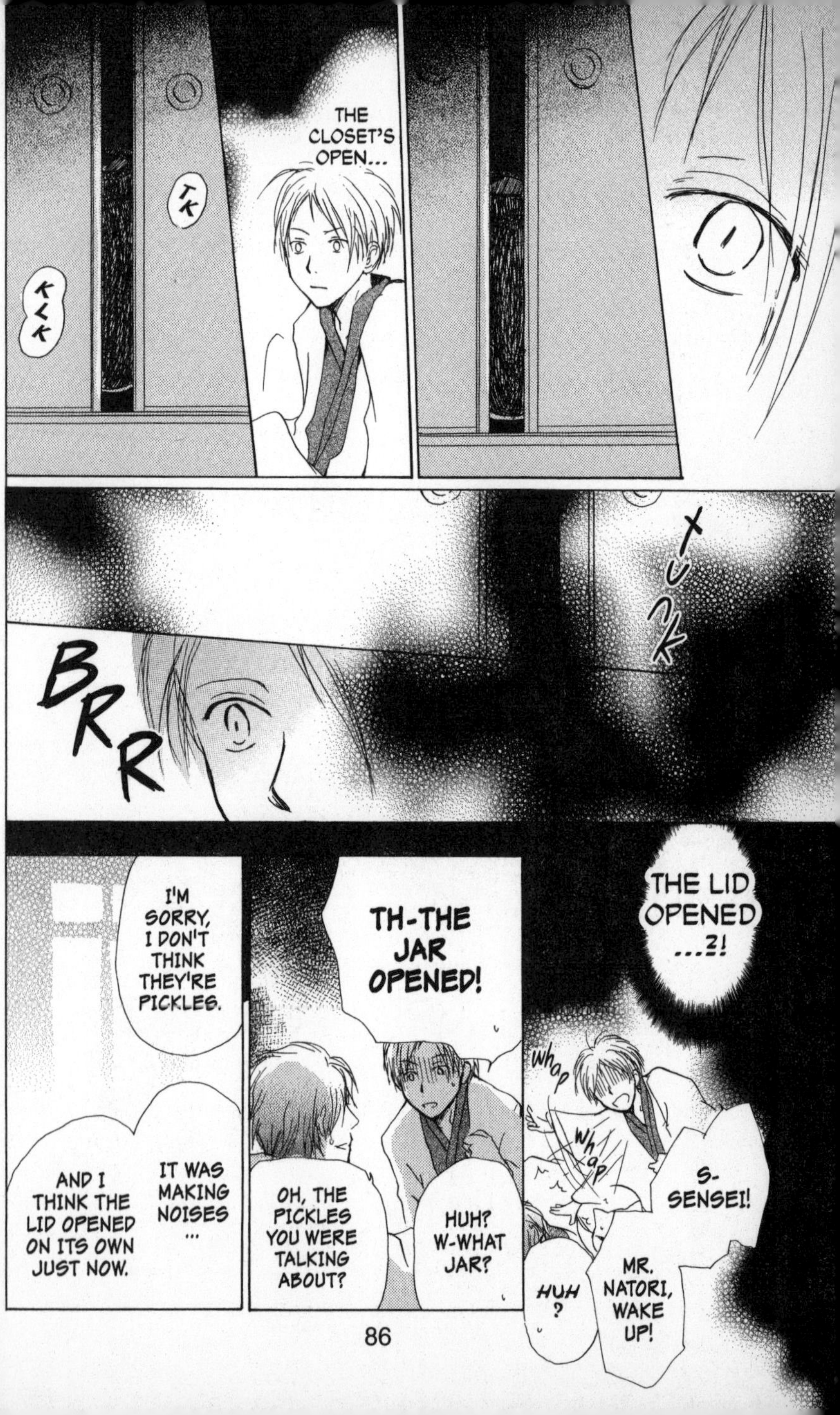
THE CLOSET'S OPEN...
TK
KKK
XUNK
BRR
THE LID OPENED ...?!
whap
whap
S-SENSEI!
MR. NATORI, WAKE UP!
HUH?
TH-THE JAR OPENED!
HUH? W-WHAT JAR?
OH, THE PICKLES YOU WERE TALKING ABOUT?
I'M SORRY, I DON'T THINK THEY'RE PICKLES.
IT WAS MAKING NOISES ...
AND I THINK THE LID OPENED ON ITS OWN JUST NOW.

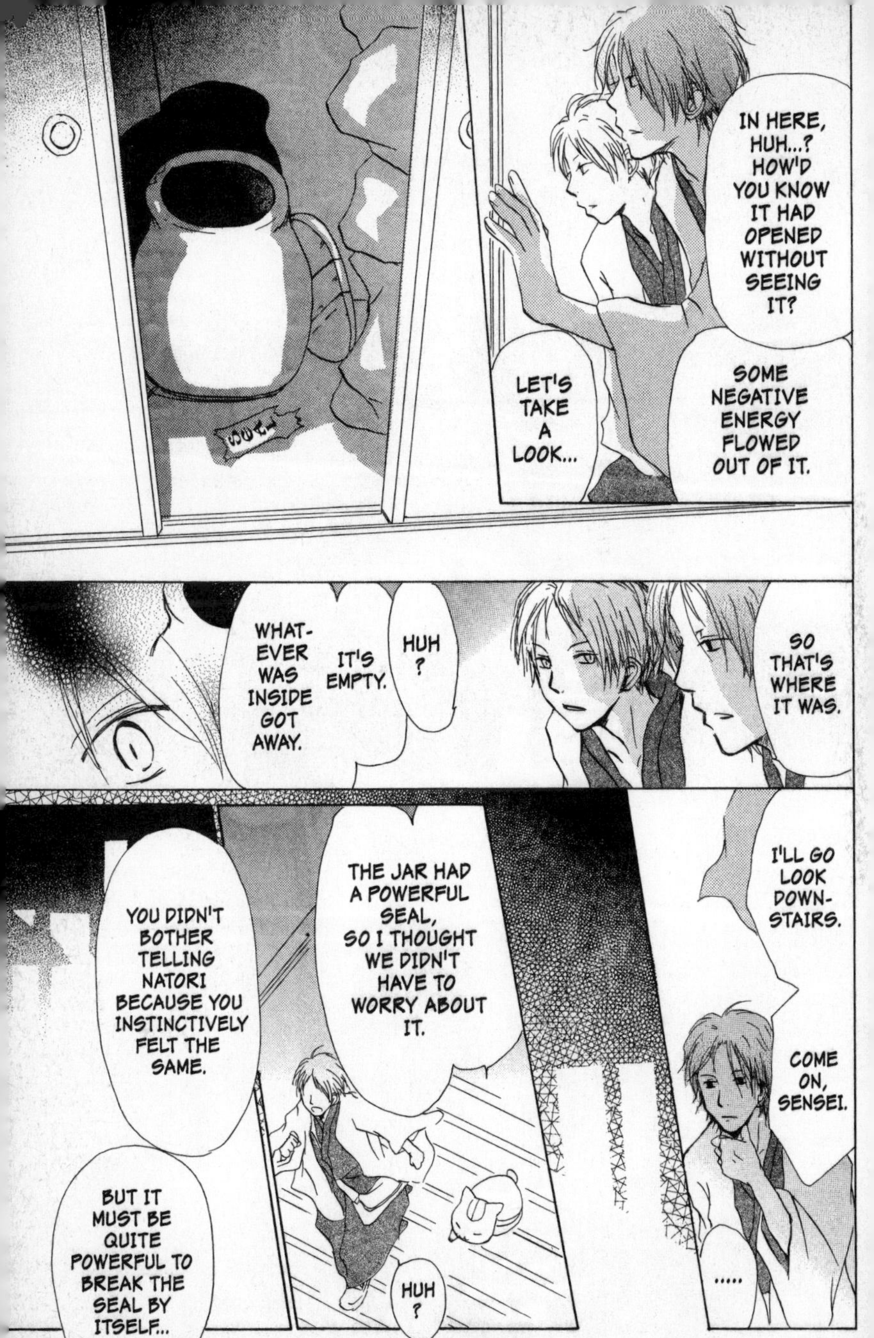
IN HERE, HUH...? HOW'D YOU KNOW IT HAD OPENED WITHOUT SEEING IT?
SOME NEGATIVE ENERGY FLOWED OUT OF IT.
LET'S TAKE A LOOK...
SO THAT'S WHERE IT WAS.
HUH?
IT'S EMPTY.
WHAT-EVER WAS INSIDE GOT AWAY.
I'LL GO LOOK DOWN-STAIRS.
COME ON, SENSEI.
.....
THE JAR HAD A POWERFUL SEAL, SO I THOUGHT WE DIDN'T HAVE TO WORRY ABOUT IT.
HUH?
YOU DIDN'T BOTHER TELLING NATORI BECAUSE YOU INSTINCTIVELY FELT THE SAME.
BUT IT MUST BE QUITE POWERFUL TO BREAK THE SEAL BY ITSELF...

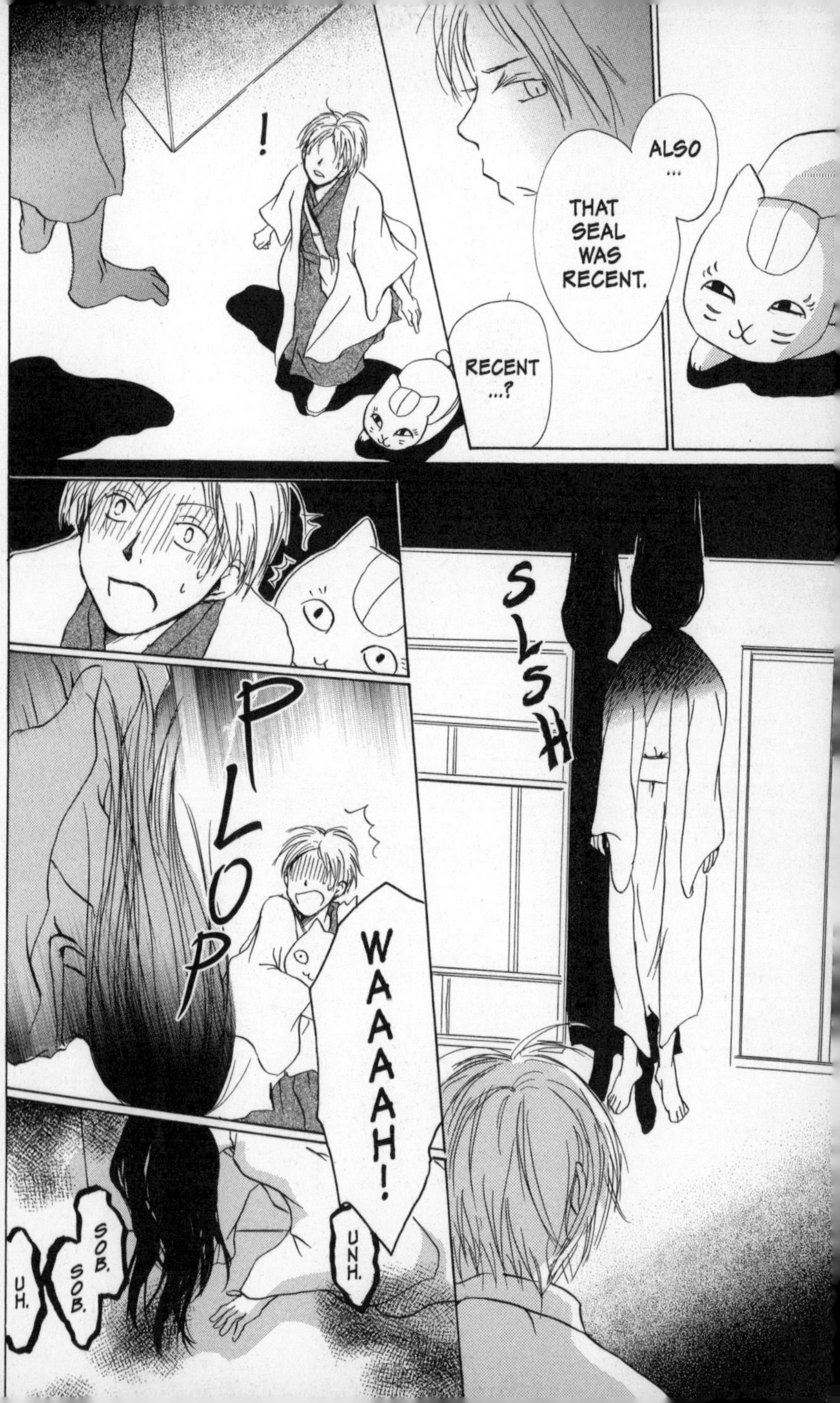
ALSO ...
THAT SEAL WAS RECENT.
RECENT ...?
!
SLSH
PLOP
WAAAAH!
UNH.
SOB. SOB.
UH.

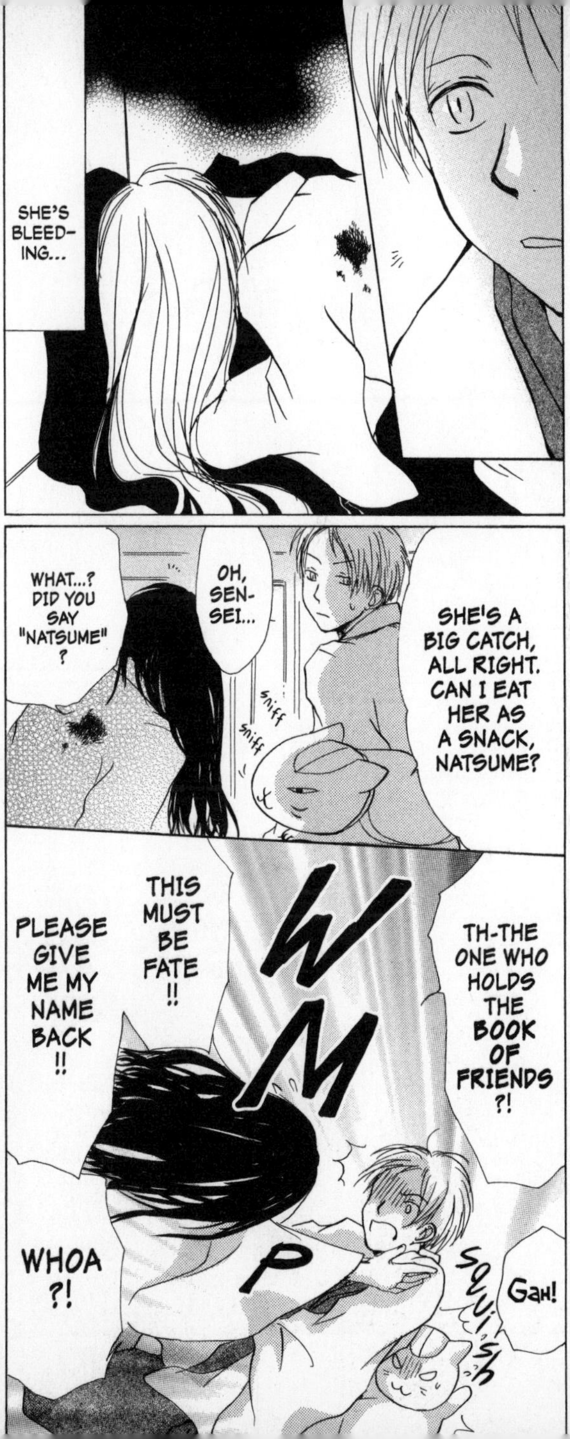
SHE'S BLEED-ING...
SHE'S A BIG CATCH, ALL RIGHT. CAN I EAT HER AS A SNACK, NATSUME?
OH, SEN-SEI...
WHAT...? DID YOU SAY "NATSUME"?
sniff
sniff
TH-THE ONE WHO HOLDS THE BOOK OF FRIENDS?!
THIS MUST BE FATE!!
PLEASE GIVE ME MY NAME BACK!!
WHOMP
Gah!
SQUISH
WHOA?!

03

❋ Interviews: part 2

I sent in my answers with a couple of rough draft samples, and a few weeks later, they faxed me their beautifully composed pages. I was shaking with joy, until I noticed that they printed my handwriting as-is. Thinking back, it should've been obvious. I became painfully aware how someone who's walking on cloud nine can be so oblivious. I was horrified that I didn't use my best handwriting. But looking at the cute colors and precise editing, the pleasantness of looking at the page made me feel happy again.

It would make me happy if you would check it out. It's now one of my cherished treasures.

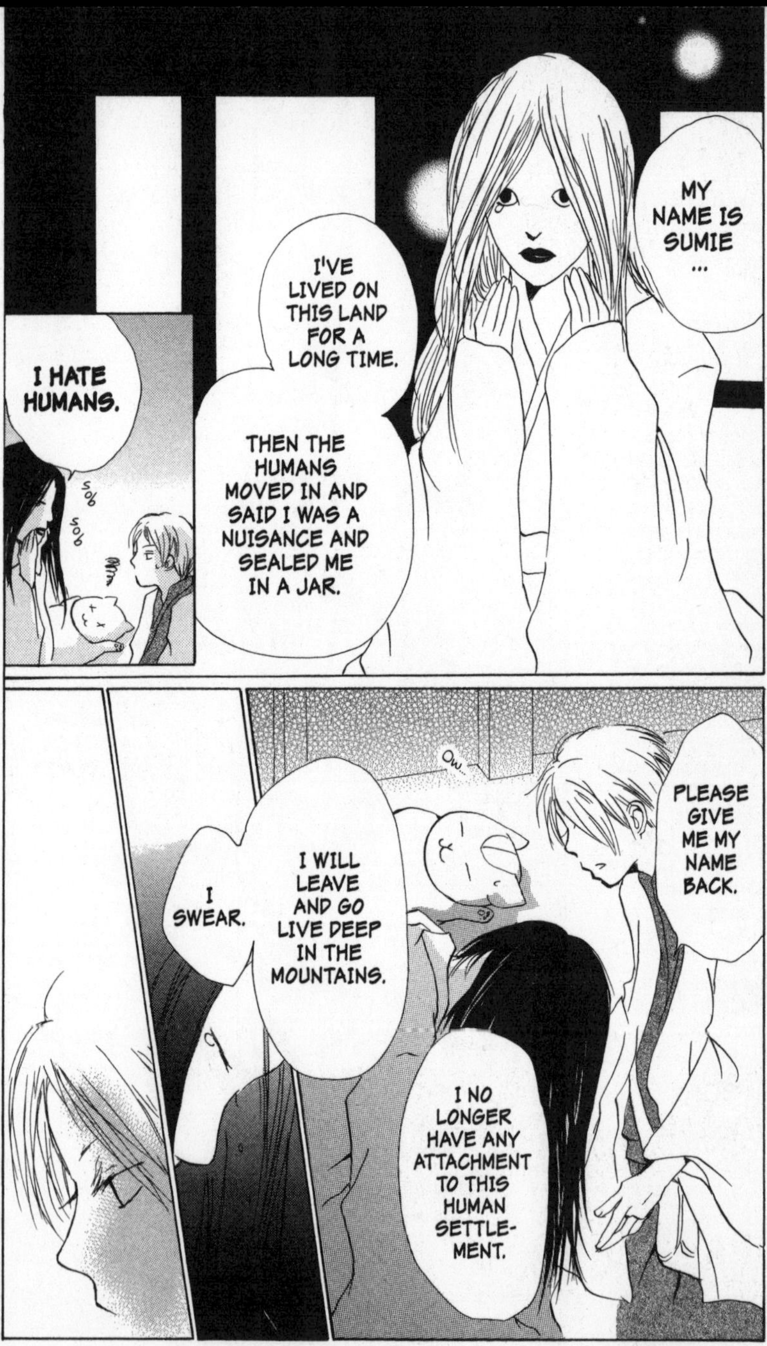
MY NAME IS SUMIE ...
I'VE LIVED ON THIS LAND FOR A LONG TIME.
THEN THE HUMANS MOVED IN AND SAID I WAS A NUISANCE AND SEALED ME IN A JAR.
I HATE HUMANS.
sob sob
PLEASE GIVE ME MY NAME BACK.
Ow...
I WILL LEAVE AND GO LIVE DEEP IN THE MOUNTAINS.
I SWEAR.
I NO LONGER HAVE ANY ATTACHMENT TO THIS HUMAN SETTLE-MENT.

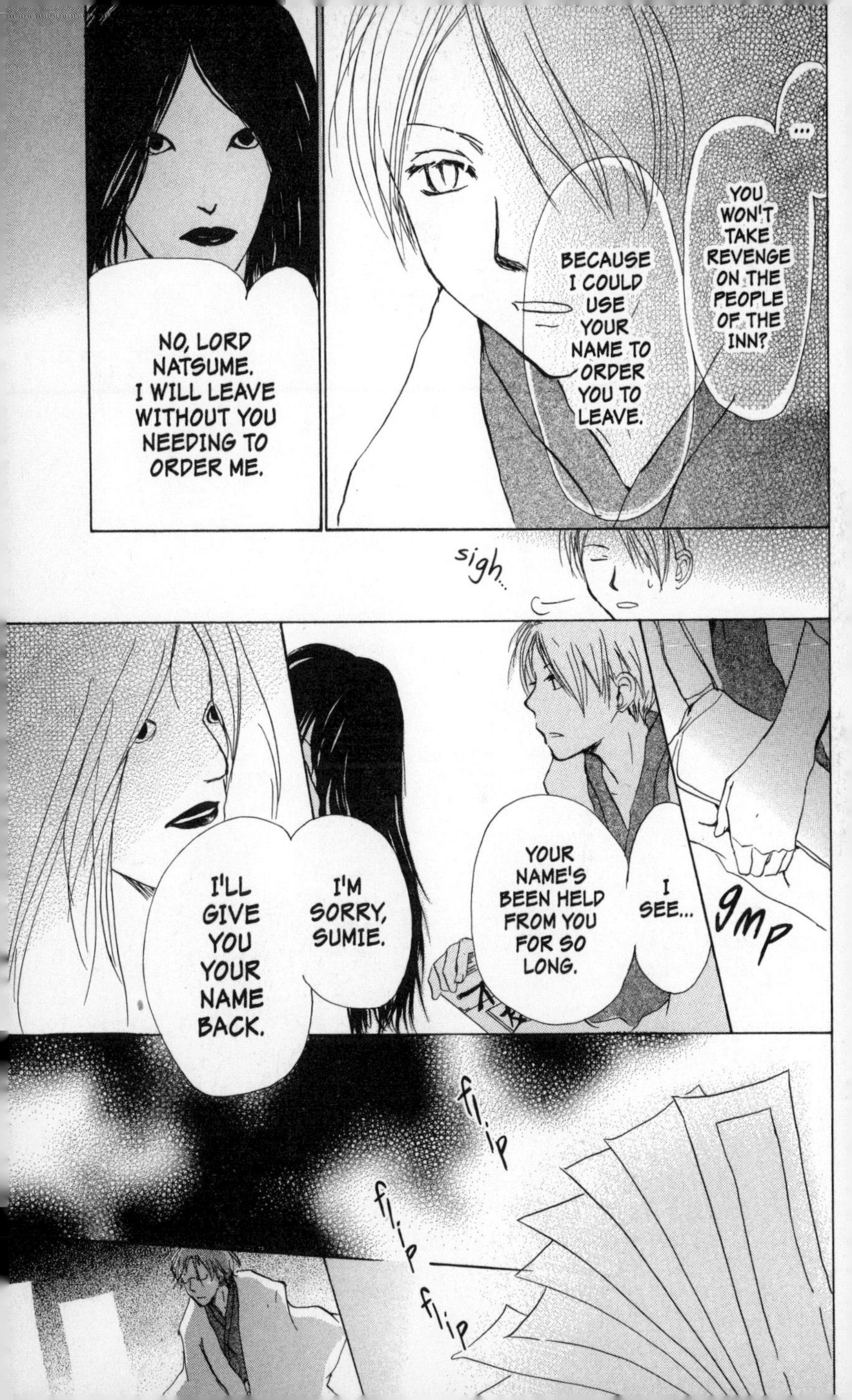
...
YOU WON'T TAKE REVENGE ON THE PEOPLE OF THE INN?
BECAUSE I COULD USE YOUR NAME TO ORDER YOU TO LEAVE.
NO, LORD NATSUME. I WILL LEAVE WITHOUT YOU NEEDING TO ORDER ME.
sigh...
gmp
I SEE...
YOUR NAME'S BEEN HELD FROM YOU FOR SO LONG.
I'M SORRY, SUMIE.
I'LL GIVE YOU YOUR NAME BACK.
flip
flip
flip

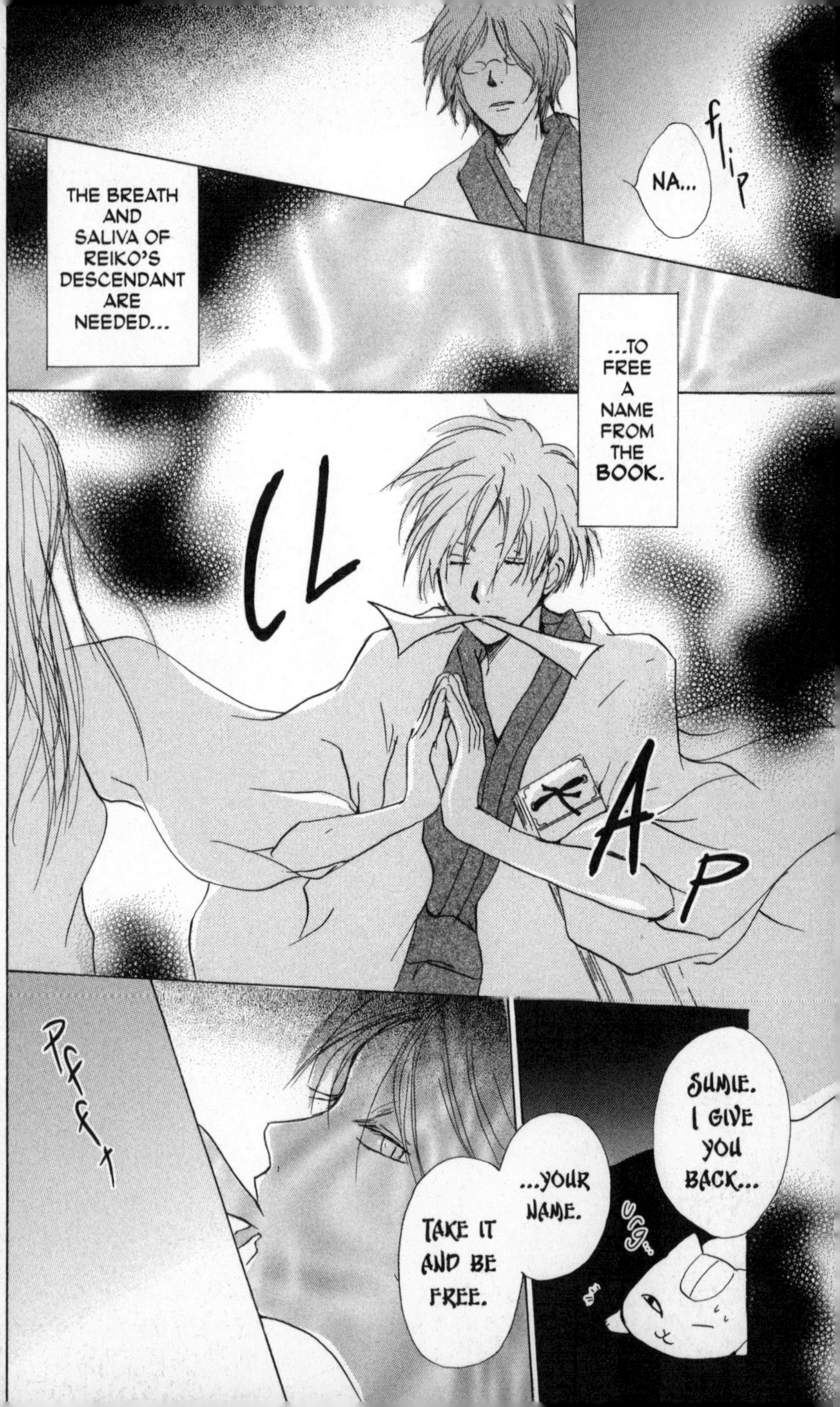
flip
NA...
THE BREATH AND SALIVA OF REIKO'S DESCENDANT ARE NEEDED...
...TO FREE A NAME FROM THE BOOK.
CLAP
SUMIE. I GIVE YOU BACK...
...YOUR NAME.
TAKE IT AND BE FREE.
urg...
Pffft

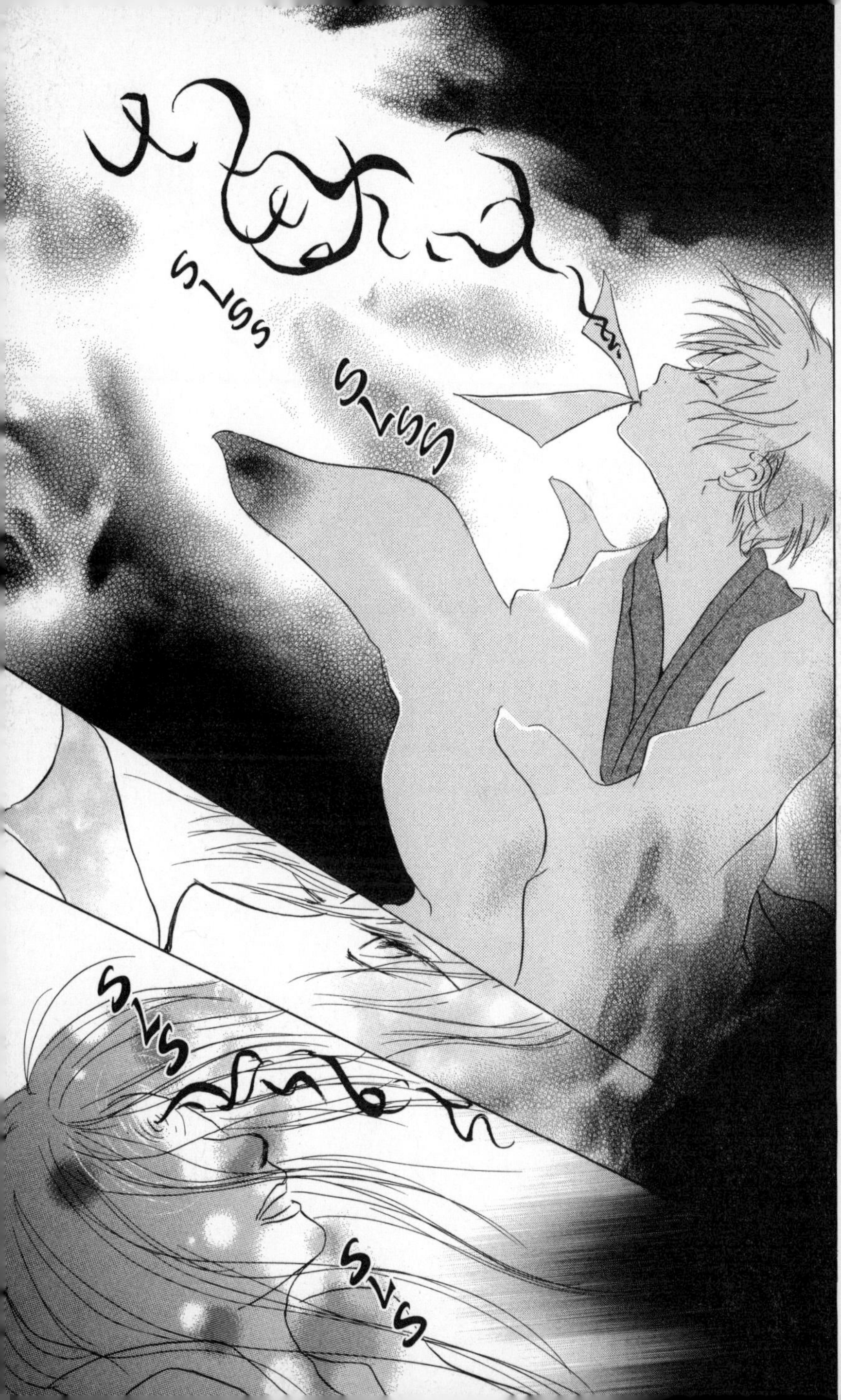

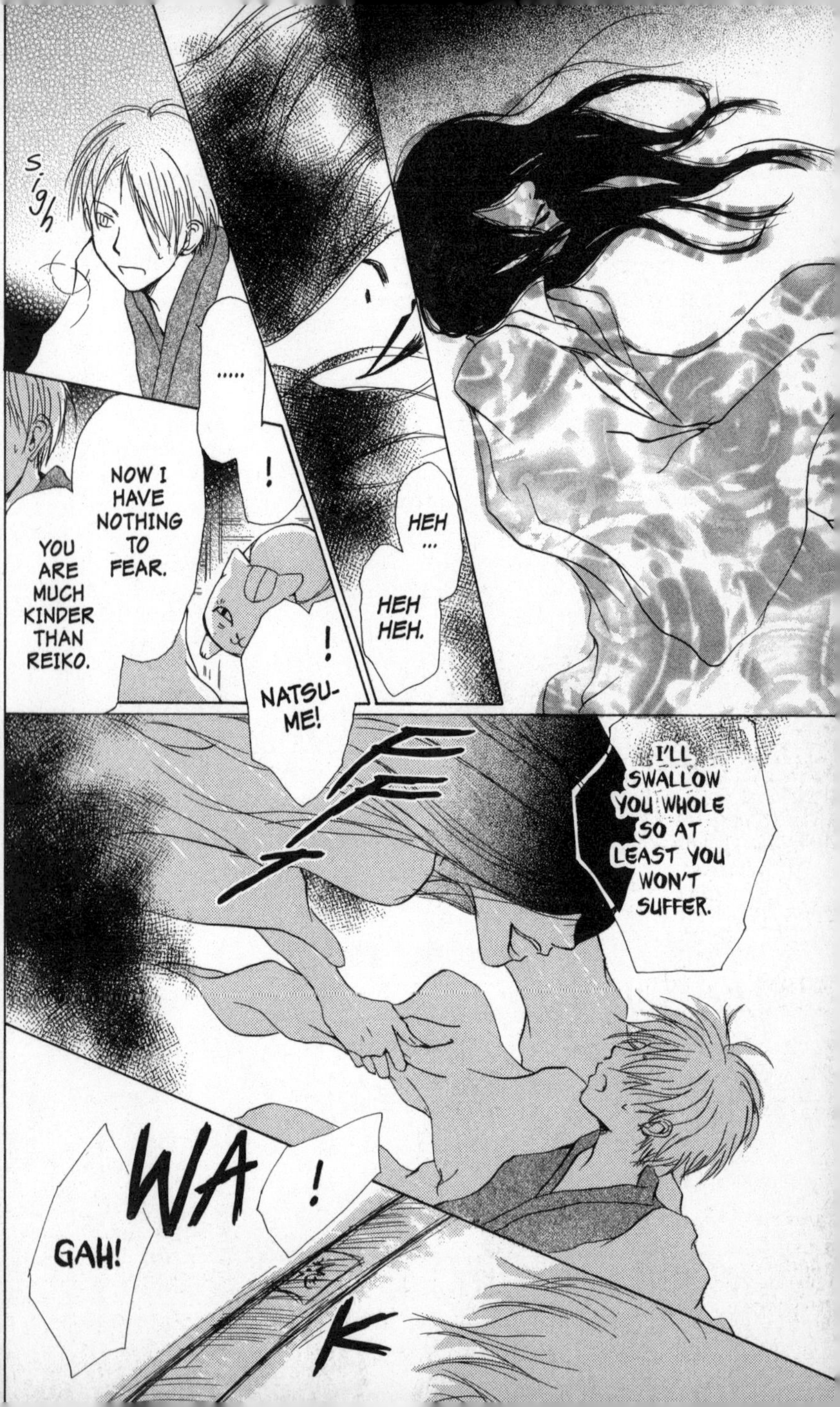
HEH ...
HEH HEH.
.....
Sigh
!
NOW I HAVE NOTHING TO FEAR.
YOU ARE MUCH KINDER THAN REIKO.
!
NATSU-ME!
FFF
I'LL SWALLOW YOU WHOLE SO AT LEAST YOU WON'T SUFFER.
WA
!
GAH!
K

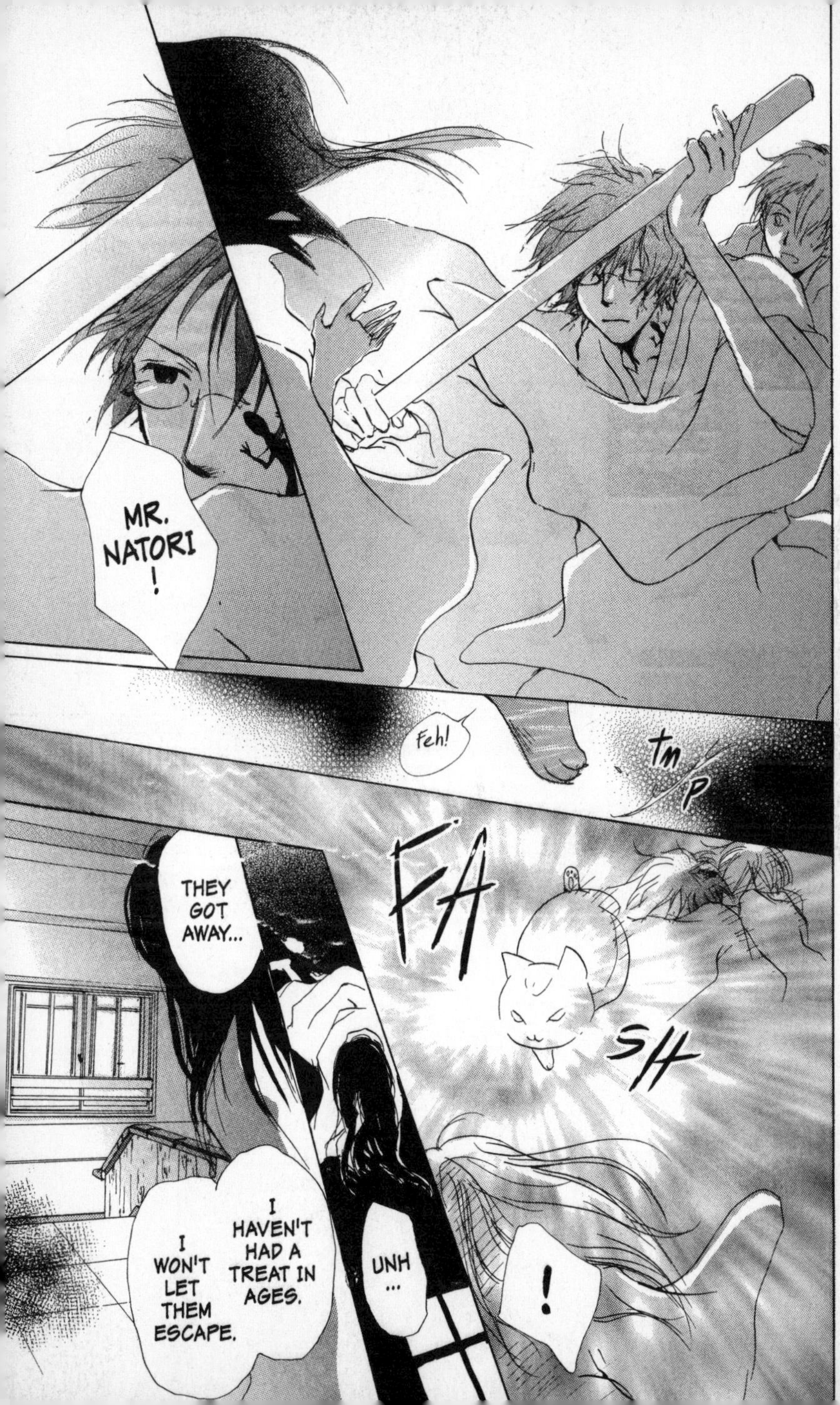

MR. NATORI!
Feh!
tmp
FASH
!
UNH ...
THEY GOT AWAY...
I HAVEN'T HAD A TREAT IN AGES.
I WON'T LET THEM ESCAPE.

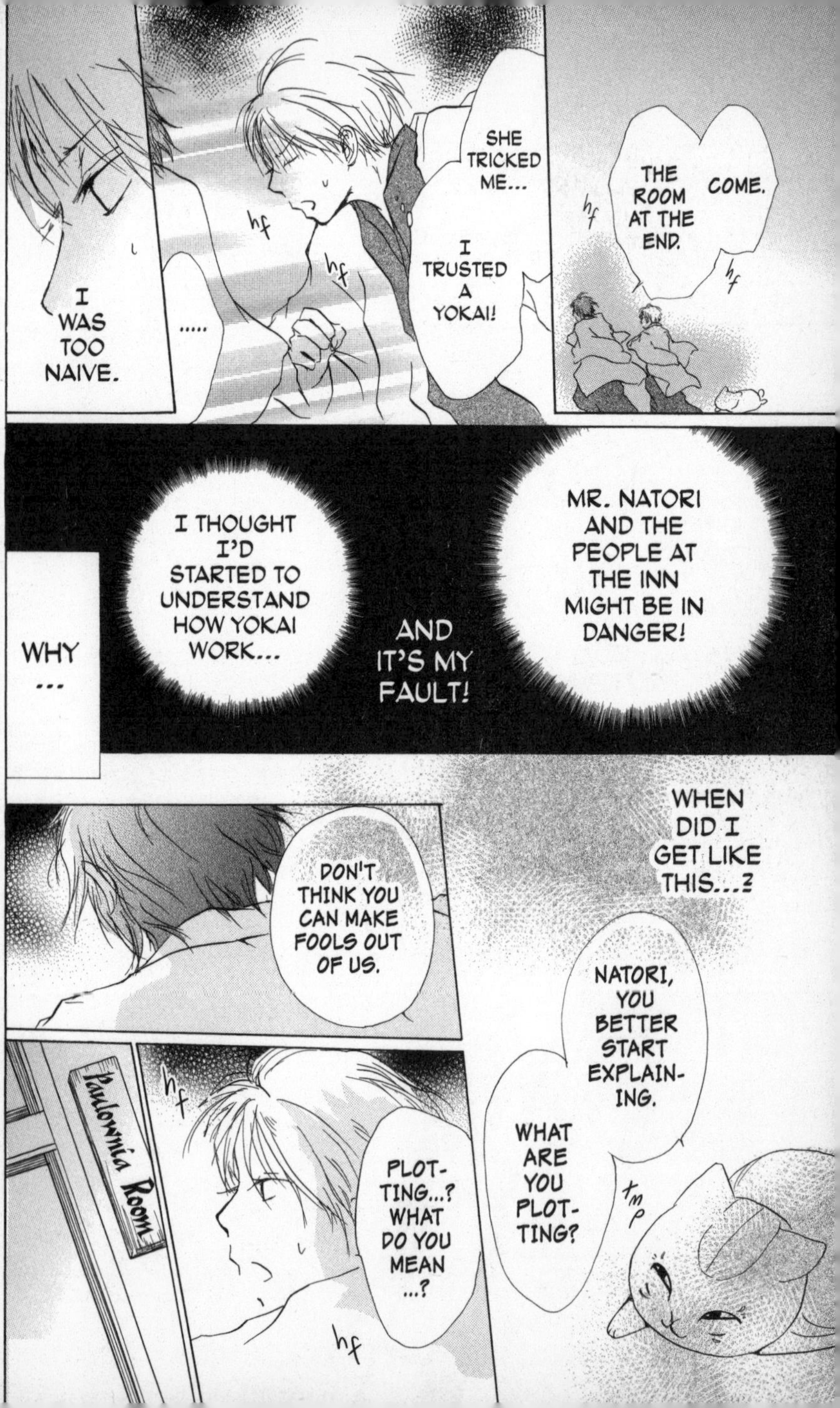
COME.
THE ROOM AT THE END.
hf
hf
SHE TRICKED ME...
I TRUSTED A YOKAI!
hf
hf
.....
I WAS TOO NAIVE.
MR. NATORI AND THE PEOPLE AT THE INN MIGHT BE IN DANGER!
AND IT'S MY FAULT!
I THOUGHT I'D STARTED TO UNDERSTAND HOW YOKAI WORK...
WHY ...
WHEN DID I GET LIKE THIS...?
DON'T THINK YOU CAN MAKE FOOLS OUT OF US.
NATORI, YOU BETTER START EXPLAINING.
WHAT ARE YOU PLOTTING?
PLOTTING...? WHAT DO YOU MEAN ...?
hf
hf
Paulownia Room

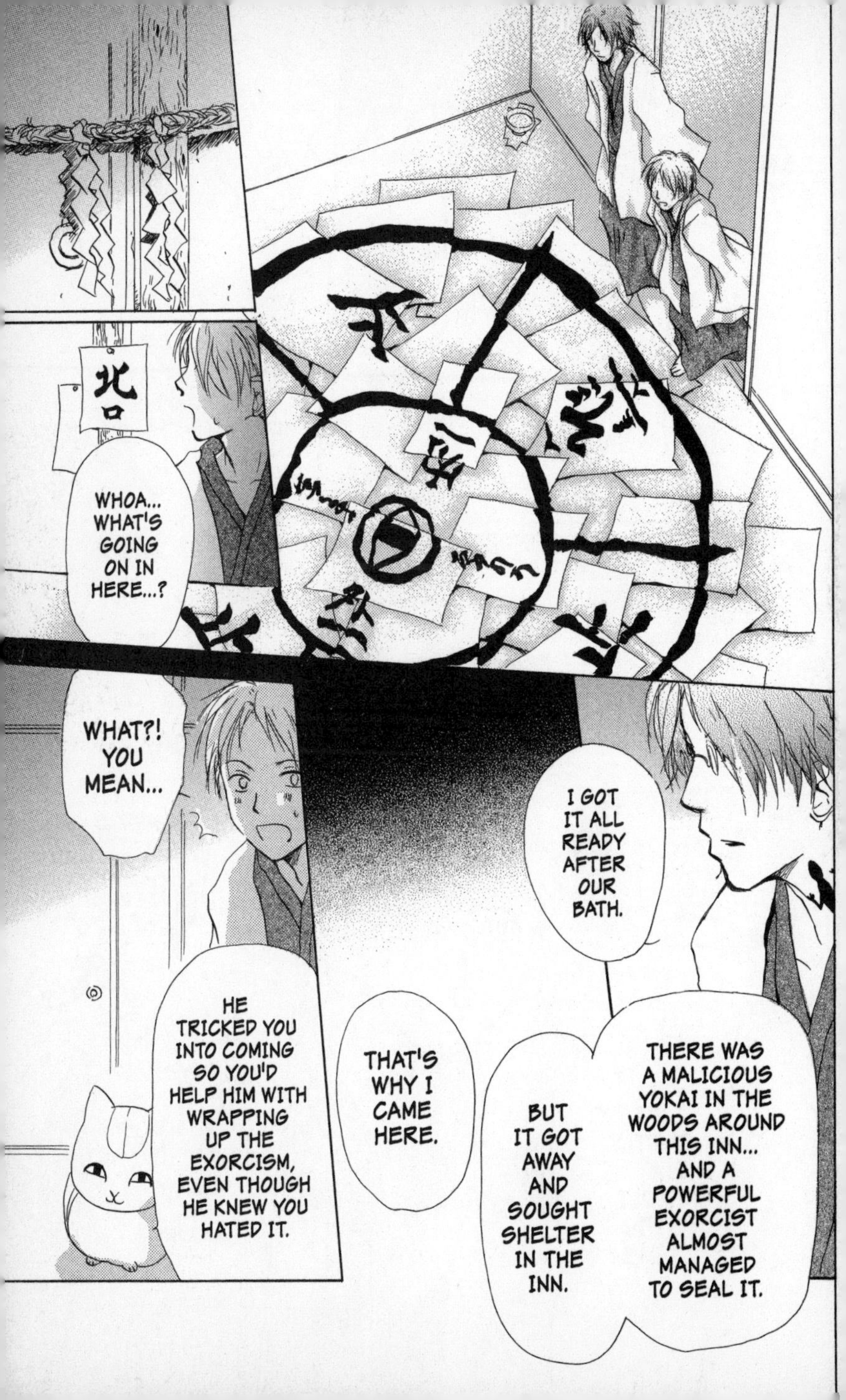

北口
WHOA... WHAT'S GOING ON IN HERE...?
I GOT IT ALL READY AFTER OUR BATH.
THERE WAS A MALICIOUS YOKAI IN THE WOODS AROUND THIS INN... AND A POWERFUL EXORCIST ALMOST MANAGED TO SEAL IT.
BUT IT GOT AWAY AND SOUGHT SHELTER IN THE INN.
THAT'S WHY I CAME HERE.
WHAT?! YOU MEAN...
HE TRICKED YOU INTO COMING SO YOU'D HELP HIM WITH WRAPPING UP THE EXORCISM, EVEN THOUGH HE KNEW YOU HATED IT.

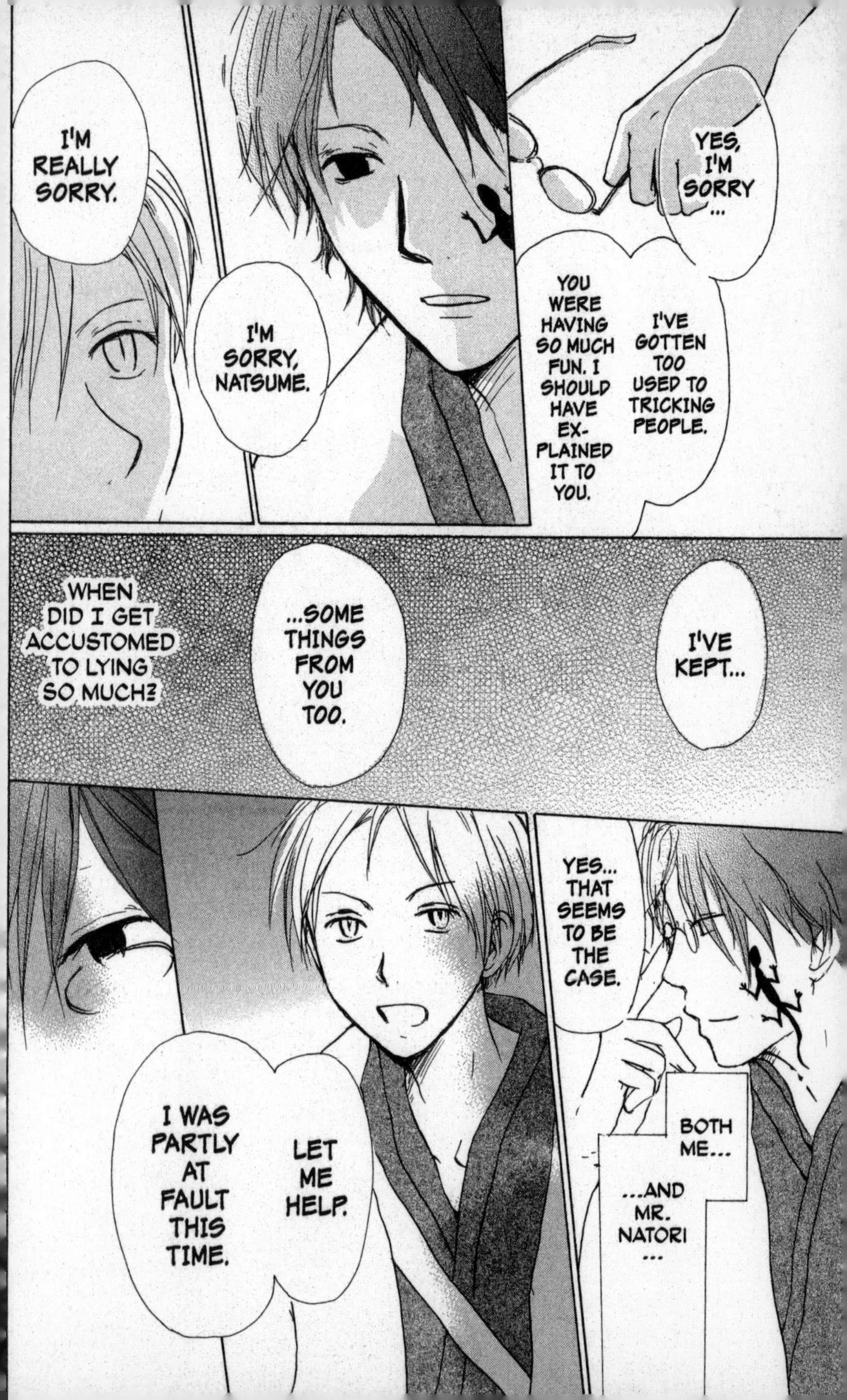
YES, I'M SORRY ...
I'VE GOTTEN TOO USED TO TRICKING PEOPLE.
YOU WERE HAVING SO MUCH FUN. I SHOULD HAVE EX-PLAINED IT TO YOU.
I'M SORRY, NATSUME.
I'M REALLY SORRY.
I'VE KEPT...
...SOME THINGS FROM YOU TOO.
WHEN DID I GET ACCUSTOMED TO LYING SO MUCH?
YES... THAT SEEMS TO BE THE CASE.
BOTH ME...
...AND MR. NATORI ...
LET ME HELP.
I WAS PARTLY AT FAULT THIS TIME.

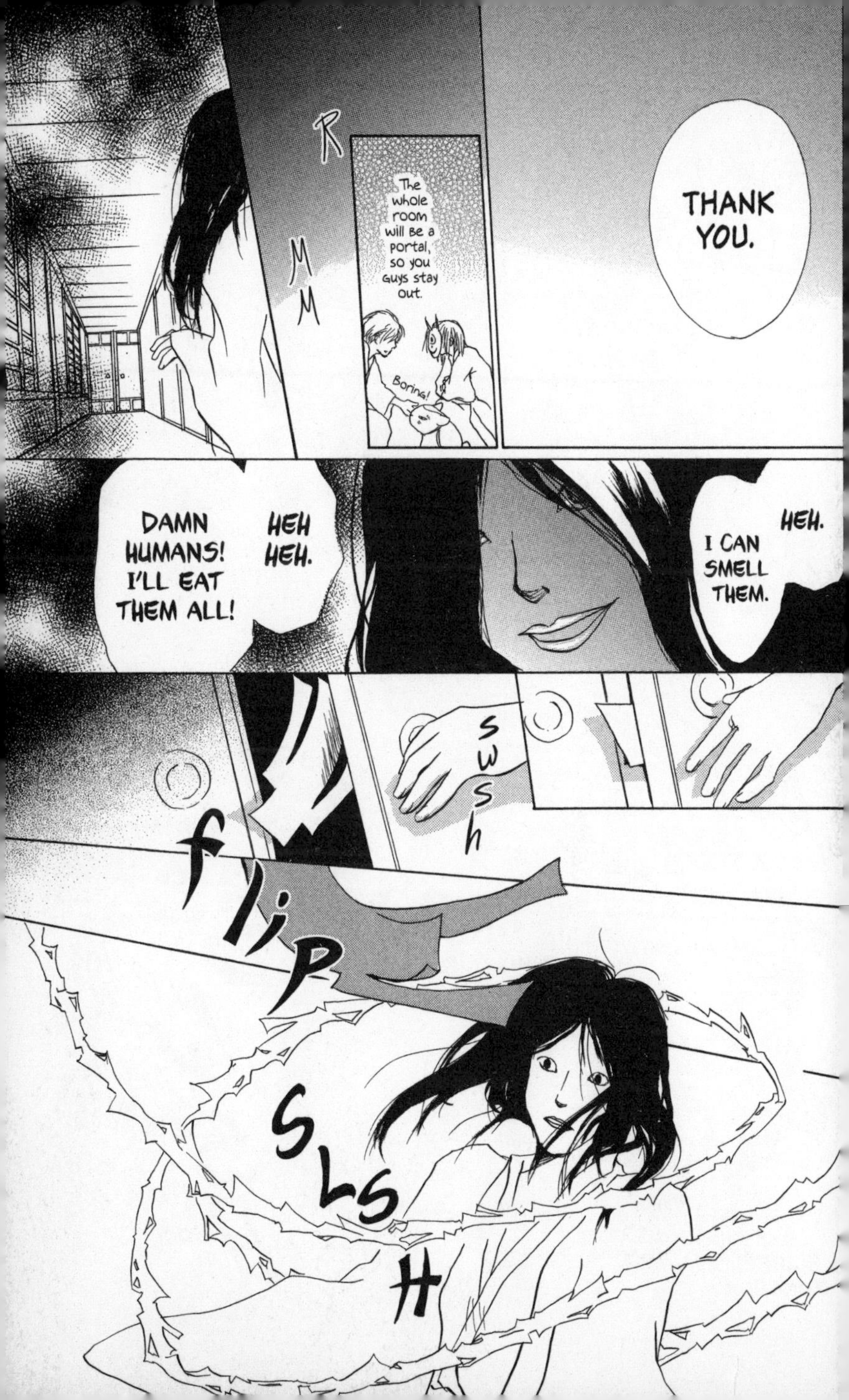

THANK YOU.
The whole room will be a portal, so you guys stay out.
Boring!
RMM
HEH.
I CAN SMELL THEM.
HEH HEH.
DAMN HUMANS! I'LL EAT THEM ALL!
SWSh
flip
SLSH

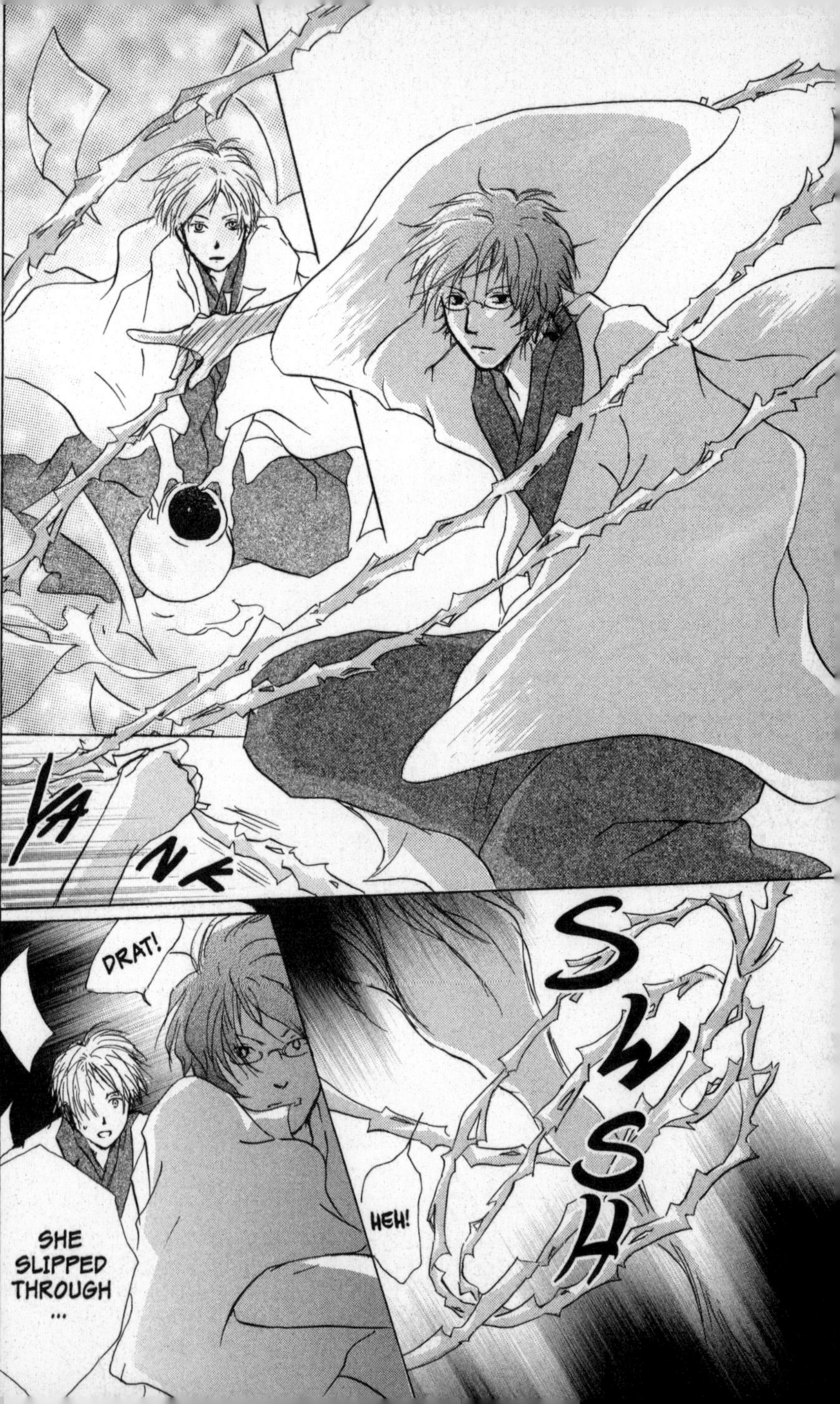
YANK
SWSH
DRAT!
HEH!
SHE SLIPPED THROUGH ...

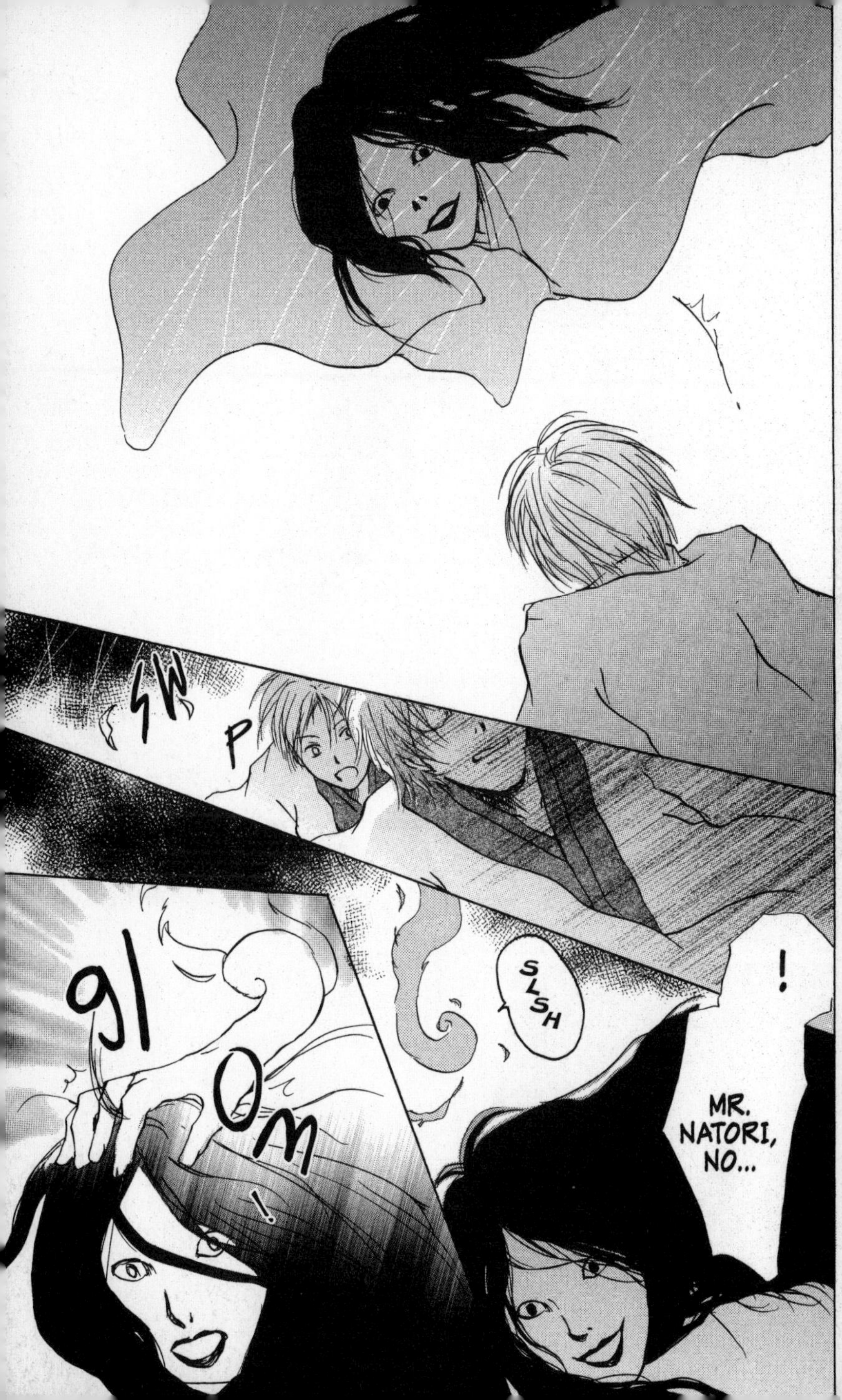
SWP
!
MR. NATORI, NO...
SLSH

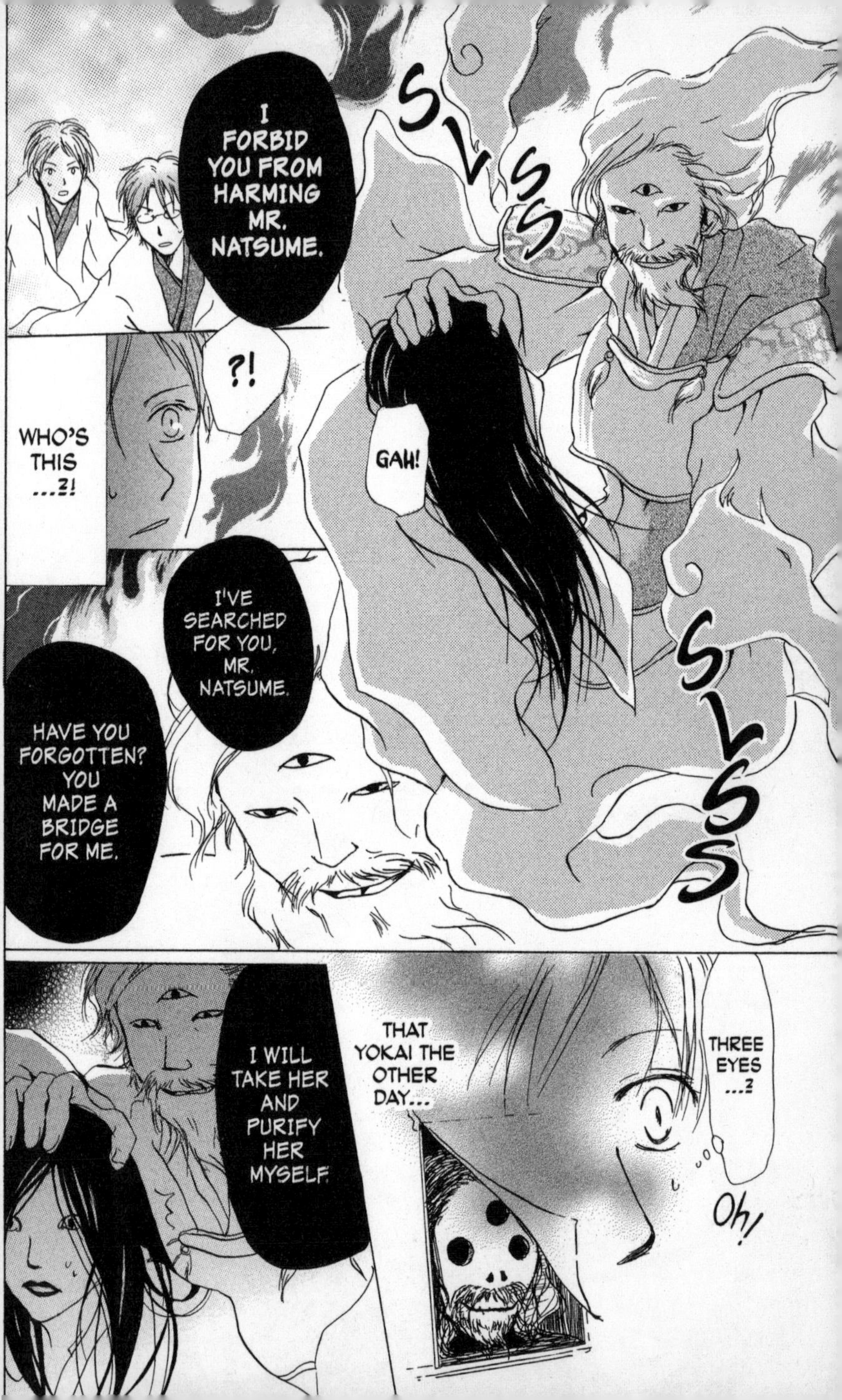
SLSS
GAH!
SLSS
I FORBID YOU FROM HARMING MR. NATSUME.
?!
WHO'S THIS ...?!
I'VE SEARCHED FOR YOU, MR. NATSUME.
HAVE YOU FORGOTTEN? YOU MADE A BRIDGE FOR ME.
THREE EYES ...?
Oh!
THAT YOKAI THE OTHER DAY...
I WILL TAKE HER AND PURIFY HER MYSELF.

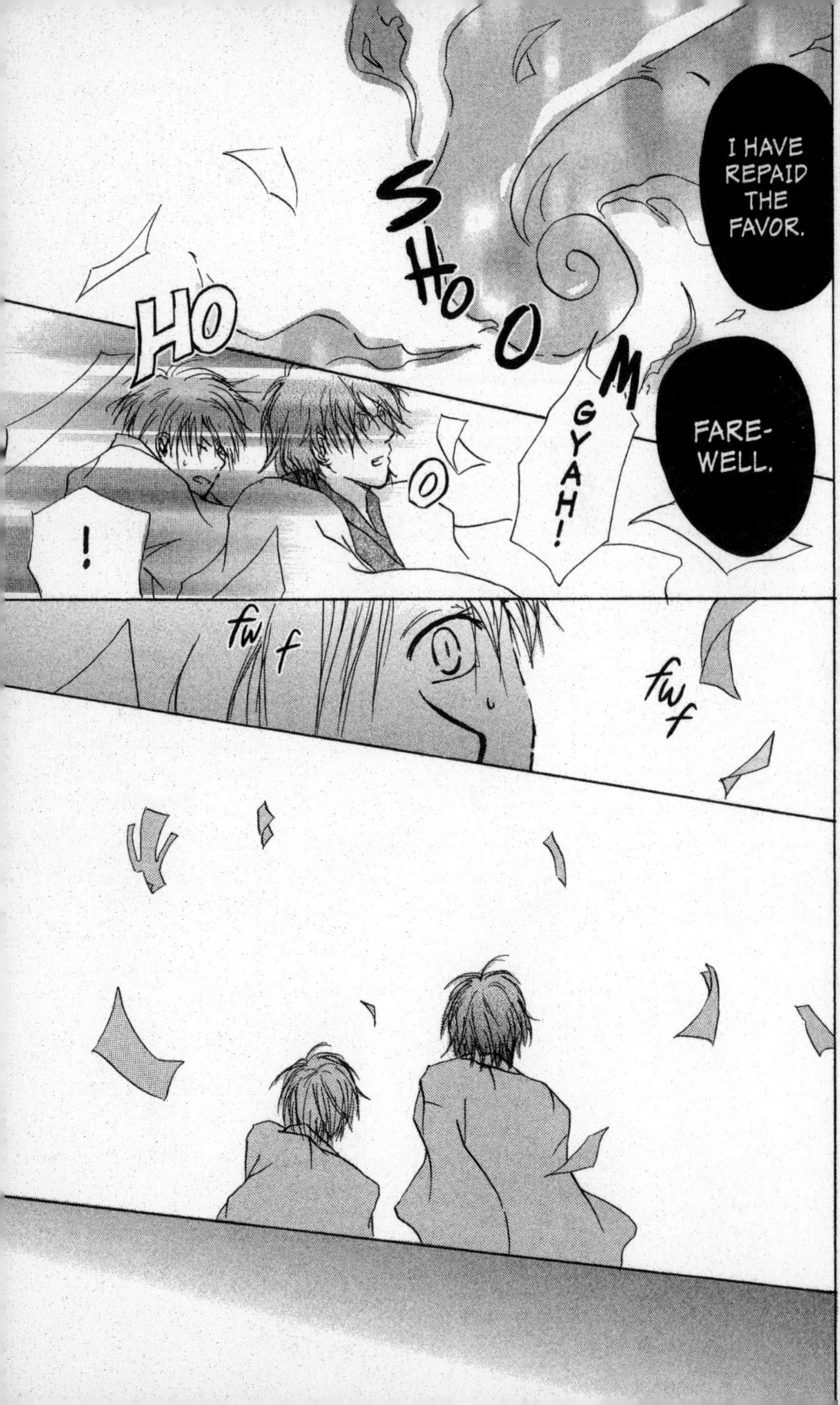
I HAVE REPAID THE FAVOR.
FARE-WELL.
SHOOOM
GYAH!
O
HO
!
fwf
fwf

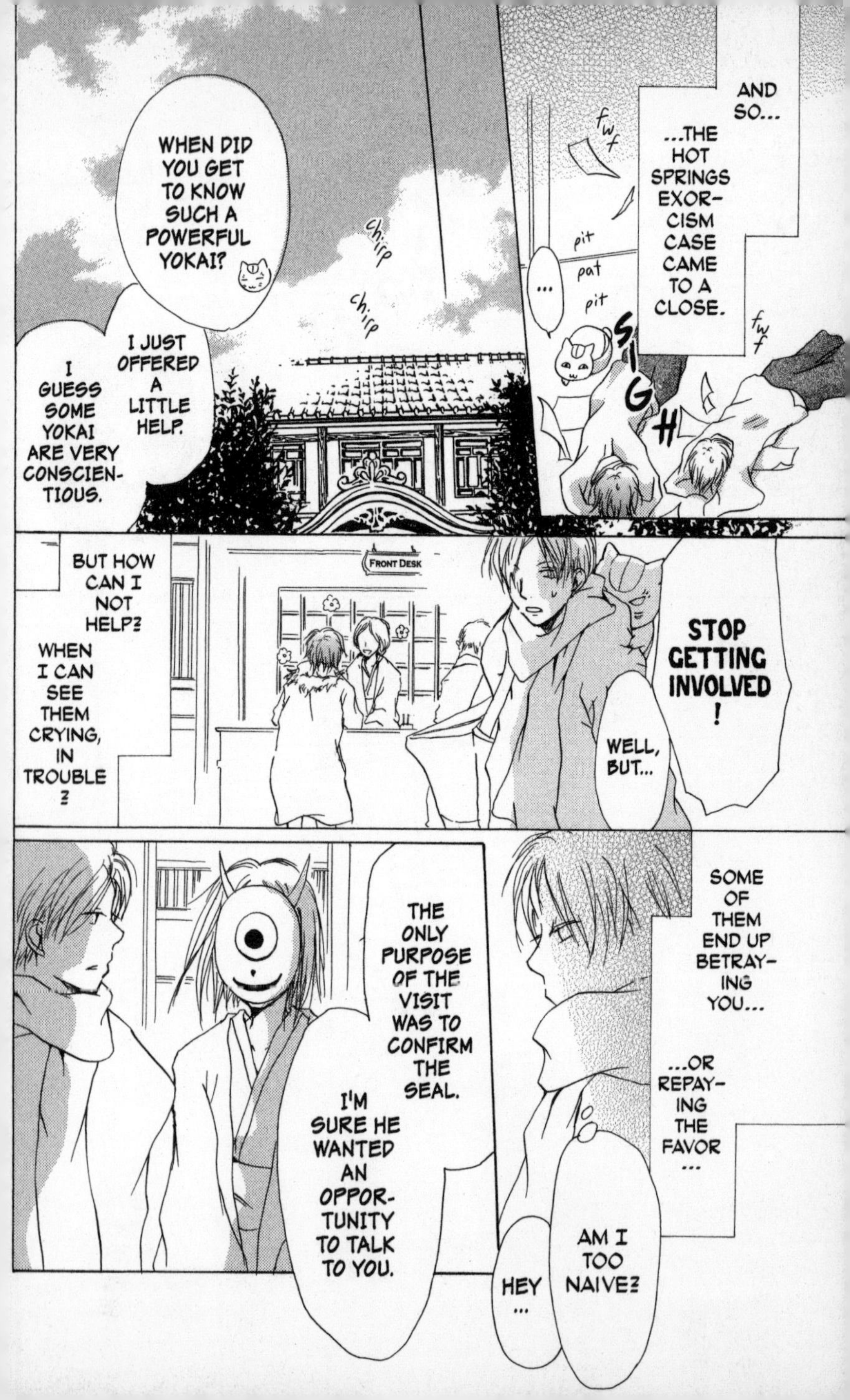
AND SO...
...THE HOT SPRINGS EXOR-CISM CASE CAME TO A CLOSE.
fwf
pit pat pit
...
SIGH
fwf
chirp chirp
WHEN DID YOU GET TO KNOW SUCH A POWERFUL YOKAI?
I JUST OFFERED A LITTLE HELP.
I GUESS SOME YOKAI ARE VERY CONSCIEN-TIOUS.
FRONT DESK
STOP GETTING INVOLVED!
WELL, BUT...
BUT HOW CAN I NOT HELP?
WHEN I CAN SEE THEM CRYING, IN TROUBLE?
SOME OF THEM END UP BETRAY-ING YOU...
...OR REPAY-ING THE FAVOR...
AM I TOO NAIVE?
HEY...
THE ONLY PURPOSE OF THE VISIT WAS TO CONFIRM THE SEAL.
I'M SURE HE WANTED AN OPPOR-TUNITY TO TALK TO YOU.

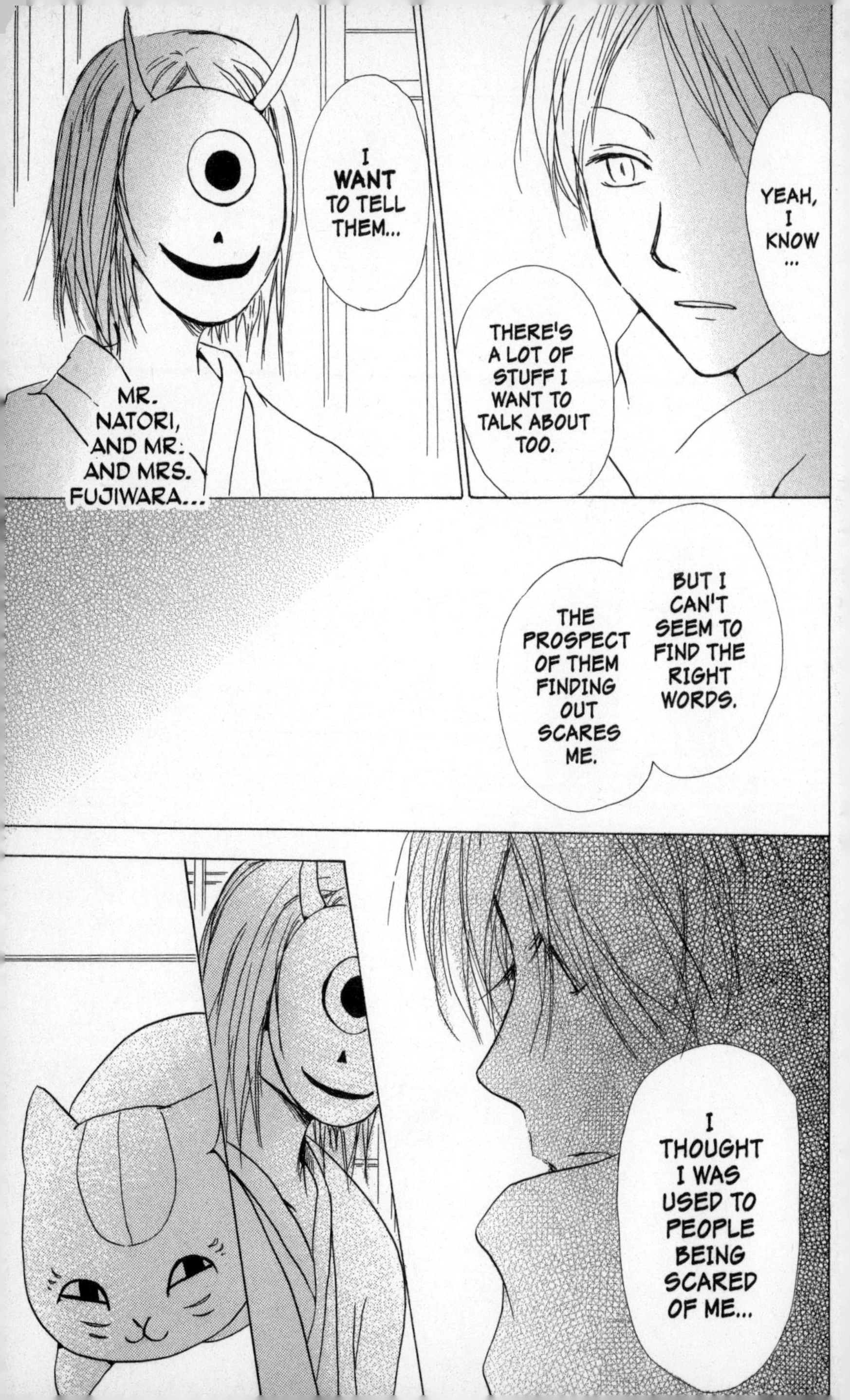
YEAH, I KNOW ...
THERE'S A LOT OF STUFF I WANT TO TALK ABOUT TOO.
I WANT TO TELL THEM...
MR. NATORI, AND MR. AND MRS. FUJIWARA...
BUT I CAN'T SEEM TO FIND THE RIGHT WORDS.
THE PROSPECT OF THEM FINDING OUT SCARES ME.
I THOUGHT I WAS USED TO PEOPLE BEING SCARED OF ME...

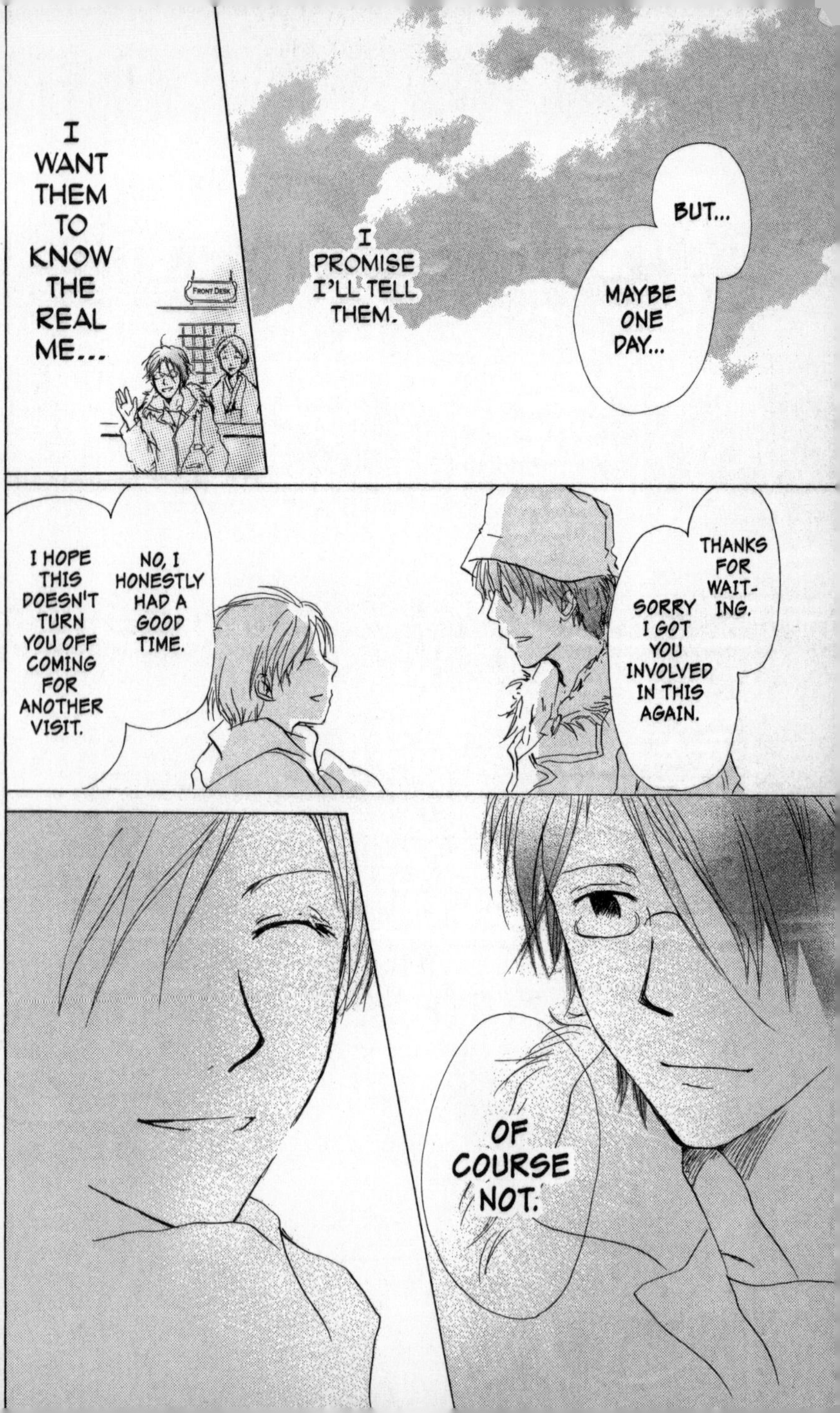
BUT...
MAYBE ONE DAY...
I PROMISE I'LL TELL THEM.
FRONT DESK
I WANT THEM TO KNOW THE REAL ME...
THANKS FOR WAIT-ING.
SORRY I GOT YOU INVOLVED IN THIS AGAIN.
NO, I HONESTLY HAD A GOOD TIME.
I HOPE THIS DOESN'T TURN YOU OFF COMING FOR ANOTHER VISIT.
OF COURSE NOT.

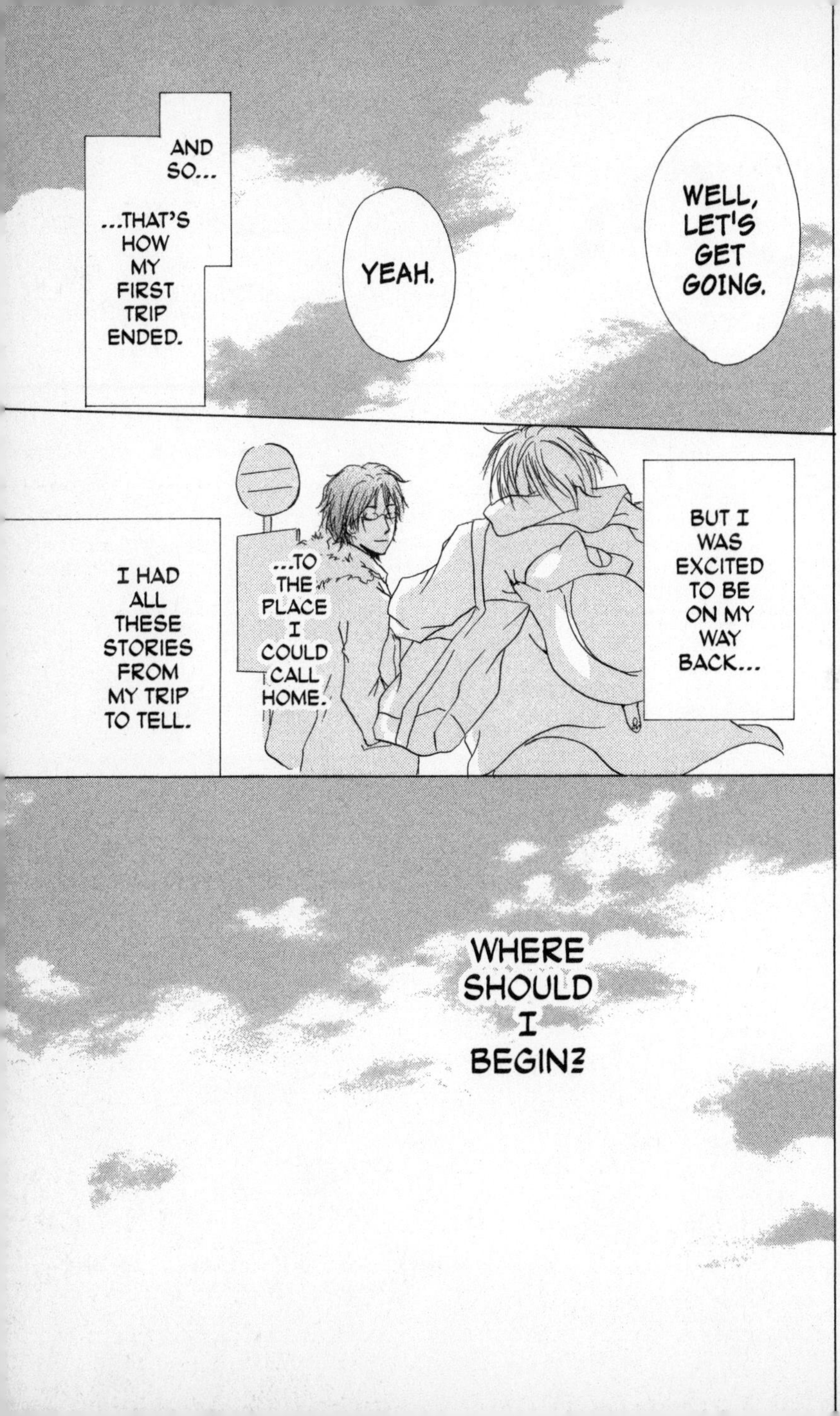
WELL, LET'S GET GOING.
YEAH.
AND SO...
...THAT'S HOW MY FIRST TRIP ENDED.
BUT I WAS EXCITED TO BE ON MY WAY BACK...
...TO THE PLACE I COULD CALL HOME.
I HAD ALL THESE STORIES FROM MY TRIP TO TELL.
WHERE SHOULD I BEGIN?

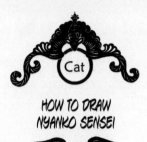

Cat

HOW TO DRAW NYANKO SENSEI

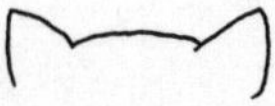

①The ears slightly flattened

↓

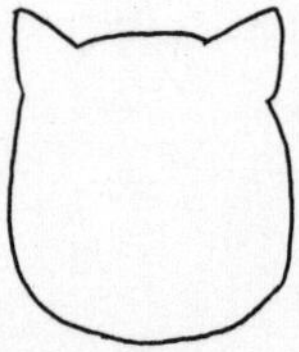

②Quite plump in the jowls

↓

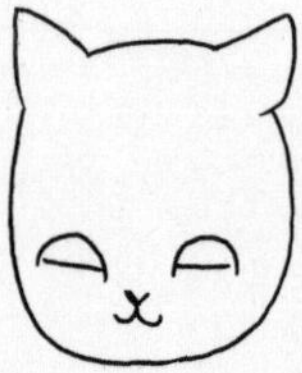

③Big forehead, the eyes placed low

↓

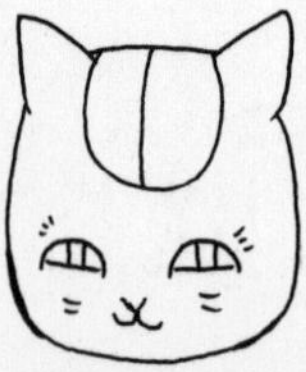

④He gets too cute if the pupils are too large, so keep them ambiguously creepy

←

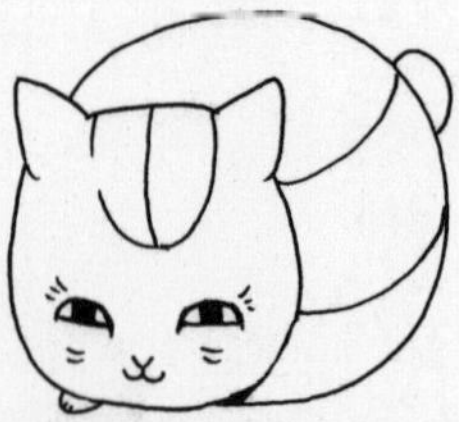

⑤2.5 heads tall!

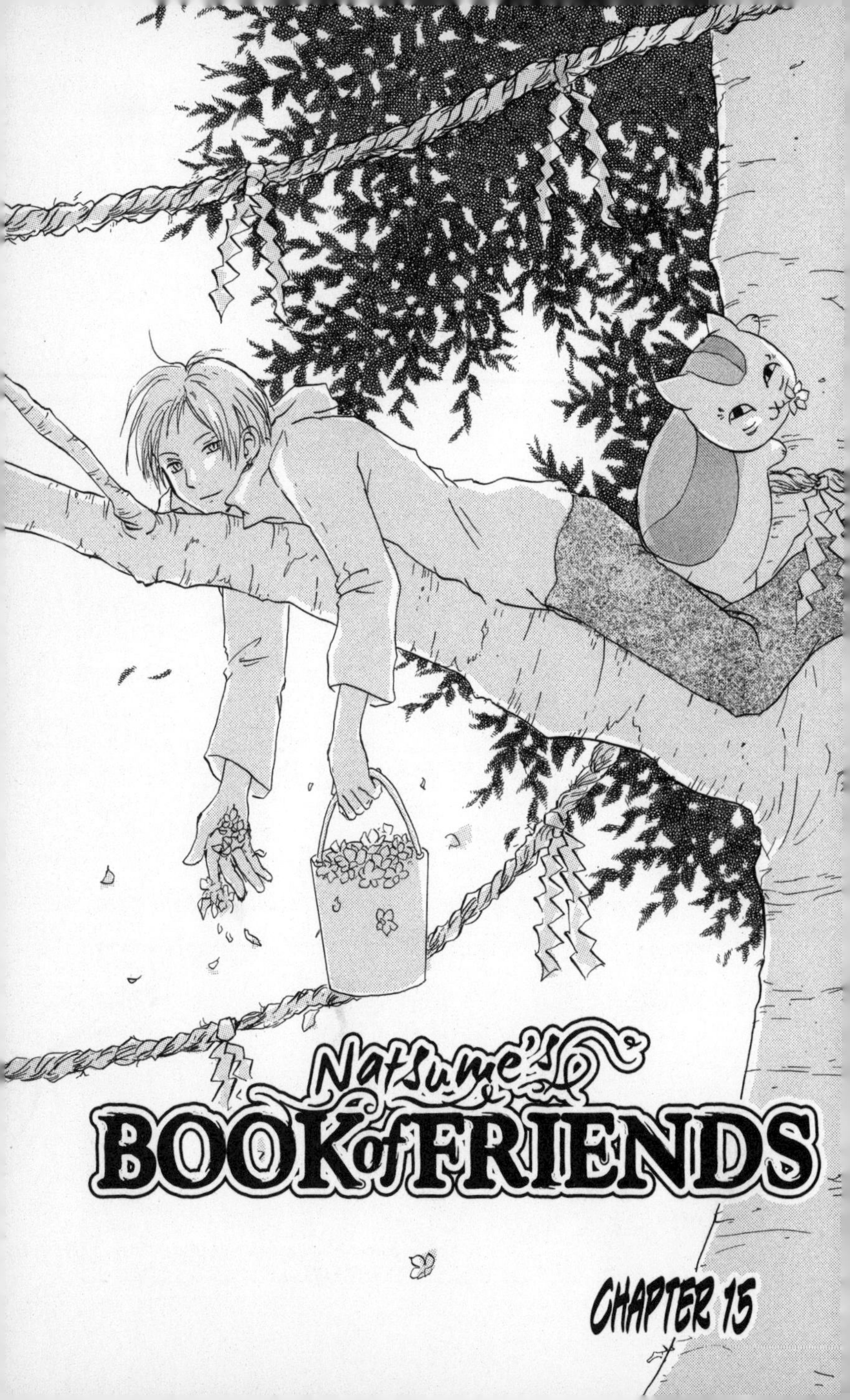
Natsume's
BOOK of FRIENDS
CHAPTER 15

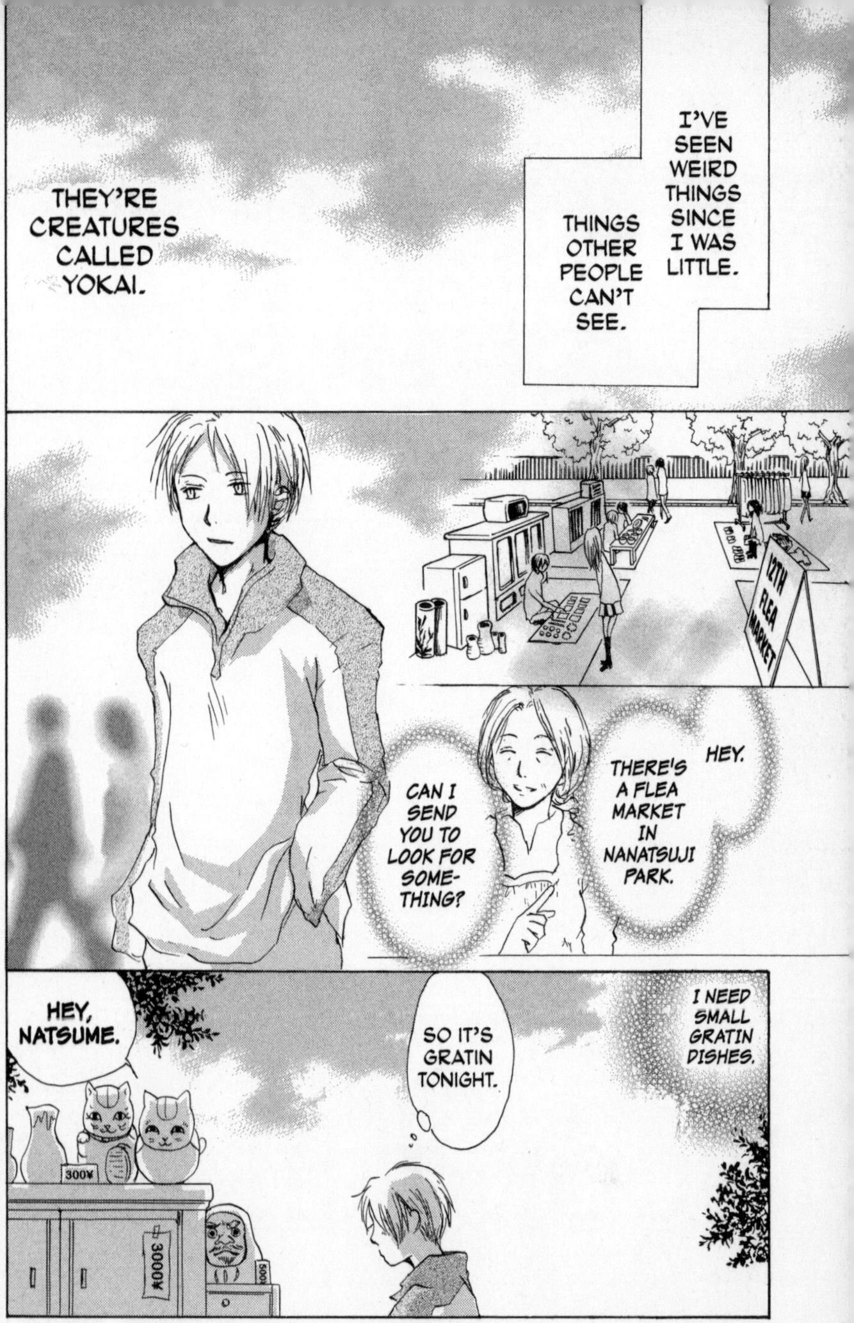
I'VE SEEN WEIRD THINGS SINCE I WAS LITTLE.
THINGS OTHER PEOPLE CAN'T SEE.
THEY'RE CREATURES CALLED YOKAI.
12TH FLEA MARKET
HEY.
THERE'S A FLEA MARKET IN NANATSUJI PARK.
CAN I SEND YOU TO LOOK FOR SOME-THING?
I NEED SMALL GRATIN DISHES.
SO IT'S GRATIN TONIGHT.
HEY, NATSUME.
300¥
3000¥

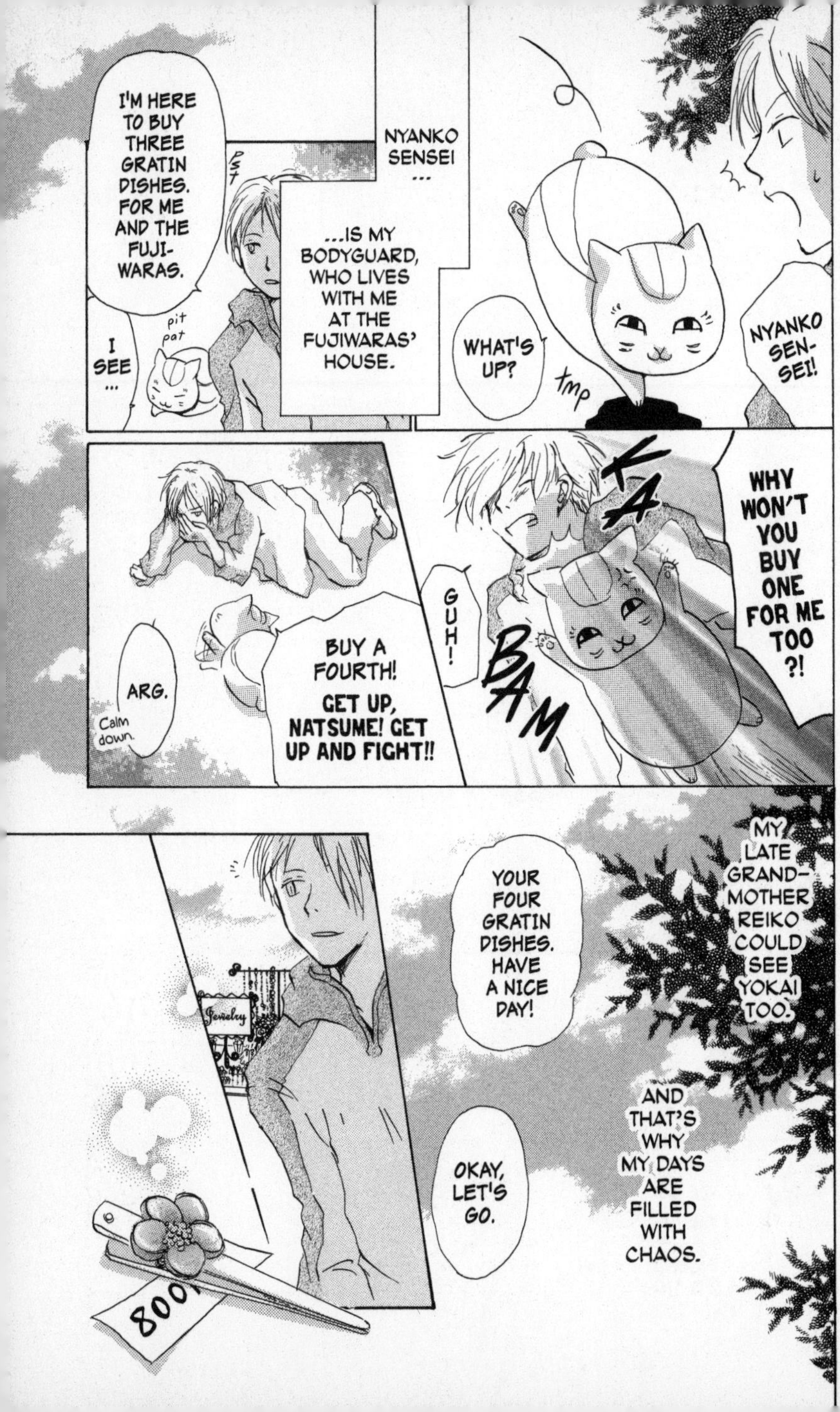
NYANKO SENSEI!
WHAT'S UP?
tmp
NYANKO SENSEI ...
...IS MY BODYGUARD, WHO LIVES WITH ME AT THE FUJIWARAS' HOUSE.
I'M HERE TO BUY THREE GRATIN DISHES. FOR ME AND THE FUJIWARAS.
pst
I SEE ...
pit pat
WHY WON'T YOU BUY ONE FOR ME TOO ?!
KA
BAM
GUH!
BUY A FOURTH!
GET UP, NATSUME! GET UP AND FIGHT!!
ARG.
Calm down.
MY LATE GRANDMOTHER REIKO COULD SEE YOKAI TOO.
YOUR FOUR GRATIN DISHES. HAVE A NICE DAY!
AND THAT'S WHY MY DAYS ARE FILLED WITH CHAOS.
OKAY, LET'S GO.
Jewelry
800

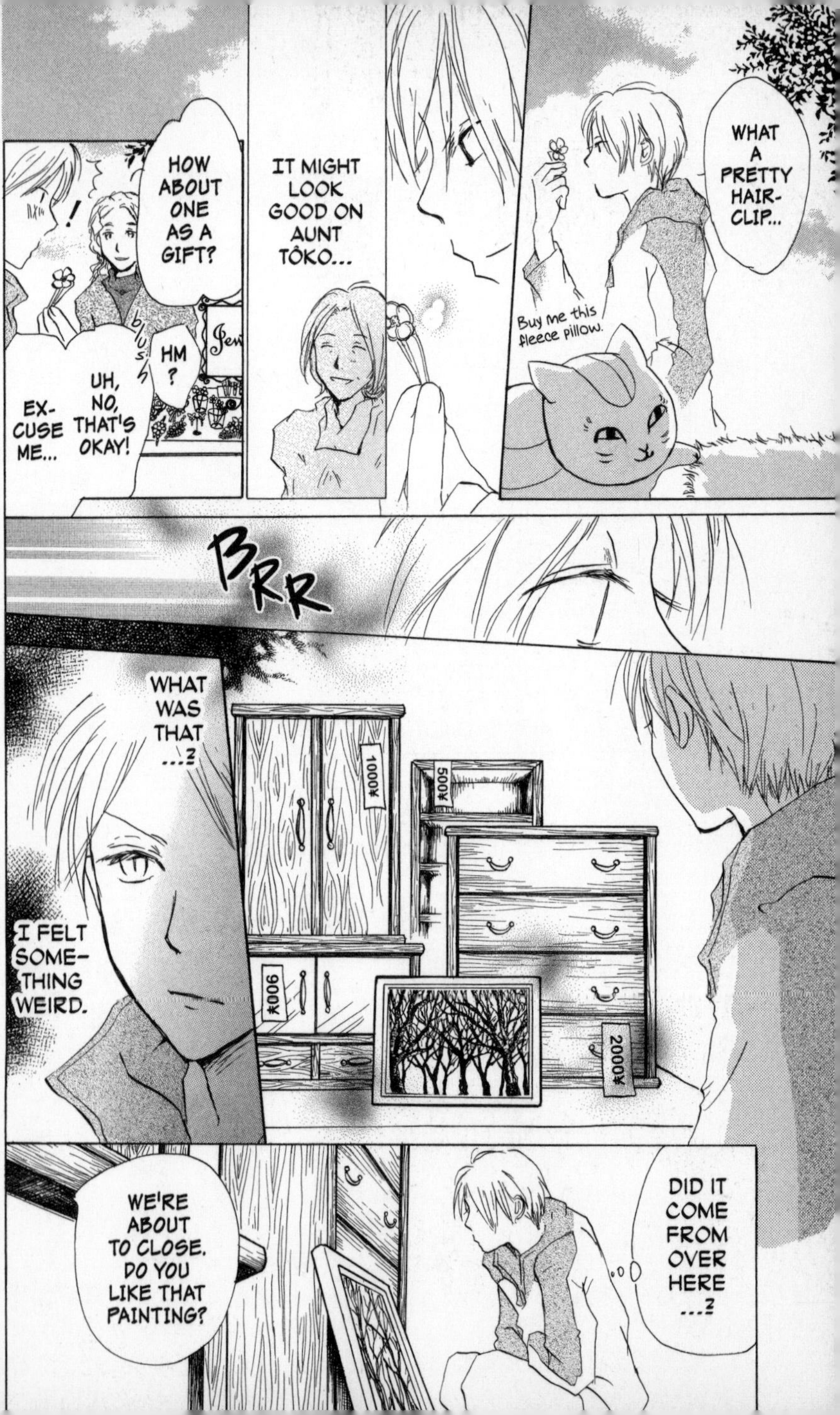

WHAT A PRETTY HAIR-CLIP...
Buy me this fleece pillow.
IT MIGHT LOOK GOOD ON AUNT TÔKO...
HOW ABOUT ONE AS A GIFT?
HM?
blush
UH, NO, THAT'S OKAY!
EX-CUSE ME...
BRR
WHAT WAS THAT...?
I FELT SOME-THING WEIRD.
1000¥
500¥
900¥
2000¥
DID IT COME FROM OVER HERE...?
WE'RE ABOUT TO CLOSE. DO YOU LIKE THAT PAINTING?

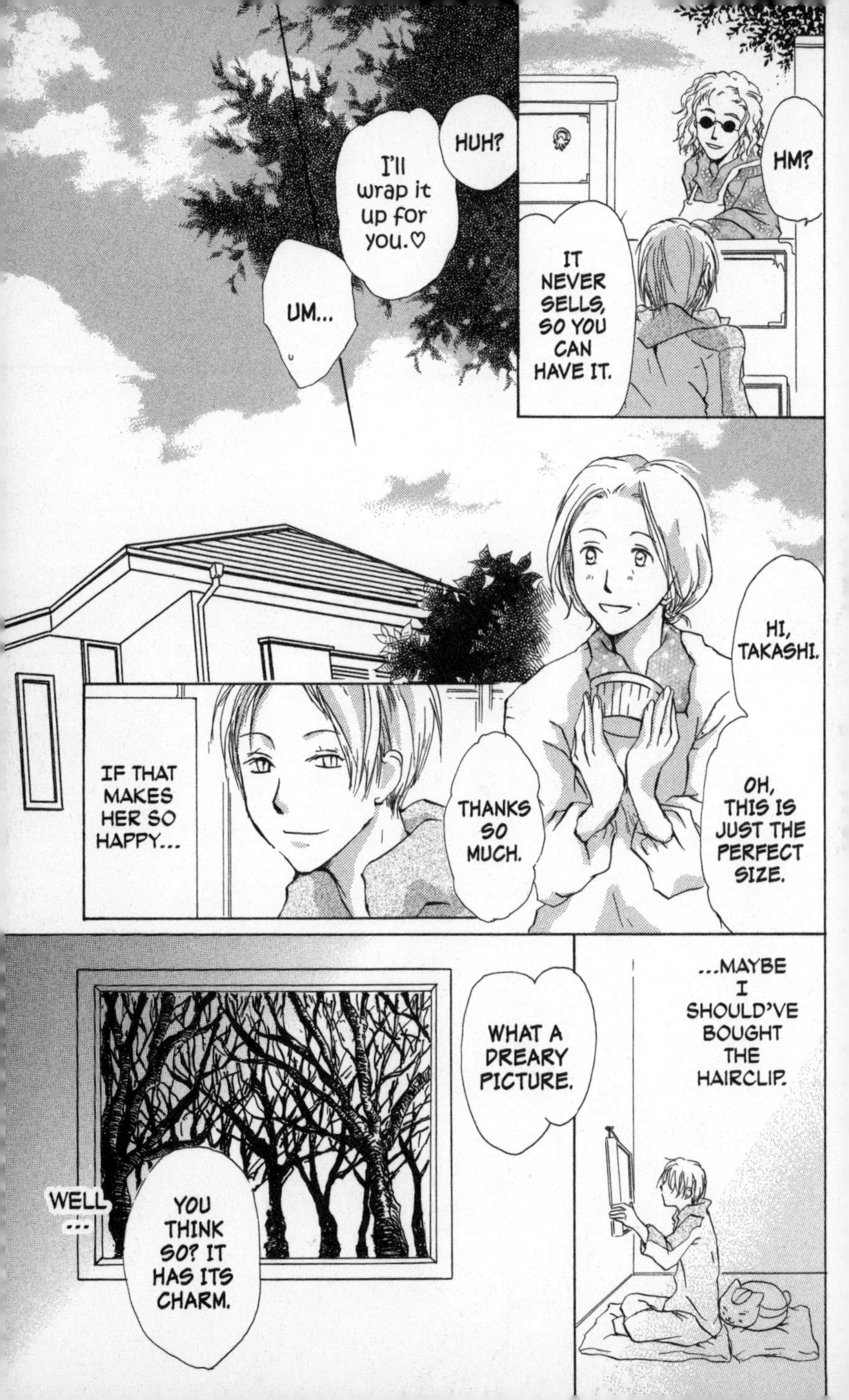
HM?
IT NEVER SELLS, SO YOU CAN HAVE IT.
HUH?
I'll wrap it up for you.♡
UM...
HI, TAKASHI.
OH, THIS IS JUST THE PERFECT SIZE.
THANKS SO MUCH.
IF THAT MAKES HER SO HAPPY...
...MAYBE I SHOULD'VE BOUGHT THE HAIRCLIP.
WHAT A DREARY PICTURE.
YOU THINK SO? IT HAS ITS CHARM.
WELL...

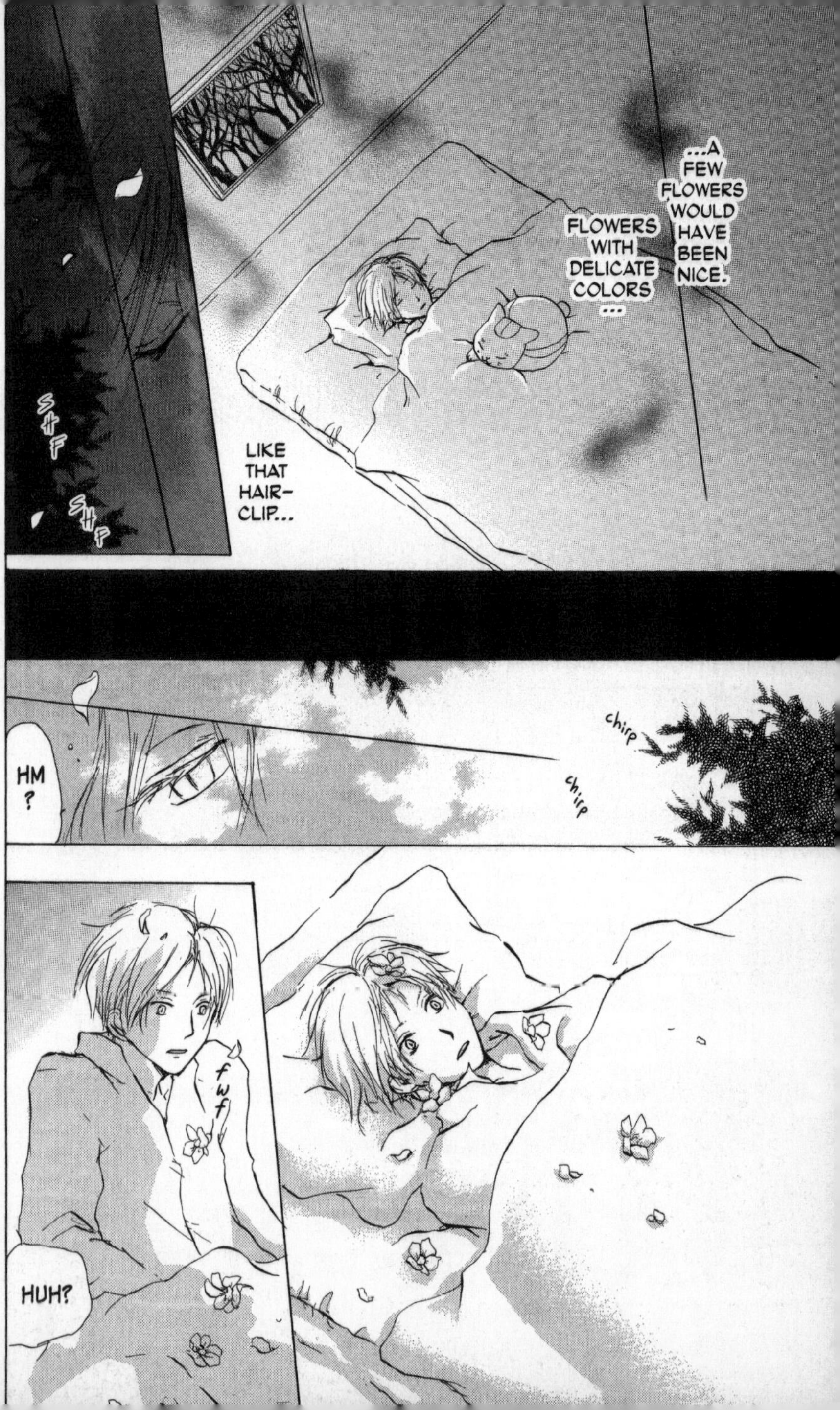
...A FEW FLOWERS WOULD HAVE BEEN NICE.
FLOWERS WITH DELICATE COLORS...
LIKE THAT HAIR-CLIP...
SHF SHF
chirp chirp
HM?
fwf
HUH?

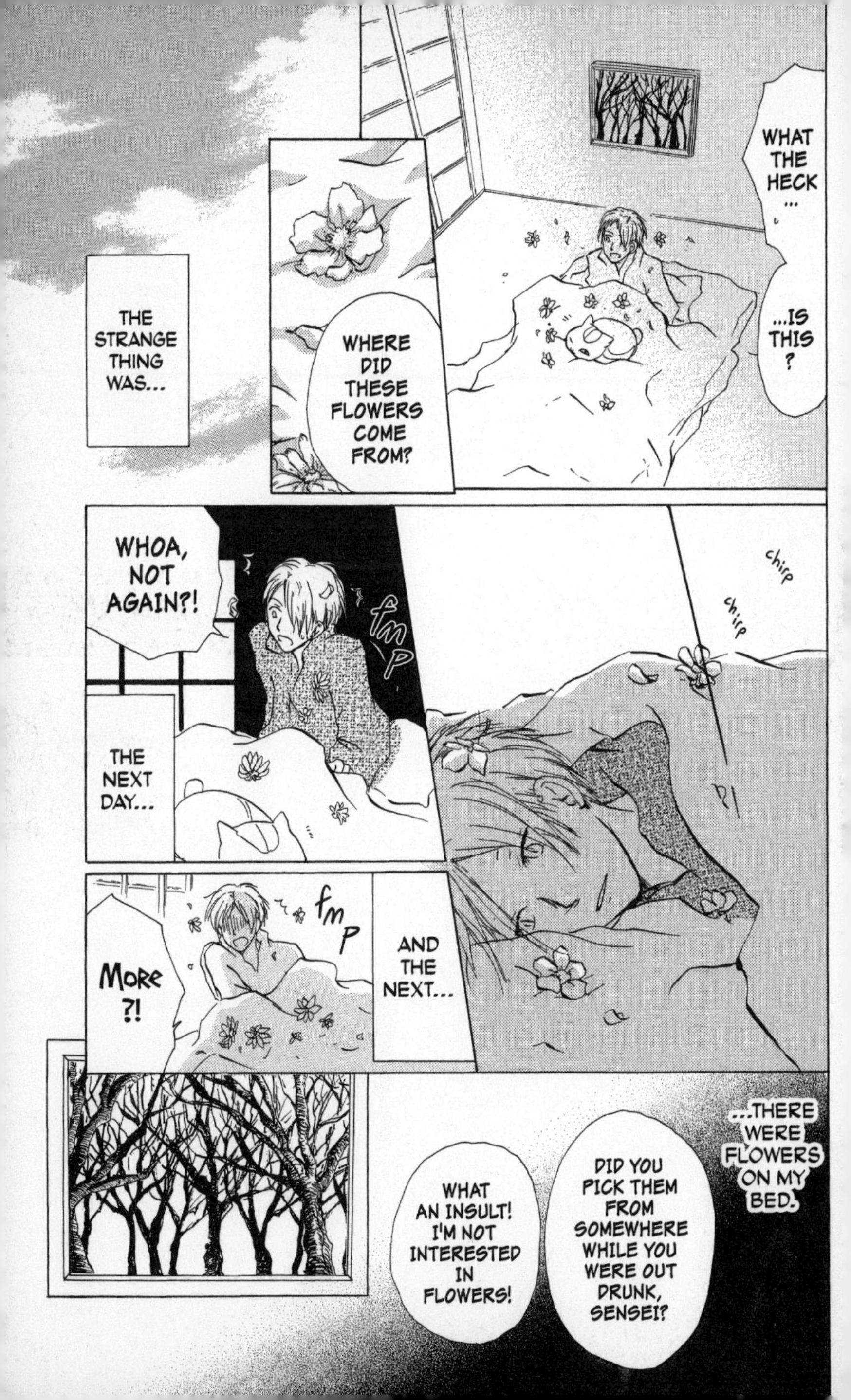
WHAT THE HECK...
...IS THIS?
WHERE DID THESE FLOWERS COME FROM?
THE STRANGE THING WAS...
chirp
chirp
WHOA, NOT AGAIN?!
fmp
THE NEXT DAY...
AND THE NEXT...
fmp
More?!
...THERE WERE FLOWERS ON MY BED.
DID YOU PICK THEM FROM SOMEWHERE WHILE YOU WERE OUT DRUNK, SENSEI?
WHAT AN INSULT! I'M NOT INTERESTED IN FLOWERS!

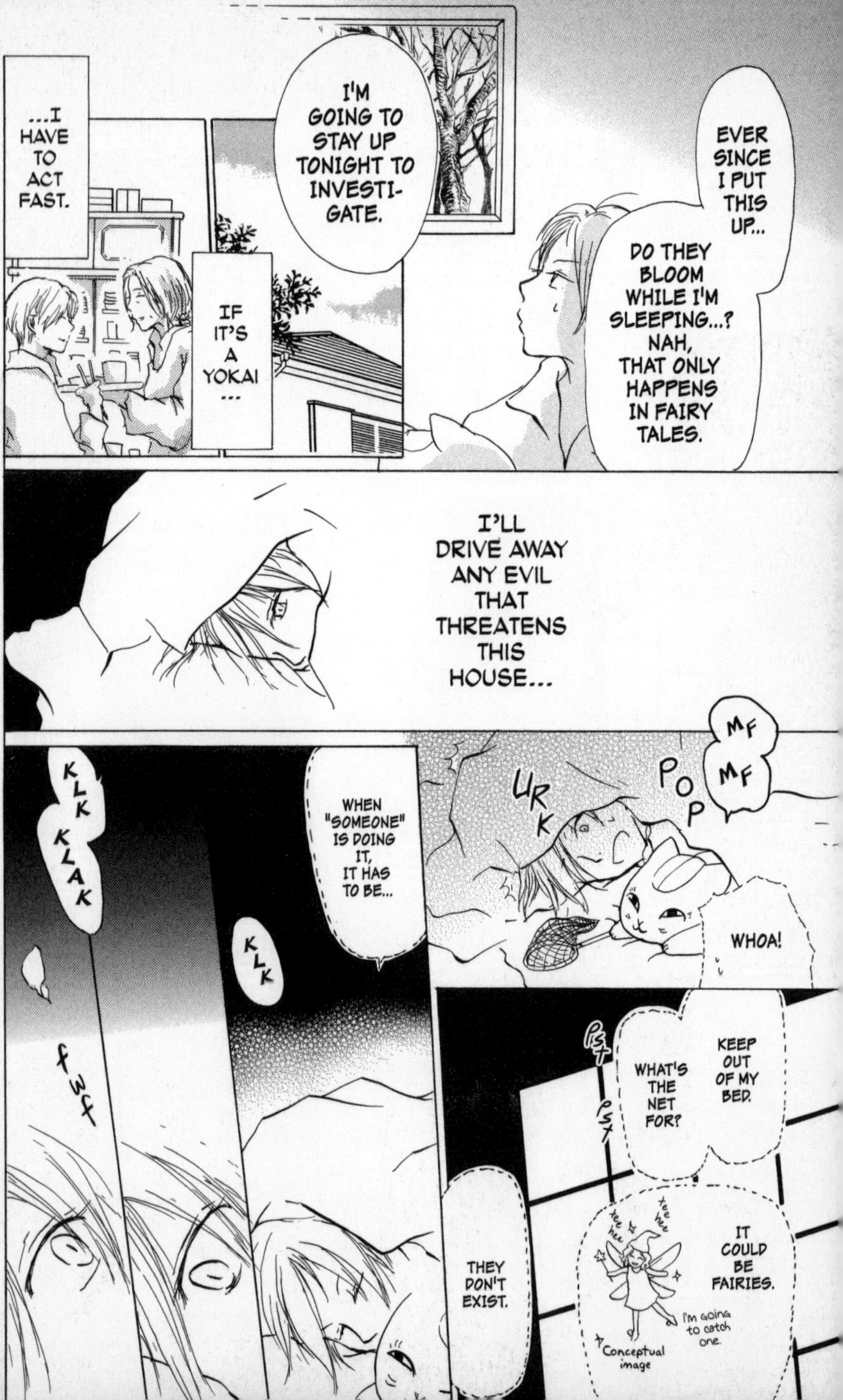
EVER SINCE I PUT THIS UP...
DO THEY BLOOM WHILE I'M SLEEPING...? NAH, THAT ONLY HAPPENS IN FAIRY TALES.
I'M GOING TO STAY UP TONIGHT TO INVESTI-GATE.
IF IT'S A YOKAI...
...I HAVE TO ACT FAST.
I'LL DRIVE AWAY ANY EVIL THAT THREATENS THIS HOUSE...
MF MF
POP
URK
WHOA!
KEEP OUT OF MY BED.
WHAT'S THE NET FOR?
PSST PSST
IT COULD BE FAIRIES.
xee hee xee hee
I'm going to catch one.
Conceptual image
THEY DON'T EXIST.
WHEN "SOMEONE" IS DOING IT, IT HAS TO BE...
KLK KLAK
KLK
fwf

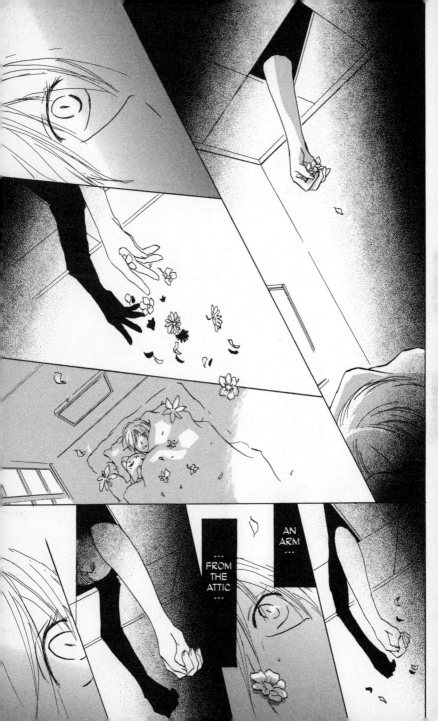

AN
ARM
...

...
FROM
THE
ATTIC
...

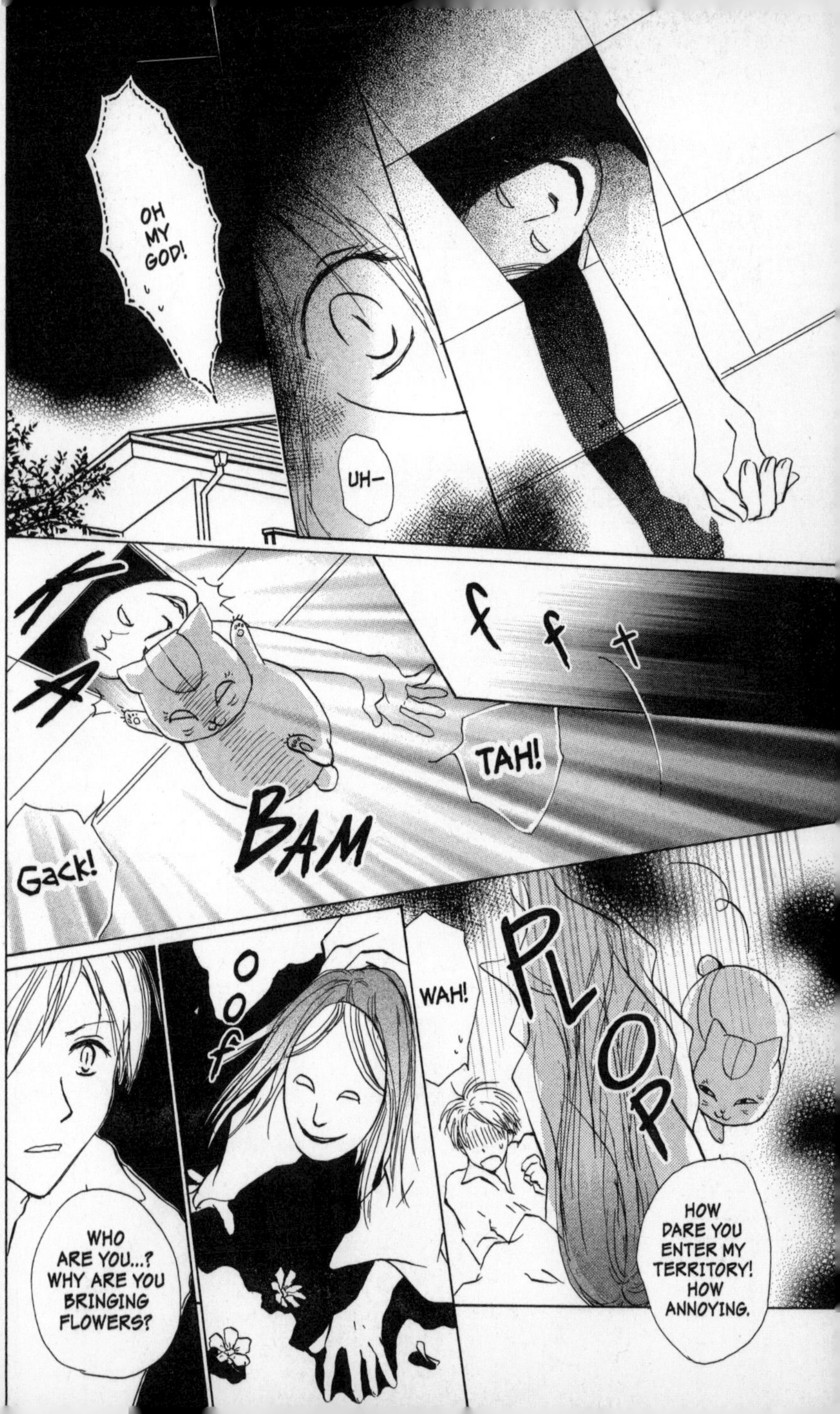
OH MY GOD!
UH—
f f t
KA
TAH!
BAM
Gack!
PLOP
WAH!
HOW DARE YOU ENTER MY TERRITORY! HOW ANNOYING.
oof
WHO ARE YOU...? WHY ARE YOU BRINGING FLOWERS?

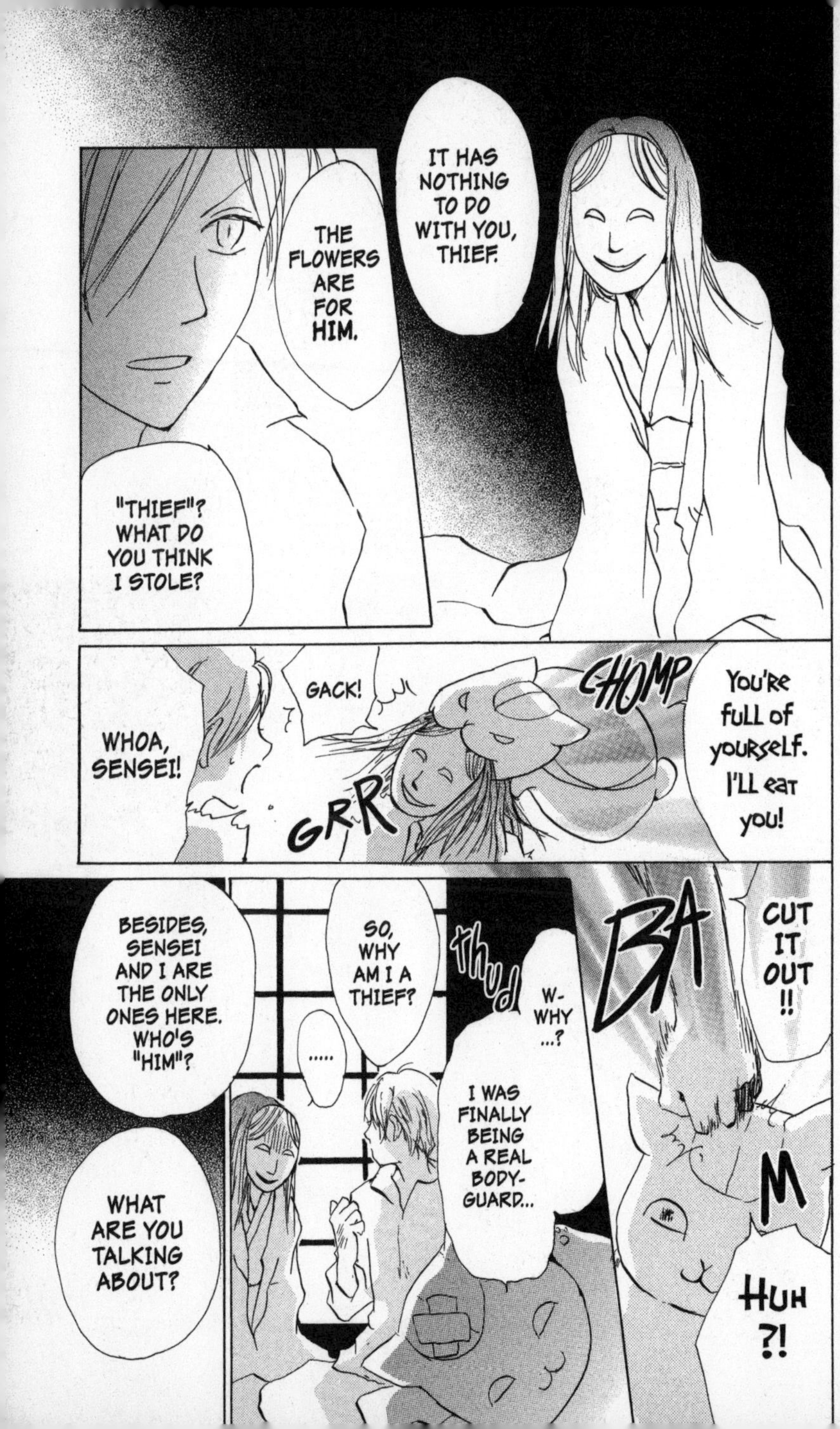
IT HAS NOTHING TO DO WITH YOU, THIEF.
THE FLOWERS ARE FOR HIM.
"THIEF"? WHAT DO YOU THINK I STOLE?
You're full of yourself. I'll eat you!
CHOMP
GRR
GACK!
WHOA, SENSEI!
CUT IT OUT !!
BA
M
HUH ?!
W-WHY ...?
I WAS FINALLY BEING A REAL BODY-GUARD...
thud
SO, WHY AM I A THIEF?
BESIDES, SENSEI AND I ARE THE ONLY ONES HERE. WHO'S "HIM"?
......
WHAT ARE YOU TALKING ABOUT?

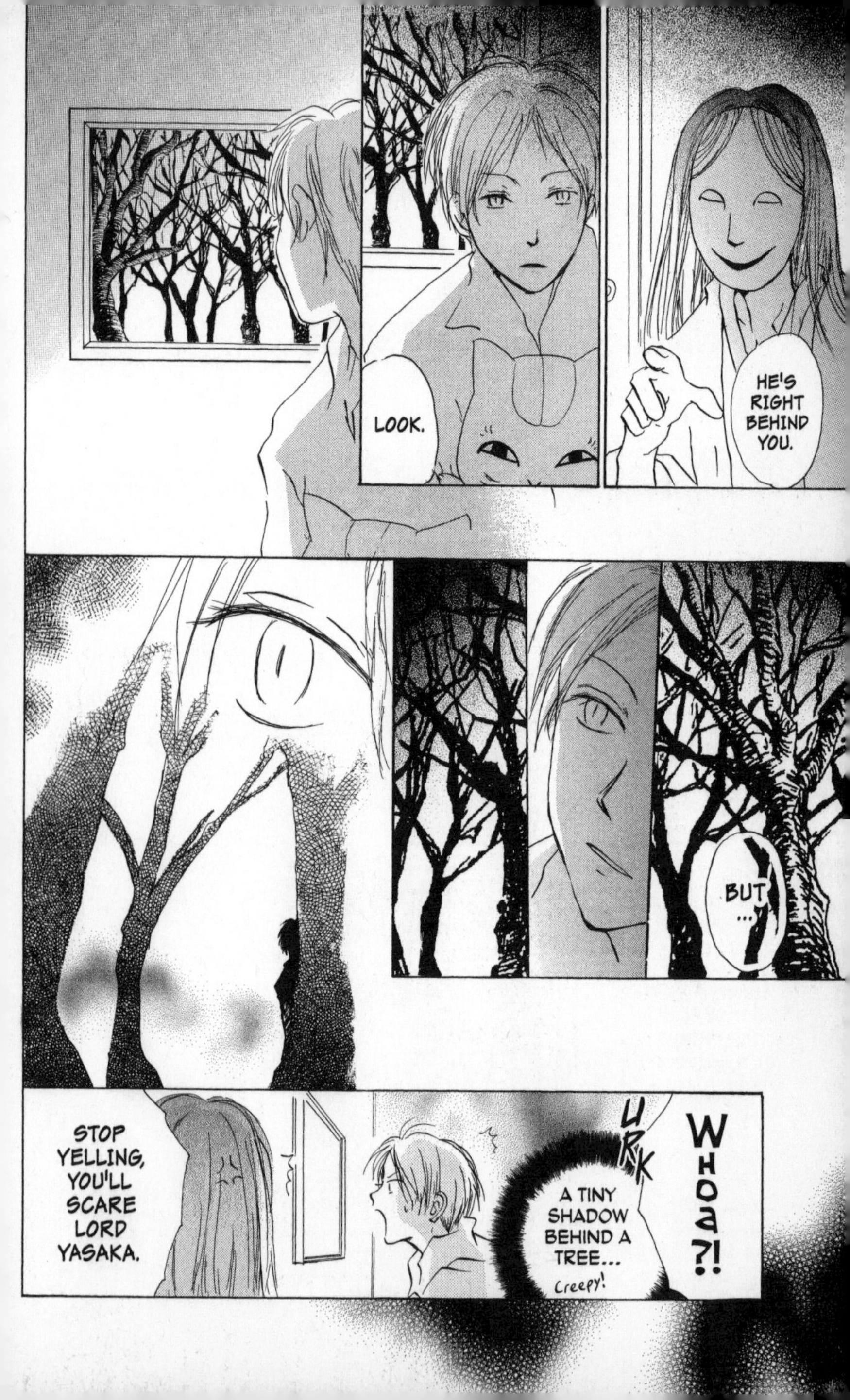
HE'S RIGHT BEHIND YOU.
LOOK.
BUT ...
WHOA?!
URK
A TINY SHADOW BEHIND A TREE...
Creepy!
STOP YELLING, YOU'LL SCARE LORD YASAKA.

04

❋The yokai in the jar

This yokai came about because I wanted to do a story where you glance over into the corner of the room and something's dangling from the ceiling. A dangling head would've been scarier, but I chose a dangling body. In which case, I had to ask myself, "Where is the head?" But this kind of story is difficult, since the excitement fades once the head is eventually revealed.

❋Male Characters

Natsume and Sensei are both male, so I get nervous when the guest characters are also male, because they make the page stuffy. I wonder how other people get around these problems? I need to study more. I feel like I stumble a lot in unexpected ways.

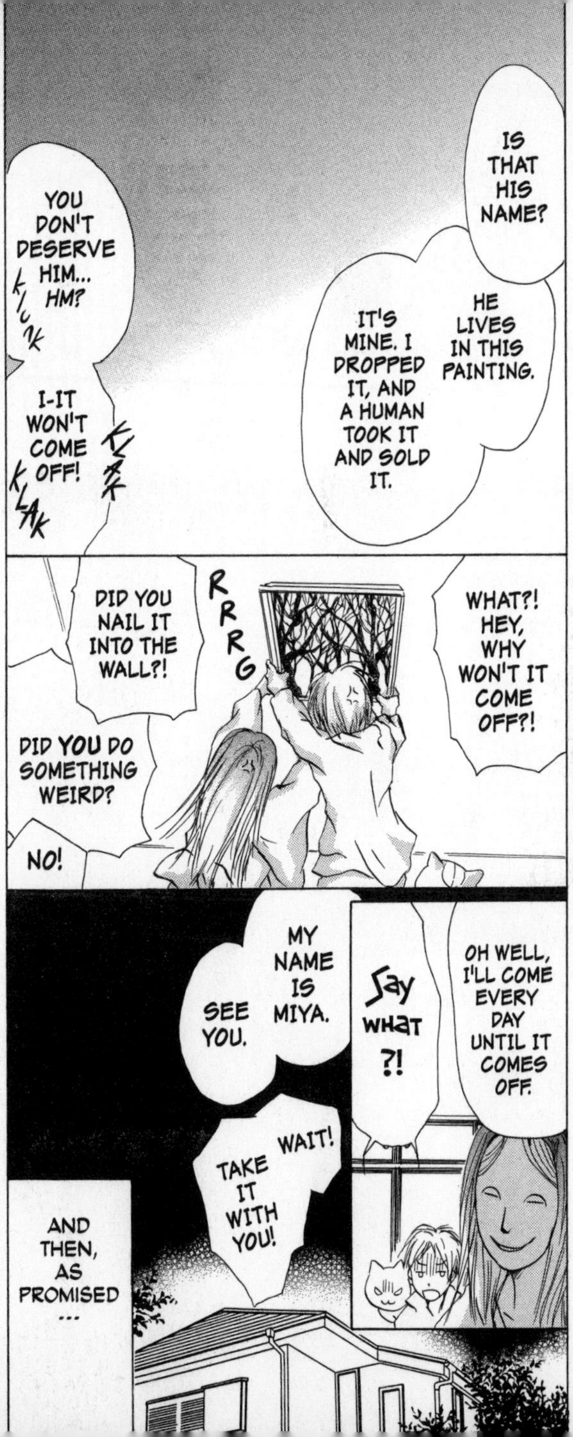
IS THAT HIS NAME?
HE LIVES IN THIS PAINTING.
IT'S MINE. I DROPPED IT, AND A HUMAN TOOK IT AND SOLD IT.
YOU DON'T DESERVE HIM... HM?
KLUNK
I-IT WON'T COME OFF!
KLAK
KLAK
WHAT?! HEY, WHY WON'T IT COME OFF?!
RRRG
DID YOU NAIL IT INTO THE WALL?!
DID YOU DO SOMETHING WEIRD?
NO!
OH WELL, I'LL COME EVERY DAY UNTIL IT COMES OFF.
Say what?!
MY NAME IS MIYA.
SEE YOU.
WAIT!
TAKE IT WITH YOU!
AND THEN, AS PROMISED...

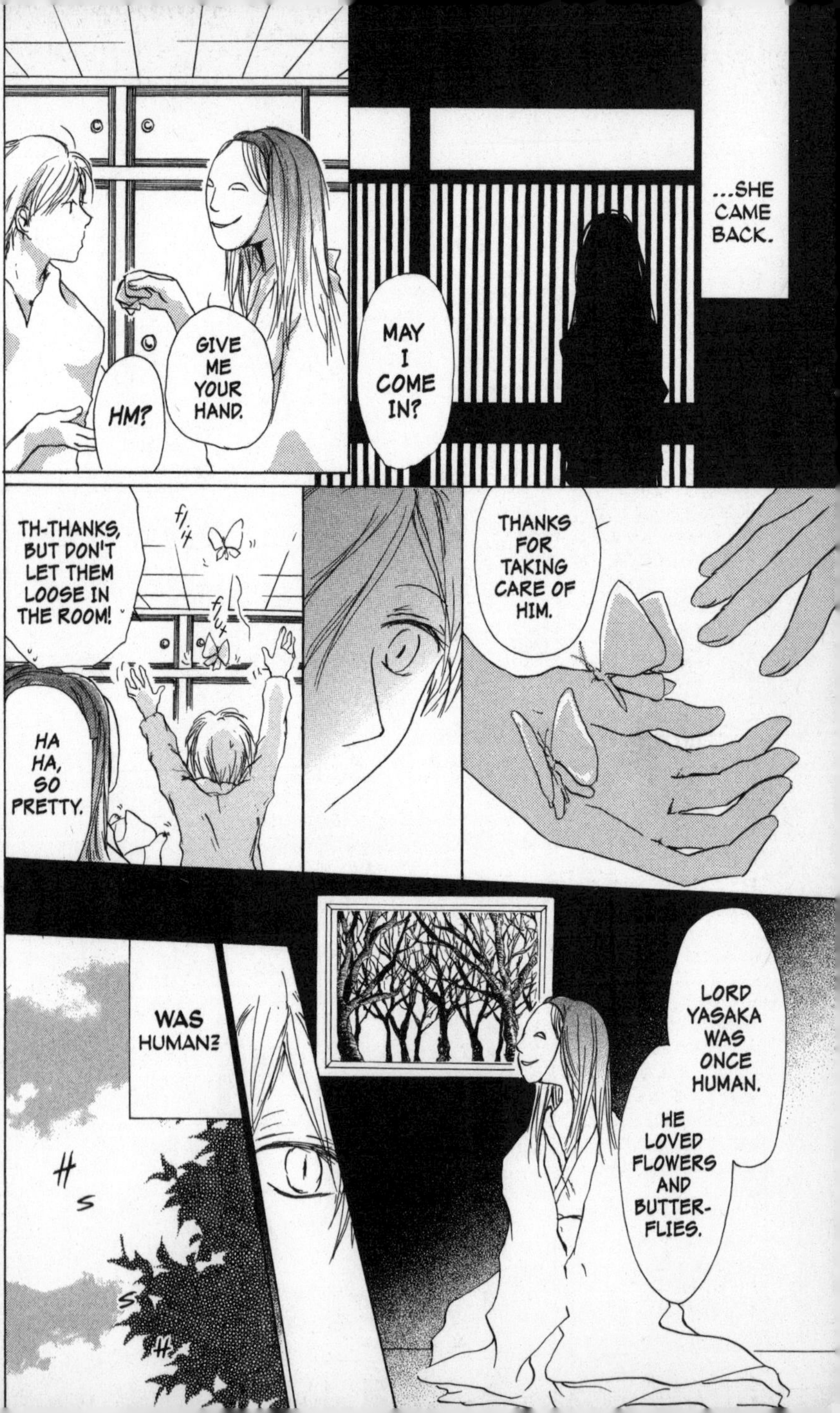
...SHE CAME BACK.
MAY I COME IN?
GIVE ME YOUR HAND.
HM?
THANKS FOR TAKING CARE OF HIM.
TH-THANKS, BUT DON'T LET THEM LOOSE IN THE ROOM!
flit
flut
HA HA, SO PRETTY.
LORD YASAKA WAS ONCE HUMAN.
HE LOVED FLOWERS AND BUTTERFLIES.
WAS HUMAN?

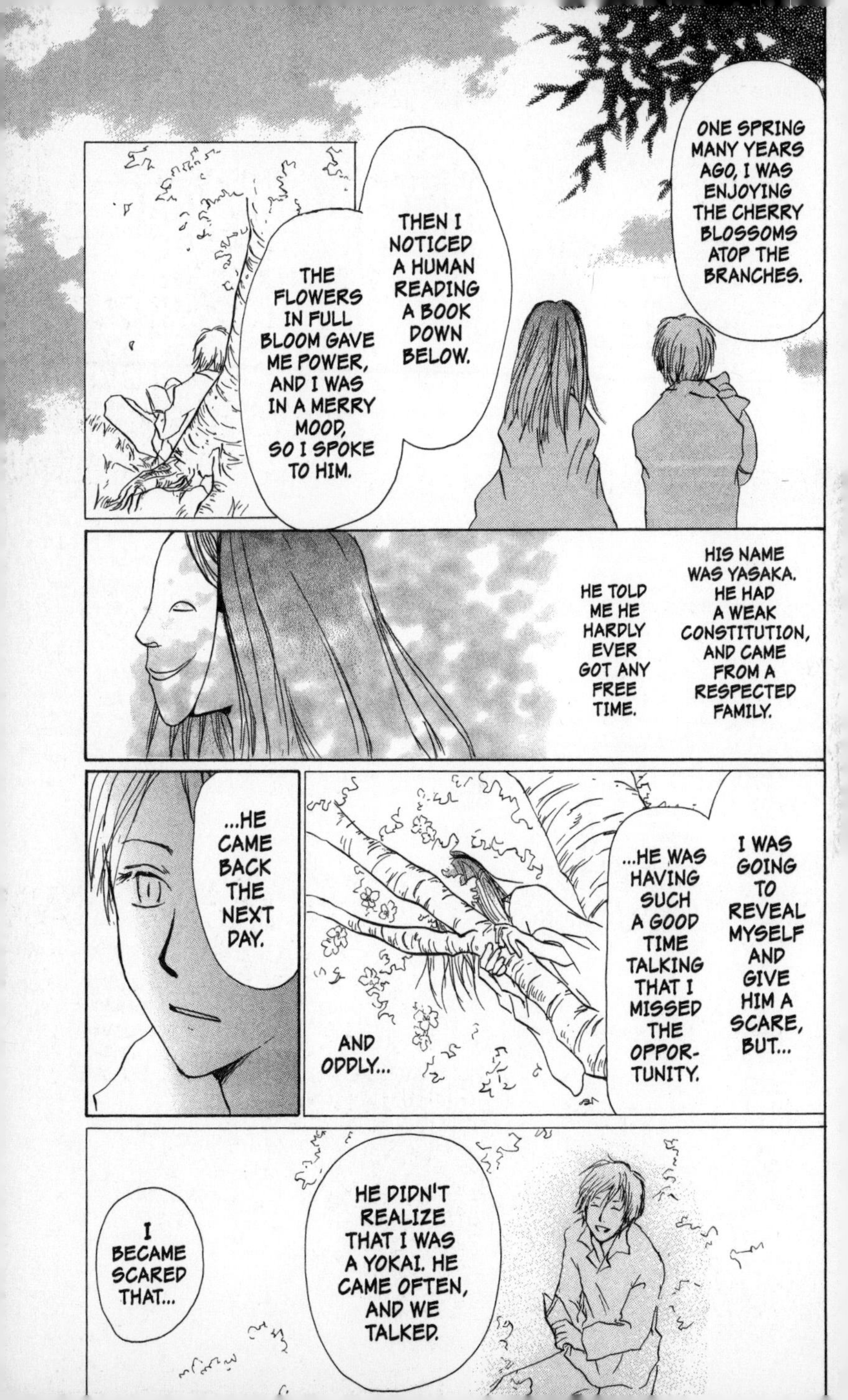
ONE SPRING MANY YEARS AGO, I WAS ENJOYING THE CHERRY BLOSSOMS ATOP THE BRANCHES.
THEN I NOTICED A HUMAN READING A BOOK DOWN BELOW.
THE FLOWERS IN FULL BLOOM GAVE ME POWER, AND I WAS IN A MERRY MOOD, SO I SPOKE TO HIM.
HIS NAME WAS YASAKA. HE HAD A WEAK CONSTITUTION, AND CAME FROM A RESPECTED FAMILY.
HE TOLD ME HE HARDLY EVER GOT ANY FREE TIME.
I WAS GOING TO REVEAL MYSELF AND GIVE HIM A SCARE, BUT...
...HE WAS HAVING SUCH A GOOD TIME TALKING THAT I MISSED THE OPPOR-TUNITY.
AND ODDLY...
...HE CAME BACK THE NEXT DAY.
HE DIDN'T REALIZE THAT I WAS A YOKAI. HE CAME OFTEN, AND WE TALKED.
I BECAME SCARED THAT...

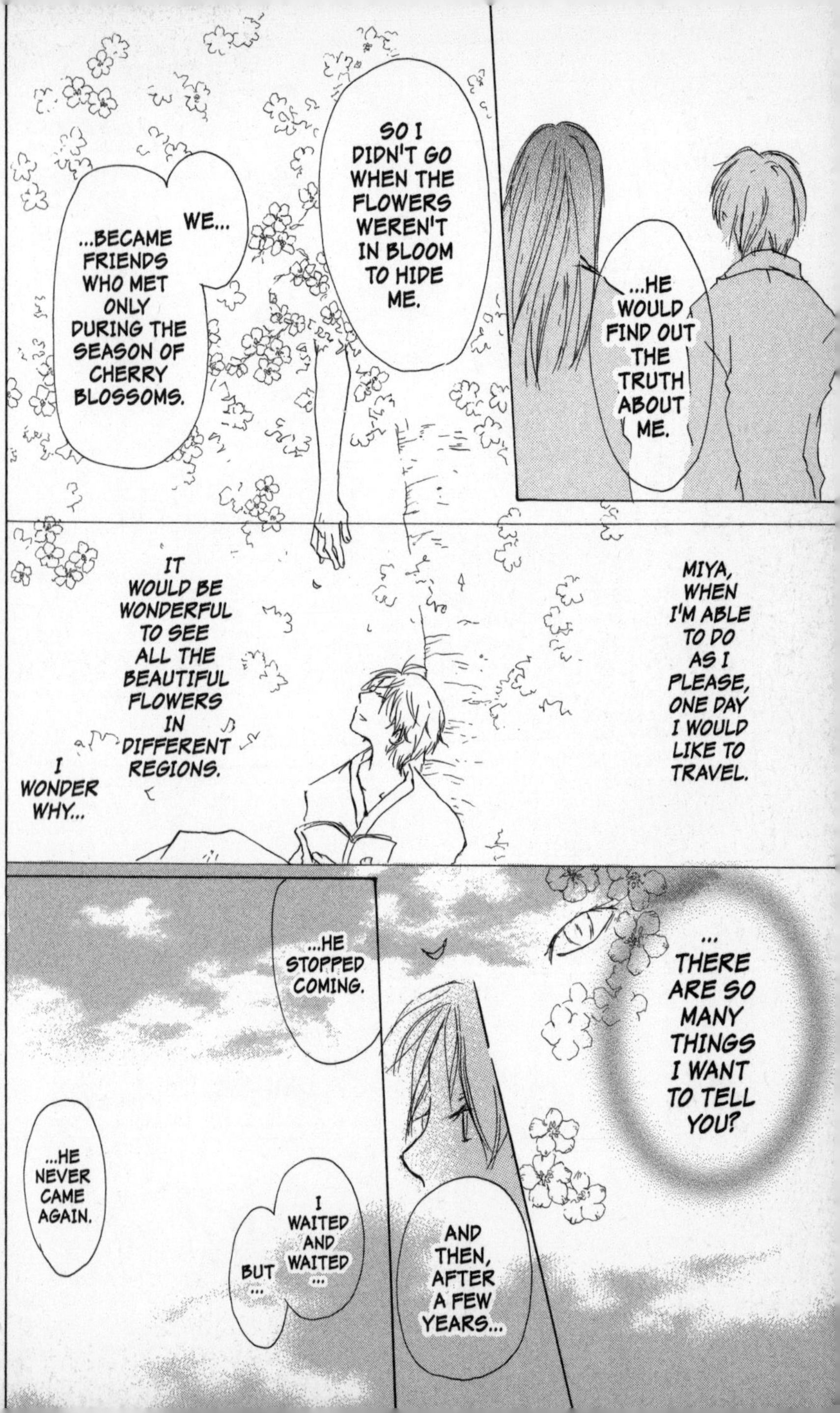
...HE WOULD FIND OUT THE TRUTH ABOUT ME.
SO I DIDN'T GO WHEN THE FLOWERS WEREN'T IN BLOOM TO HIDE ME.
WE...
...BECAME FRIENDS WHO MET ONLY DURING THE SEASON OF CHERRY BLOSSOMS.
MIYA, WHEN I'M ABLE TO DO AS I PLEASE, ONE DAY I WOULD LIKE TO TRAVEL.
IT WOULD BE WONDERFUL TO SEE ALL THE BEAUTIFUL FLOWERS IN DIFFERENT REGIONS.
I WONDER WHY...
...THERE ARE SO MANY THINGS I WANT TO TELL YOU?
AND THEN, AFTER A FEW YEARS...
...HE STOPPED COMING.
I WAITED AND WAITED...
BUT...
...HE NEVER CAME AGAIN.

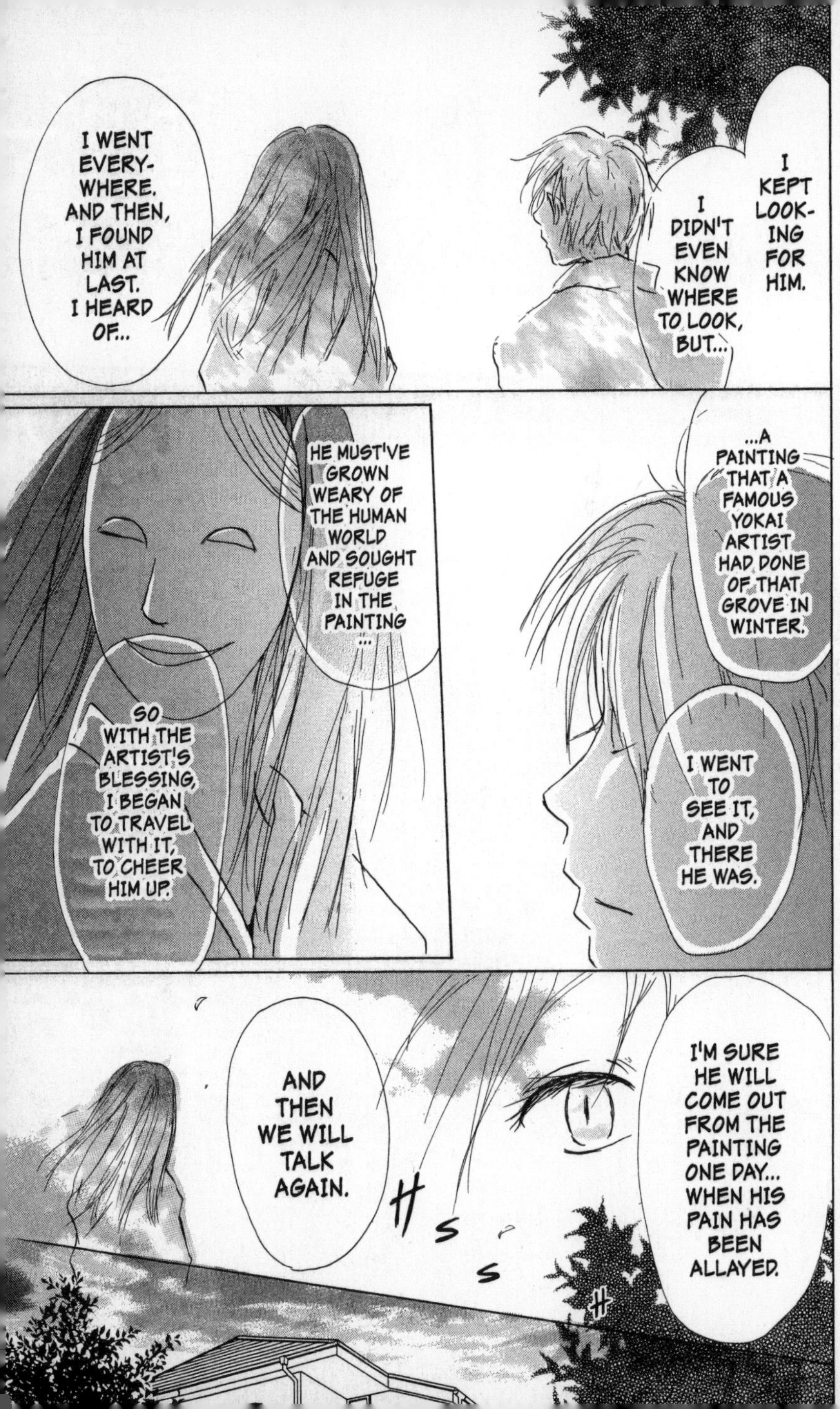
I KEPT LOOKING FOR HIM.
I DIDN'T EVEN KNOW WHERE TO LOOK, BUT...
I WENT EVERYWHERE. AND THEN, I FOUND HIM AT LAST. I HEARD OF...
...A PAINTING THAT A FAMOUS YOKAI ARTIST HAD DONE OF THAT GROVE IN WINTER.
I WENT TO SEE IT, AND THERE HE WAS.
HE MUST'VE GROWN WEARY OF THE HUMAN WORLD AND SOUGHT REFUGE IN THE PAINTING...
SO WITH THE ARTIST'S BLESSING, I BEGAN TO TRAVEL WITH IT, TO CHEER HIM UP.
I'M SURE HE WILL COME OUT FROM THE PAINTING ONE DAY... WHEN HIS PAIN HAS BEEN ALLAYED.
AND THEN WE WILL TALK AGAIN.

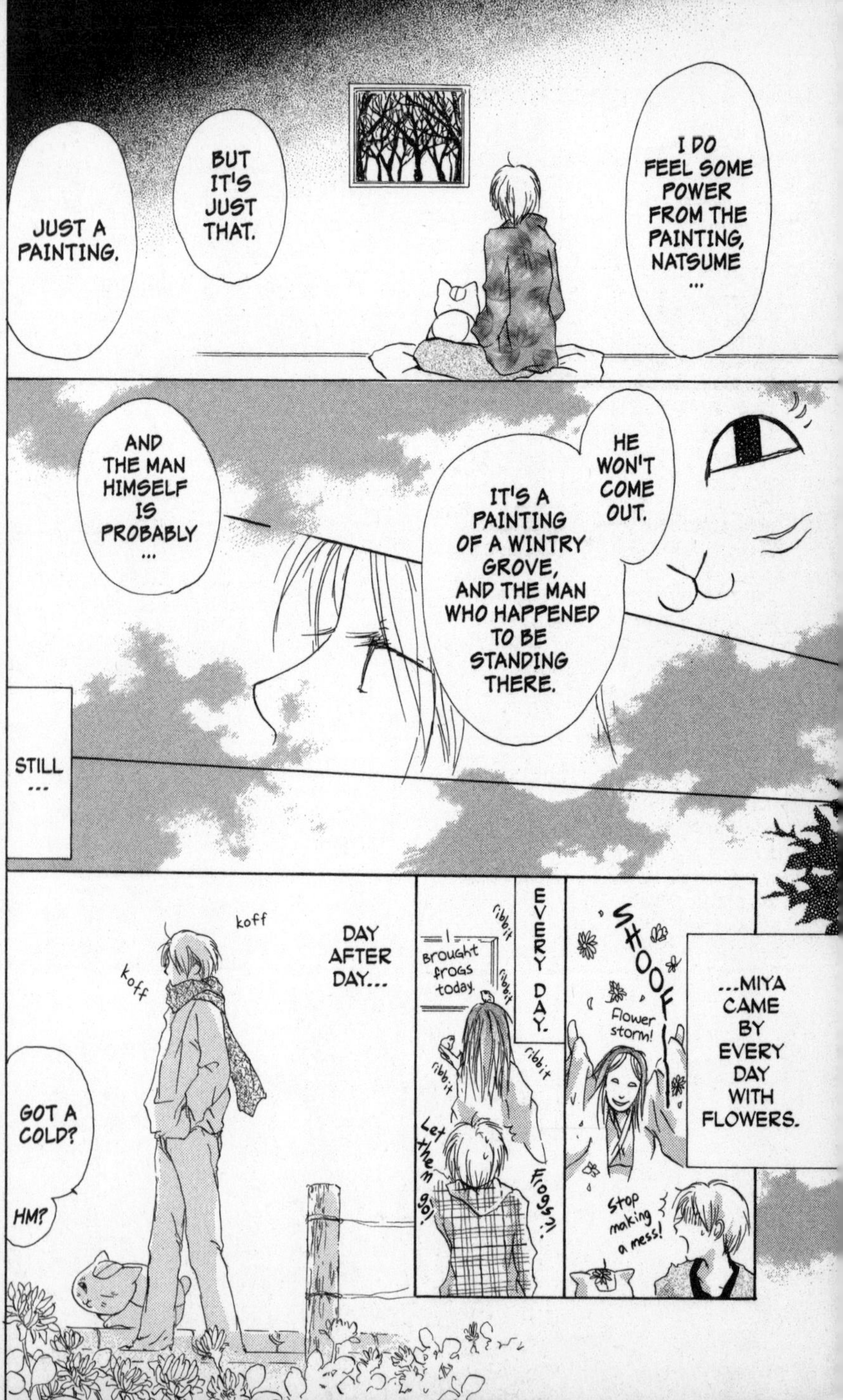

I DO FEEL SOME POWER FROM THE PAINTING, NATSUME...
BUT IT'S JUST THAT.
JUST A PAINTING.
HE WON'T COME OUT.
IT'S A PAINTING OF A WINTRY GROVE, AND THE MAN WHO HAPPENED TO BE STANDING THERE.
AND THE MAN HIMSELF IS PROBABLY...
STILL...
...MIYA CAME BY EVERY DAY WITH FLOWERS.
SHOOF!
Flower storm!
Stop making a mess!
EVERY DAY.
I brought frogs today.
ribbit
ribbit
ribbit
ribbit
Frogs?!
Let them go!
DAY AFTER DAY...
koff
koff
GOT A COLD?
HM?

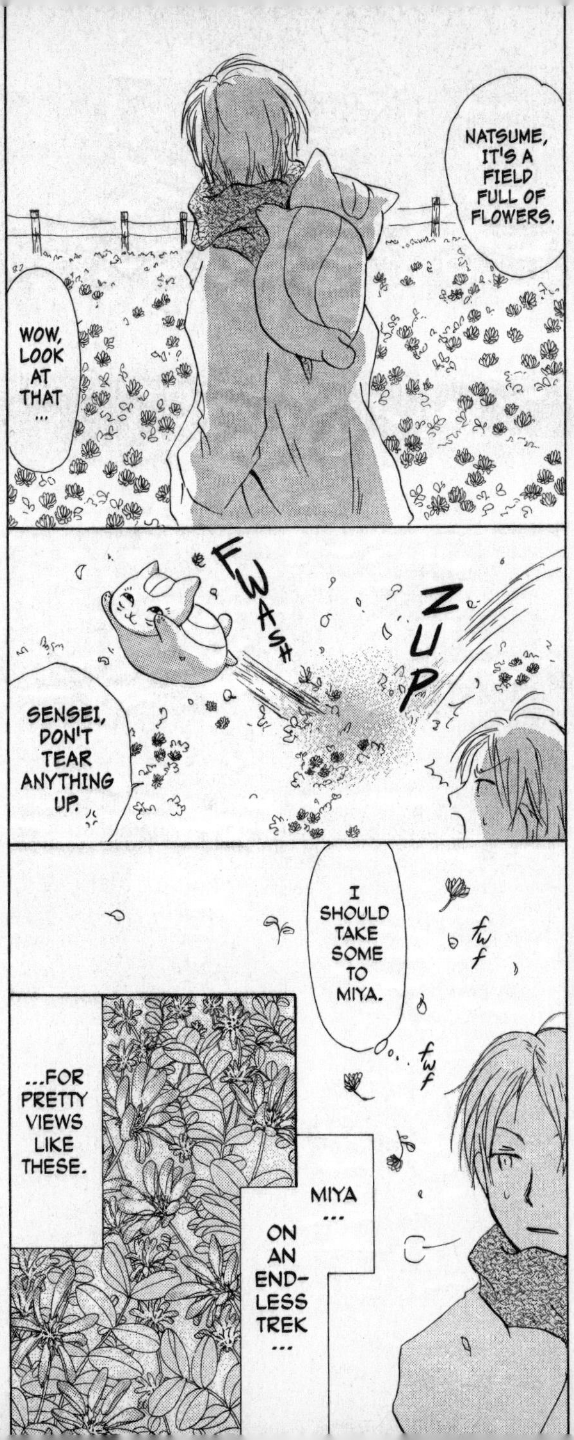
NATSUME, IT'S A FIELD FULL OF FLOWERS.
WOW, LOOK AT THAT ...
ZUP
FWASH
SENSEI, DON'T TEAR ANYTHING UP.
I SHOULD TAKE SOME TO MIYA.
fwf
fwf
MIYA ...
ON AN END-LESS TREK ...
...FOR PRETTY VIEWS LIKE THESE.

05

❋Tokyo!

I live in the provinces, and I hardly ever get to meet the editorial staff. So when I visit Tokyo, I take the opportunity to talk to them. Since I love to create manga, sometimes I ask the most straightforward questions, bordering on impolite. But often, they answer just as passionately, inspiring me to a surprising extent. I work really hard with my editor, agonizing over everything, to get the privilege to submit my work. When I discovered that they put just as much care into the production side of things, details that I never even realized, it renewed my will to work harder.

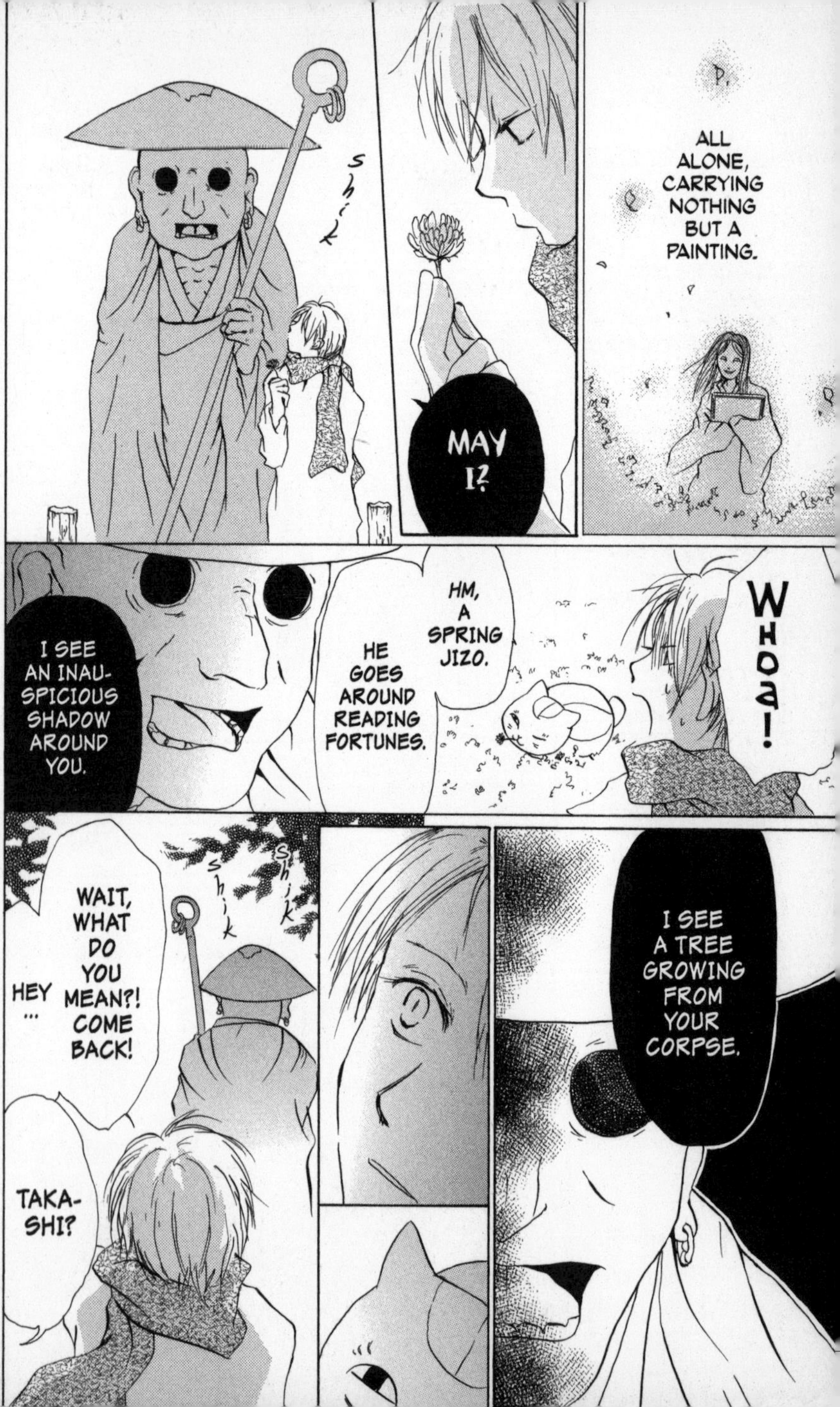
ALL ALONE, CARRYING NOTHING BUT A PAINTING.
MAY I?
shik
WHOA!
HM, A SPRING JIZO.
HE GOES AROUND READING FORTUNES.
I SEE AN INAU-SPICIOUS SHADOW AROUND YOU.
I SEE A TREE GROWING FROM YOUR CORPSE.
shik
shik
WAIT, WHAT DO YOU MEAN?! COME BACK!
HEY...
TAKA-SHI?

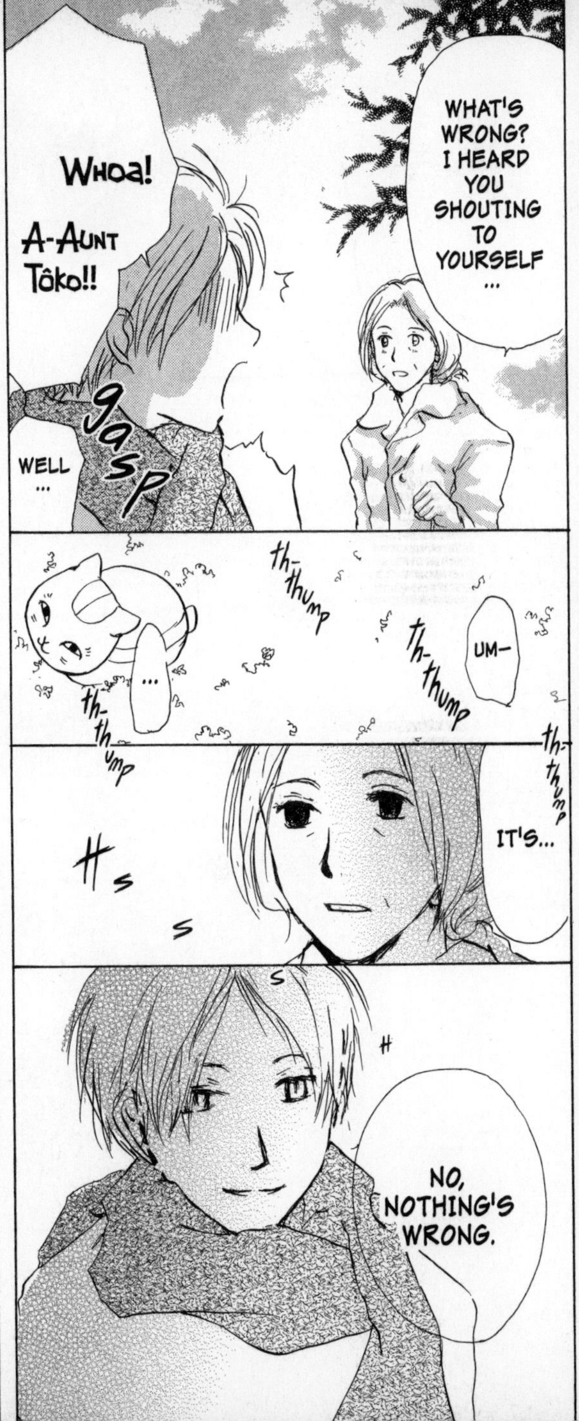
WHAT'S WRONG? I HEARD YOU SHOUTING TO YOURSELF ...
WHOA!
A-AUNT TÔKO!!
gasp
WELL ...
UM-
th-thump
th-thump
...
th-thump
th-thump
IT'S...
H
s
s
s
H
NO, NOTHING'S WRONG.

06

❋Natsume's clothes

Natsume mainly wears his school uniform and collared shirts in the summer. But actually, he likes street punk clothes. We're starting to see glimpses of Aunt Tôko spoiling him by buying him lots of new track-suits. I tend to avoid clothes with patterns since I often can't get the page to look right. I liked to have my characters wear the same kind of clothes all the time. But these days, with the advice of my assistants, I'm beginning to have more fun getting them to use different kinds of screen tones.

A boy projects a cool image of him-self, yet wears a cutely patterned scarf... I've discov-ered for the first time how fun it is to imagine these aspects.

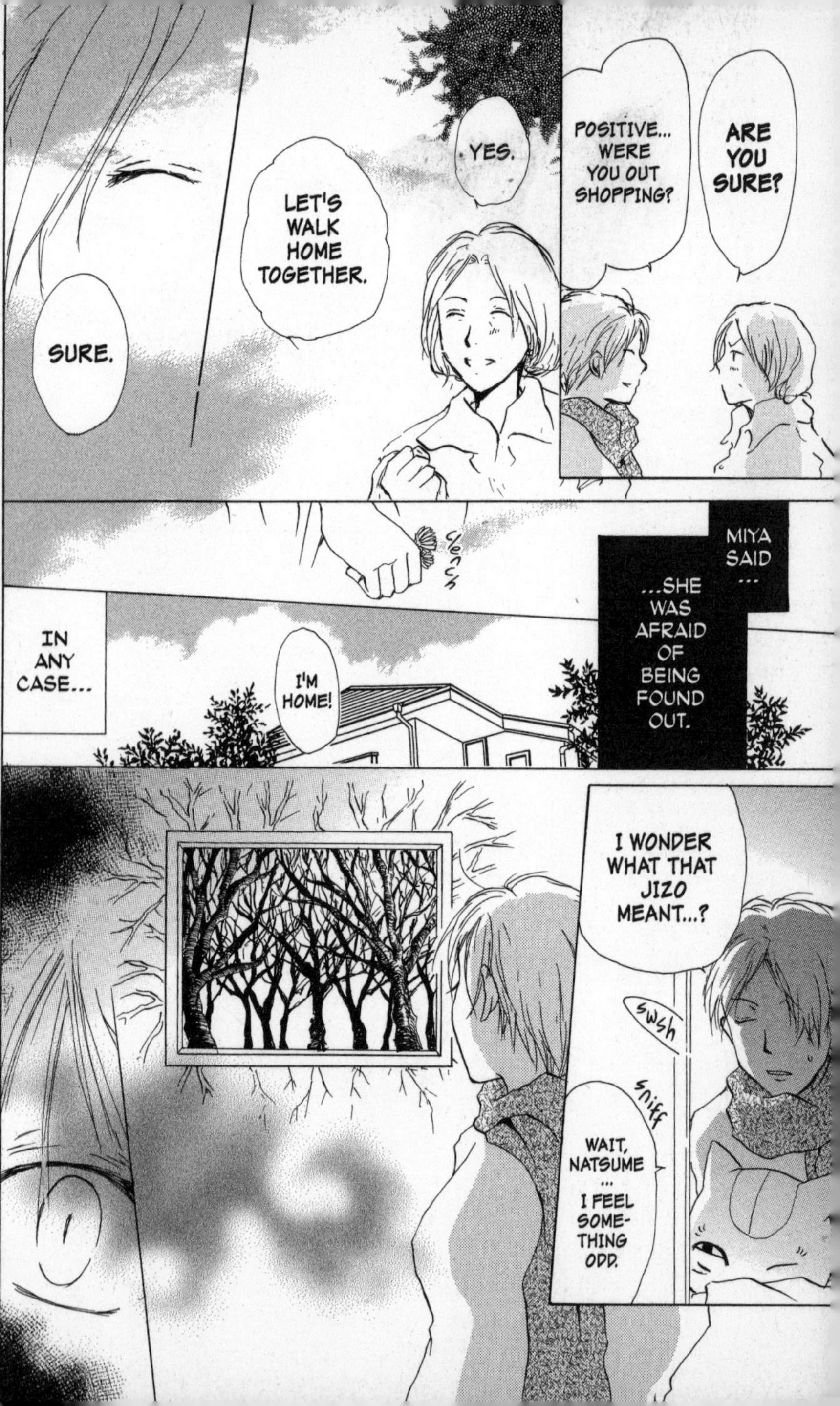
ARE YOU SURE?
POSITIVE... WERE YOU OUT SHOPPING?
YES.
LET'S WALK HOME TOGETHER.
SURE.
clench
MIYA SAID...
...SHE WAS AFRAID OF BEING FOUND OUT.
I'M HOME!
IN ANY CASE...
I WONDER WHAT THAT JIZO MEANT...?
swsh
sniff
WAIT, NATSUME... I FEEL SOME-THING ODD.

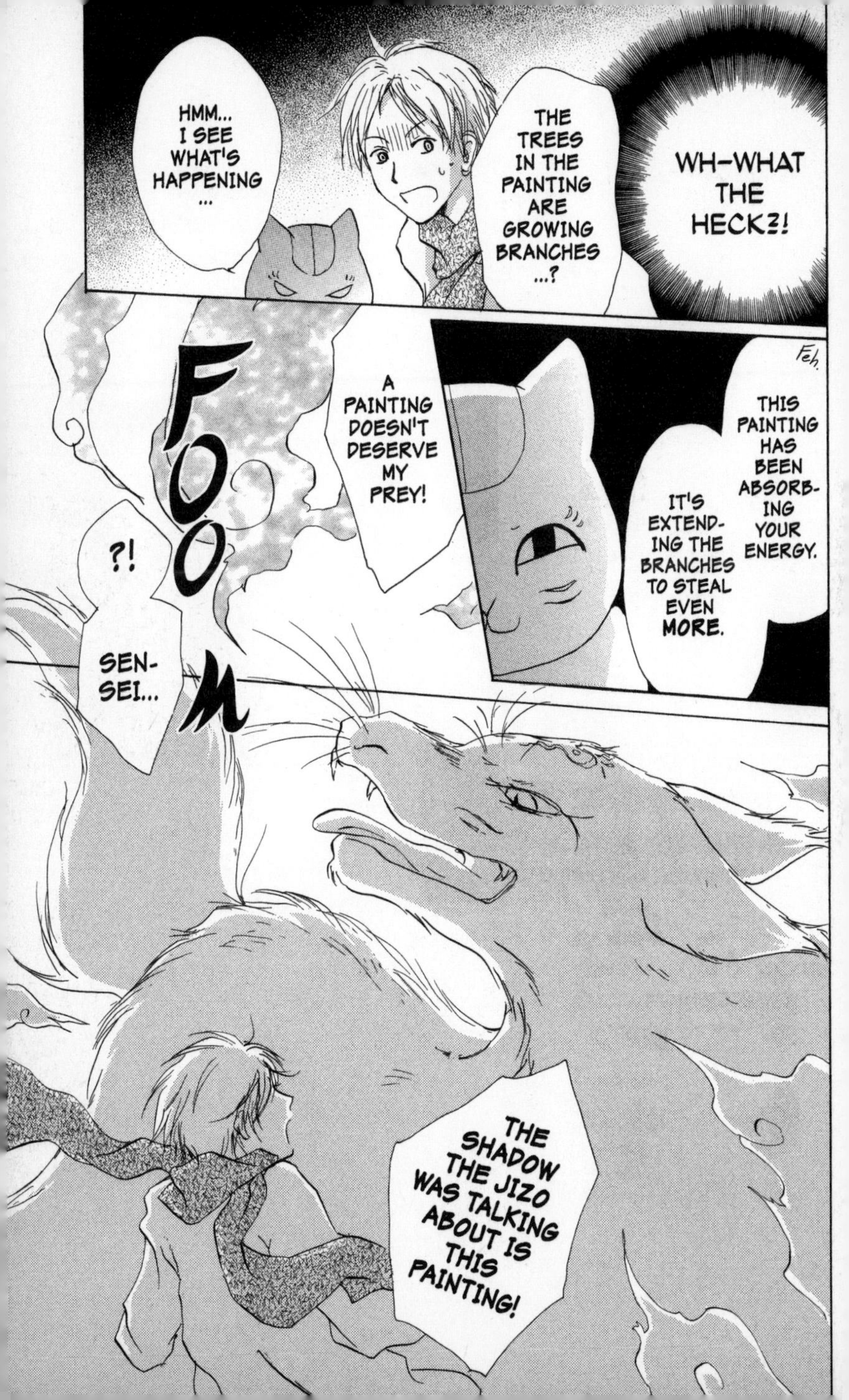
WH-WHAT THE HECK?!
THE TREES IN THE PAINTING ARE GROWING BRANCHES...?
HMM... I SEE WHAT'S HAPPENING...
Feh.
THIS PAINTING HAS BEEN ABSORBING YOUR ENERGY.
IT'S EXTENDING THE BRANCHES TO STEAL EVEN MORE.
A PAINTING DOESN'T DESERVE MY PREY!
FOOM
?!
SEN-SEI...
THE SHADOW THE JIZO WAS TALKING ABOUT IS THIS PAINTING!

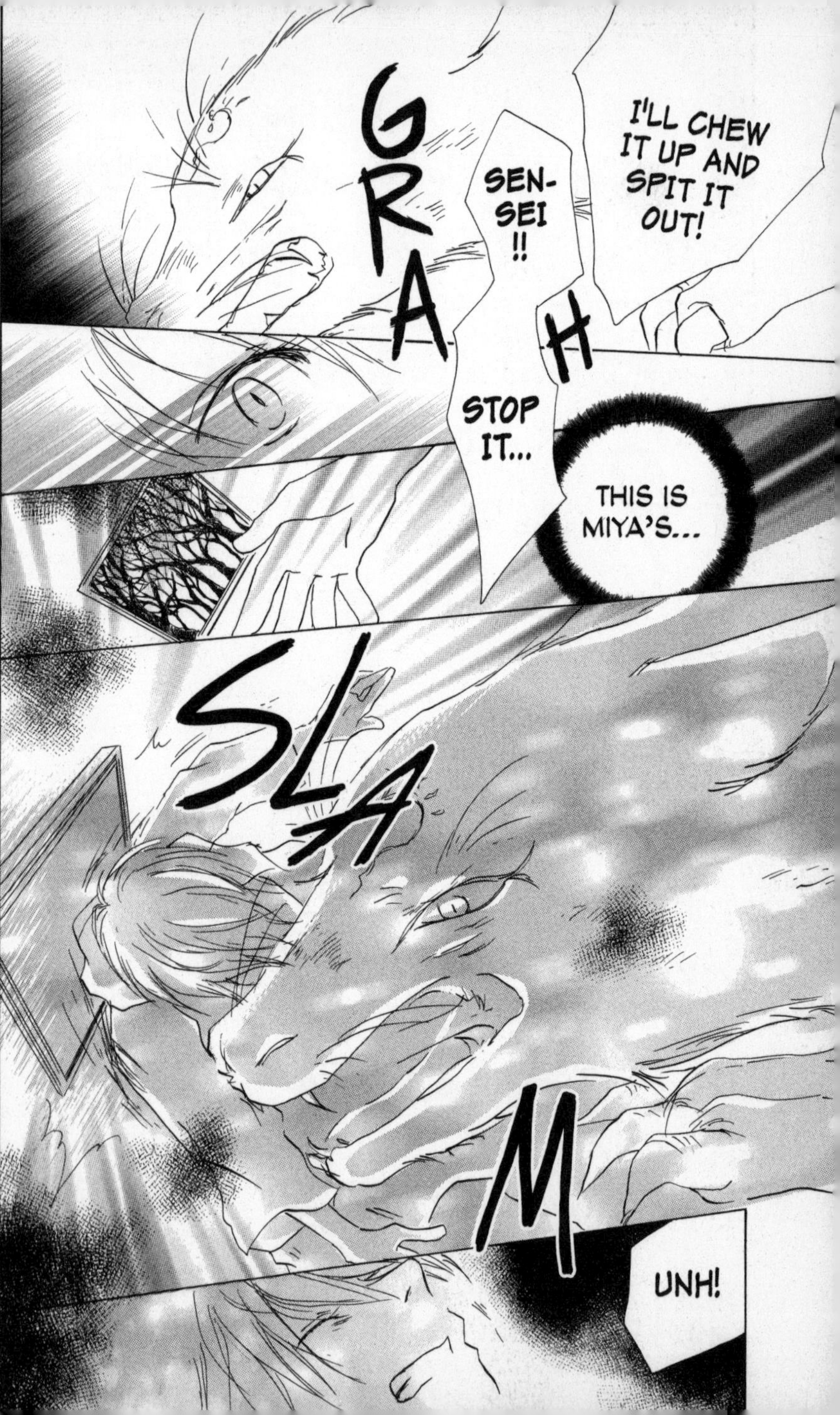
I'LL CHEW IT UP AND SPIT IT OUT!
SEN-SEI !!
GRAH
STOP IT...
THIS IS MIYA'S...
SLAM
UNH!

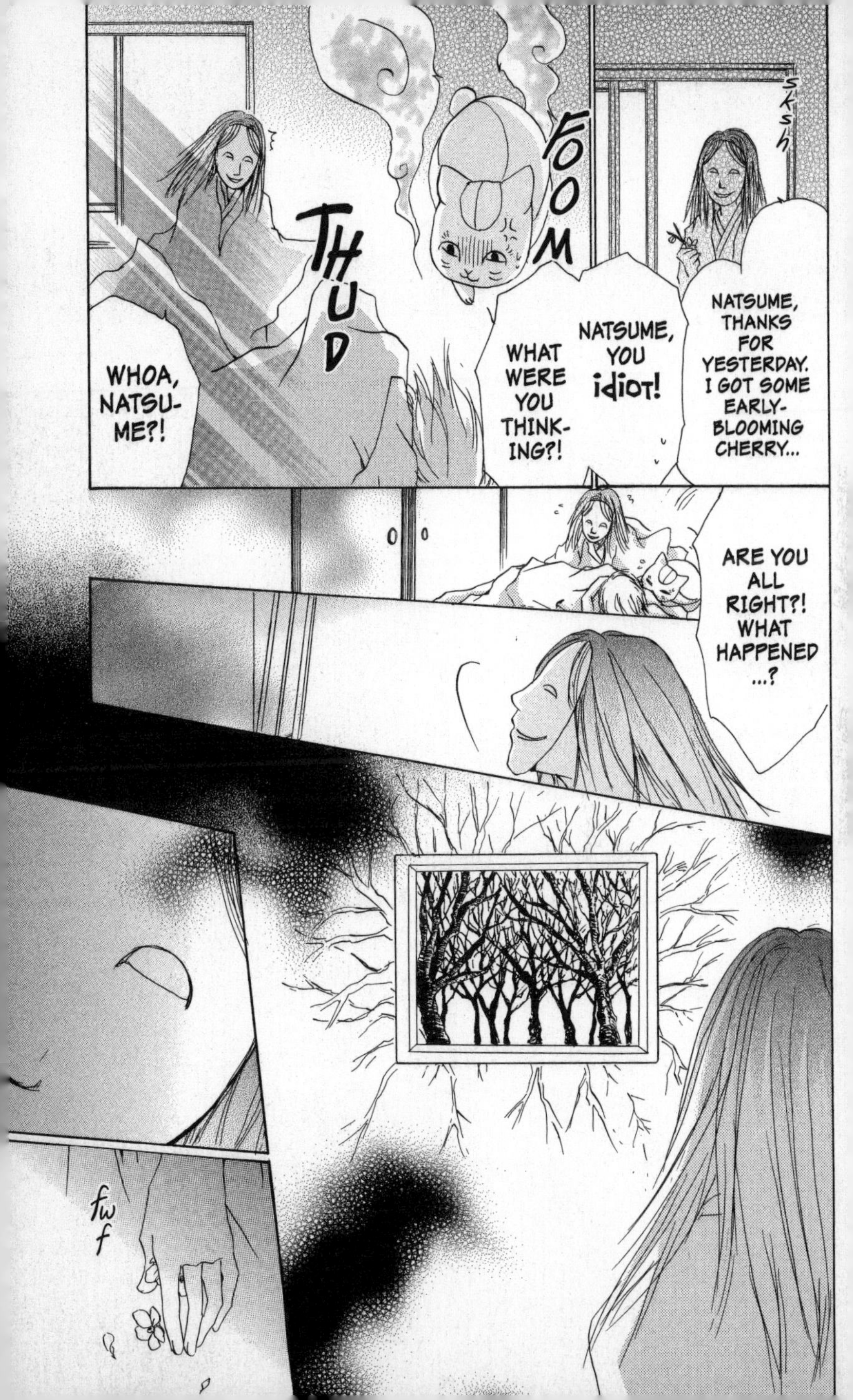

sksh
NATSUME, THANKS FOR YESTERDAY. I GOT SOME EARLY-BLOOMING CHERRY...
NATSUME, YOU idiot!
WHAT WERE YOU THINKING?!
FOOM
THUD
WHOA, NATSU-ME?!
ARE YOU ALL RIGHT?! WHAT HAPPENED ...?
fwf

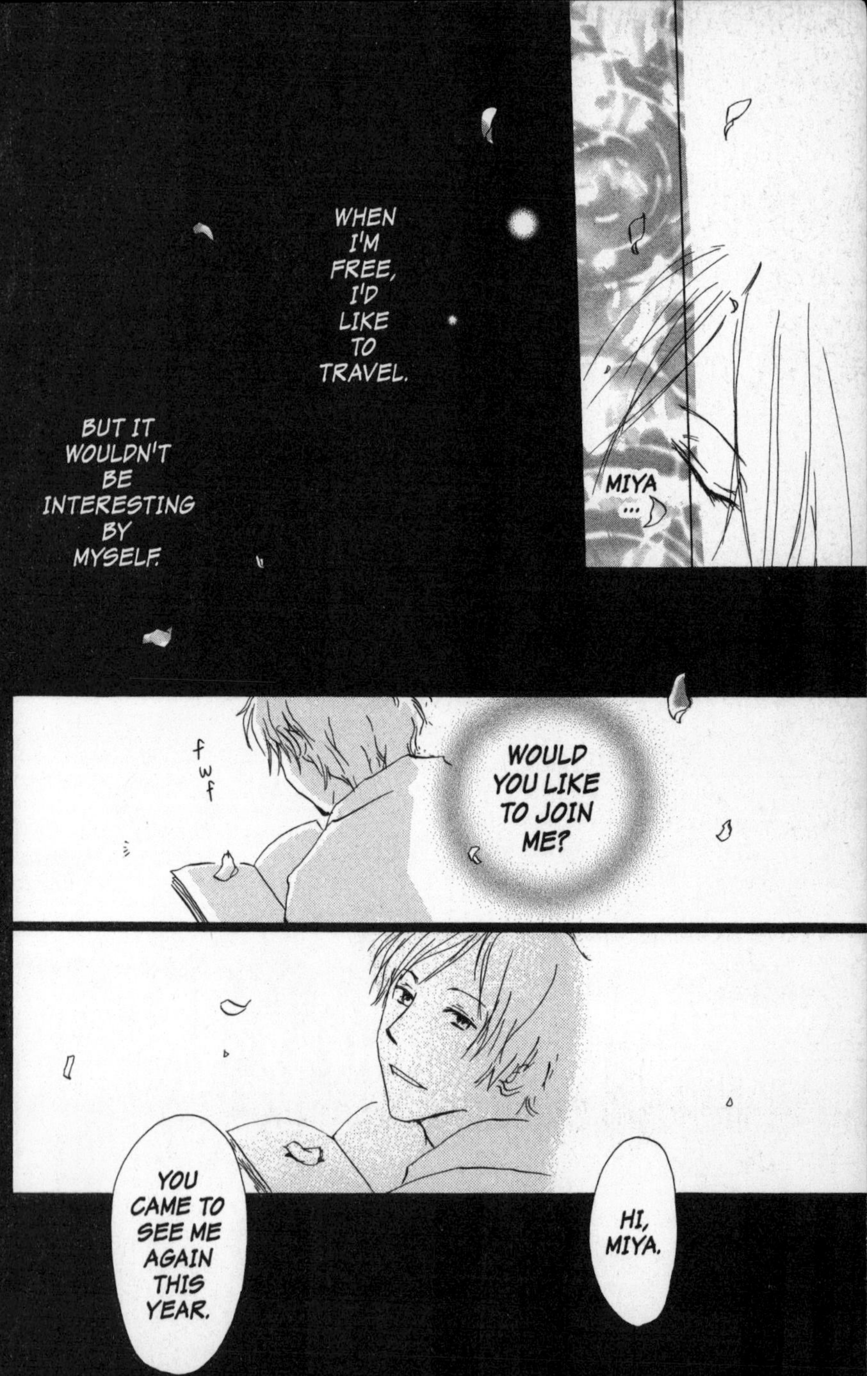
MIYA...
WHEN I'M FREE, I'D LIKE TO TRAVEL.
BUT IT WOULDN'T BE INTERESTING BY MYSELF.
WOULD YOU LIKE TO JOIN ME?
fwf
HI, MIYA.
YOU CAME TO SEE ME AGAIN THIS YEAR.

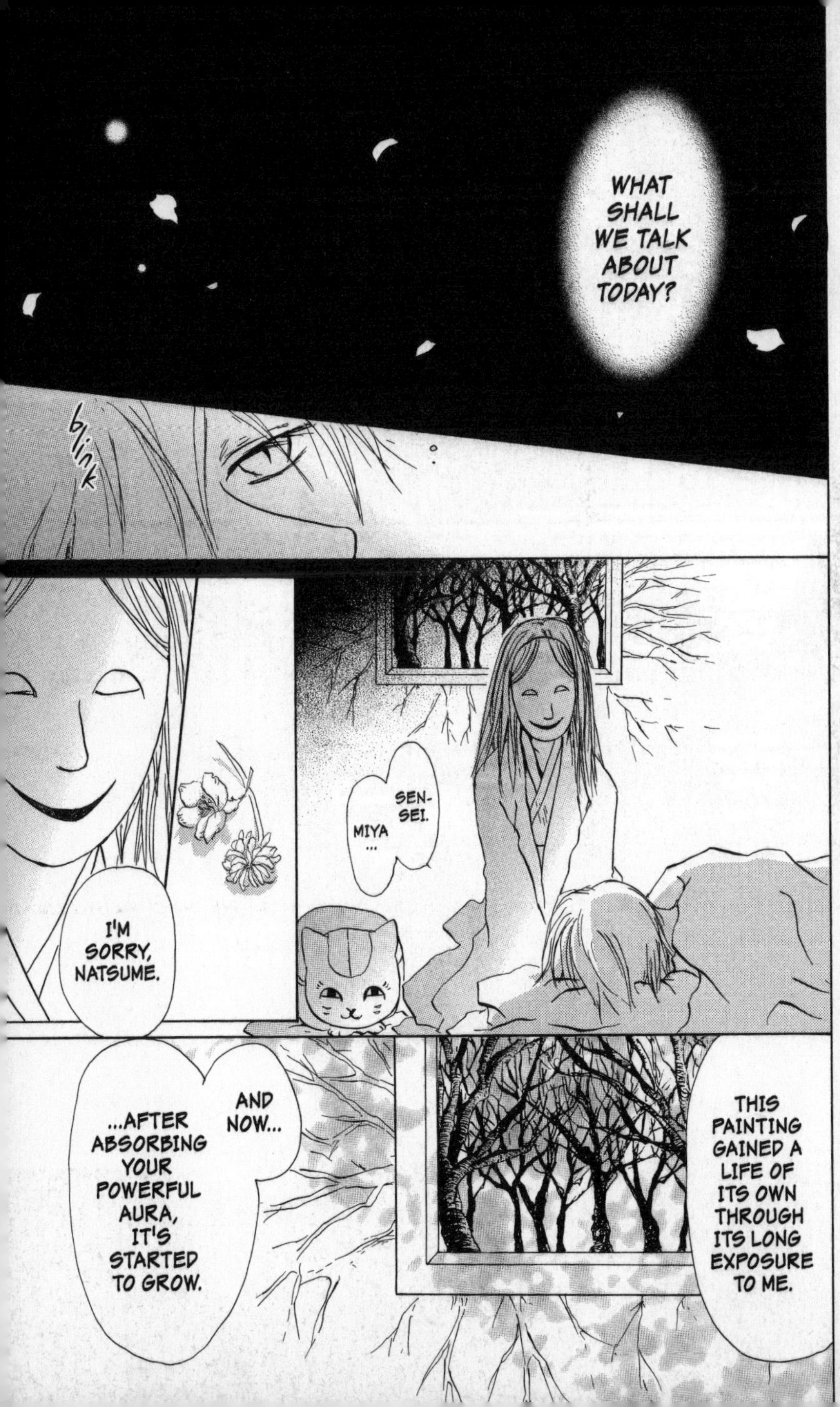
WHAT SHALL WE TALK ABOUT TODAY?
blink
SEN-SEI.
MIYA ...
I'M SORRY, NATSUME.
THIS PAINTING GAINED A LIFE OF ITS OWN THROUGH ITS LONG EXPOSURE TO ME.
AND NOW...
...AFTER ABSORBING YOUR POWERFUL AURA, IT'S STARTED TO GROW.

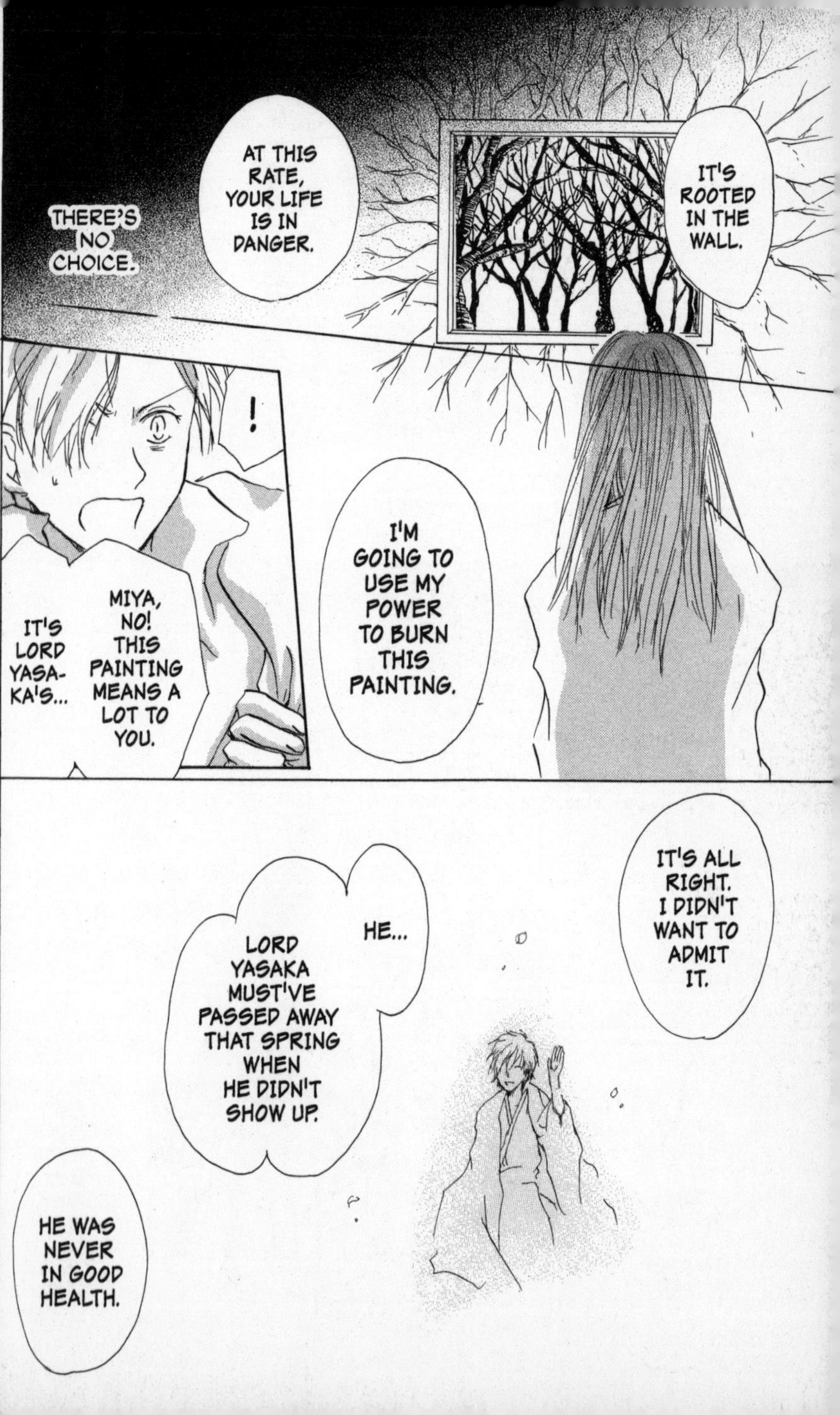
IT'S ROOTED IN THE WALL.
AT THIS RATE, YOUR LIFE IS IN DANGER.
THERE'S NO CHOICE.
I'M GOING TO USE MY POWER TO BURN THIS PAINTING.
!
MIYA, NO! THIS PAINTING MEANS A LOT TO YOU.
IT'S LORD YASAKA'S...
IT'S ALL RIGHT. I DIDN'T WANT TO ADMIT IT.
HE...
LORD YASAKA MUST'VE PASSED AWAY THAT SPRING WHEN HE DIDN'T SHOW UP.
HE WAS NEVER IN GOOD HEALTH.

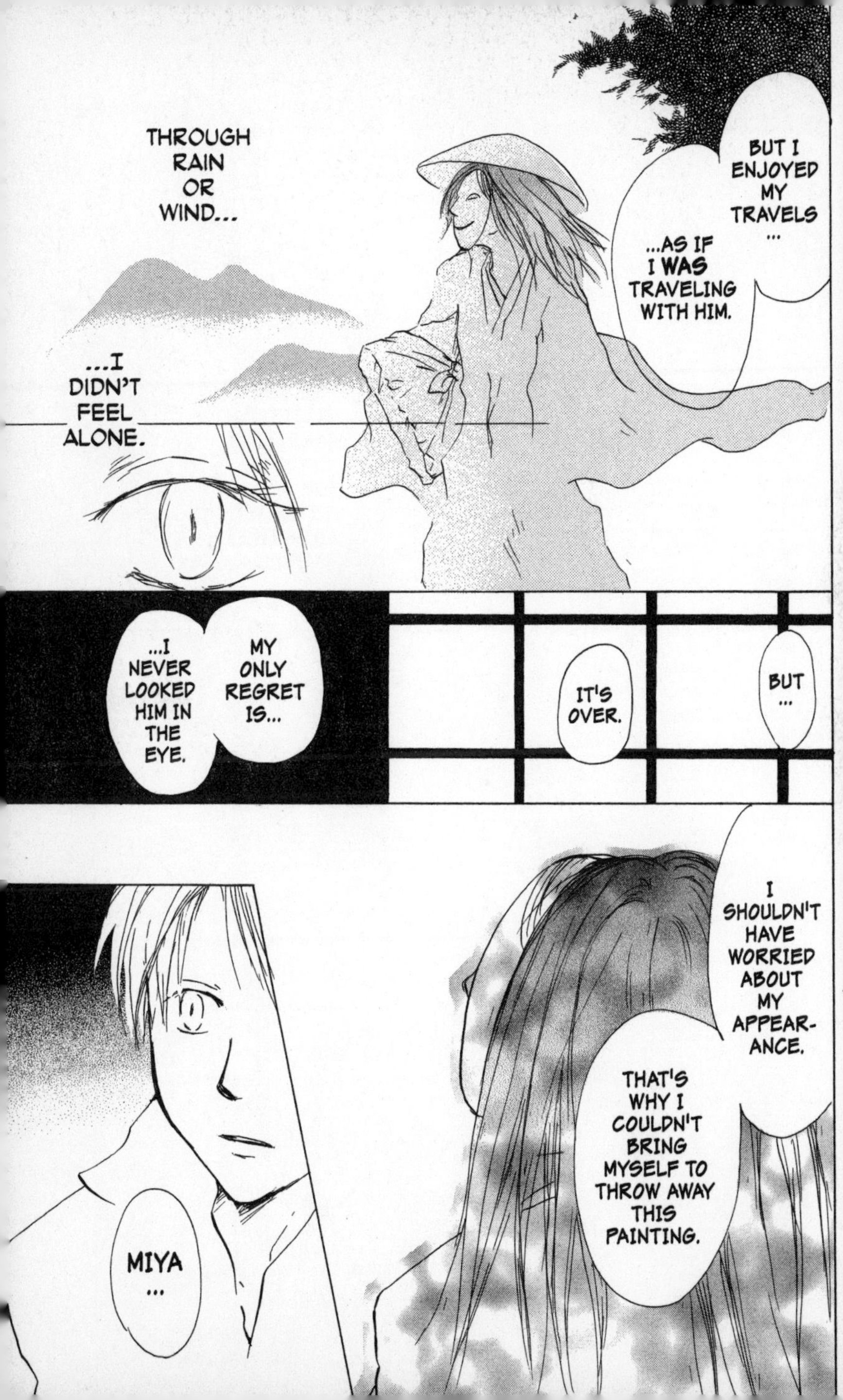
BUT I ENJOYED MY TRAVELS ...
...AS IF I WAS TRAVELING WITH HIM.
THROUGH RAIN OR WIND...
...I DIDN'T FEEL ALONE.
BUT ...
IT'S OVER.
MY ONLY REGRET IS...
...I NEVER LOOKED HIM IN THE EYE.
I SHOULDN'T HAVE WORRIED ABOUT MY APPEARANCE.
THAT'S WHY I COULDN'T BRING MYSELF TO THROW AWAY THIS PAINTING.
MIYA ...

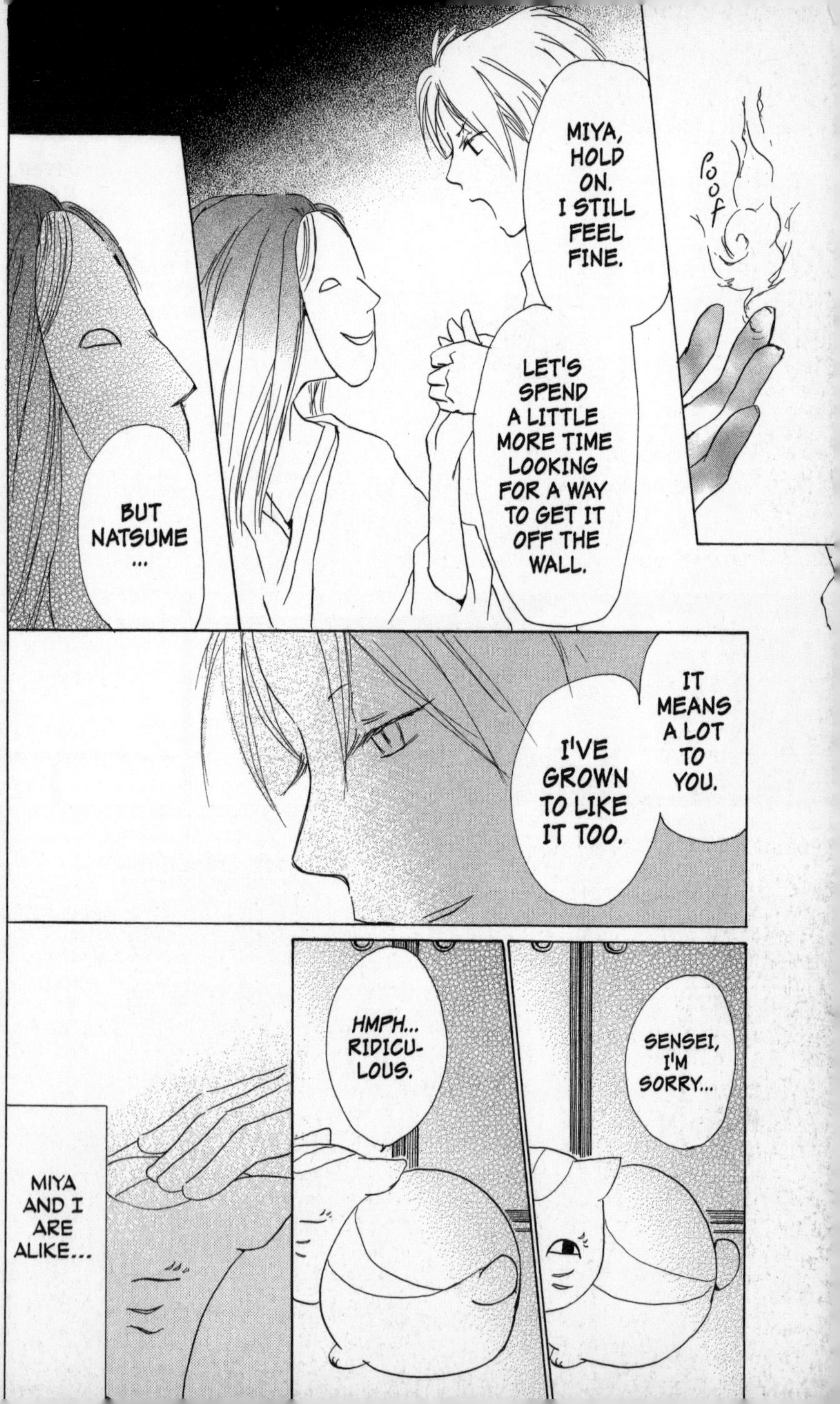
Poof
MIYA, HOLD ON. I STILL FEEL FINE.
LET'S SPEND A LITTLE MORE TIME LOOKING FOR A WAY TO GET IT OFF THE WALL.
BUT NATSUME ...
IT MEANS A LOT TO YOU.
I'VE GROWN TO LIKE IT TOO.
SENSEI, I'M SORRY...
HMPH... RIDICULOUS.
MIYA AND I ARE ALIKE...

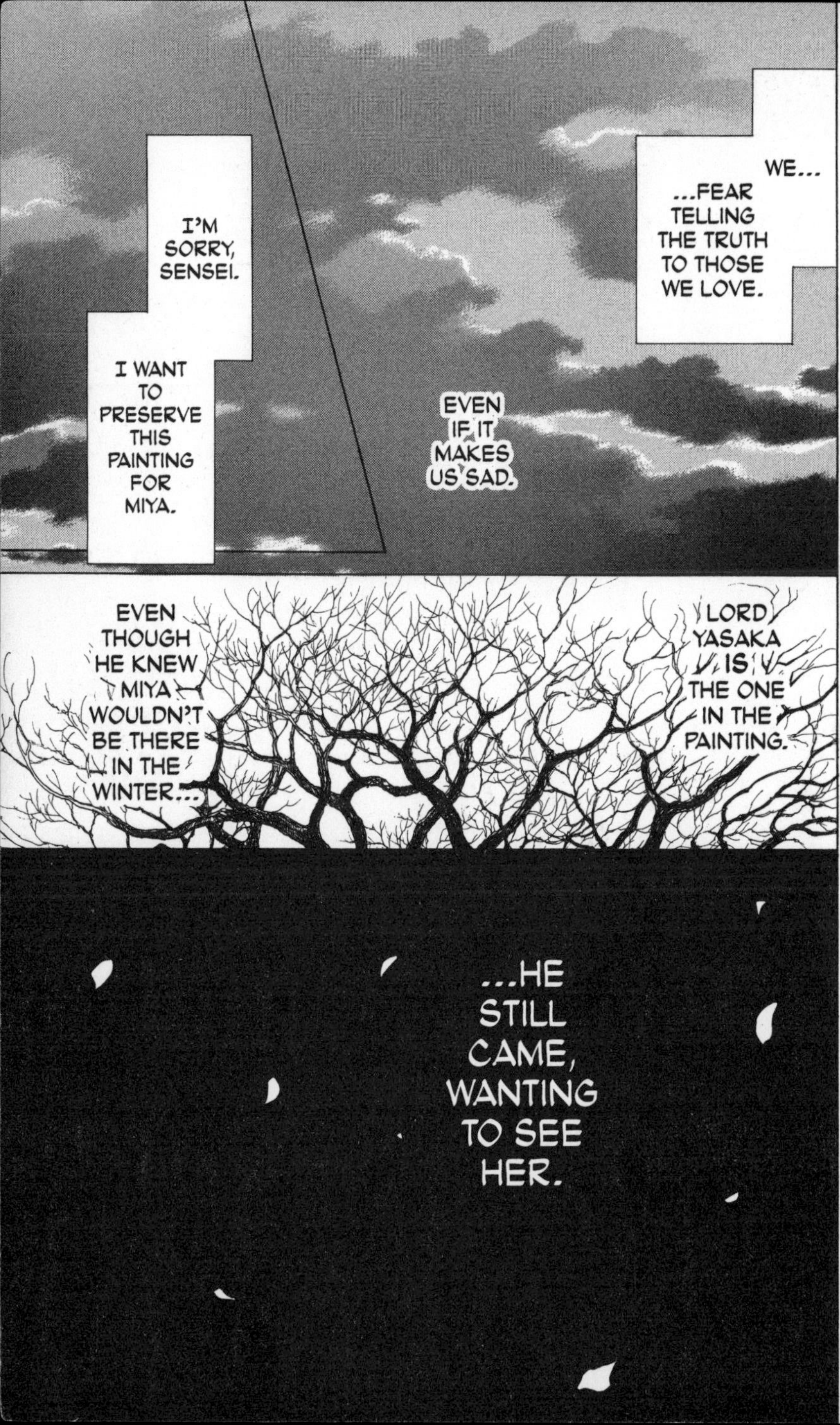
WE...
...FEAR TELLING THE TRUTH TO THOSE WE LOVE.
EVEN IF IT MAKES US SAD.
I'M SORRY, SENSEI.
I WANT TO PRESERVE THIS PAINTING FOR MIYA.
LORD YASAKA IS THE ONE IN THE PAINTING.
EVEN THOUGH HE KNEW MIYA WOULDN'T BE THERE IN THE WINTER...
...HE STILL CAME, WANTING TO SEE HER.

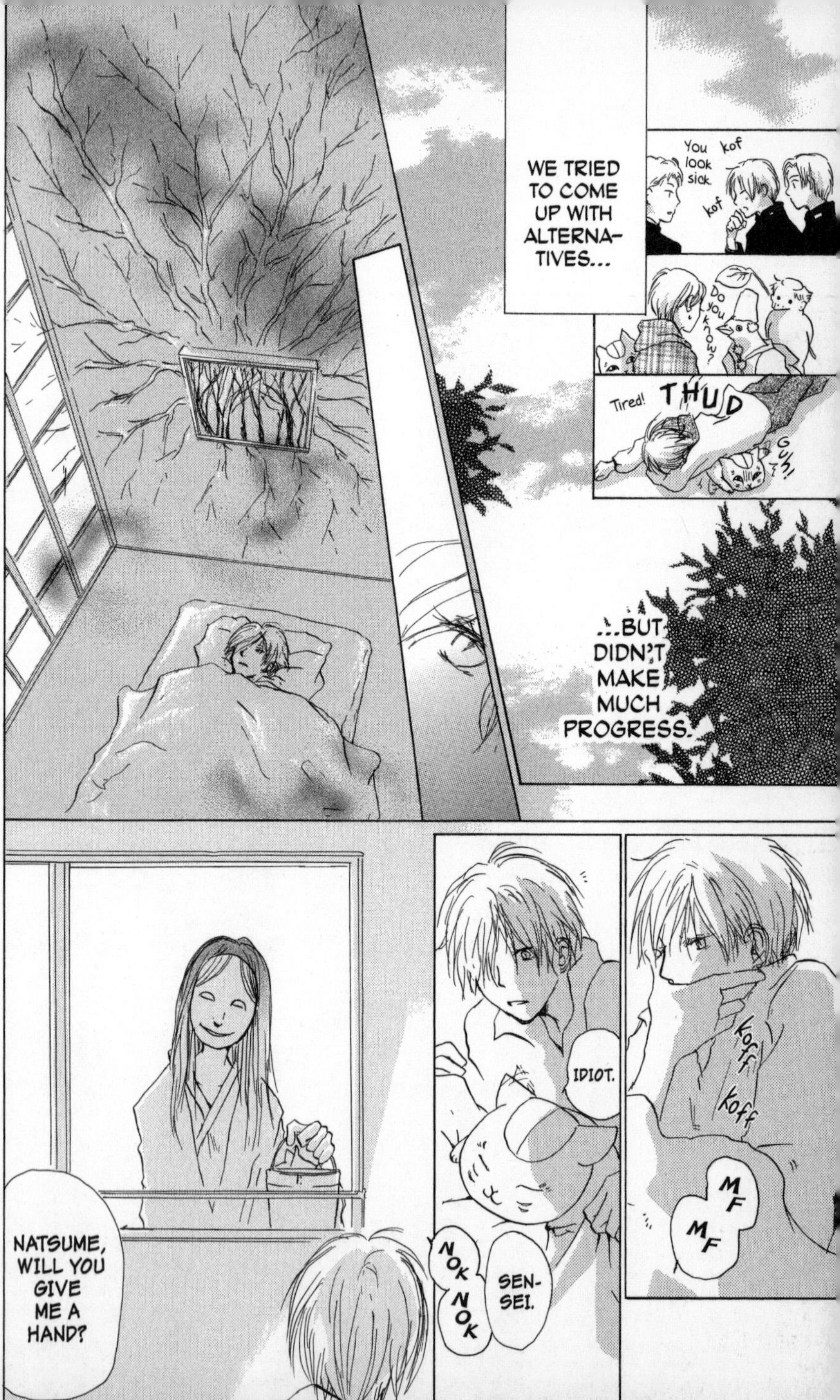
WE TRIED TO COME UP WITH ALTERNATIVES...
You look sick.
kof
kof
Do you know?
Tired!
THUD
Guh!
...BUT DIDN'T MAKE MUCH PROGRESS.
koff koff
MF MF
IDIOT.
SEN-SEI.
NOK NOK
NATSUME, WILL YOU GIVE ME A HAND?

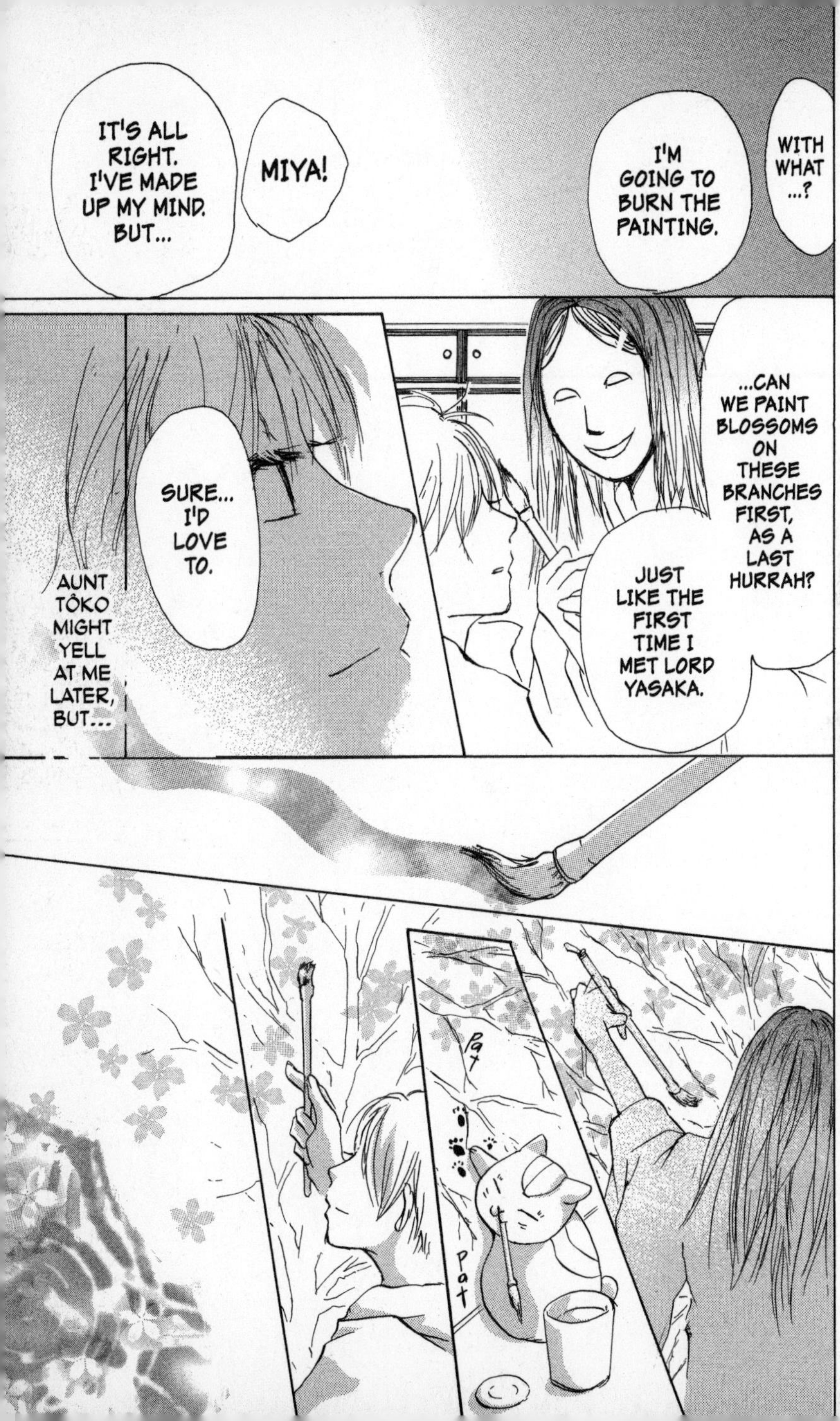
WITH WHAT ...?
I'M GOING TO BURN THE PAINTING.
MIYA!
IT'S ALL RIGHT. I'VE MADE UP MY MIND. BUT...
...CAN WE PAINT BLOSSOMS ON THESE BRANCHES FIRST, AS A LAST HURRAH?
JUST LIKE THE FIRST TIME I MET LORD YASAKA.
SURE... I'D LOVE TO.
AUNT TÔKO MIGHT YELL AT ME LATER, BUT...
Pat
Pat

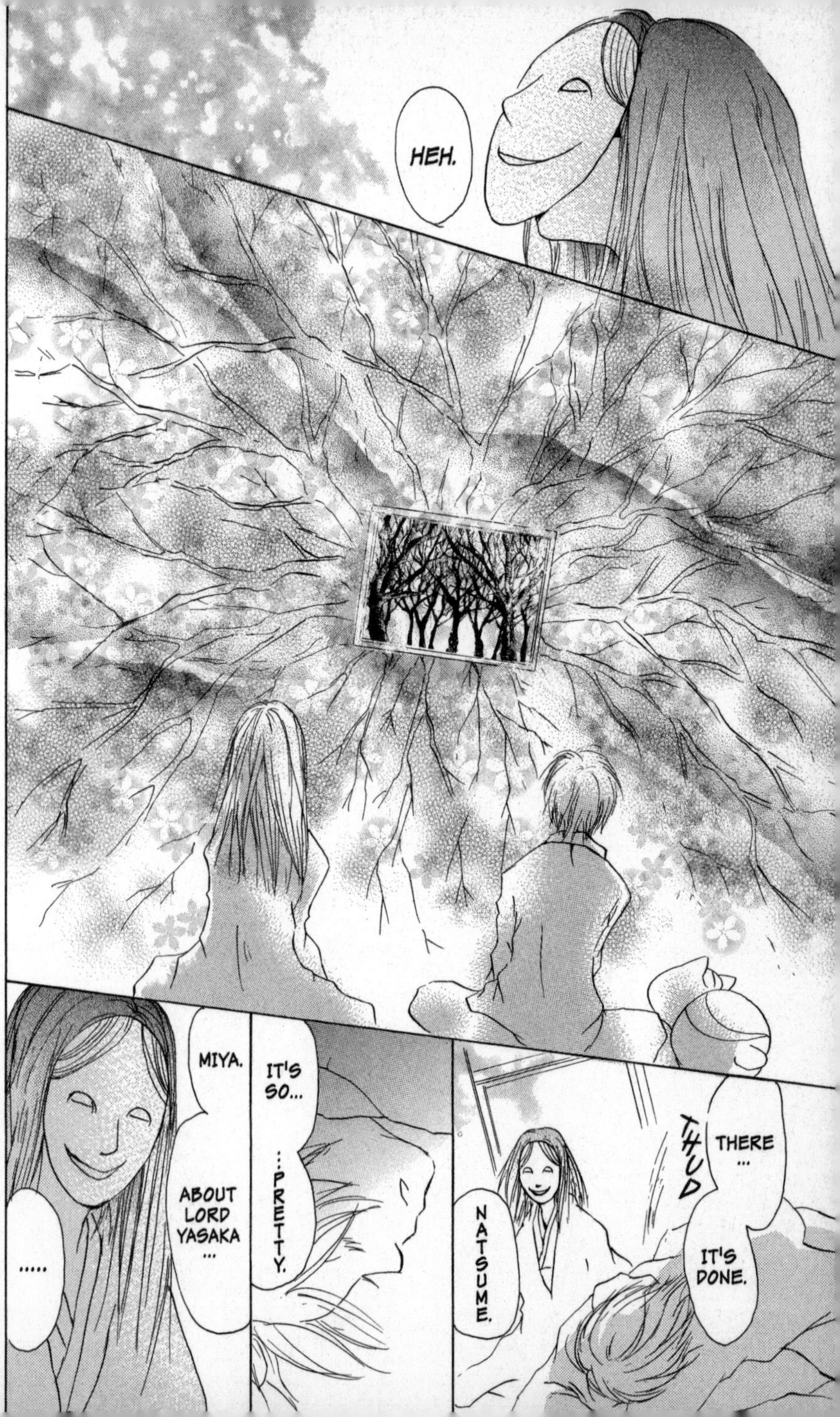
HEH.
THERE ...
THUD
IT'S DONE.
NATSUME.
IT'S SO...
...PRETTY.
MIYA.
ABOUT LORD YASAKA ...
.....

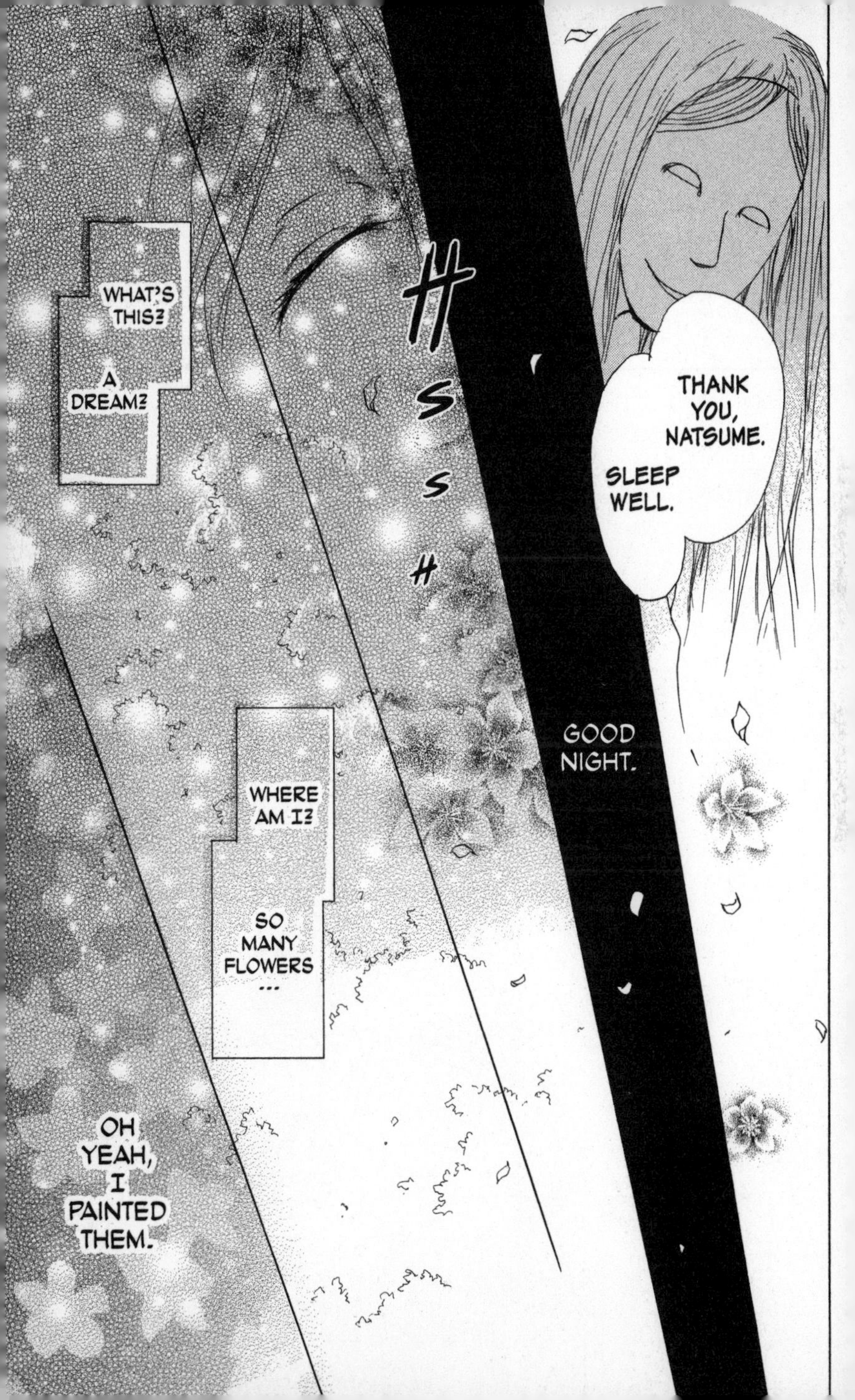
THANK YOU, NATSUME.
SLEEP WELL.
GOOD NIGHT.
HSSH
WHAT'S THIS?
A DREAM?
WHERE AM I?
SO MANY FLOWERS...
OH YEAH, I PAINTED THEM.

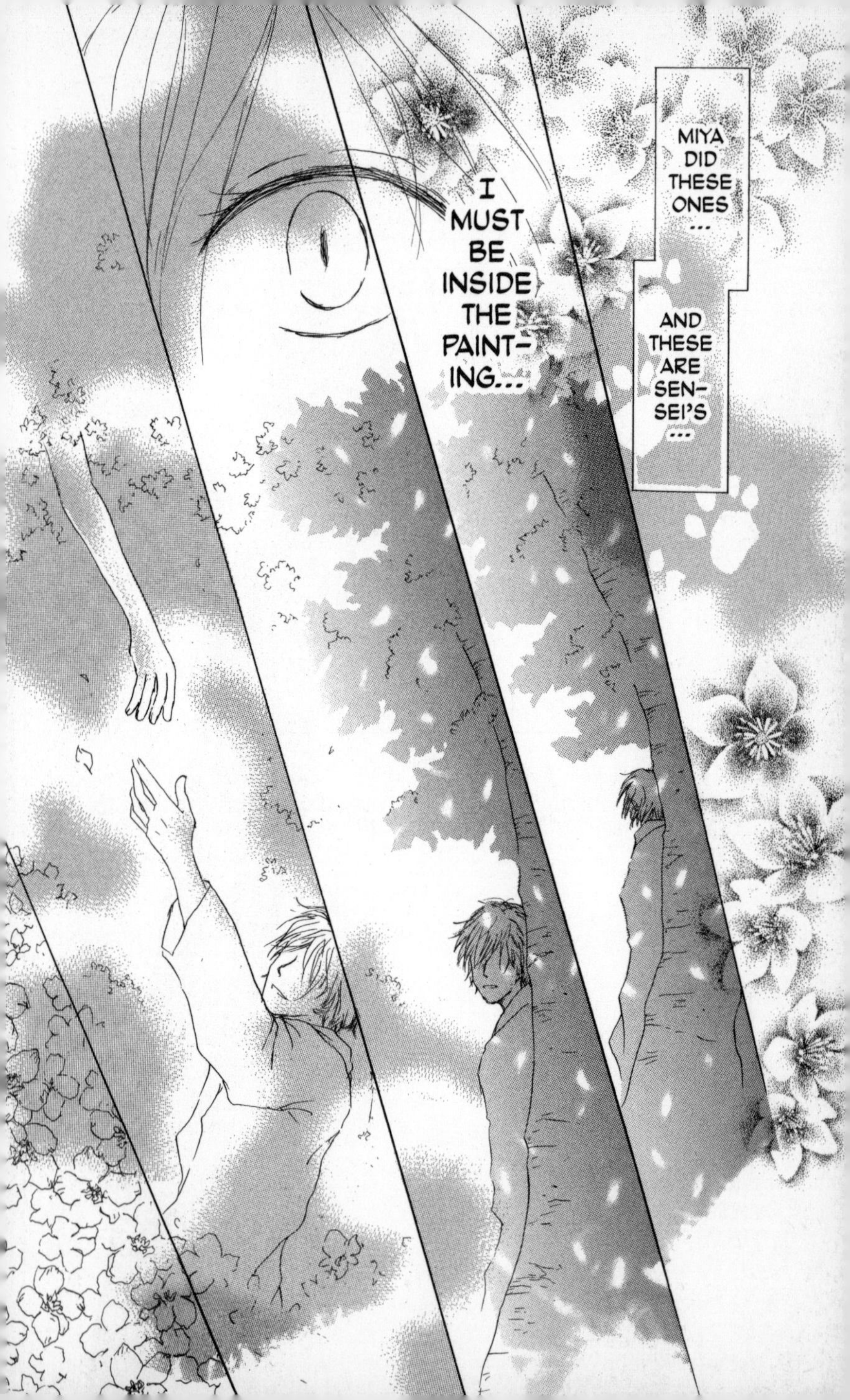
MIYA DID THESE ONES...
AND THESE ARE SEN-SEI'S...
I MUST BE INSIDE THE PAINT-ING...

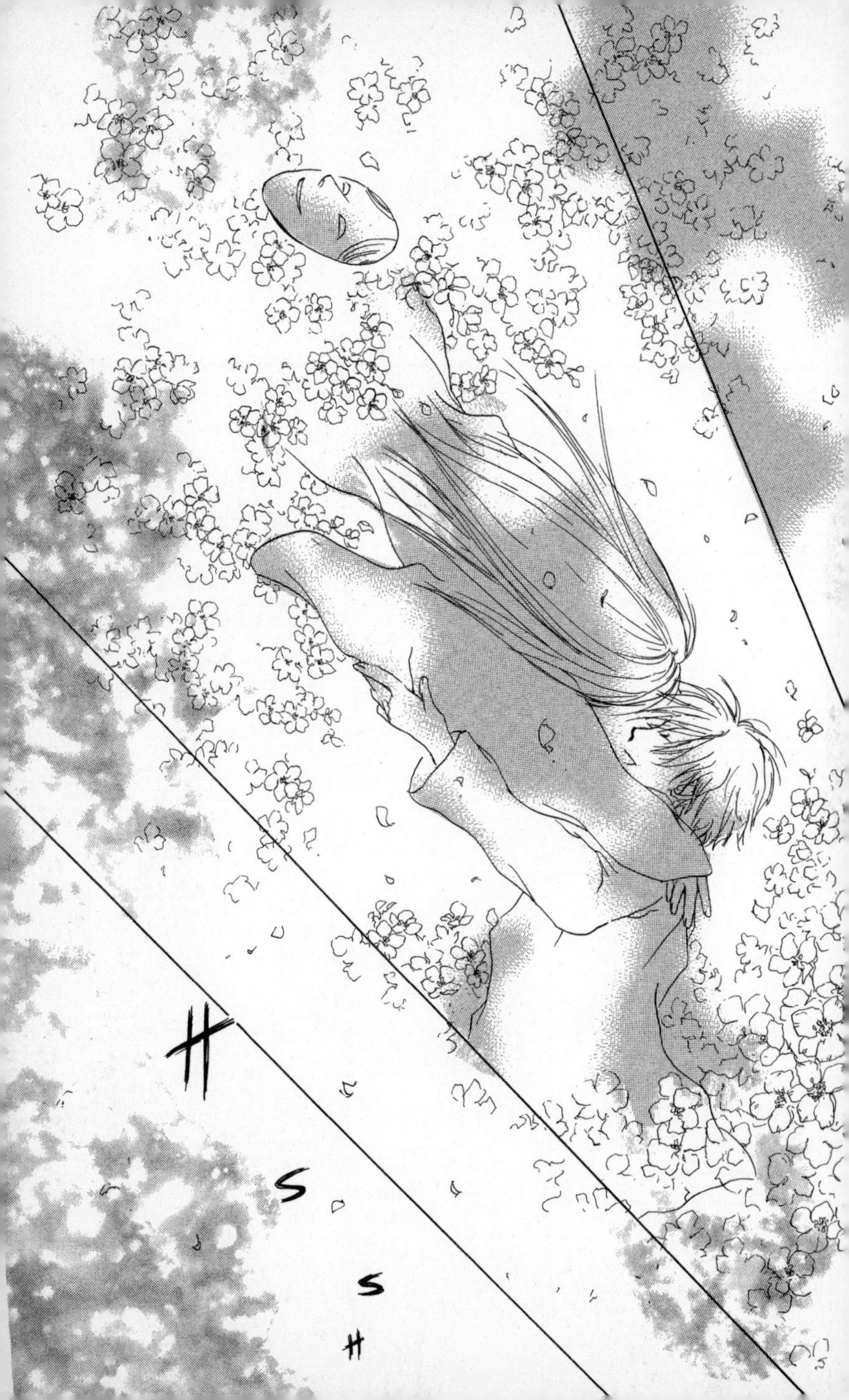
HSSH

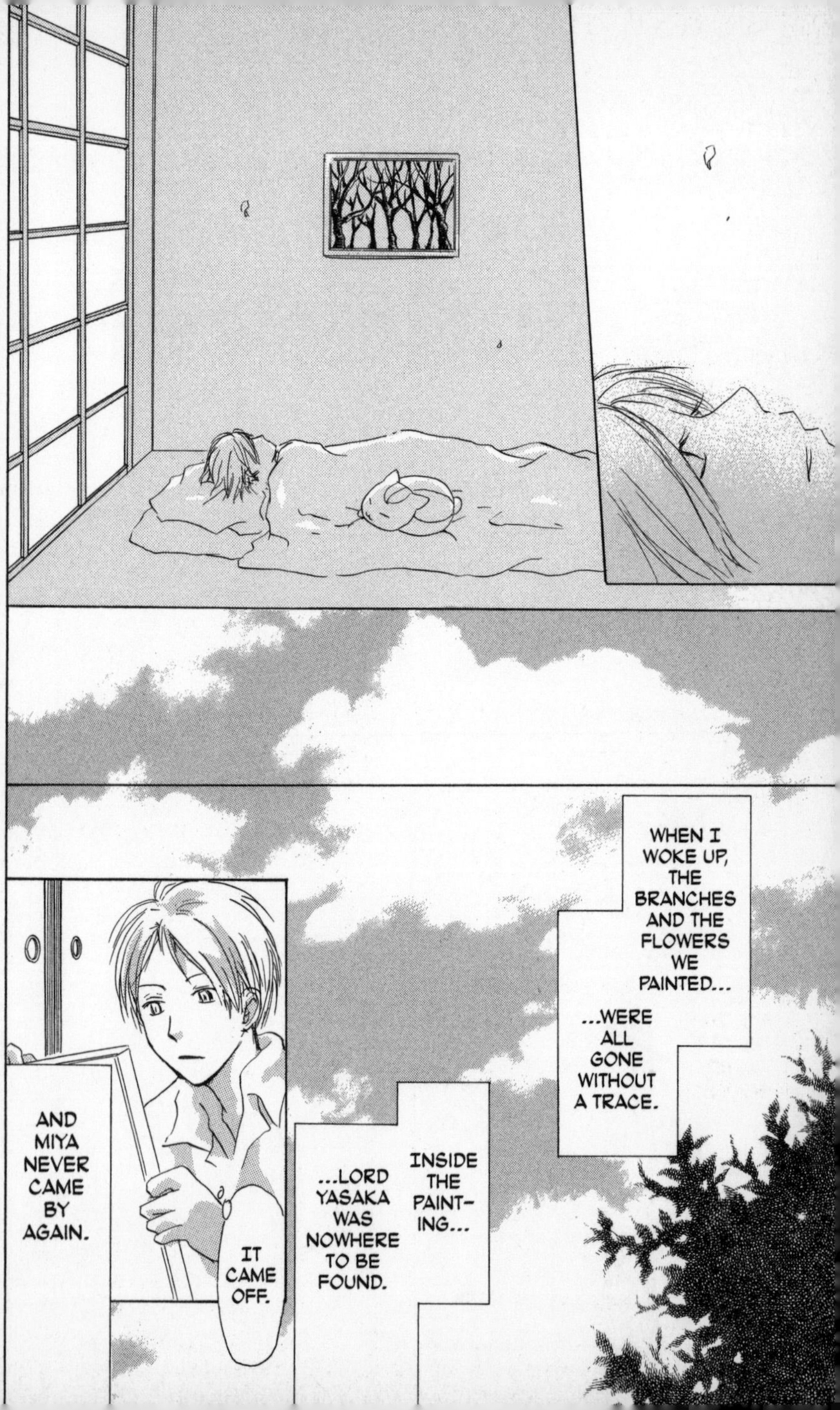
WHEN I WOKE UP, THE BRANCHES AND THE FLOWERS WE PAINTED...
...WERE ALL GONE WITHOUT A TRACE.
INSIDE THE PAINT-ING...
...LORD YASAKA WAS NOWHERE TO BE FOUND.
IT CAME OFF.
AND MIYA NEVER CAME BY AGAIN.

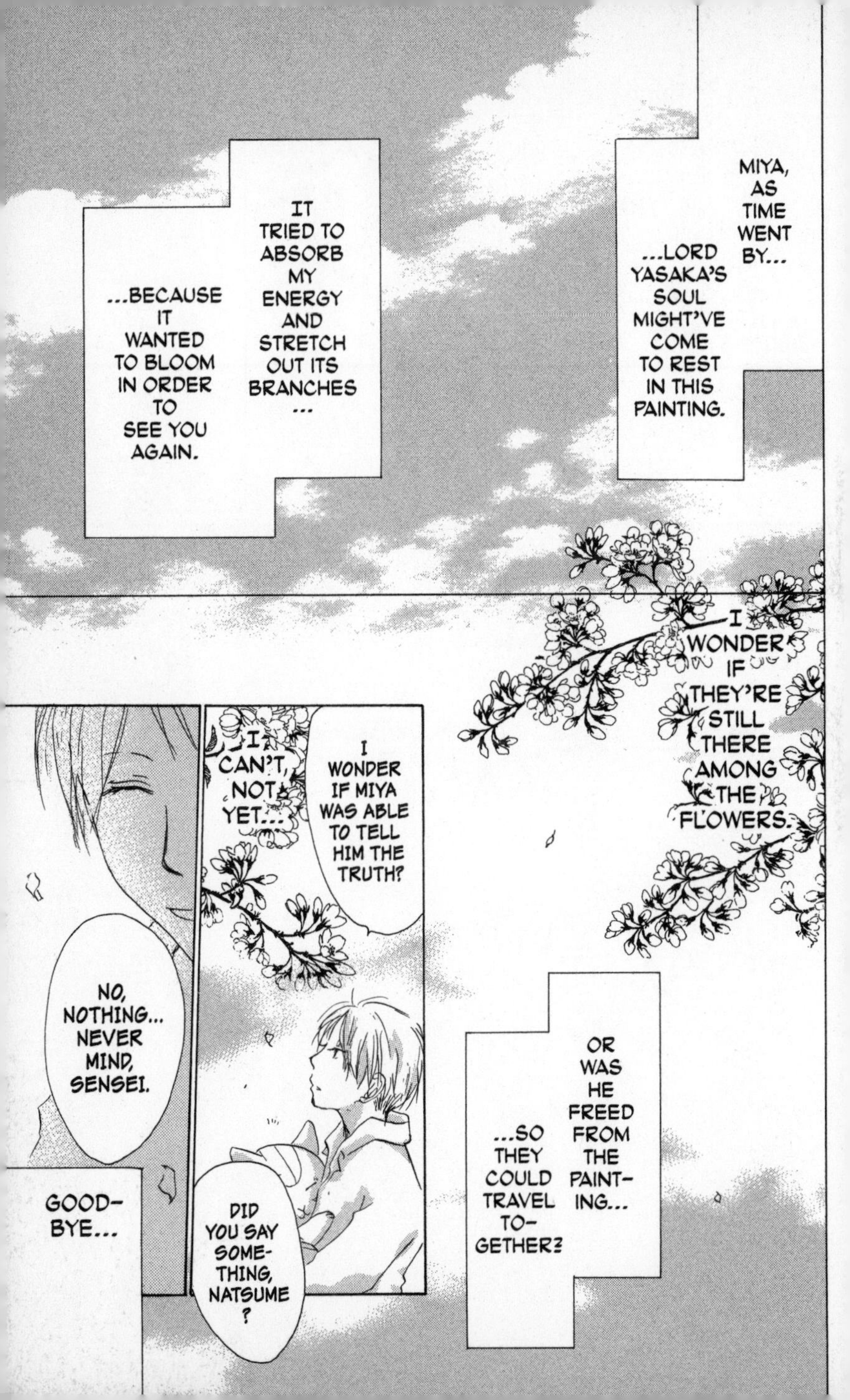
MIYA, AS TIME WENT BY...
...LORD YASAKA'S SOUL MIGHT'VE COME TO REST IN THIS PAINTING.
IT TRIED TO ABSORB MY ENERGY AND STRETCH OUT ITS BRANCHES...
...BECAUSE IT WANTED TO BLOOM IN ORDER TO SEE YOU AGAIN.
I WONDER IF THEY'RE STILL THERE AMONG THE FLOWERS.
OR WAS HE FREED FROM THE PAINTING...
...SO THEY COULD TRAVEL TOGETHER?
I WONDER IF MIYA WAS ABLE TO TELL HIM THE TRUTH?
I CAN'T, NOT YET...
DID YOU SAY SOMETHING, NATSUME?
NO, NOTHING... NEVER MIND, SENSEI.
GOOD-BYE...

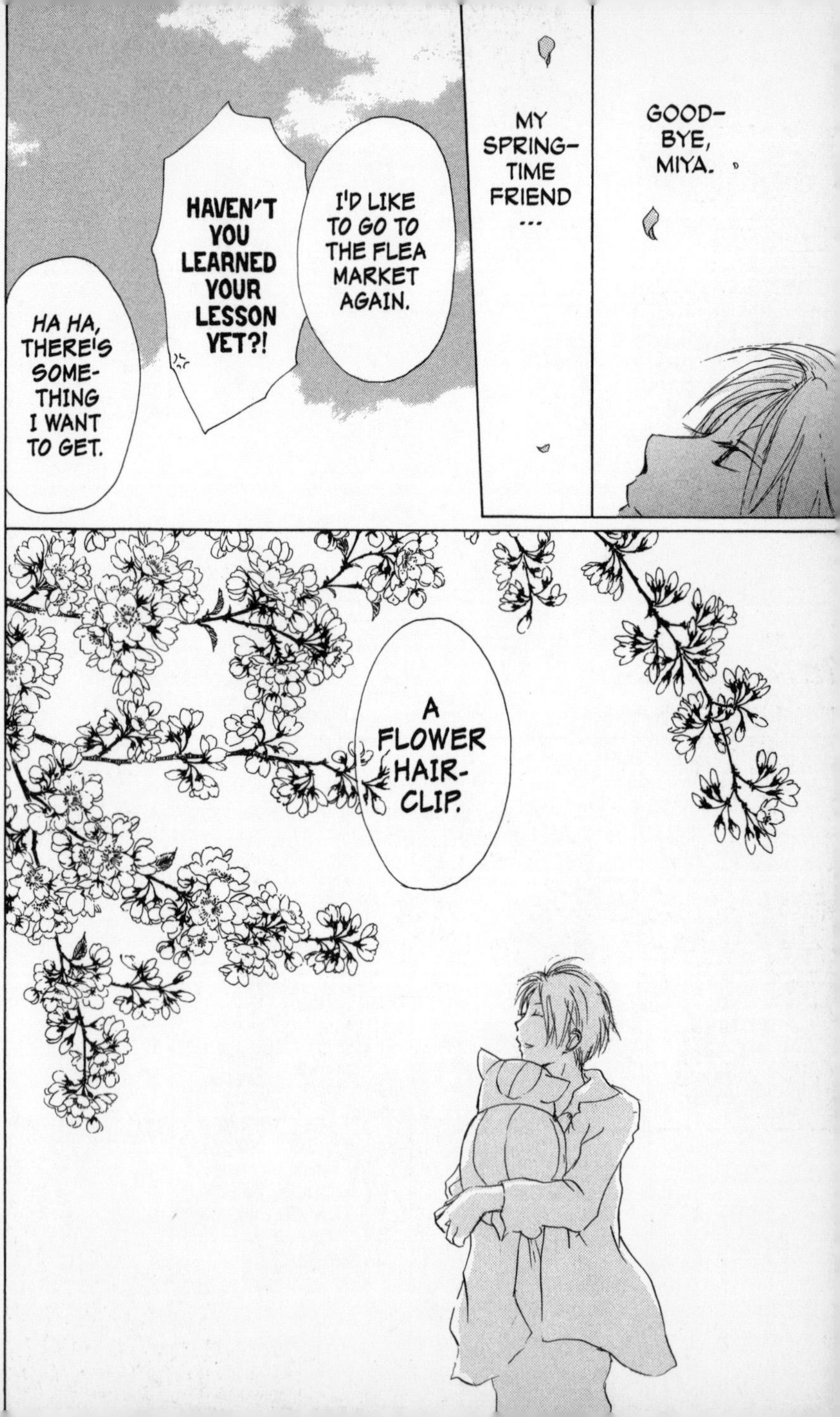
GOOD-BYE, MIYA.
MY SPRING-TIME FRIEND...
I'D LIKE TO GO TO THE FLEA MARKET AGAIN.
HAVEN'T YOU LEARNED YOUR LESSON YET?!
HA HA, THERE'S SOME-THING I WANT TO GET.
A FLOWER HAIR-CLIP.

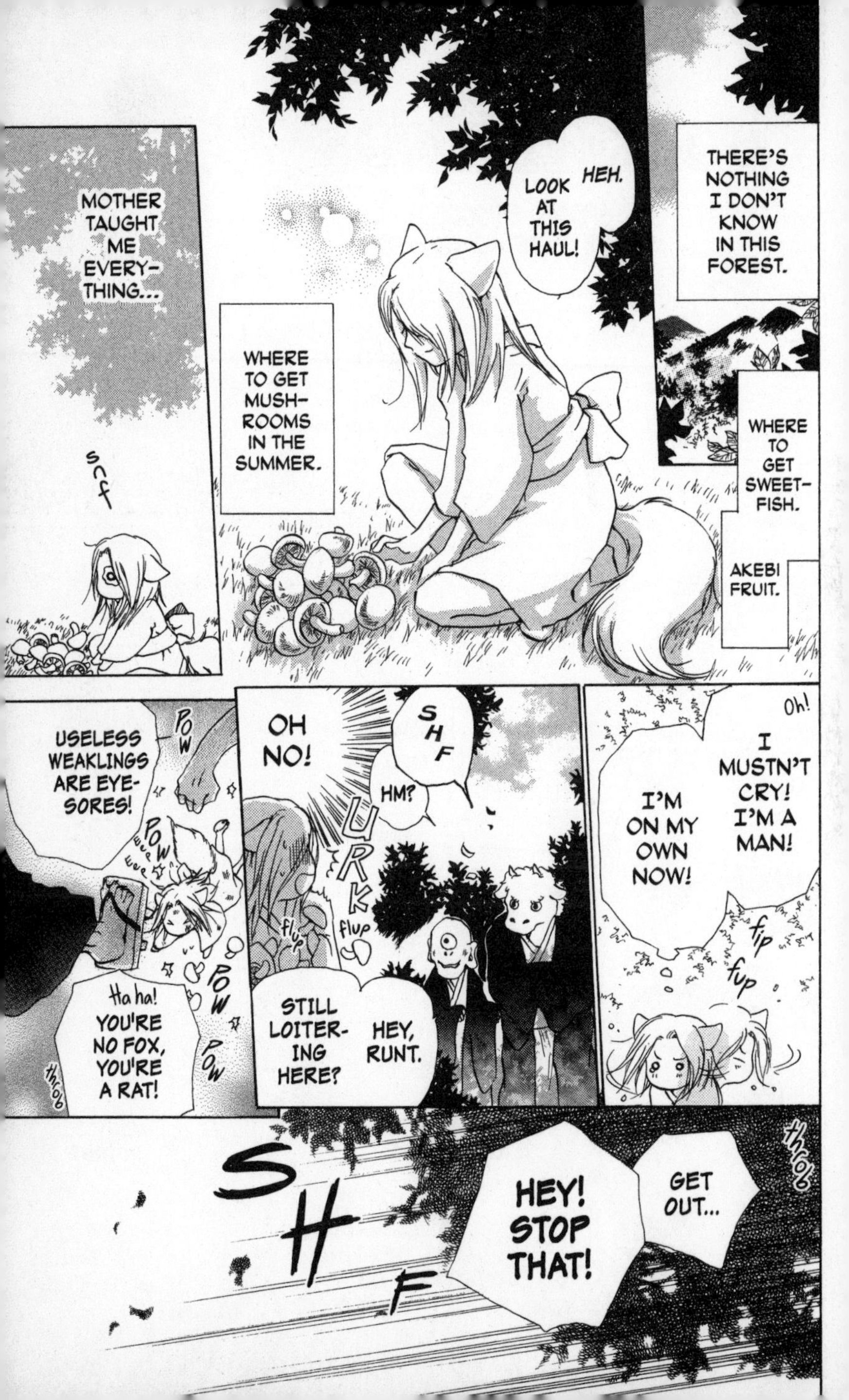
THERE'S NOTHING I DON'T KNOW IN THIS FOREST.
HEH.
LOOK AT THIS HAUL!
WHERE TO GET SWEET-FISH.
AKEBI FRUIT.
WHERE TO GET MUSH-ROOMS IN THE SUMMER.
MOTHER TAUGHT ME EVERY-THING...
Oh!
I MUSTN'T CRY! I'M A MAN!
I'M ON MY OWN NOW!
fip
fup
SHF
HM?
OH NO!
URK
flup
flup
HEY, RUNT.
STILL LOITER-ING HERE?
USELESS WEAKLINGS ARE EYE-SORES!
POW
POW
Ha ha! YOU'RE NO FOX, YOU'RE A RAT!
POW
POW
throb
throb
GET OUT...
HEY! STOP THAT!
SHF

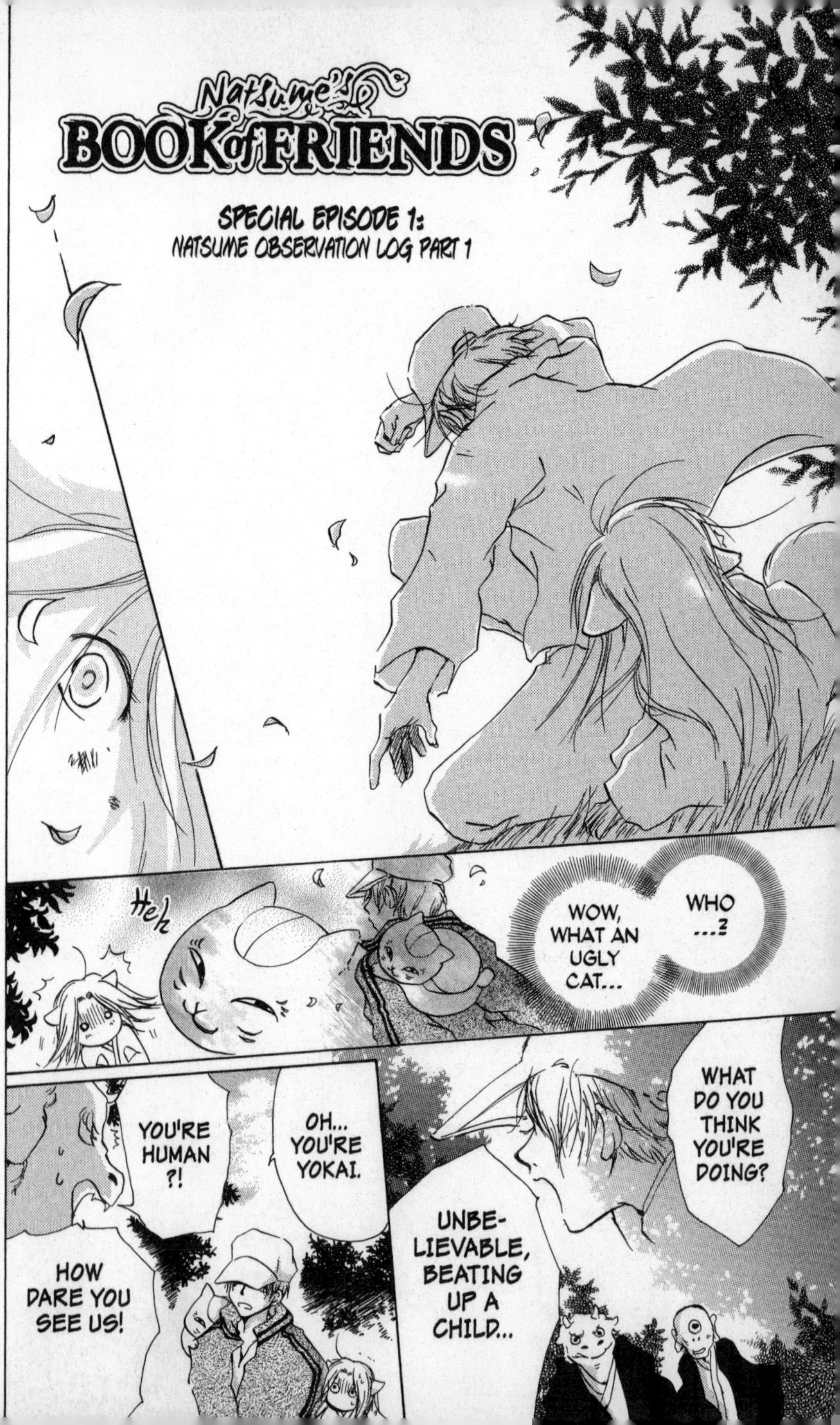
Natsume's BOOK of FRIENDS
SPECIAL EPISODE 1:
NATSUME OBSERVATION LOG PART 1
WHO ...?
WOW, WHAT AN UGLY CAT...
Heh
WHAT DO YOU THINK YOU'RE DOING?
UNBE-LIEVABLE, BEATING UP A CHILD...
OH... YOU'RE YOKAI.
YOU'RE HUMAN ?!
HOW DARE YOU SEE US!

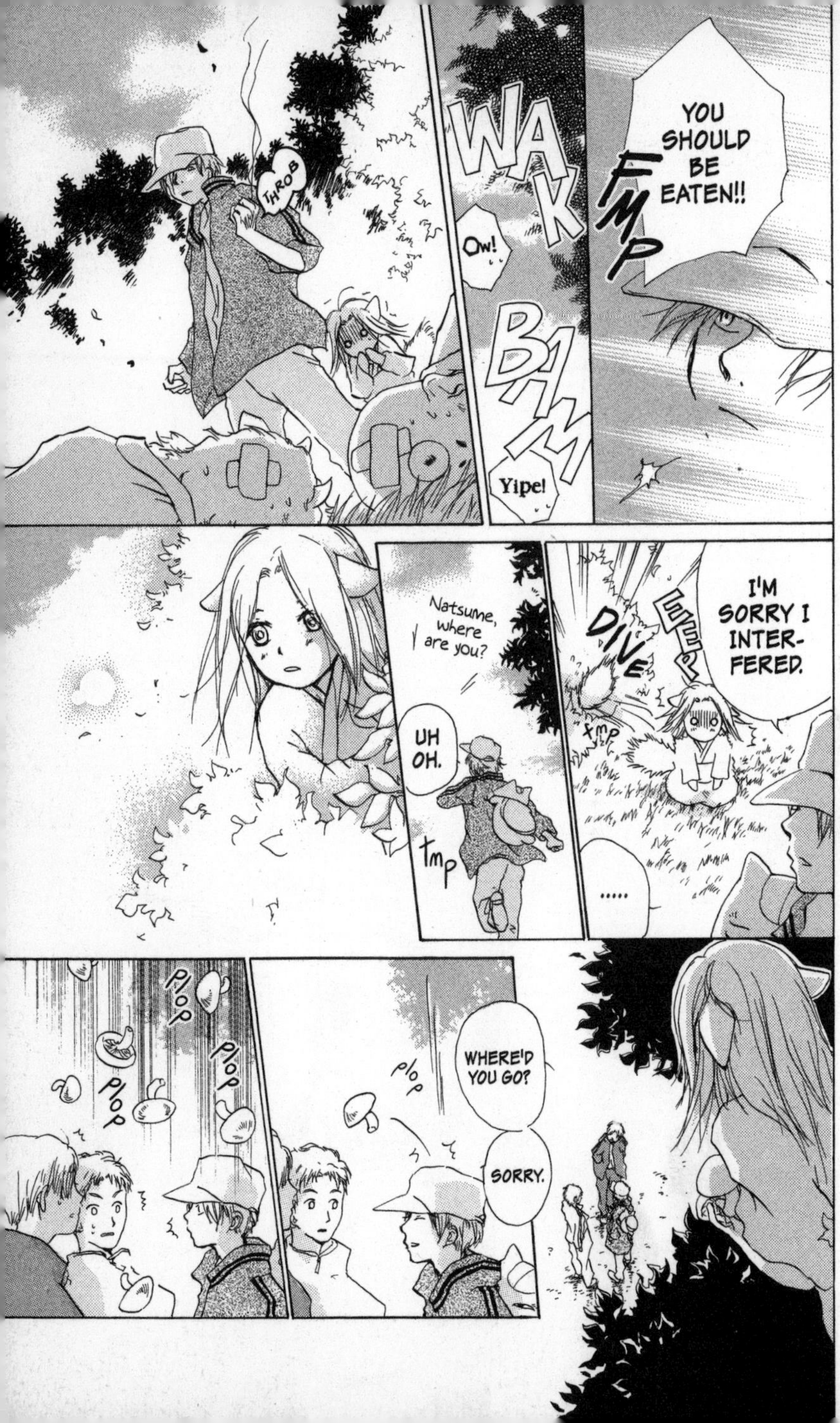
YOU SHOULD BE EATEN!!
FMP
WAK
Ow!
BAM
Yipe!
THROB
I'M SORRY I INTER-FERED.
EEP
DIVE
tmp
......
Natsume, where are you?
UH OH.
tmp
WHERE'D YOU GO?
plop
SORRY.
plop
plop
plop

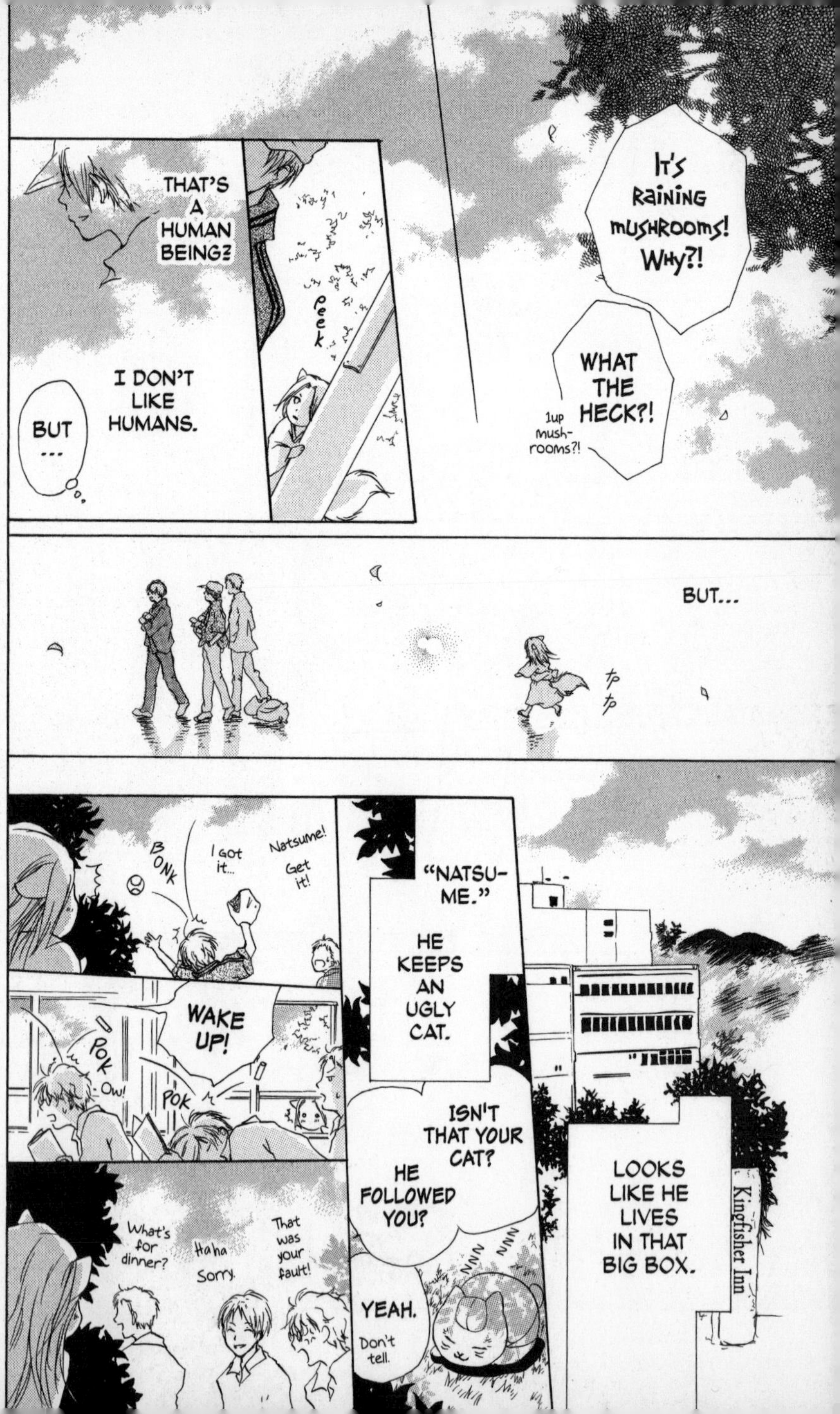
It's raining mushrooms! Why?!
WHAT THE HECK?!
1up mushrooms?!
THAT'S A HUMAN BEING?
Peek
I DON'T LIKE HUMANS.
BUT...
BUT...
tp tp
"NATSUME."
HE KEEPS AN UGLY CAT.
LOOKS LIKE HE LIVES IN THAT BIG BOX.
Kingfisher Inn
Natsume! Get it!
I got it...
BONK
WAKE UP!
POK
Ow!
POK
ISN'T THAT YOUR CAT?
HE FOLLOWED YOU?
YEAH.
Don't tell.
NNN NNN
That was your fault!
Haha Sorry.
What's for dinner?

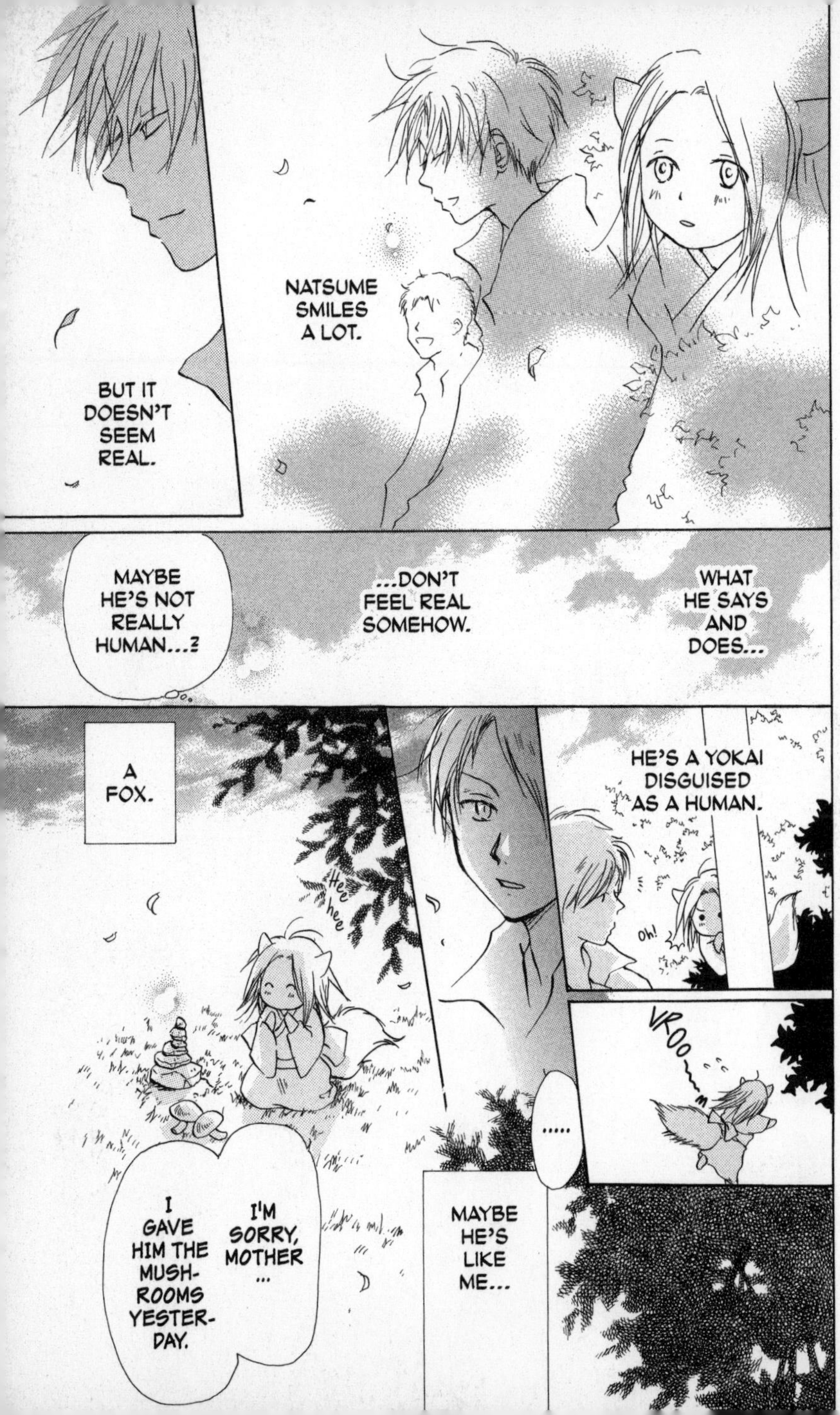
NATSUME SMILES A LOT.
BUT IT DOESN'T SEEM REAL.
WHAT HE SAYS AND DOES...
...DON'T FEEL REAL SOMEHOW.
MAYBE HE'S NOT REALLY HUMAN...?
HE'S A YOKAI DISGUISED AS A HUMAN.
Oh!
VROOO~~m
.....
MAYBE HE'S LIKE ME...
A FOX.
Hee hee
I'M SORRY, MOTHER...
I GAVE HIM THE MUSH-ROOMS YESTER-DAY.

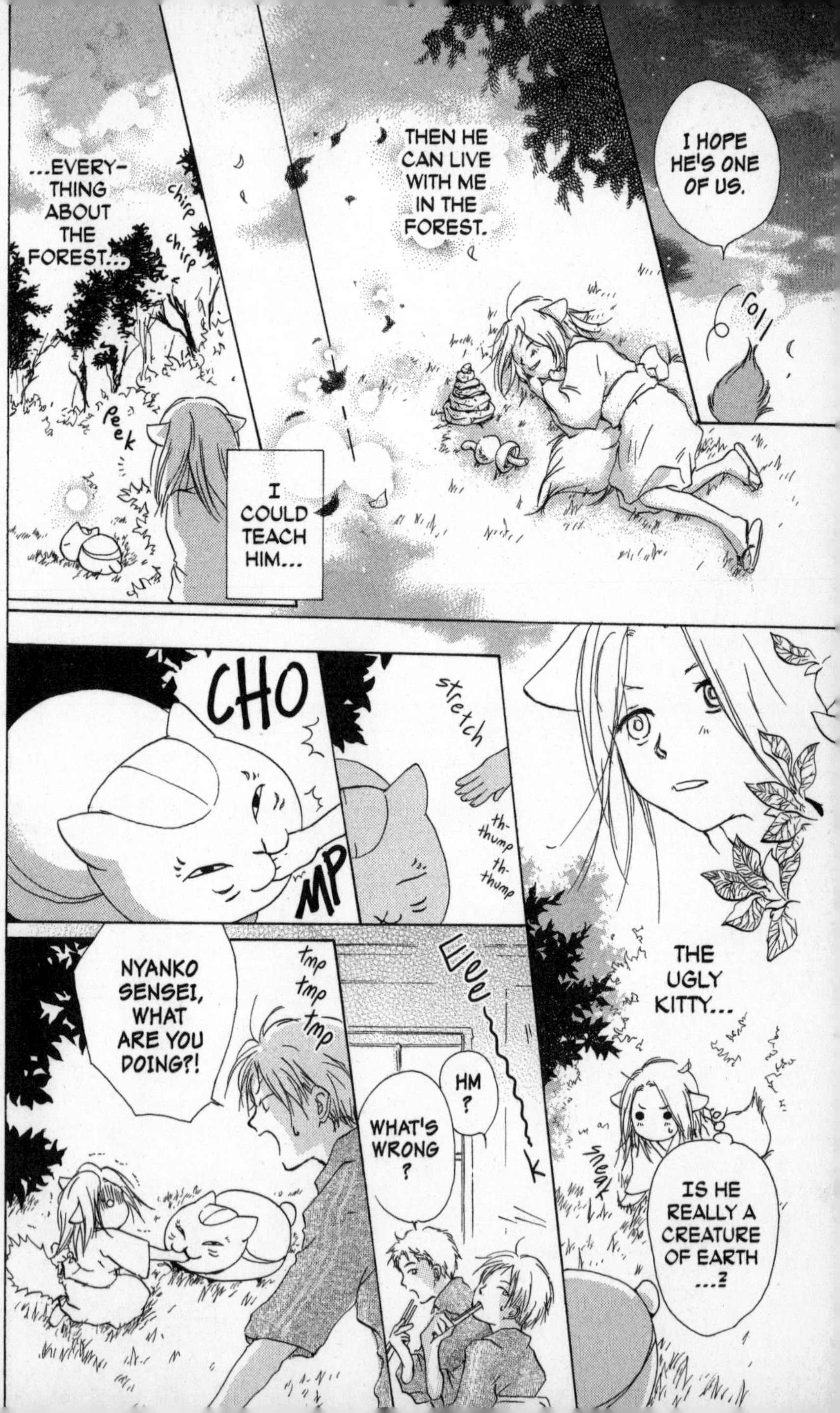
I HOPE HE'S ONE OF US.
roll
THEN HE CAN LIVE WITH ME IN THE FOREST.
I COULD TEACH HIM...
...EVERY-THING ABOUT THE FOREST...
chirp chirp
peek
THE UGLY KITTY...
sneak
IS HE REALLY A CREATURE OF EARTH...?
stretch
th-thump th-thump
CHOMP
Eeee---K
HM?
WHAT'S WRONG?
tmp tmp tmp
NYANKO SENSEI, WHAT ARE YOU DOING?!

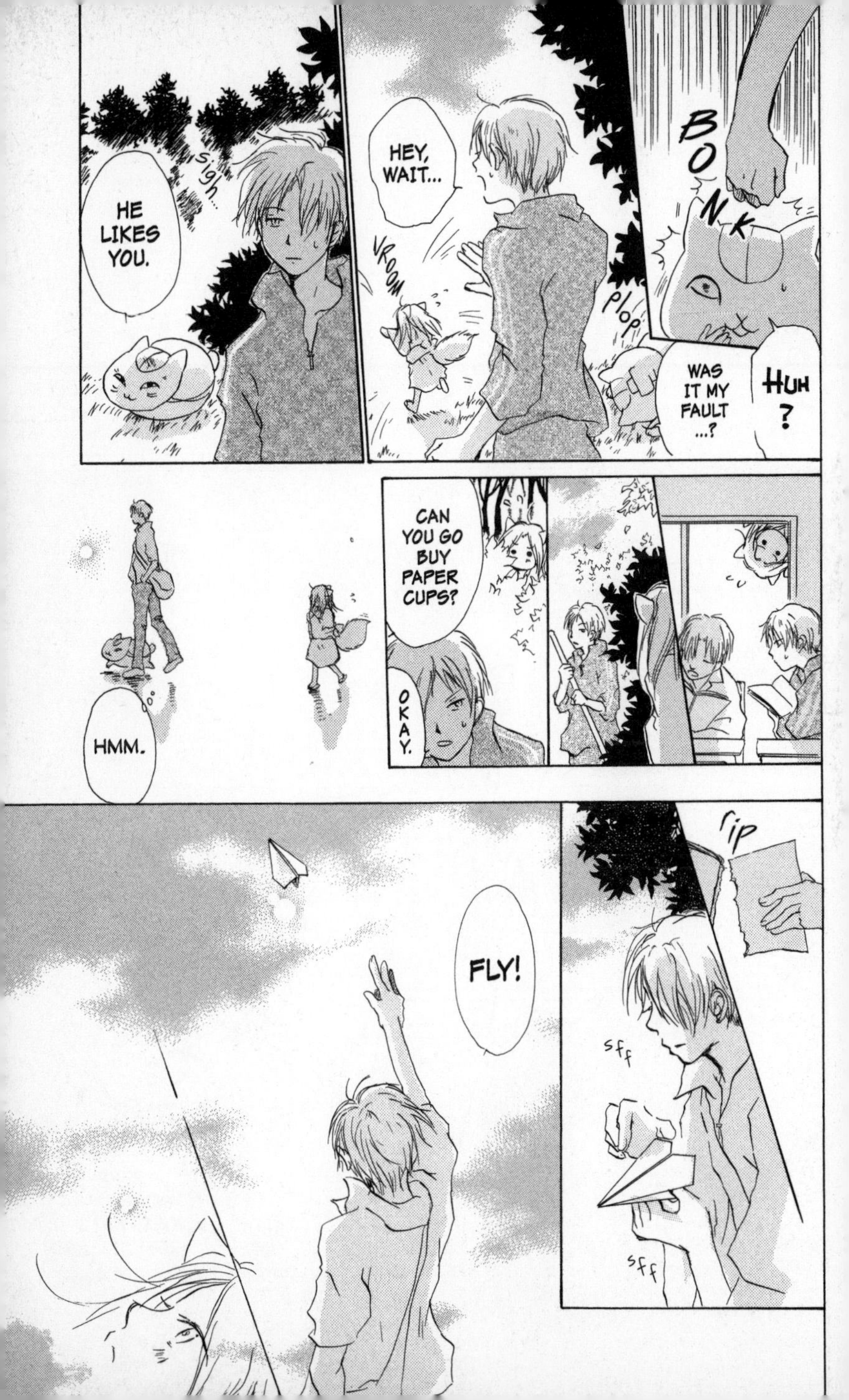
BONK
HUH?
WAS IT MY FAULT ...?
PLOP
HEY, WAIT...
VROOM
sigh...
HE LIKES YOU.
CAN YOU GO BUY PAPER CUPS?
OKAY.
HMM.
rip
sff
sff
FLY!

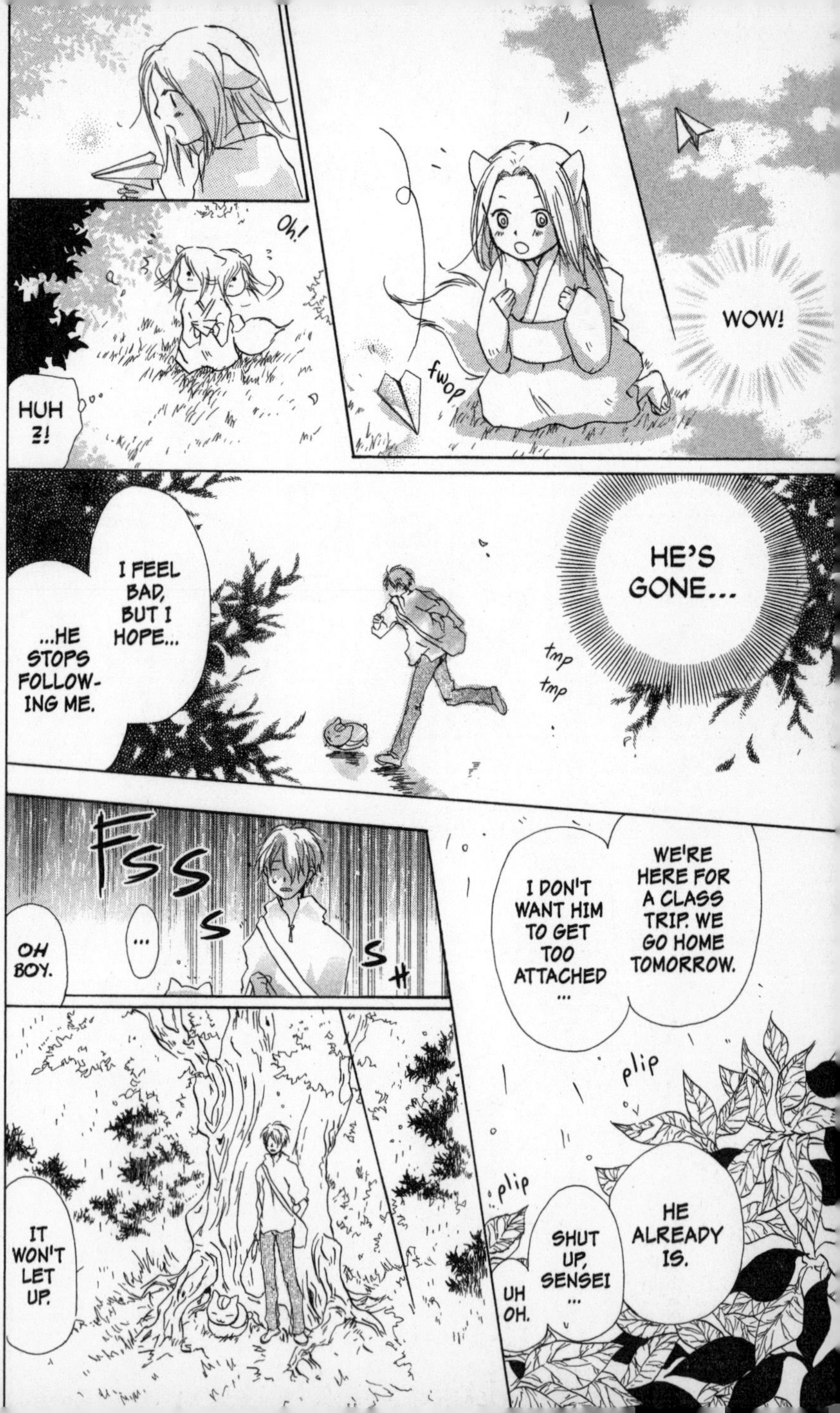
WOW!
fwop
Oh!
HUH ?!
HE'S GONE...
tmp
tmp
I FEEL BAD, BUT I HOPE...
...HE STOPS FOLLOWING ME.
WE'RE HERE FOR A CLASS TRIP. WE GO HOME TOMORROW.
I DON'T WANT HIM TO GET TOO ATTACHED...
plip
HE ALREADY IS.
plip
SHUT UP, SENSEI...
UH OH.
FSSS
SH
...
OH BOY.
IT WON'T LET UP.

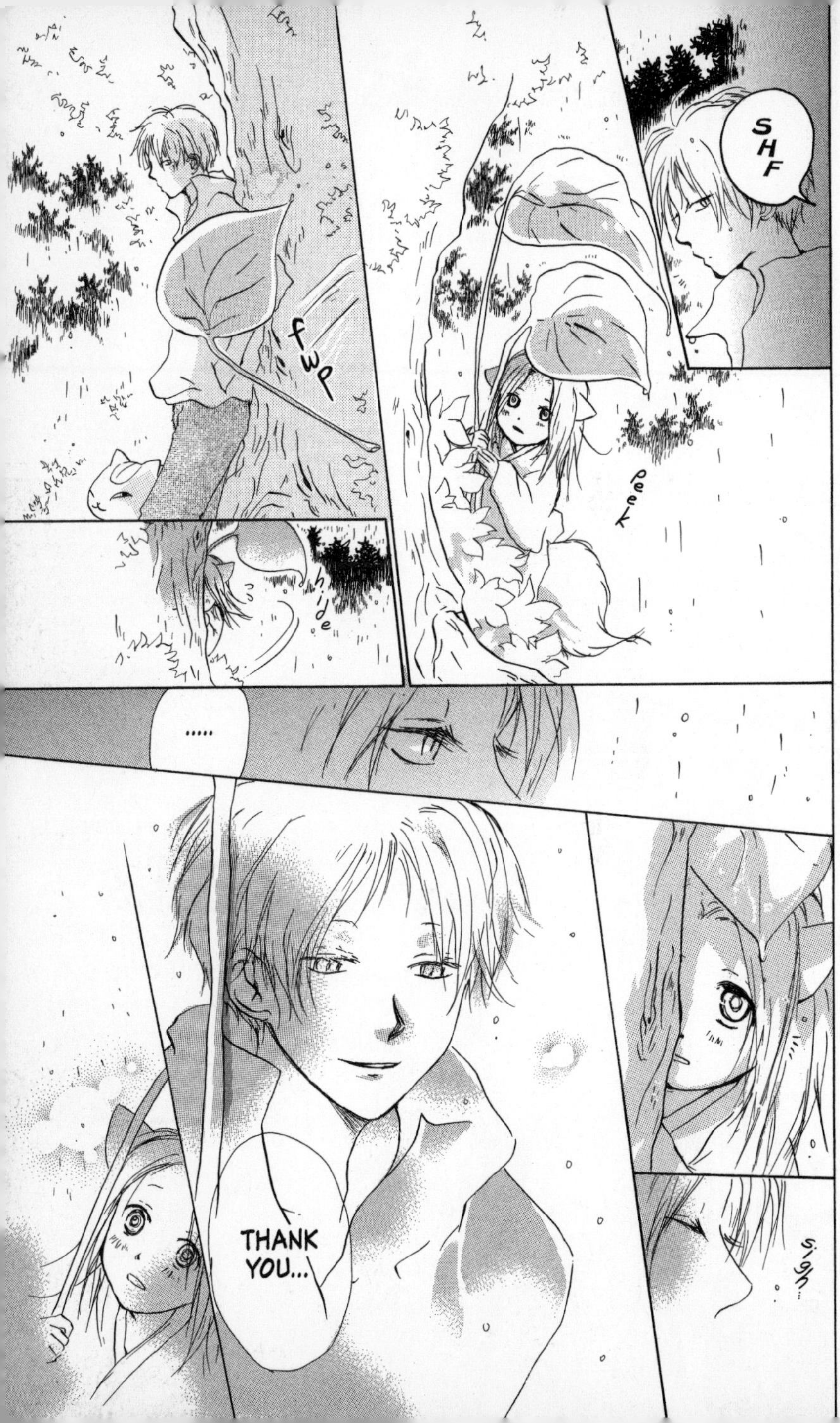
SHF
fwp
peek
hide
.....
sigh...
THANK YOU...

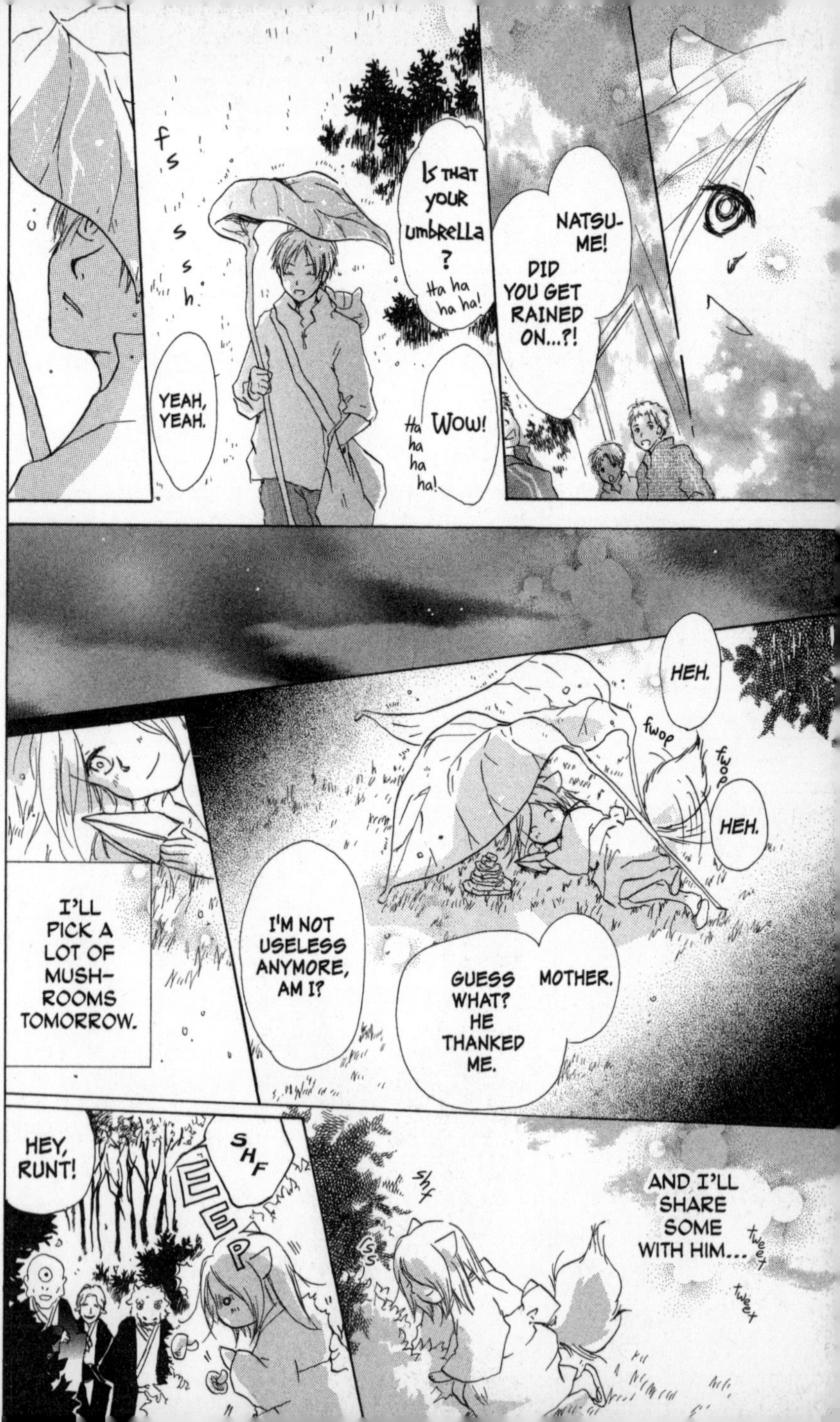
NATSU-ME!
DID YOU GET RAINED ON...?!
Is that your umbrella?
Ha ha ha ha!
WOW!
Ha ha ha ha ha!
fsssh
YEAH, YEAH.
HEH.
fwop
fwop
HEH.
MOTHER.
GUESS WHAT? HE THANKED ME.
I'M NOT USELESS ANYMORE, AM I?
I'LL PICK A LOT OF MUSH-ROOMS TOMORROW.
AND I'LL SHARE SOME WITH HIM...
tweet
tweet
shf
ss
SHF
EEEP
HEY, RUNT!

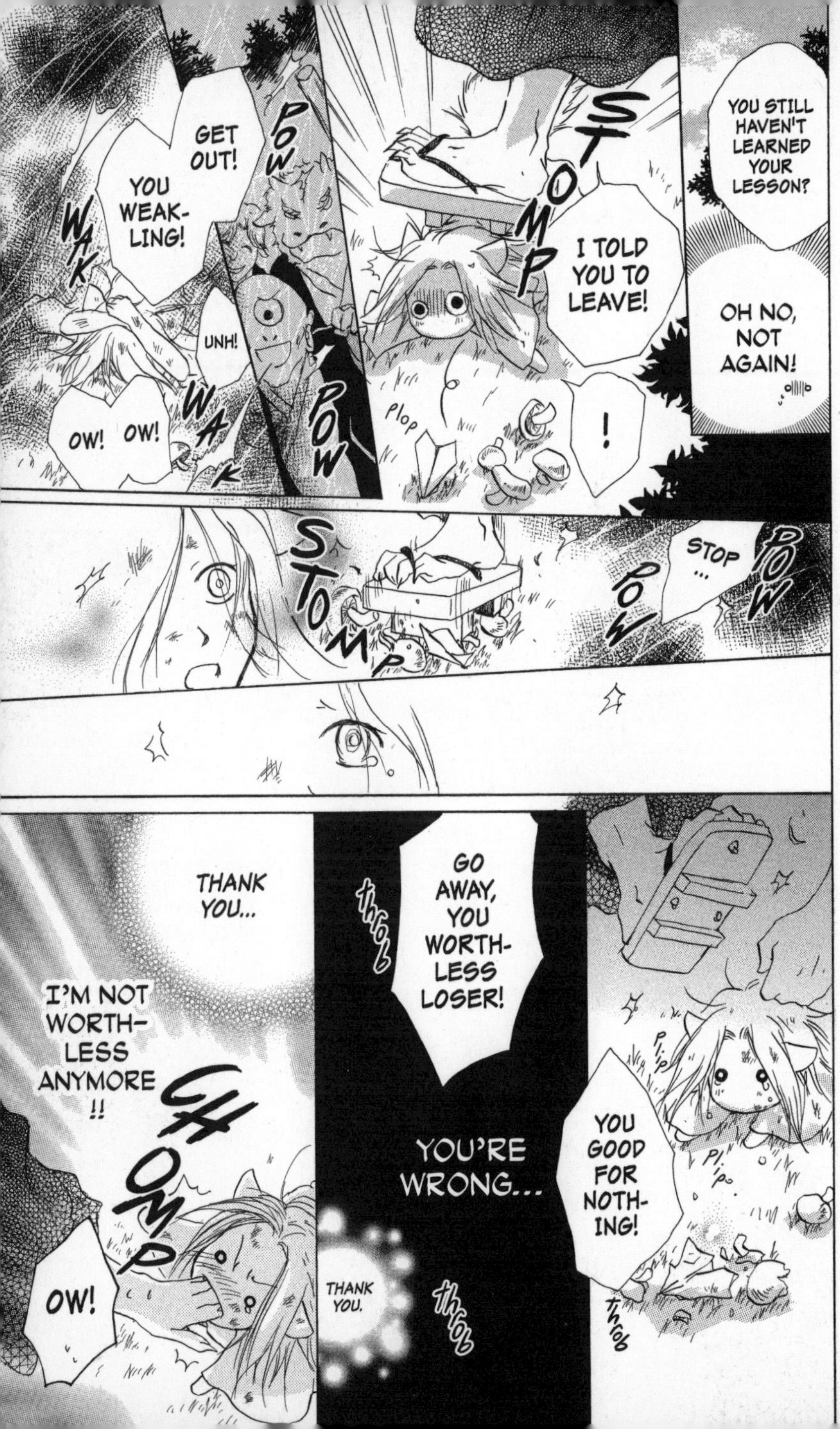
YOU STILL HAVEN'T LEARNED YOUR LESSON?
OH NO, NOT AGAIN!
STOMP
I TOLD YOU TO LEAVE!
!
Plop
POW POW
GET OUT!
YOU WEAK-LING!
UNH!
WAK WAK WAK
OW! OW!
POW POW
STOP...
STOMP
YOU GOOD FOR NOTH-ING!
Plip
Plip
throb
GO AWAY, YOU WORTH-LESS LOSER!
throb
YOU'RE WRONG...
THANK YOU.
throb
THANK YOU...
I'M NOT WORTH-LESS ANYMORE!!
CHOMP
OW!

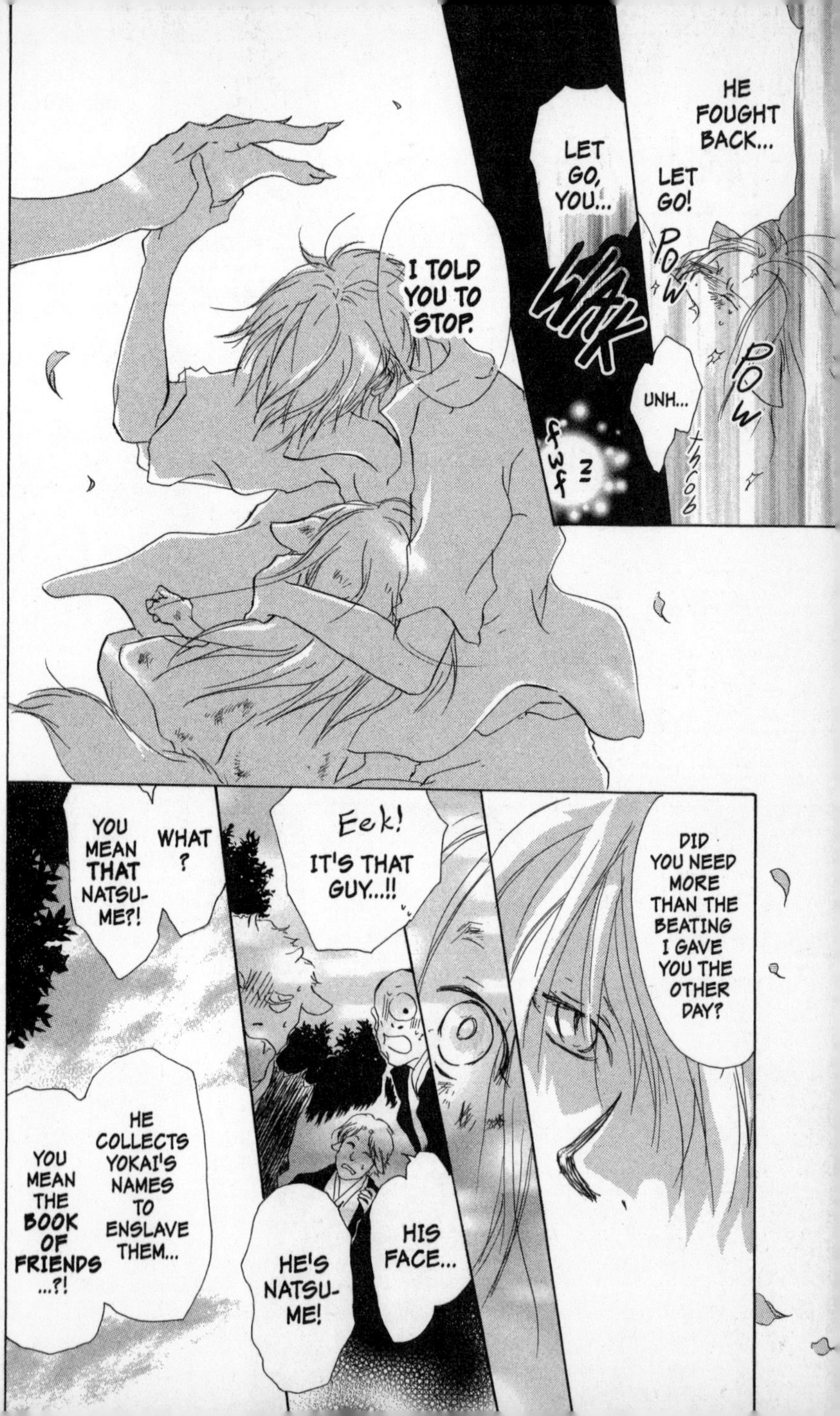
HE FOUGHT BACK...
LET GO!
LET GO, YOU...
POW
POW
WHAK
UNH...
throb
fwf
I TOLD YOU TO STOP.
DID YOU NEED MORE THAN THE BEATING I GAVE YOU THE OTHER DAY?
Eek!
IT'S THAT GUY...!!
HIS FACE...
HE'S NATSU-ME!
WHAT?
YOU MEAN THAT NATSU-ME?!
HE COLLECTS YOKAI'S NAMES TO ENSLAVE THEM...
YOU MEAN THE BOOK OF FRIENDS...?!

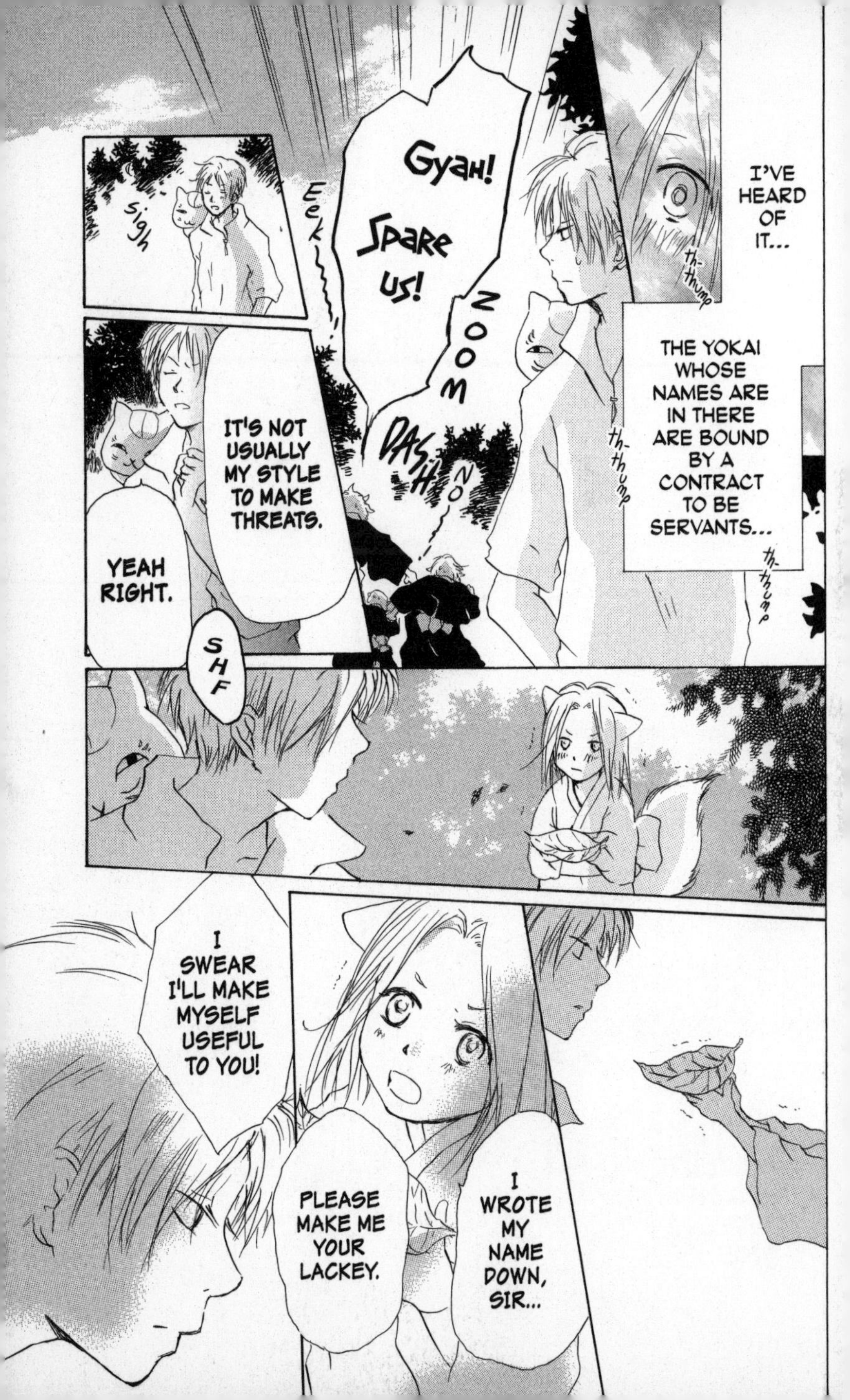
I'VE HEARD OF IT...
th-thump
THE YOKAI WHOSE NAMES ARE IN THERE ARE BOUND BY A CONTRACT TO BE SERVANTS...
th-thump
th-thump
Gyah!
Spare us!
ZOOM
DASH
Eek
No
sigh
IT'S NOT USUALLY MY STYLE TO MAKE THREATS.
YEAH RIGHT.
SHF
I WROTE MY NAME DOWN, SIR...
PLEASE MAKE ME YOUR LACKEY.
I SWEAR I'LL MAKE MYSELF USEFUL TO YOU!

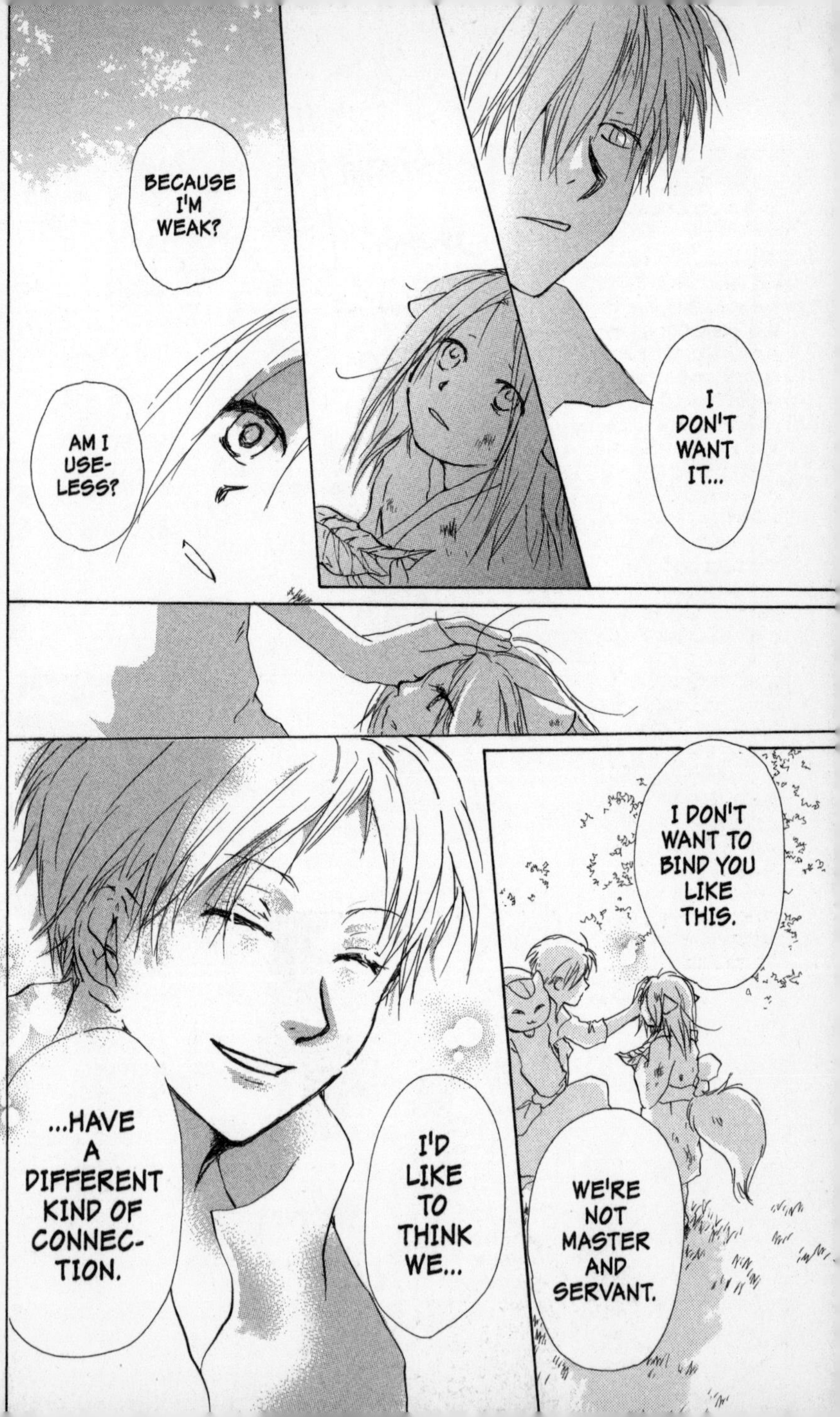
I DON'T WANT IT...
BECAUSE I'M WEAK?
AM I USELESS?
I DON'T WANT TO BIND YOU LIKE THIS.
WE'RE NOT MASTER AND SERVANT.
I'D LIKE TO THINK WE...
...HAVE A DIFFERENT KIND OF CONNECTION.

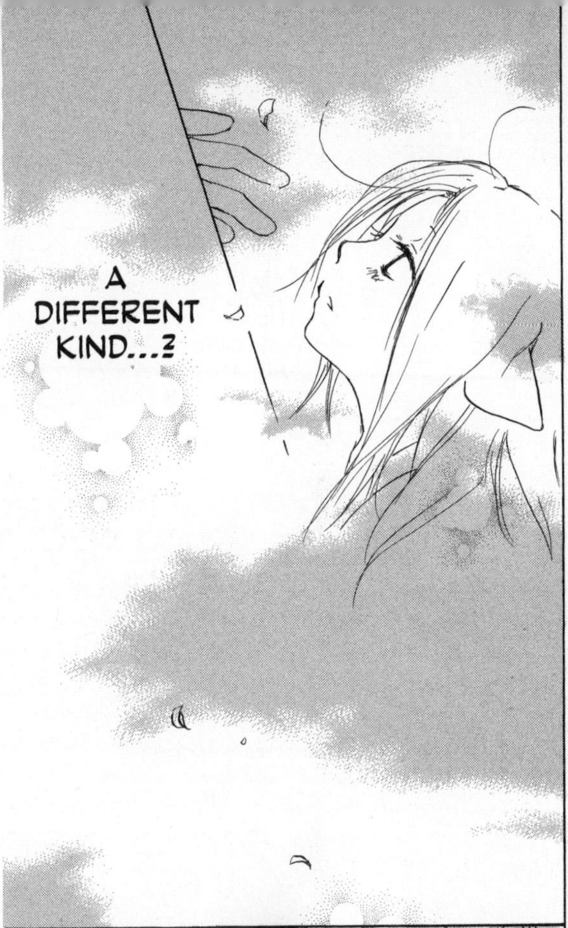
A DIFFERENT KIND...?

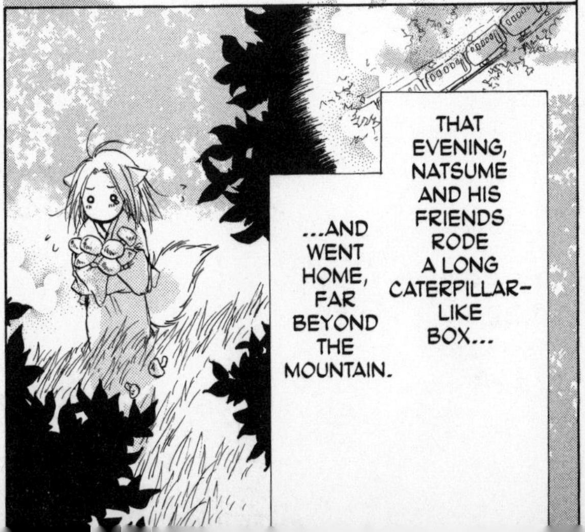
THAT EVENING, NATSUME AND HIS FRIENDS RODE A LONG CATERPILLAR-LIKE BOX...
...AND WENT HOME, FAR BEYOND THE MOUNTAIN.

07

❀Um, enclosures...

There was another big development for me and Natsume. It was something I assumed would never happen, and made me fall over with joy. The magazine *LaLa* has an amazing concept of sometimes including a drama CD as a bonus, and they made one for Natsume too! I'm sure some of the readers also fell over with surprise.

I loved anime when I was little, but since I live in the provinces, I don't get as much anime on TV these days as they do in Tokyo. I was a willing fan but was forced into ignorance about the recent trends, and I worried about what I should do.

← Continued in part 08

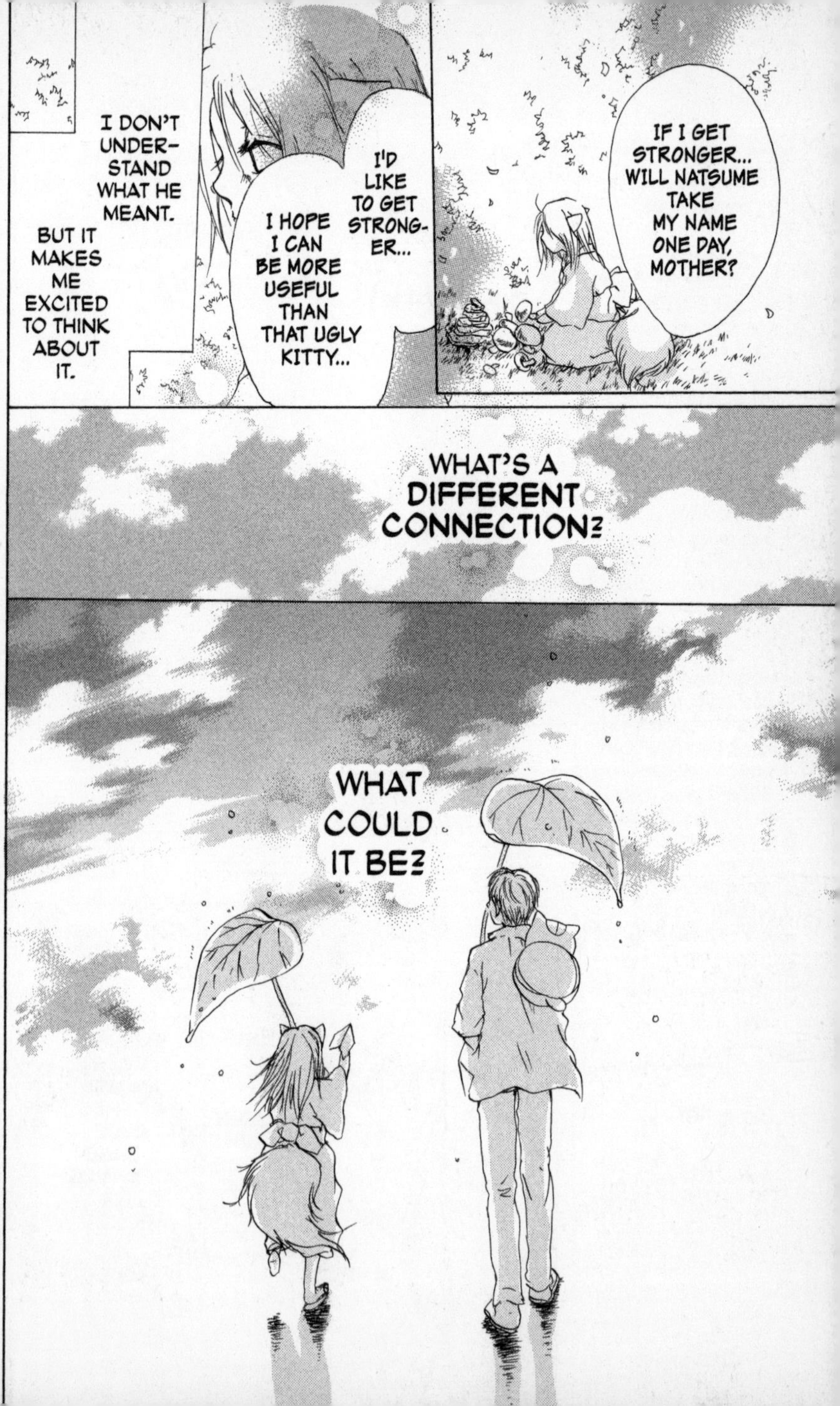
IF I GET STRONGER... WILL NATSUME TAKE MY NAME ONE DAY, MOTHER?
I'D LIKE TO GET STRONG-ER...
I HOPE I CAN BE MORE USEFUL THAN THAT UGLY KITTY...
I DON'T UNDER-STAND WHAT HE MEANT.
BUT IT MAKES ME EXCITED TO THINK ABOUT IT.
WHAT'S A DIFFERENT CONNECTION?
WHAT COULD IT BE?

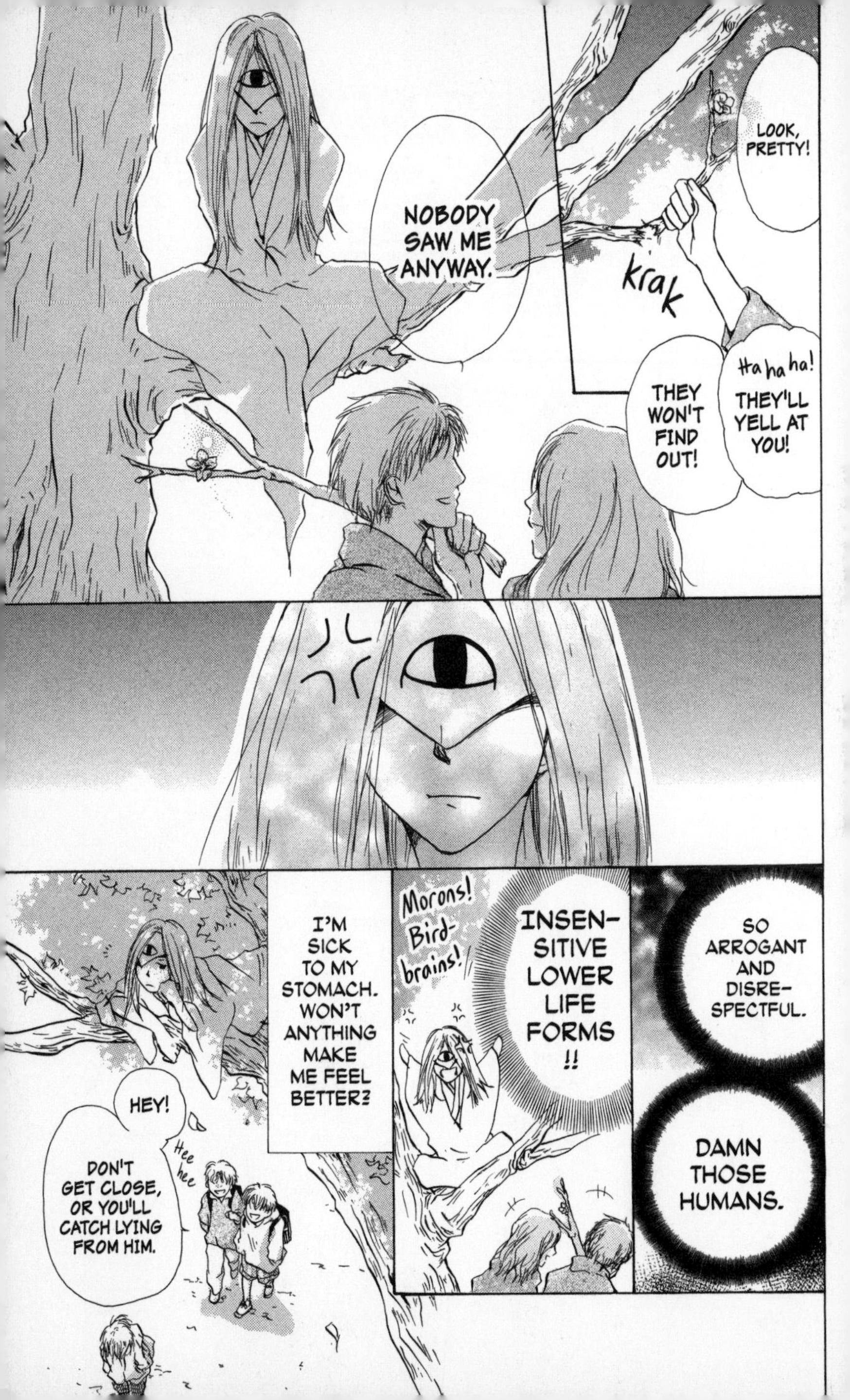
LOOK, PRETTY!
krak
Ha ha ha! THEY'LL YELL AT YOU!
THEY WON'T FIND OUT!
NOBODY SAW ME ANYWAY.
SO ARROGANT AND DISRE-SPECTFUL.
DAMN THOSE HUMANS.
INSEN-SITIVE LOWER LIFE FORMS !!
Morons! Bird-brains!
I'M SICK TO MY STOMACH. WON'T ANYTHING MAKE ME FEEL BETTER?
HEY!
DON'T GET CLOSE, OR YOU'LL CATCH LYING FROM HIM.
Hee hee

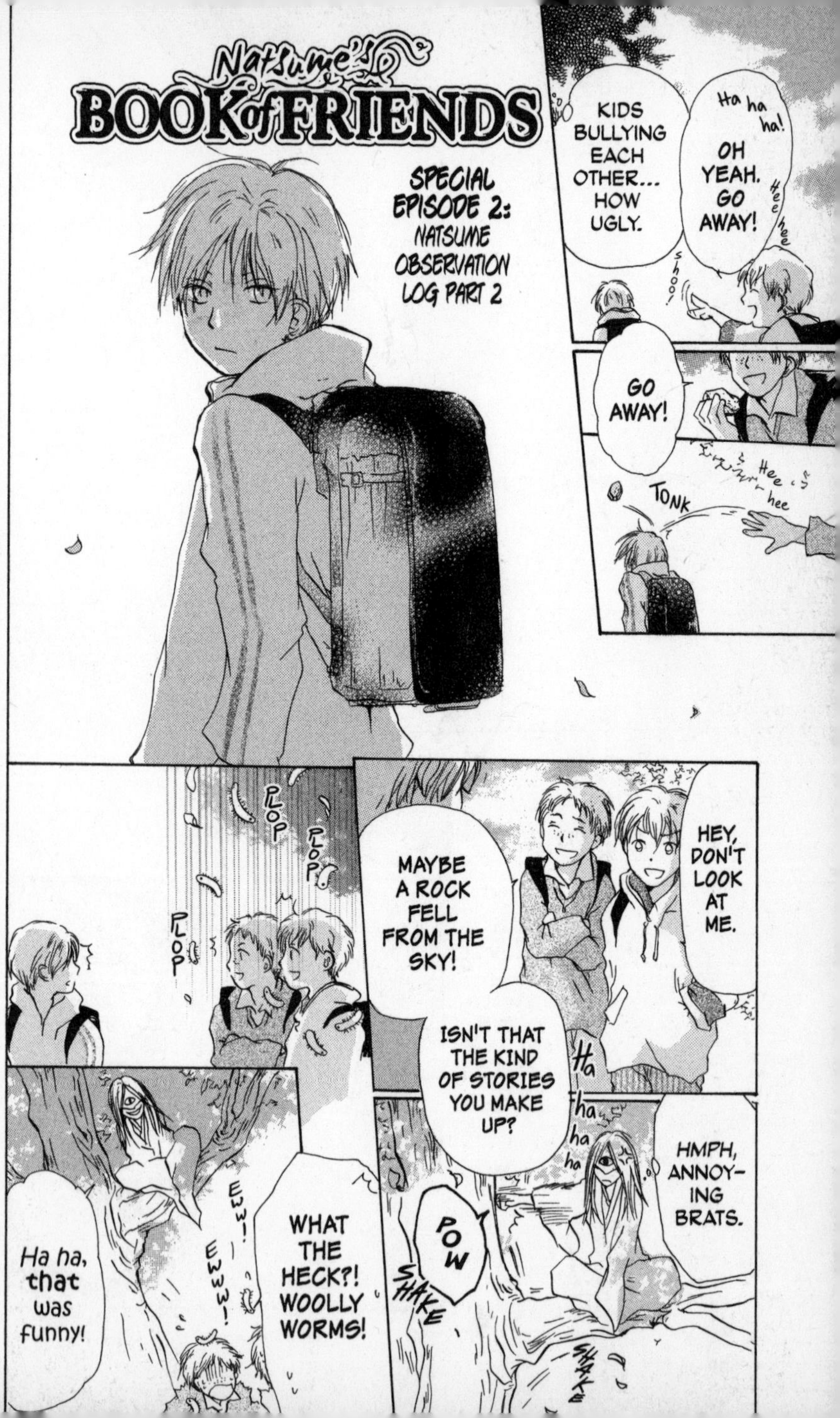
KIDS BULLYING EACH OTHER... HOW UGLY.
Ha ha ha!
OH YEAH. GO AWAY!
Hee hee
shoo!
GO AWAY!
Hee hee
TONK
Natsume's BOOK of FRIENDS
SPECIAL EPISODE 2: NATSUME OBSERVATION LOG PART 2
HEY, DON'T LOOK AT ME.
MAYBE A ROCK FELL FROM THE SKY!
ISN'T THAT THE KIND OF STORIES YOU MAKE UP?
Ha ha ha ha
PLOP PLOP
PLOP
HMPH, ANNOYING BRATS.
POW
SHAKE
SHAKE
WHAT THE HECK?! WOOLLY WORMS!
EWW!
EWWW!
Ha ha, that was funny!

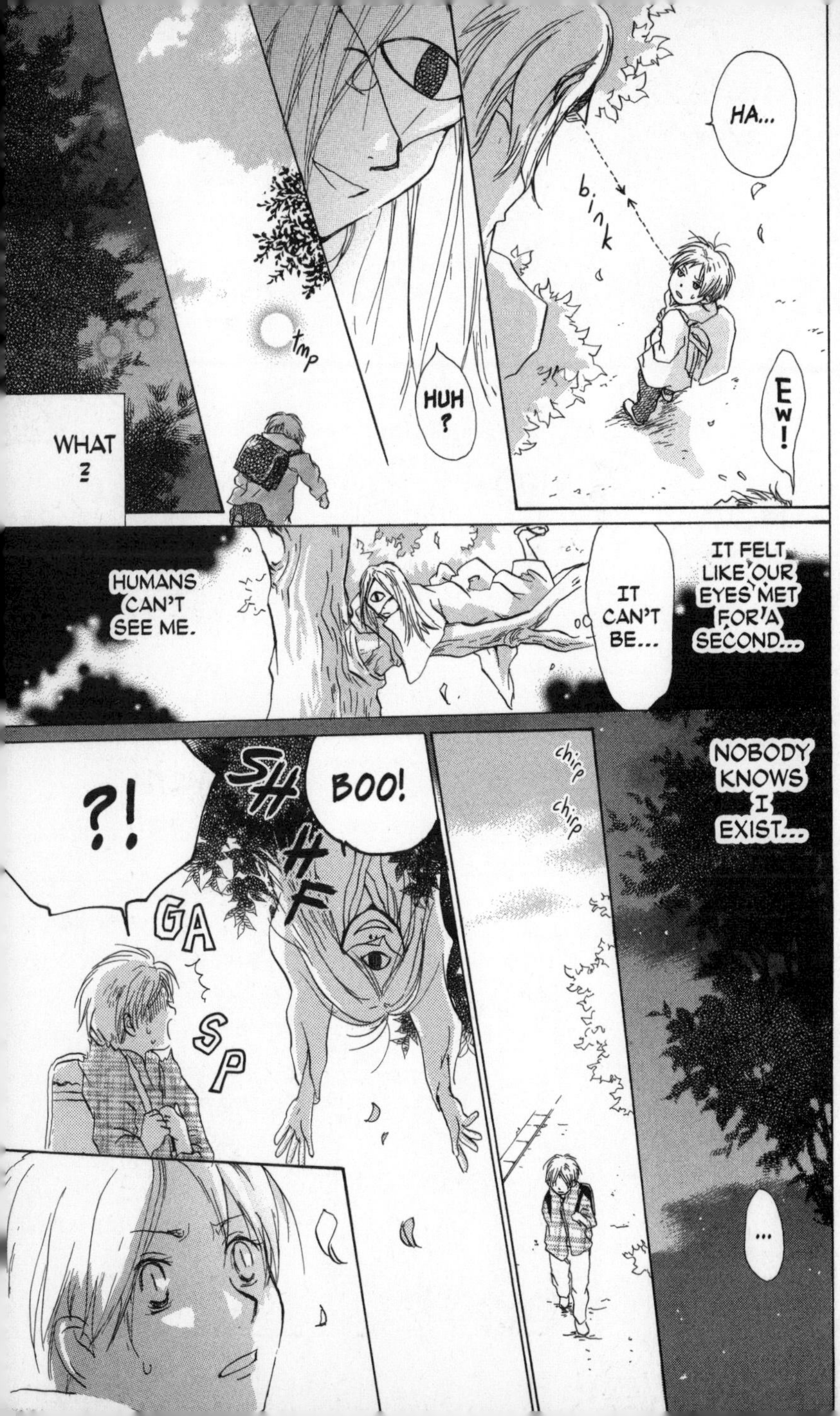
HA...
bink
EW!
HUH?
tmp
WHAT?
IT FELT LIKE OUR EYES MET FOR A SECOND...
IT CAN'T BE...
HUMANS CAN'T SEE ME.
NOBODY KNOWS I EXIST...
chirp
chirp
...
BOO!
SHHF
?!
GASP

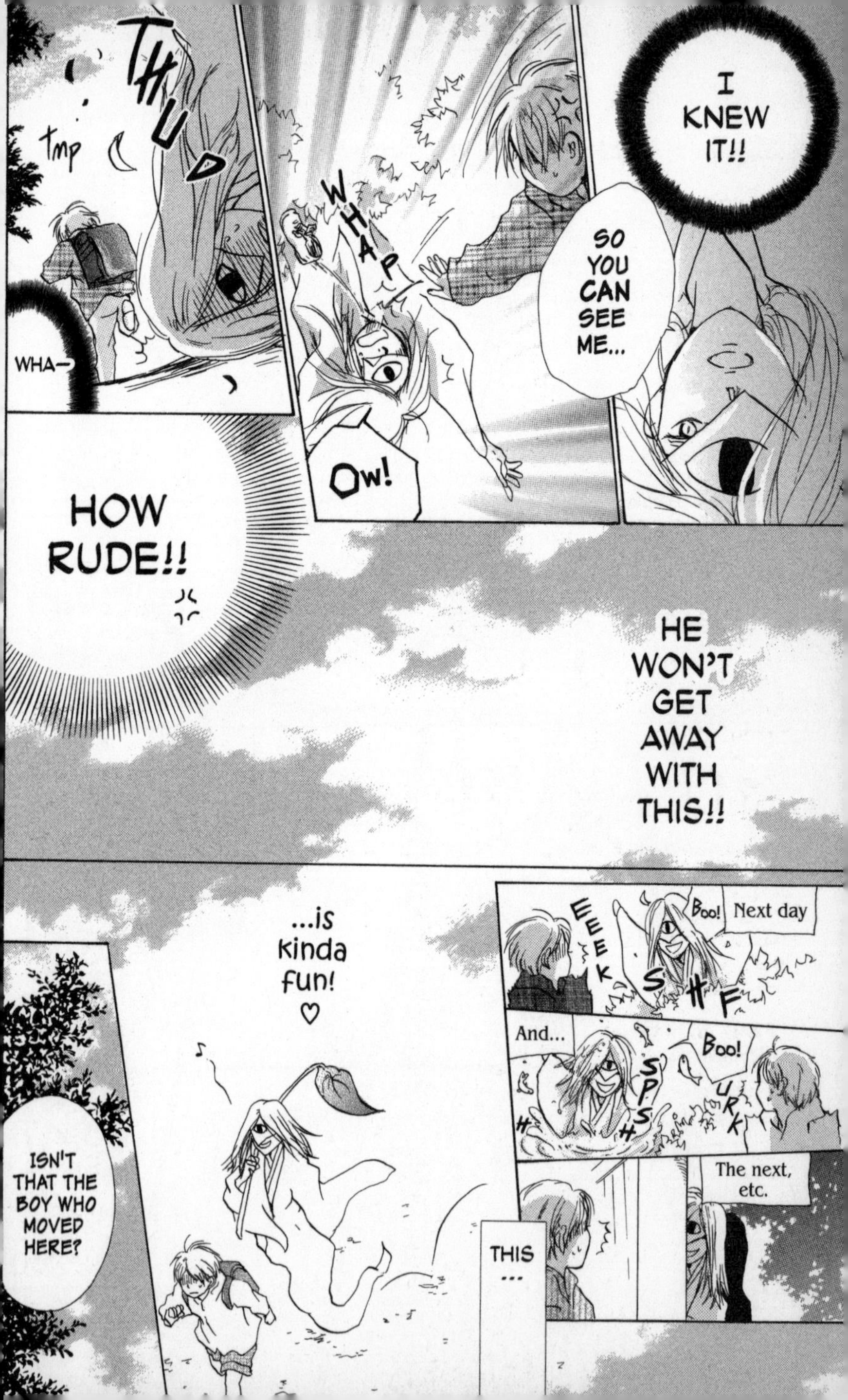
I KNEW IT!!
SO YOU CAN SEE ME...
WHAP
Ow!
THUD
tmp
WHA—
HOW RUDE!!
HE WON'T GET AWAY WITH THIS!!
Next day
Boo!
EEEEK
SHF
And...
Boo!
SPSH
URK
SPSH
The next, etc.
THIS...
...is kinda fun! ♡
ISN'T THAT THE BOY WHO MOVED HERE?

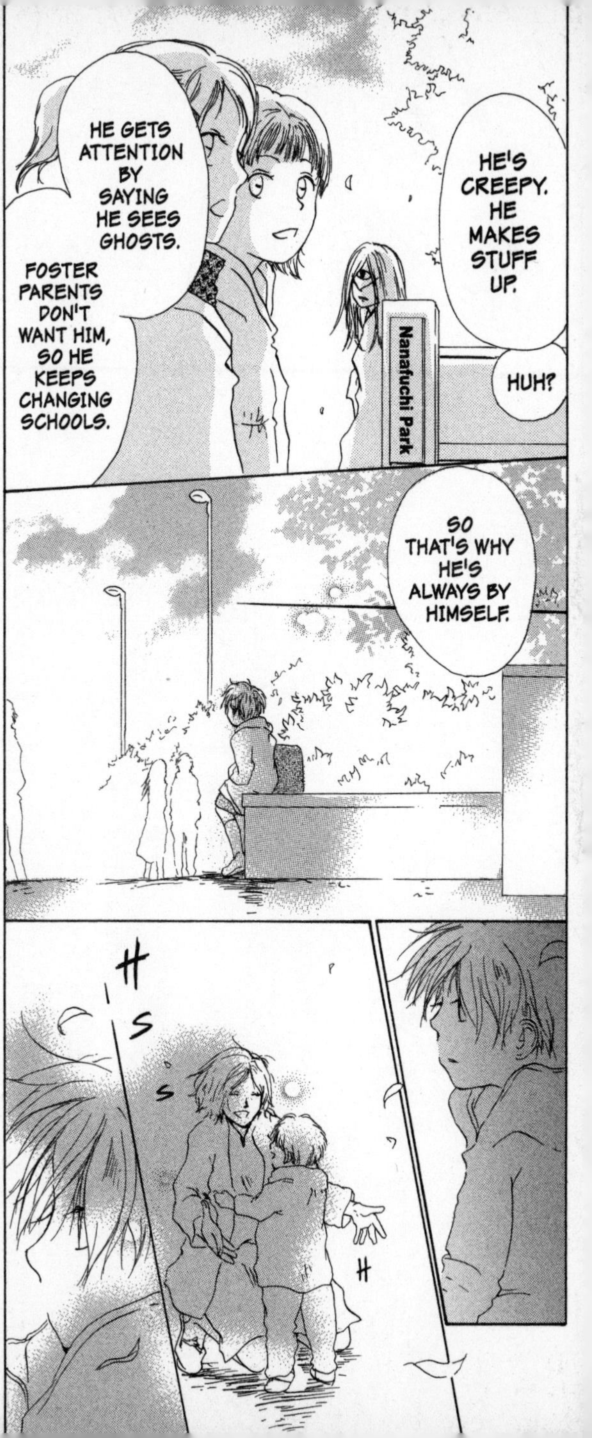
HE'S CREEPY. HE MAKES STUFF UP.
HUH?
HE GETS ATTENTION BY SAYING HE SEES GHOSTS.
FOSTER PARENTS DON'T WANT HIM, SO HE KEEPS CHANGING SCHOOLS.
Nanafuchi Park
SO THAT'S WHY HE'S ALWAYS BY HIMSELF.
H
S
S
H

08

Working with the general nuances I felt, opinions from others, and the wonderful voices of candidates the CD production company offered, we were able to smoothly decide the direction we wanted to take. I was afraid there might be discrepancies from what the readers had imagined, but I was so happy to be involved in a different form of Natsume.

It'll be included in the October issue of LaLa, on sale in August 2007. So please check it out if you're interested.

It turned out to be a wonderful incarnation of "The Swallow Underwater" thanks to the voice actors and the staff.

Thanks to everyone for their support.

End of 1/4 columns.

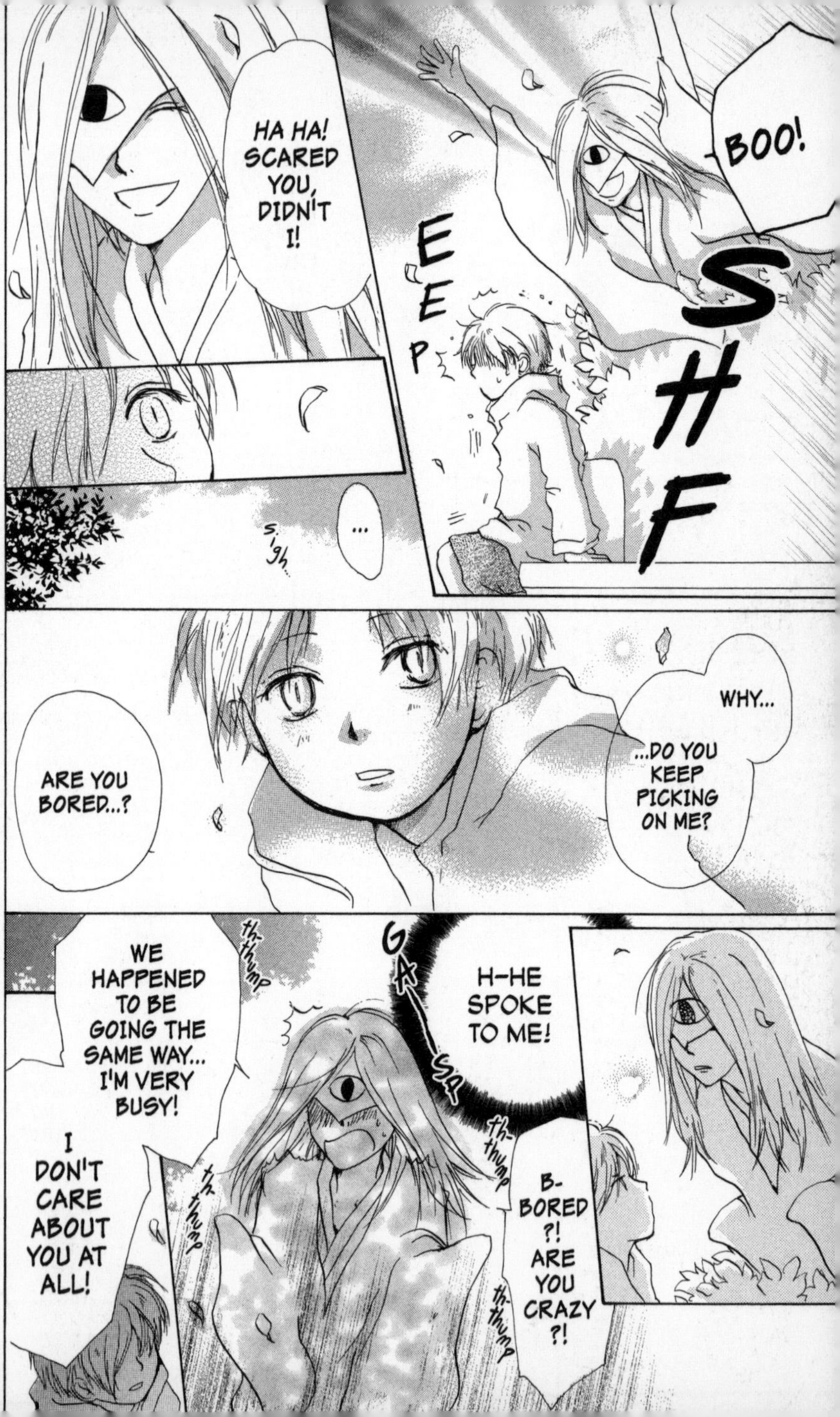
BOO!
SHF
EEEP
HA HA! SCARED YOU, DIDN'T I!
...
sigh...
WHY...
...DO YOU KEEP PICKING ON ME?
ARE YOU BORED...?
GASA
H-HE SPOKE TO ME!
th-thump
B-BORED?! ARE YOU CRAZY?!
th-thump
th-thump
th-thump
WE HAPPENED TO BE GOING THE SAME WAY... I'M VERY BUSY!
I DON'T CARE ABOUT YOU AT ALL!

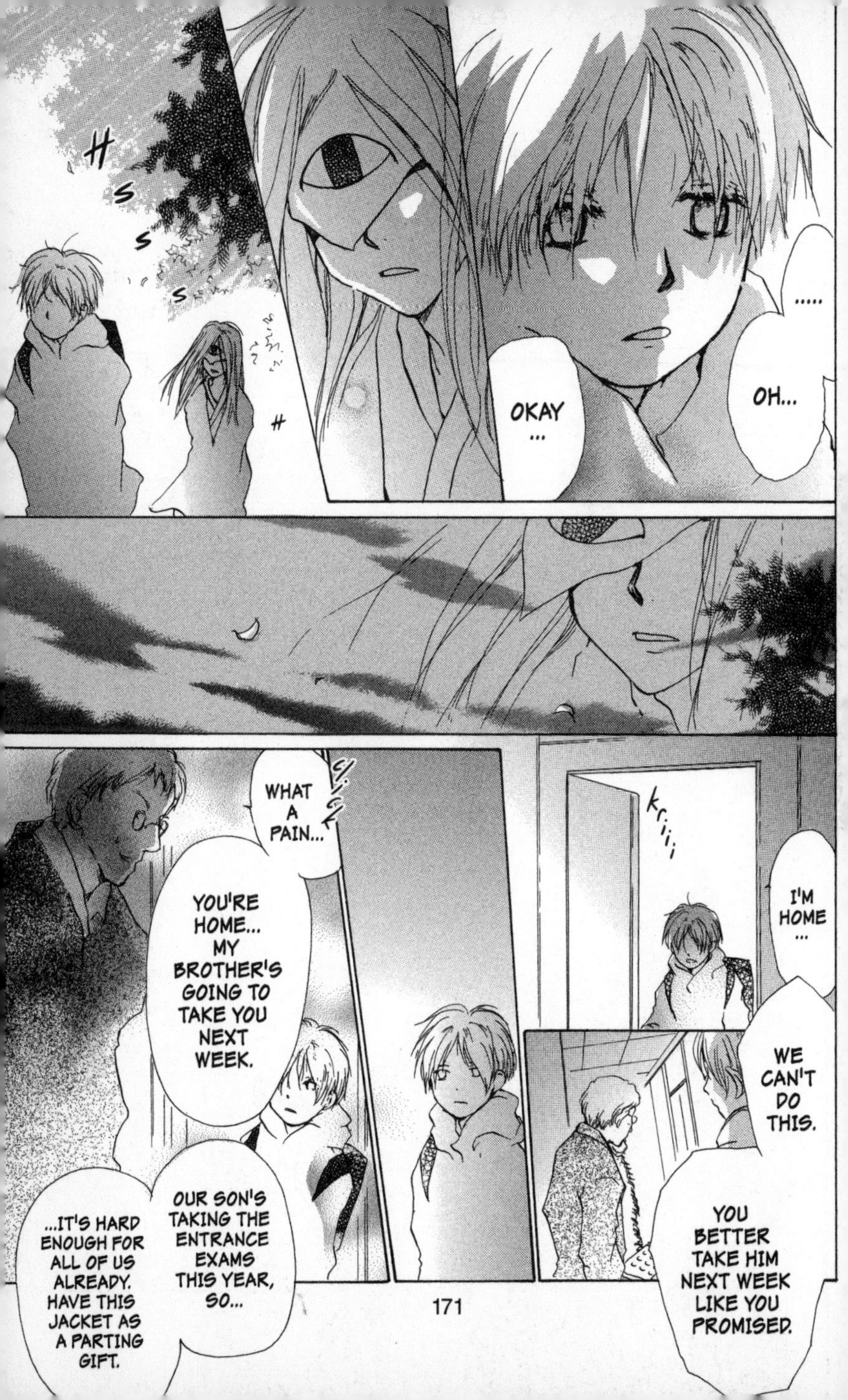
.....
OH...
OKAY ...
HSSS
H
I'M HOME ...
WE CAN'T DO THIS.
YOU BETTER TAKE HIM NEXT WEEK LIKE YOU PROMISED.
WHAT A PAIN...
YOU'RE HOME... MY BROTHER'S GOING TO TAKE YOU NEXT WEEK.
OUR SON'S TAKING THE ENTRANCE EXAMS THIS YEAR, SO...
...IT'S HARD ENOUGH FOR ALL OF US ALREADY. HAVE THIS JACKET AS A PARTING GIFT.

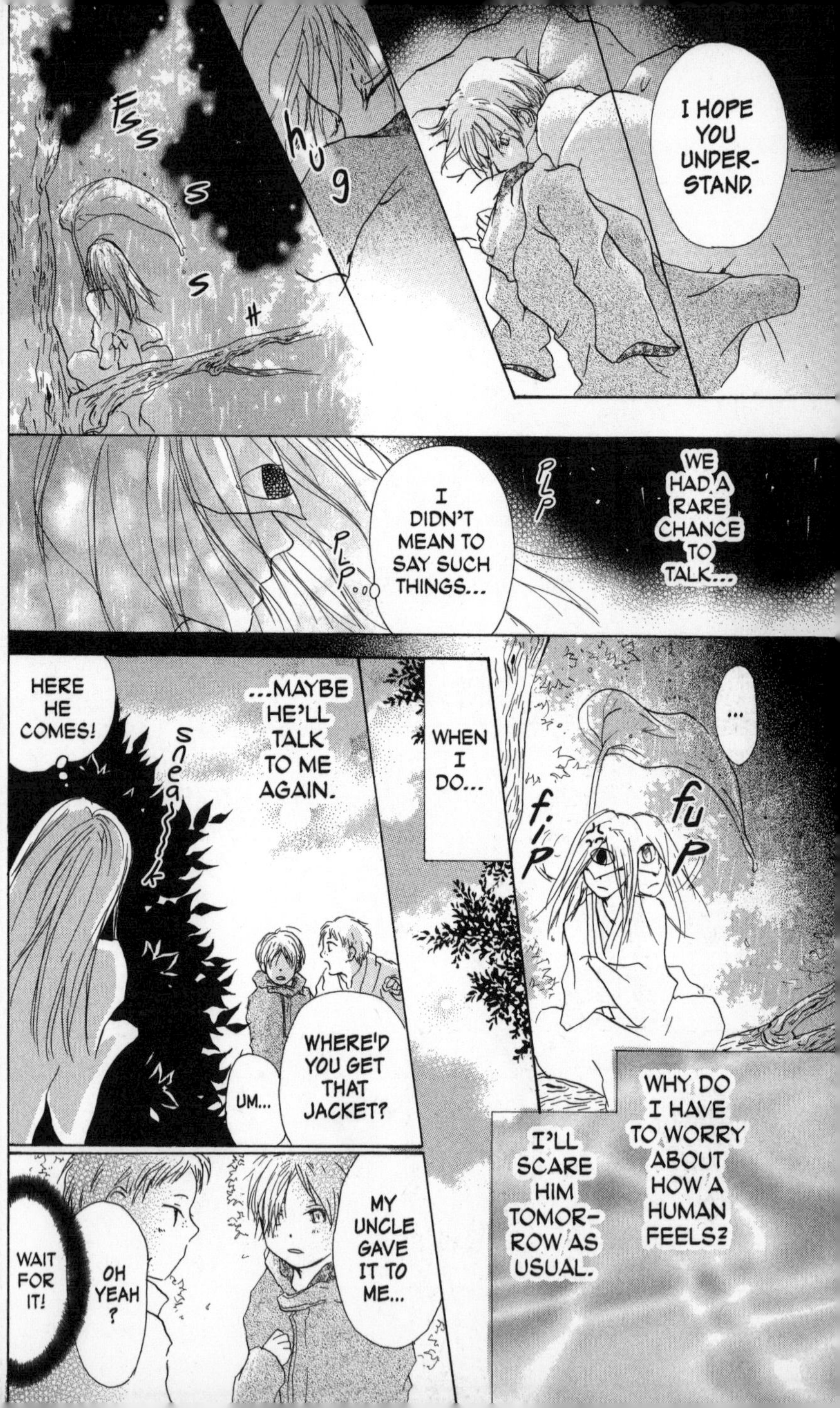

I HOPE YOU UNDER-STAND.
hug
Fssssh
WE HAD A RARE CHANCE TO TALK...
PLP
I DIDN'T MEAN TO SAY SUCH THINGS...
PLP
...
fup
flip
WHEN I DO...
...MAYBE HE'LL TALK TO ME AGAIN.
HERE HE COMES!
sneak
WHERE'D YOU GET THAT JACKET?
UM...
WHY DO I HAVE TO WORRY ABOUT HOW A HUMAN FEELS?
I'LL SCARE HIM TOMOR-ROW AS USUAL.
MY UNCLE GAVE IT TO ME...
OH YEAH?
WAIT FOR IT!

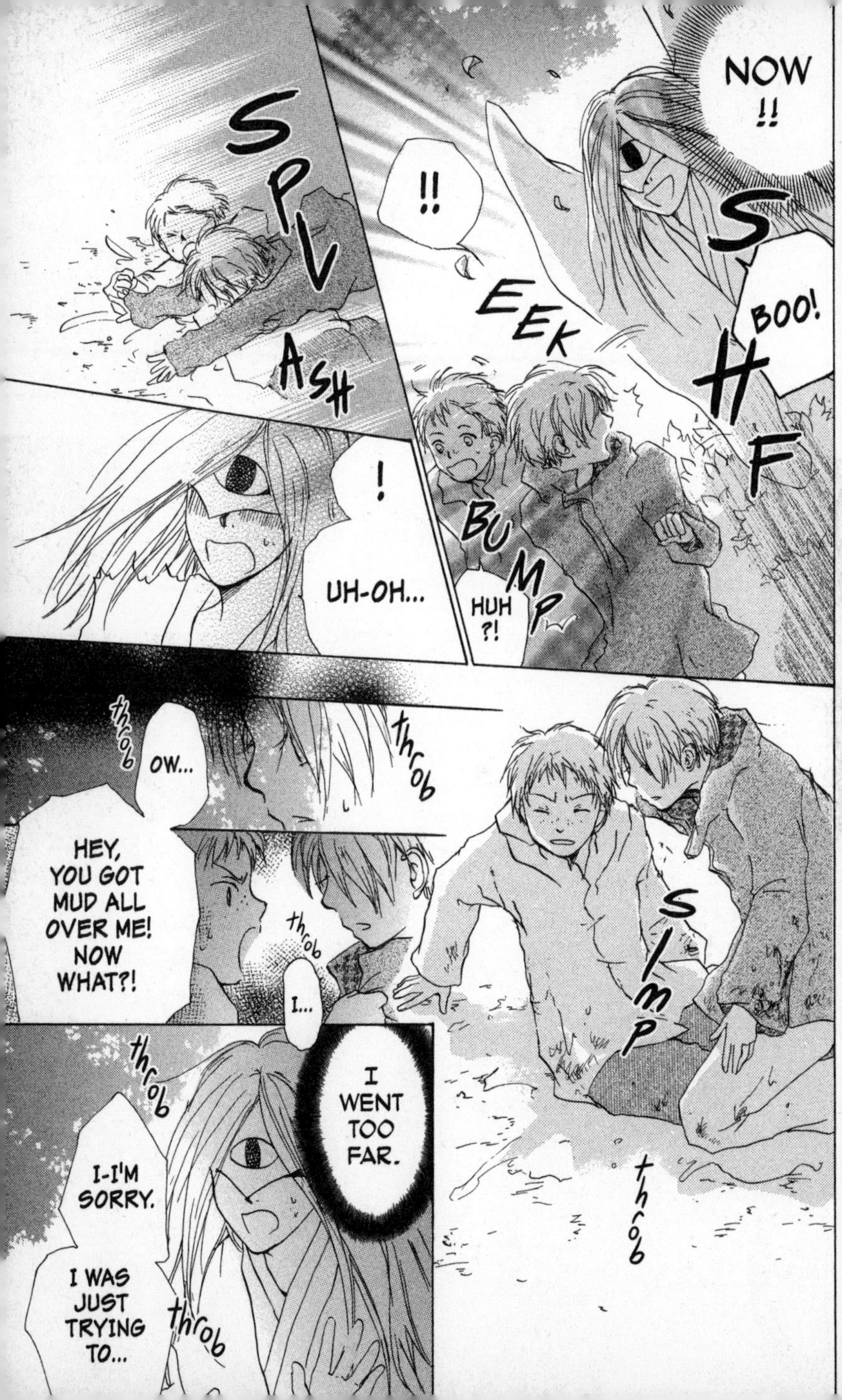
NOW !!
SHF
BOO!
!!
EEK
BUMP
HUH ?!
SPLASH
!
UH-OH...
SLMP
throb
throb
OW...
throb
HEY, YOU GOT MUD ALL OVER ME! NOW WHAT?!
throb
I...
throb
I WENT TOO FAR.
I-I'M SORRY.
I WAS JUST TRYING TO...
throb

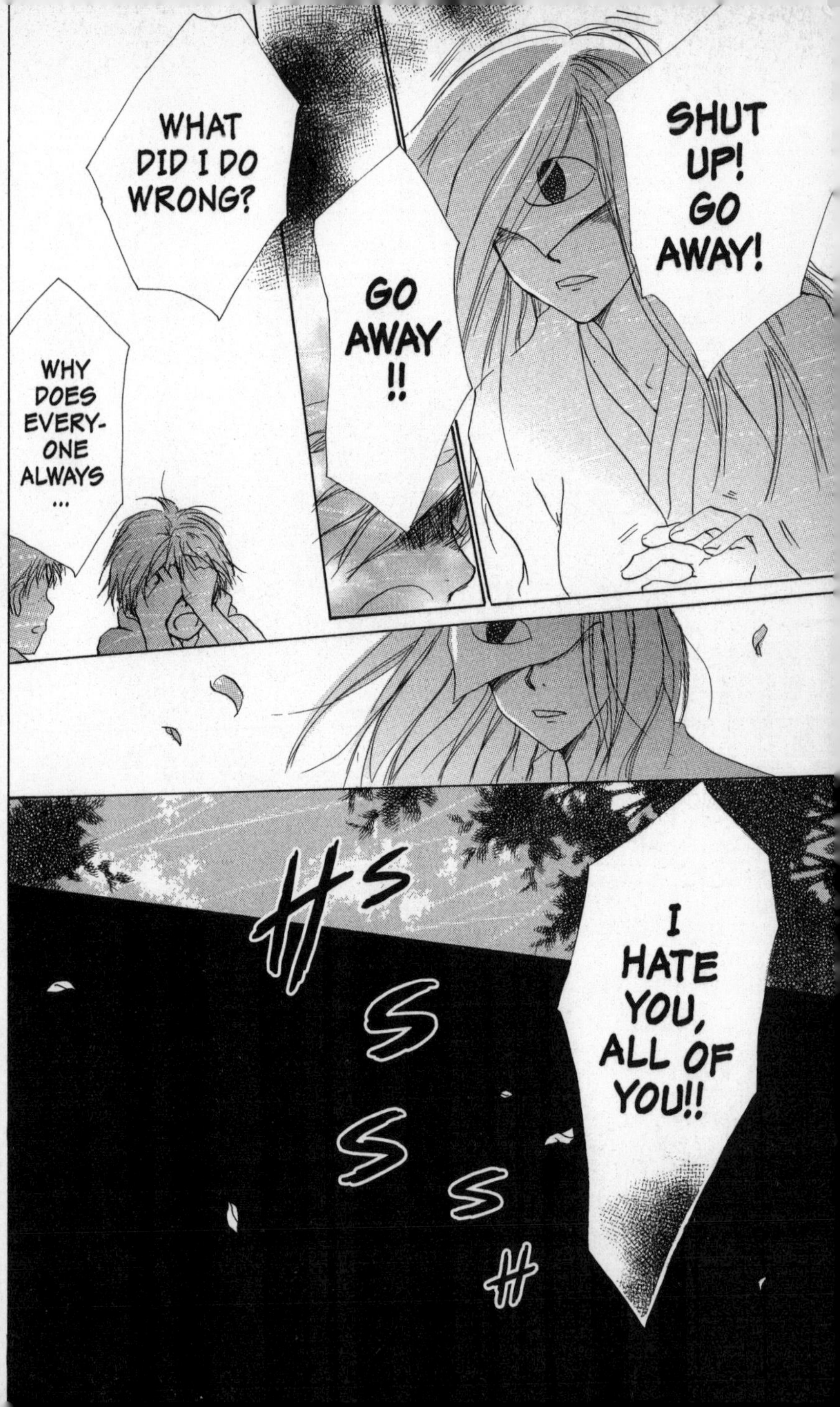
SHUT UP! GO AWAY!
GO AWAY !!
WHAT DID I DO WRONG?
WHY DOES EVERY-ONE ALWAYS ...
I HATE YOU, ALL OF YOU!!
HSSSSH

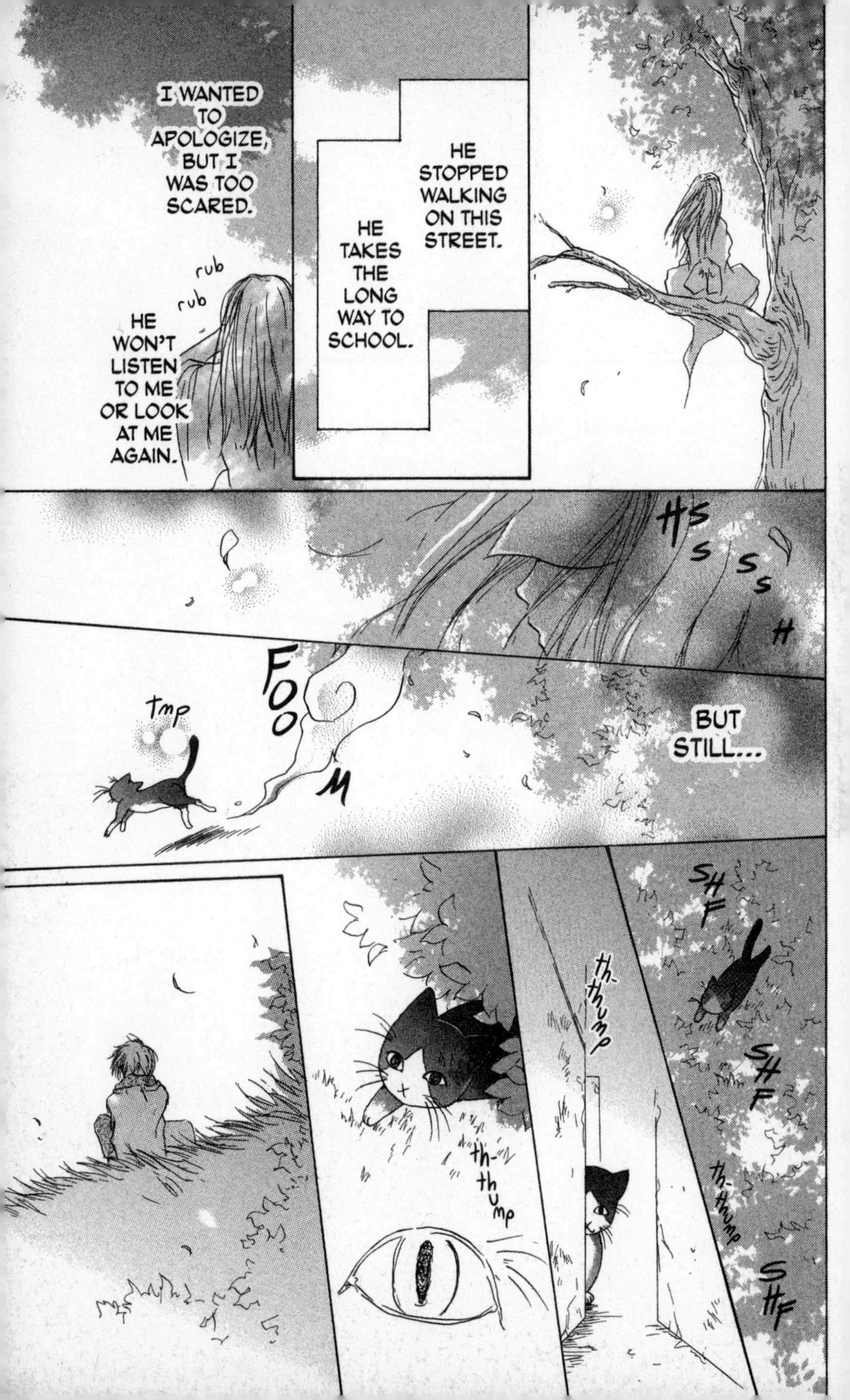
HE STOPPED WALKING ON THIS STREET.
HE TAKES THE LONG WAY TO SCHOOL.
I WANTED TO APOLOGIZE, BUT I WAS TOO SCARED.
rub
rub
HE WON'T LISTEN TO ME OR LOOK AT ME AGAIN.
HSSSSH
BUT STILL...
FOOM
tmp
SHF
SHF
th-thump
SHF
th-thump
th-thump

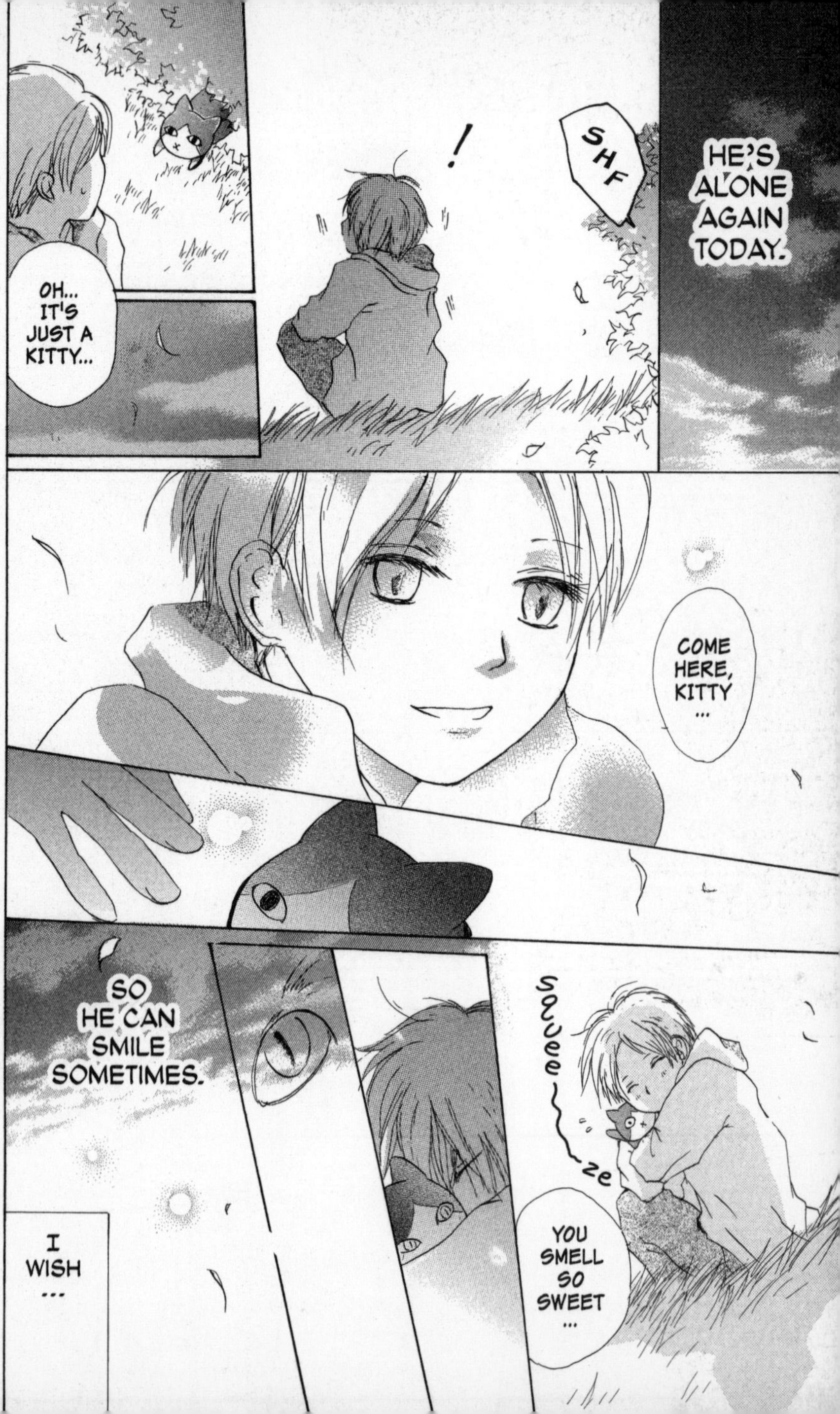

HE'S ALONE AGAIN TODAY.
SHF
!
OH... IT'S JUST A KITTY...
COME HERE, KITTY ...
SQuee~ze
YOU SMELL SO SWEET ...
SO HE CAN SMILE SOMETIMES.
I WISH ...

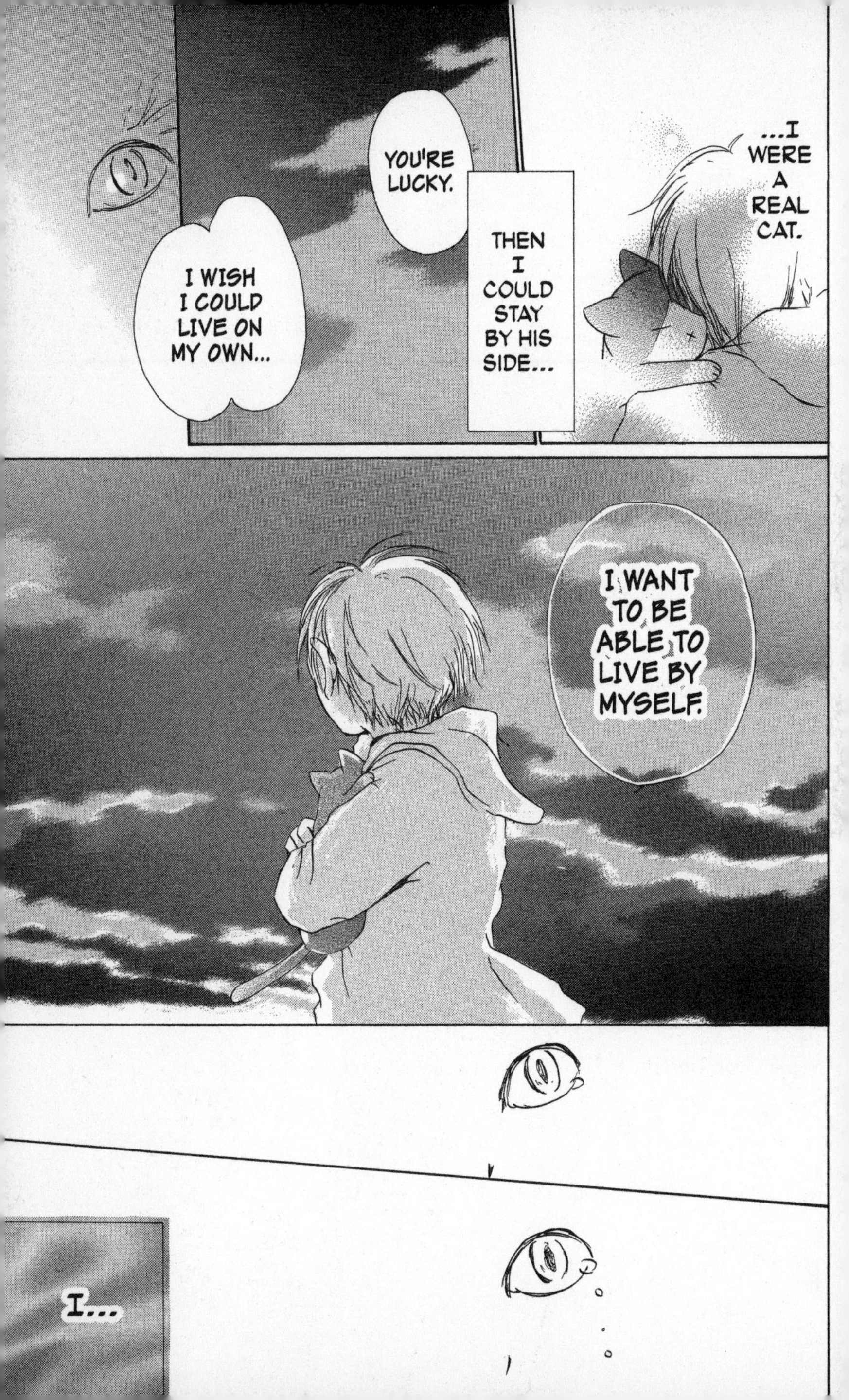
...I WERE A REAL CAT.
THEN I COULD STAY BY HIS SIDE...
YOU'RE LUCKY.
I WISH I COULD LIVE ON MY OWN...
I WANT TO BE ABLE TO LIVE BY MYSELF.
I...

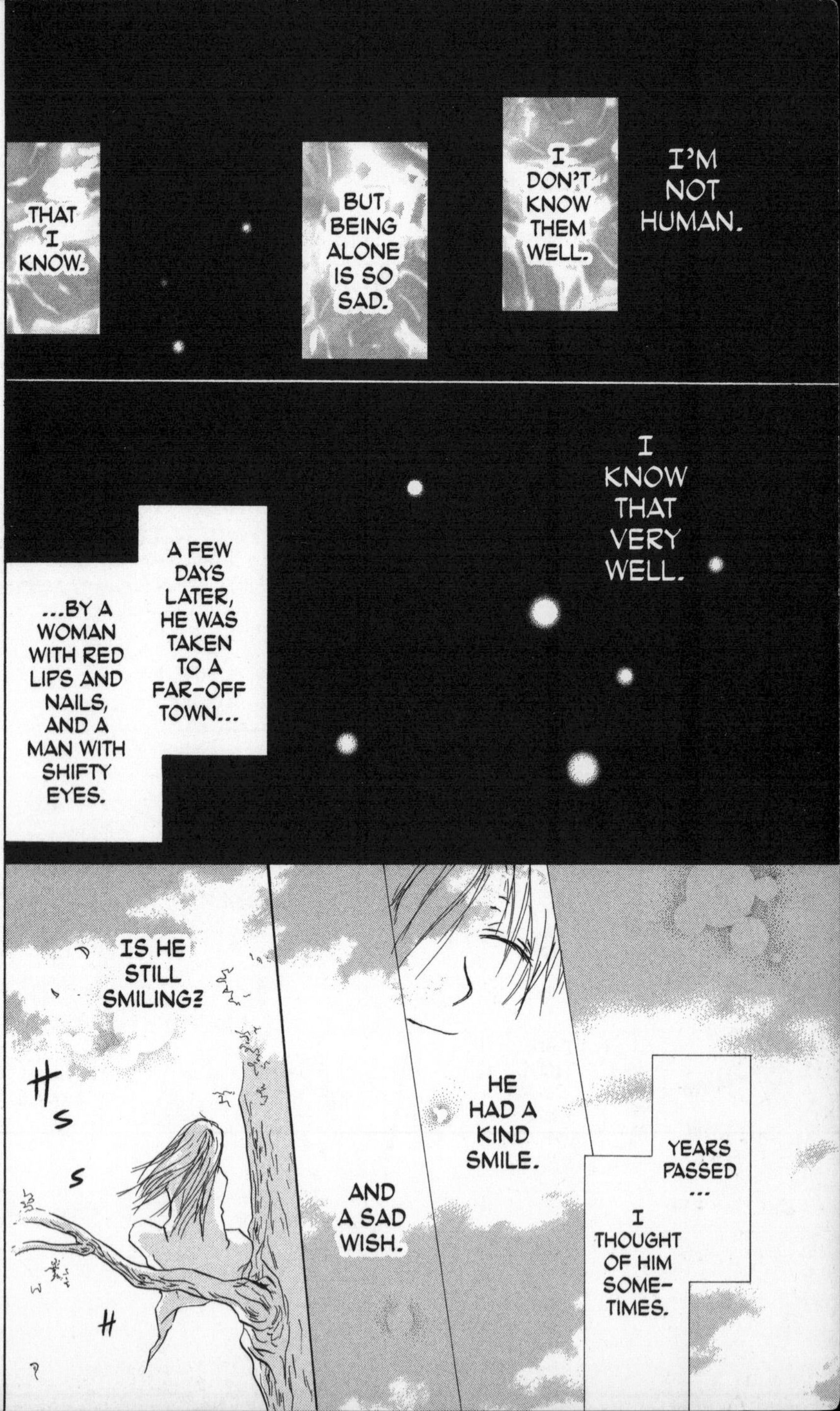
I'M NOT HUMAN.
I DON'T KNOW THEM WELL.
BUT BEING ALONE IS SO SAD.
THAT I KNOW.
I KNOW THAT VERY WELL.
A FEW DAYS LATER, HE WAS TAKEN TO A FAR-OFF TOWN...
...BY A WOMAN WITH RED LIPS AND NAILS, AND A MAN WITH SHIFTY EYES.
YEARS PASSED...
I THOUGHT OF HIM SOME-TIMES.
HE HAD A KIND SMILE.
AND A SAD WISH.
IS HE STILL SMILING?
HSSH

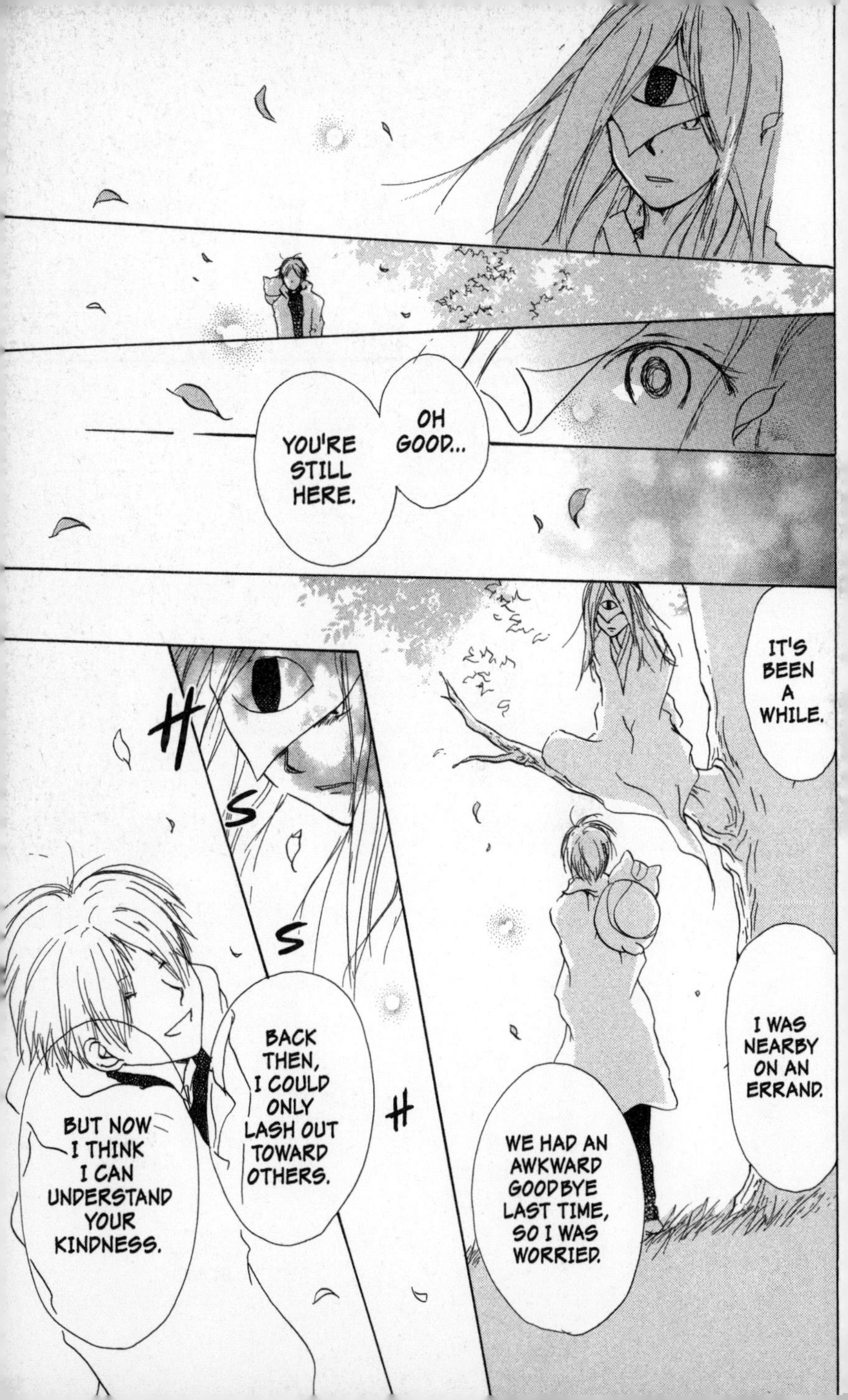
OH GOOD...
YOU'RE STILL HERE.
IT'S BEEN A WHILE.
I WAS NEARBY ON AN ERRAND.
WE HAD AN AWKWARD GOODBYE LAST TIME, SO I WAS WORRIED.
HSSH
BACK THEN, I COULD ONLY LASH OUT TOWARD OTHERS.
BUT NOW I THINK I CAN UNDERSTAND YOUR KINDNESS.

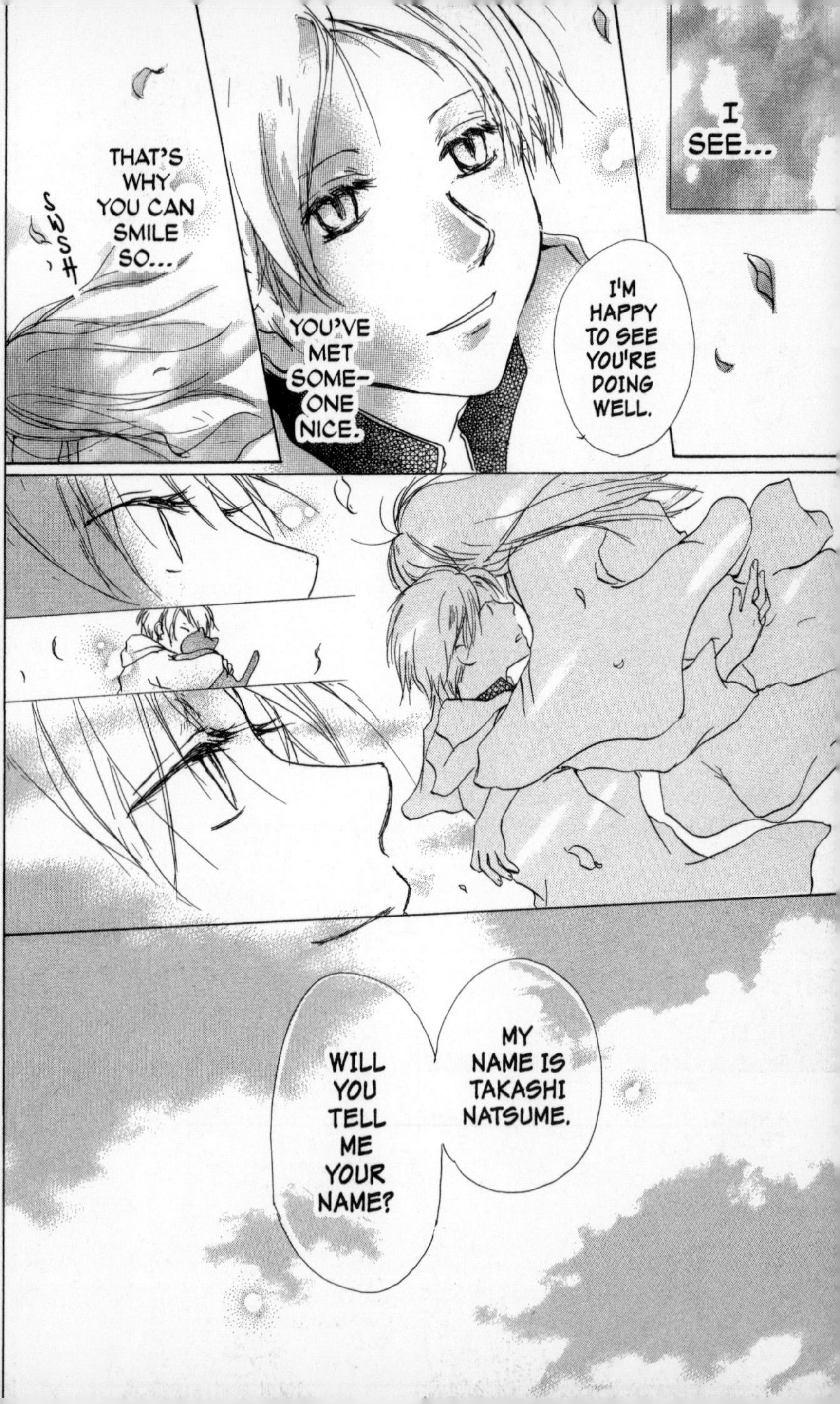
I SEE...
I'M HAPPY TO SEE YOU'RE DOING WELL.
YOU'VE MET SOME-ONE NICE.
THAT'S WHY YOU CAN SMILE SO...
SWSH
MY NAME IS TAKASHI NATSUME.
WILL YOU TELL ME YOUR NAME?

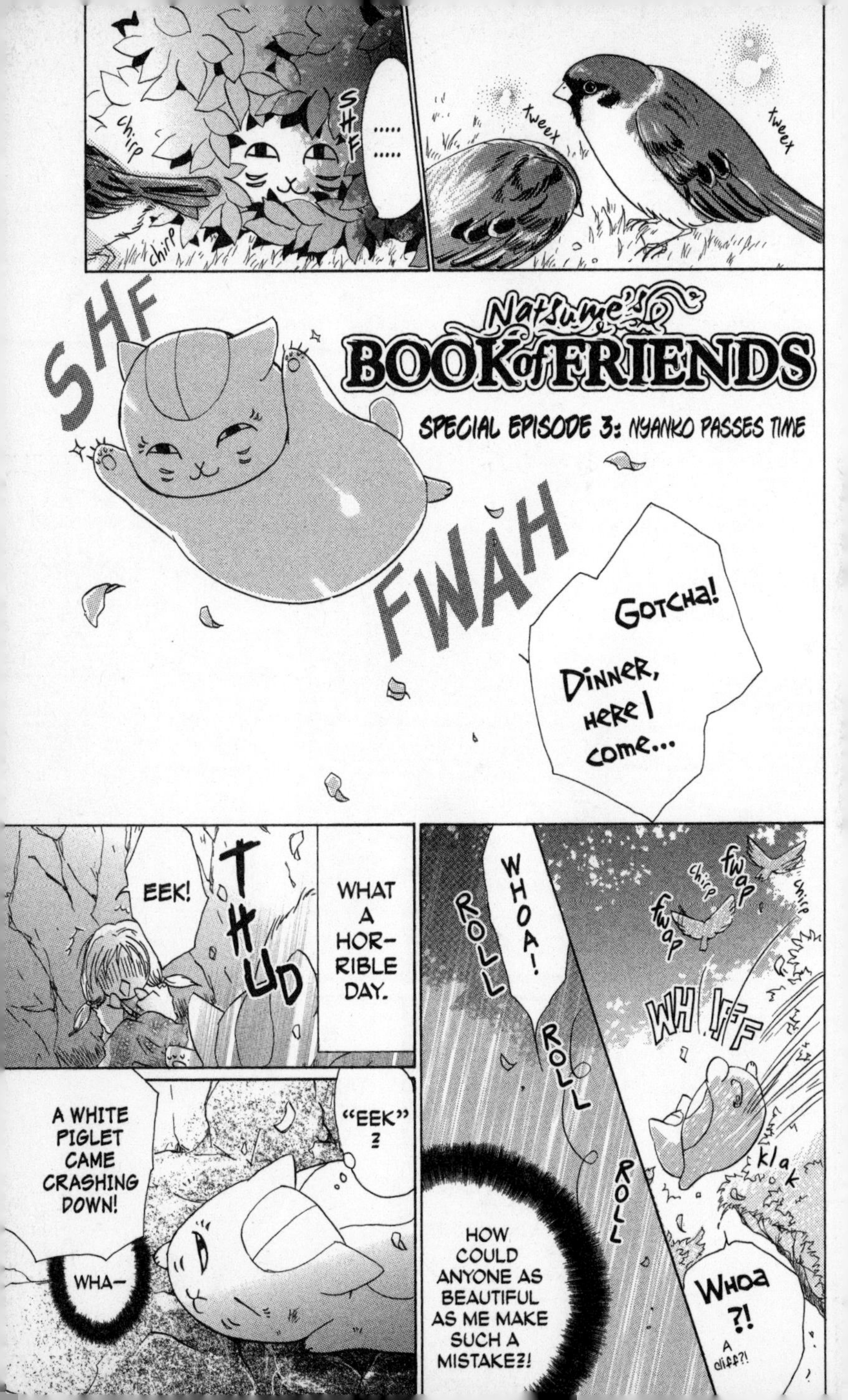
tweet
tweet
......
......
SHF
chirp
chirp
Natsume's BOOK of FRIENDS
SPECIAL EPISODE 3: NYANKO PASSES TIME
Gotcha!
Dinner, here I come...
FWAH
SHF
WHOA!
ROLL
ROLL
ROLL
fwap
chirp
chirp
fwap
WHIFF
klak
Whoa?!
A cliff?!
HOW COULD ANYONE AS BEAUTIFUL AS ME MAKE SUCH A MISTAKE?!
WHAT A HOR-RIBLE DAY.
THUD
EEK!
"EEK"?
A WHITE PIGLET CAME CRASHING DOWN!
WHA-

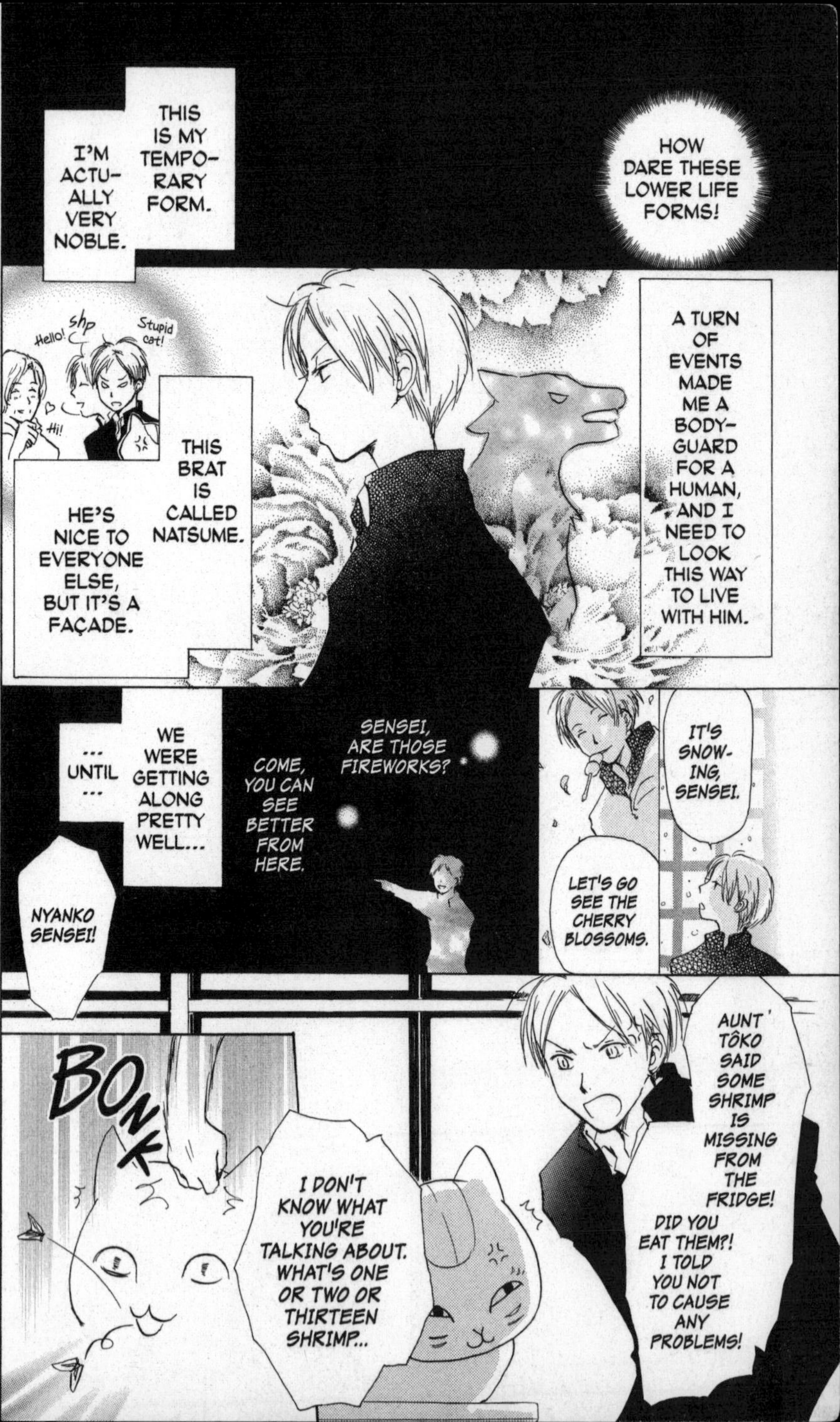
HOW DARE THESE LOWER LIFE FORMS!
THIS IS MY TEMPORARY FORM.
I'M ACTUALLY VERY NOBLE.
A TURN OF EVENTS MADE ME A BODYGUARD FOR A HUMAN, AND I NEED TO LOOK THIS WAY TO LIVE WITH HIM.
THIS BRAT IS CALLED NATSUME.
Stupid cat!
shp
Hello!
Hi!
HE'S NICE TO EVERYONE ELSE, BUT IT'S A FAÇADE.
IT'S SNOWING, SENSEI.
LET'S GO SEE THE CHERRY BLOSSOMS.
SENSEI, ARE THOSE FIREWORKS?
COME, YOU CAN SEE BETTER FROM HERE.
WE WERE GETTING ALONG PRETTY WELL...
... UNTIL ...
NYANKO SENSEI!
AUNT TÔKO SAID SOME SHRIMP IS MISSING FROM THE FRIDGE!
DID YOU EAT THEM?! I TOLD YOU NOT TO CAUSE ANY PROBLEMS!
I DON'T KNOW WHAT YOU'RE TALKING ABOUT. WHAT'S ONE OR TWO OR THIRTEEN SHRIMP...
BONK

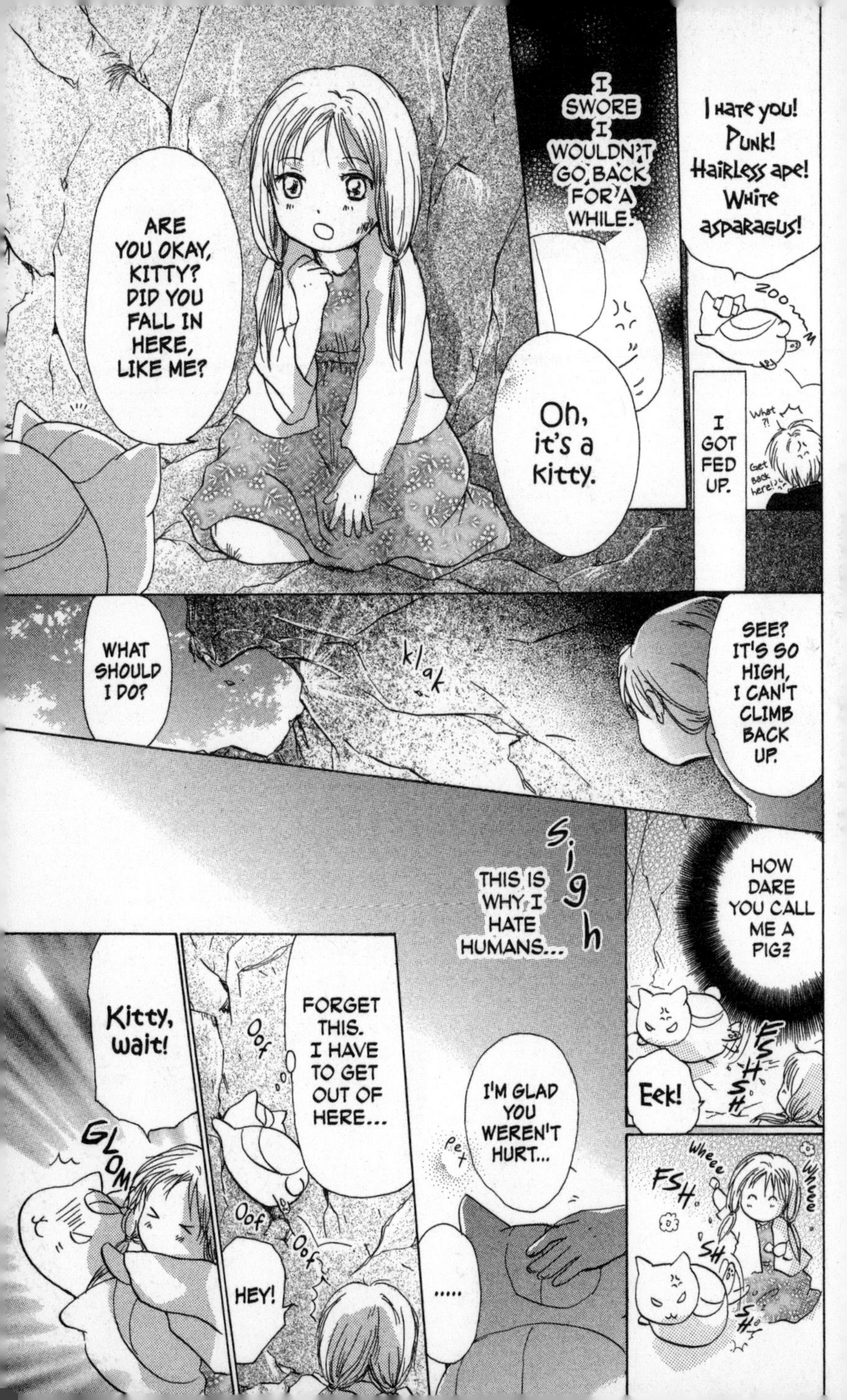

I hate you! Punk! Hairless ape! White asparagus!
ZOOOM
I GOT FED UP.
What?!
Get back here!!
I SWORE I WOULDN'T GO BACK FOR A WHILE!
Oh, it's a kitty.
ARE YOU OKAY, KITTY? DID YOU FALL IN HERE, LIKE ME?
SEE? IT'S SO HIGH, I CAN'T CLIMB BACK UP.
klak
WHAT SHOULD I DO?
HOW DARE YOU CALL ME A PIG?
FSHH SHH
Eek!
Wheee
FSH
SH
Wheee
SH
THIS IS WHY I HATE HUMANS...
sigh
I'M GLAD YOU WEREN'T HURT...
pet
.....
FORGET THIS. I HAVE TO GET OUT OF HERE...
Oof
Oof
Oof
HEY!
Kitty, wait!
GLOM

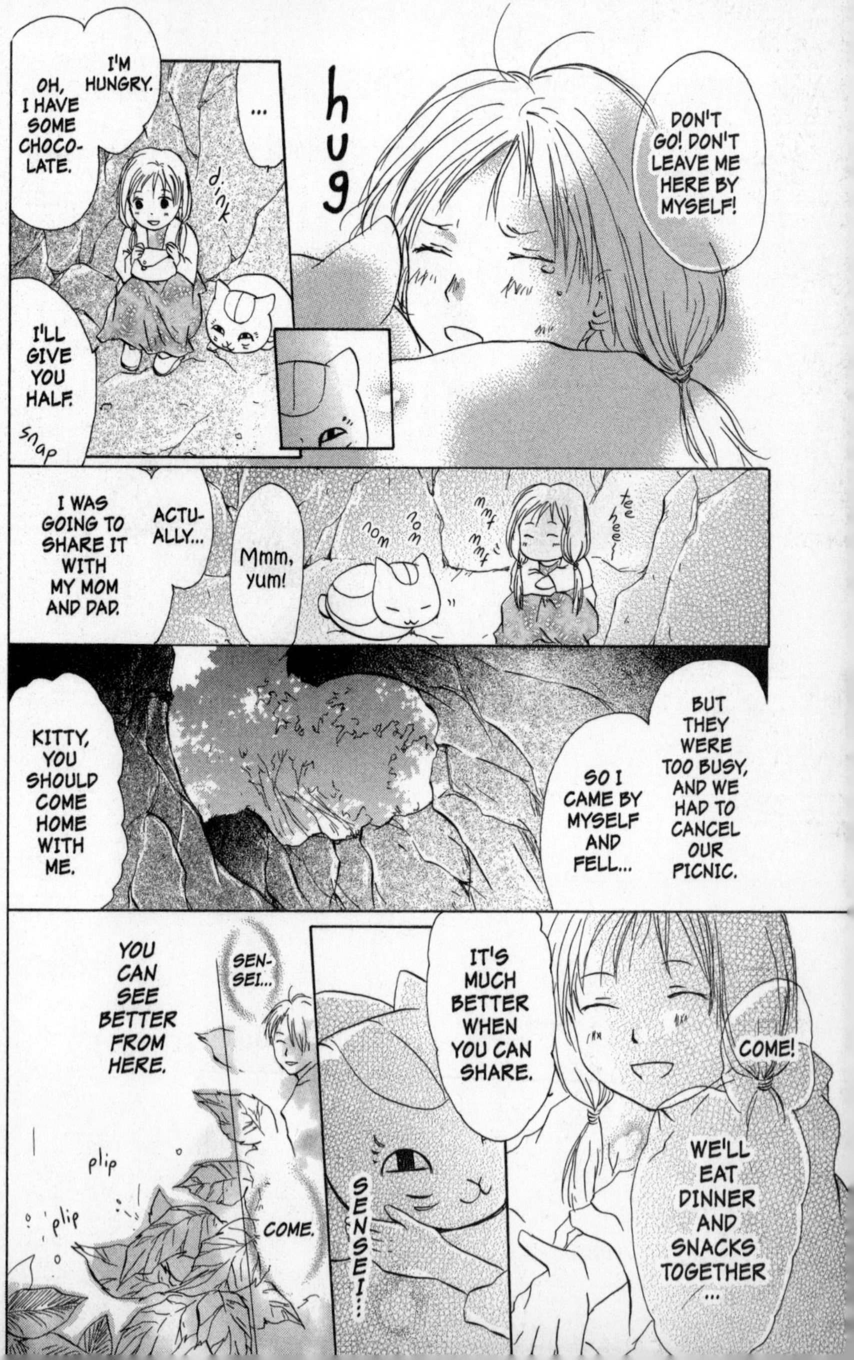
hug
DON'T GO! DON'T LEAVE ME HERE BY MYSELF!
...
dink
I'M HUNGRY.
OH, I HAVE SOME CHOCO-LATE.
I'LL GIVE YOU HALF.
snap
tee hee~
mmf mmf
nom nom
Mmm, yum!
ACTU-ALLY...
I WAS GOING TO SHARE IT WITH MY MOM AND DAD.
BUT THEY WERE TOO BUSY, AND WE HAD TO CANCEL OUR PICNIC.
SO I CAME BY MYSELF AND FELL...
KITTY, YOU SHOULD COME HOME WITH ME.
COME!
IT'S MUCH BETTER WHEN YOU CAN SHARE.
WE'LL EAT DINNER AND SNACKS TOGETHER...
SENSEI...
SEN-SEI...
YOU CAN SEE BETTER FROM HERE.
plip
plip
COME.

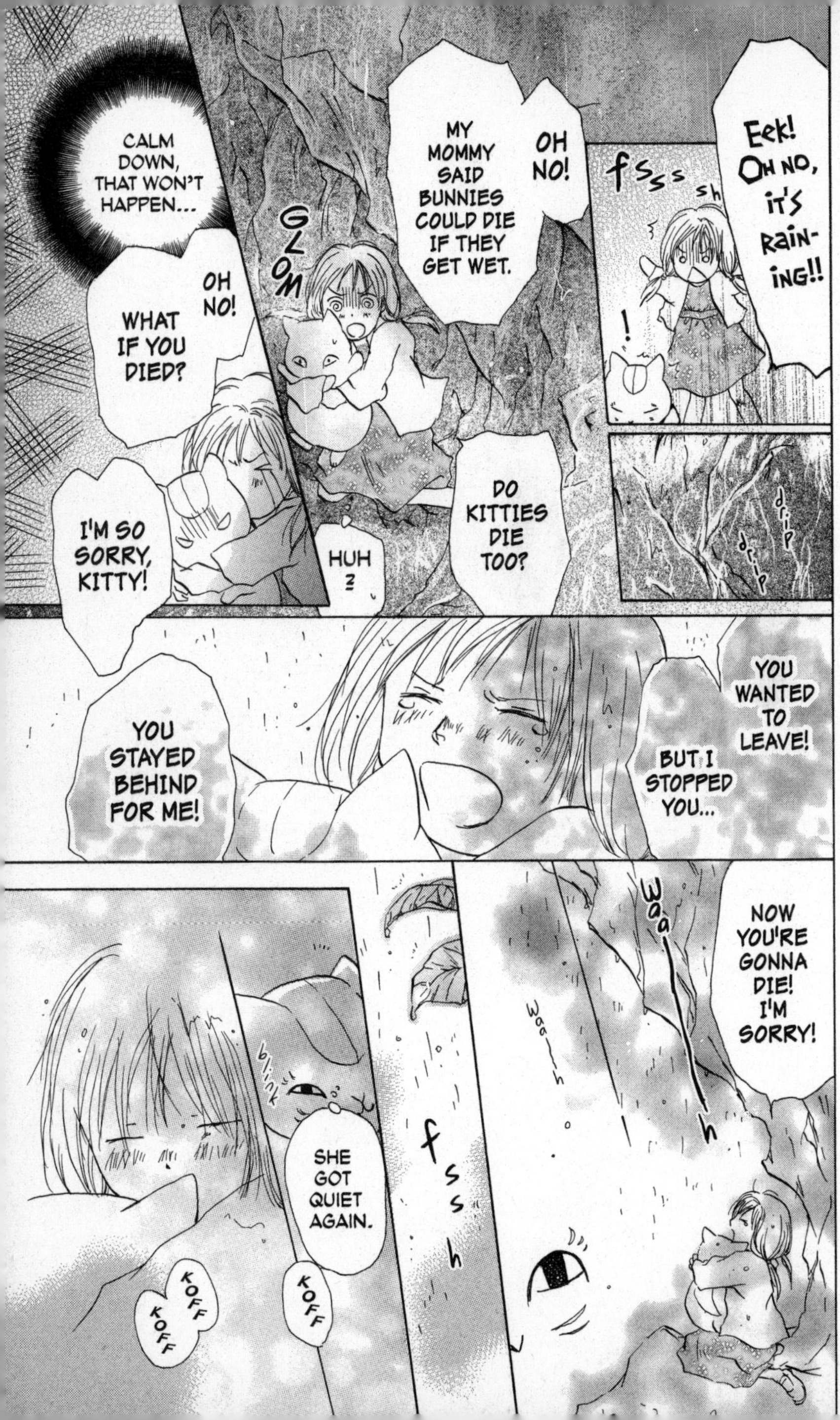
Eek! Oh no, it's raining!!
fsssh
!
drip drip
OH NO!
MY MOMMY SAID BUNNIES COULD DIE IF THEY GET WET.
GLOM
DO KITTIES DIE TOO?
HUH?
CALM DOWN, THAT WON'T HAPPEN...
OH NO!
WHAT IF YOU DIED?
I'M SO SORRY, KITTY!
YOU WANTED TO LEAVE!
BUT I STOPPED YOU...
YOU STAYED BEHIND FOR ME!
NOW YOU'RE GONNA DIE! I'M SORRY!
Waa—h
Waa—h
fssh
blink
SHE GOT QUIET AGAIN.
KOFF
KOFF KOFF

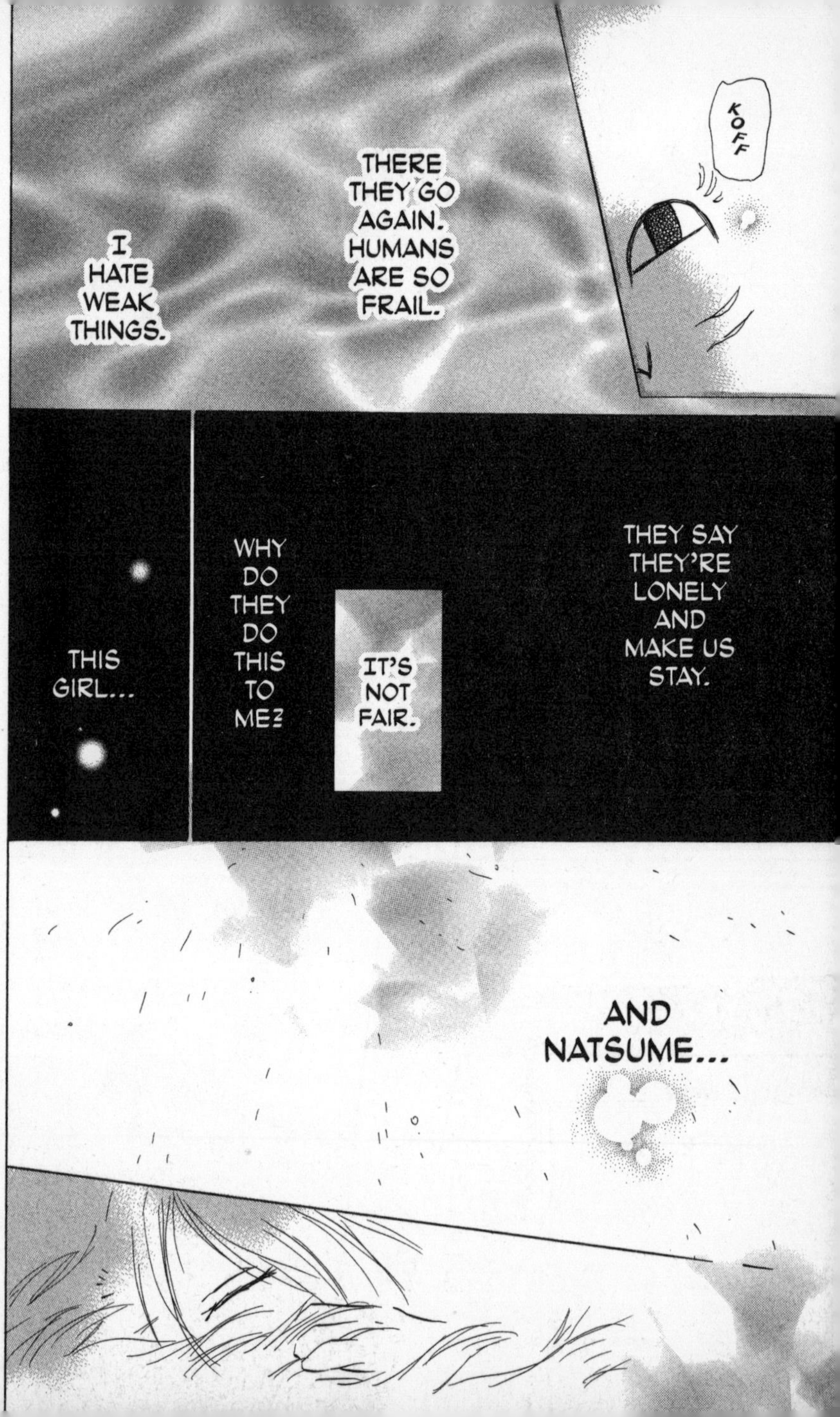
KOFF
THERE THEY GO AGAIN. HUMANS ARE SO FRAIL.
I HATE WEAK THINGS.
THEY SAY THEY'RE LONELY AND MAKE US STAY.
IT'S NOT FAIR.
WHY DO THEY DO THIS TO ME?
THIS GIRL...
AND NATSUME...

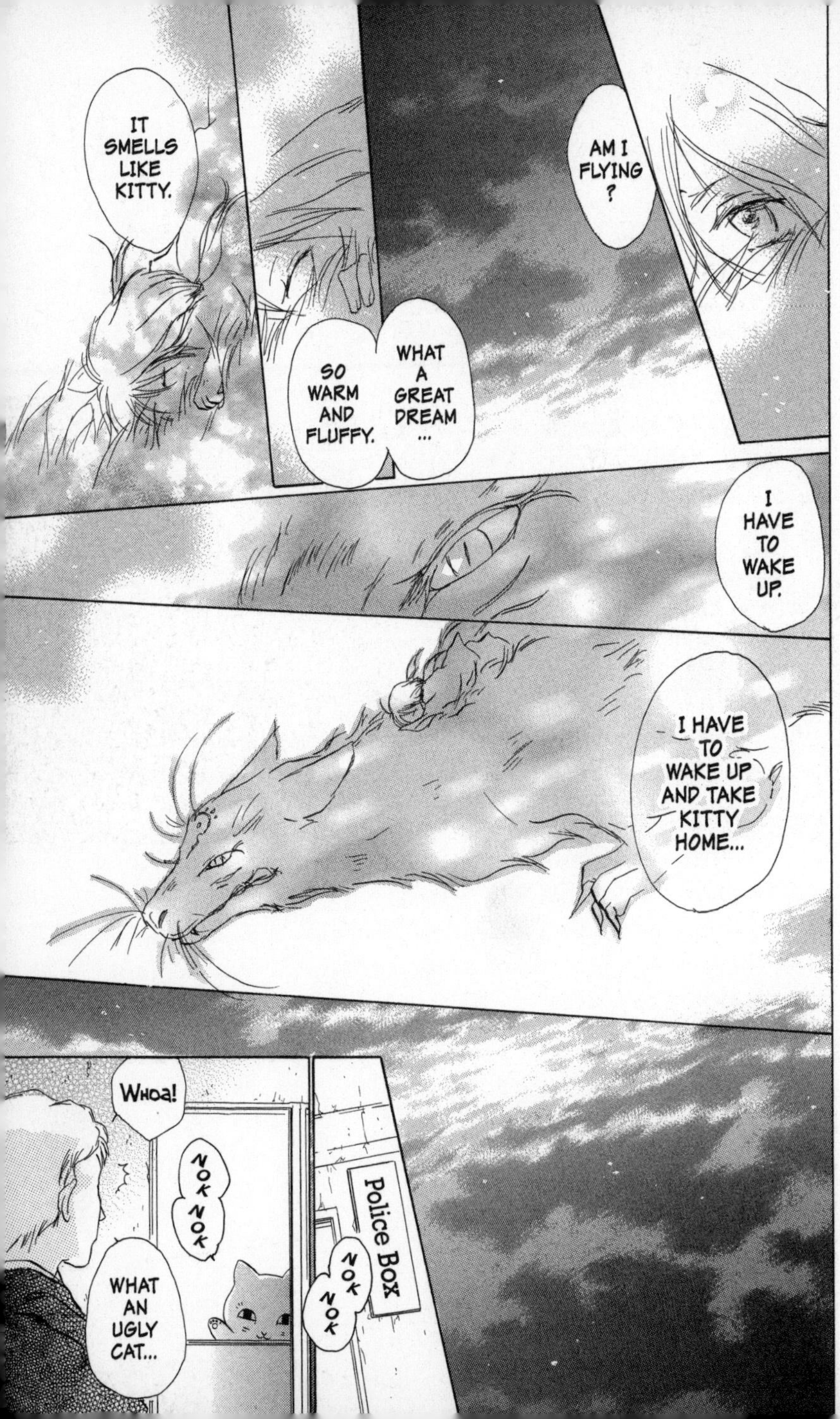
AM I FLYING?
WHAT A GREAT DREAM...
SO WARM AND FLUFFY.
IT SMELLS LIKE KITTY.
I HAVE TO WAKE UP.
I HAVE TO WAKE UP AND TAKE KITTY HOME...
Whoa!
NOK NOK
Police Box
NOK NOK
WHAT AN UGLY CAT...

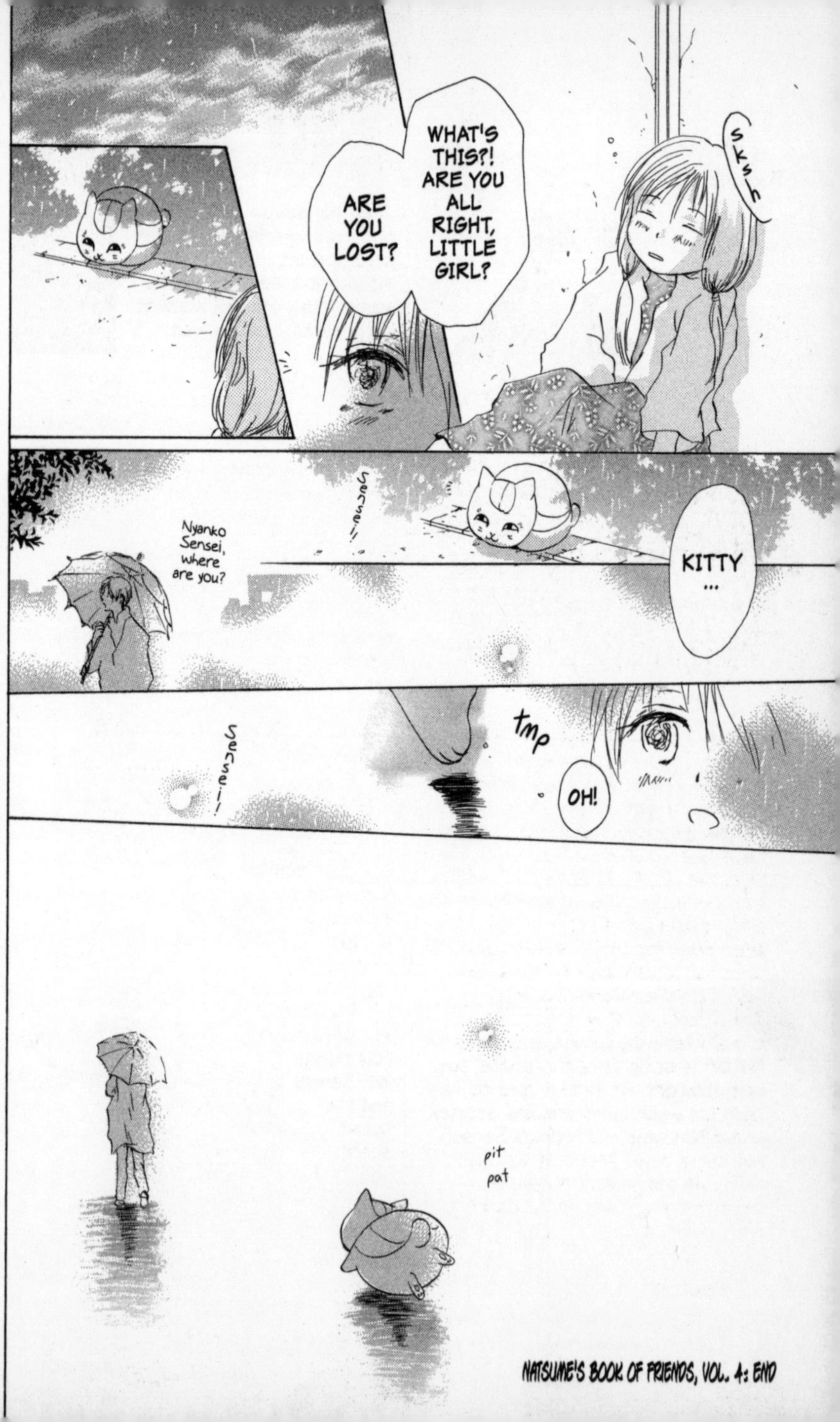
sksh
WHAT'S THIS?! ARE YOU ALL RIGHT, LITTLE GIRL?
ARE YOU LOST?
KITTY ...
Sensei!!
Nyanko Sensei, where are you?
OH!
tmp
Sensei!!
pit pat
NATSUME'S BOOK OF FRIENDS, VOL. 4: END

AFTERWORD

CHAPTER 13
Melting in Spring

I was fortunate enough that they published this as a separate booklet insert in the magazine. When I took the meticulously crafted booklet in my hands, I was moved.

Since it was an insert, I kept in mind that people may be reading it for the first time. I had a really hard time with it, and at first the yokai had possessed some other object, but it didn't have good chemistry with Natsume. When I switched to the snow bunny, it worked.

I gave him rabbit ears because I wanted to include a scene where he was standing behind a paper screen, the ears looking like ogre horns. But I was so busy editing it down that I forgot to reinsert the scene. I had fun drawing roly-poly things like Sensei and the snow bunny.

CHAPTER 14
Natsume Goes to the Hot Springs

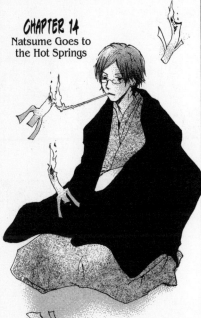

Natsume went on his first overnight trip. I wanted to try all sorts of things since Natori was making a repeat appearance, but then I was given the chance to have Natsume be the first manga in that month's issue. Since it's an important slot, I aimed for a story suitable for first-time readers. The two of them have gotten so used to lying with smiles on their faces, but they're finally realizing that there's something inherently wrong with that. Natori is good at giving advice, but not comfort. At first, I used to feel oddly sad when I was drawing stories about Natsume and Nyanko Sensei, but these days I feel that way with Natsume and Natori. Maybe that means they're starting to understand each other.

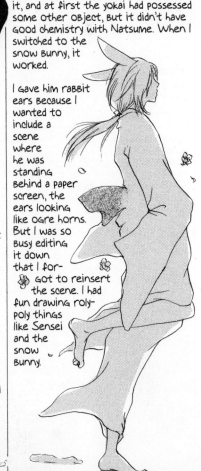

CHAPTER 15 The Man Among the Cherry Blossoms

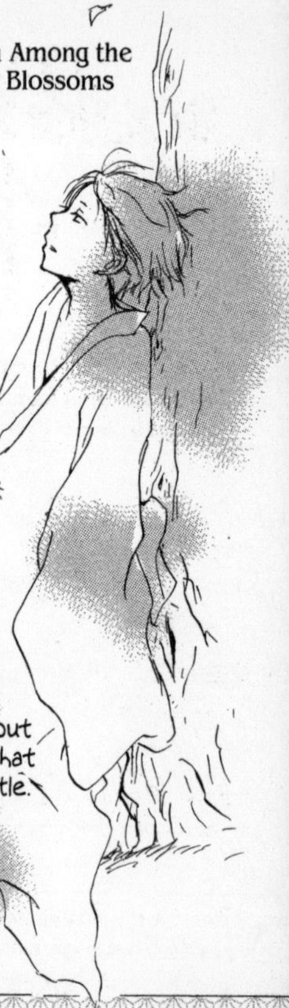

There were a bunch of soft stories in a row, so I wanted something with a little sting. I considered a story about a tree growing out of Natsume, but then it looked unexpectedly painful, so I changed it to blooming flowers. And then... I was actually asked to do the magazine cover! (I was super elated, but also scared that I wasn't worthy.) So I decided a story that celebrated with flowers would be appropriate. I love stereotypical creepy stories like strange shadowy figures inside paintings.

○ SPECIAL EPISODE 1

Working on a 16-page story was challenging and exciting in a different way, and I had fun. I was so happy that I could draw Natsume from someone else's perspective. He should always be slightly prickly.

○ SPECIAL EPISODE 2

With only 16 pages to work with, I was worried that my layout would be full of small panels, so I chose to draw kids. I feel that Natsume had a different coping mechanism when he was little.

○ SPECIAL EPISODE 3

I was nervous about doing an 8-page story. All the short episodes have a kid theme. It was fun to draw a troubling day for Nyanko Sensei.

I was finally able to pass the three-volume threshold with Natsume, thanks to my determined and patient editors and readers. I remember how I cried from joy when my editor told me volume I would get my first belly band around the dust jacket.

Special thanks to:
Tamao Ohki
Chika
Mr. Sato
My sister
Thank you so much.

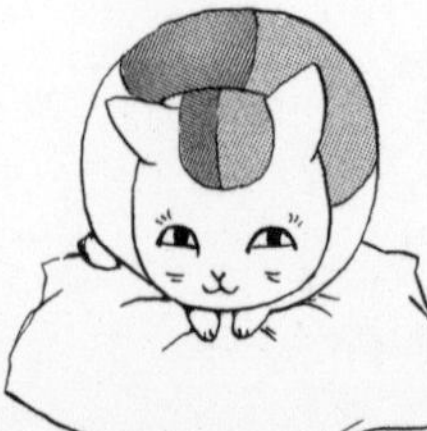

I'll take the greatest care to make an interesting manga. Please continue to support it!

Thank you so much.

Yuki Midorikawa
緑川ゆき

AFTERWORD: END

Natsume's BOOK of FRIENDS

VOLUME 4 END NOTES

PAGE 13, PANEL 8: *Guardian statues*
Statues are often found outside of Shinto shrines as guardians against evil. The designs are Chinese in origin.

PAGE 72, PANEL 6: *Family bath*
Public baths and hot springs are very common in Japan and come in various types. Family baths are essentially private hot springs (*onsen*) for families, couples, groups, etc.

PAGE 80, PANEL 1: *Rakkyo*
Pickled shallots served as a condiment.

PAGE 80, PANEL 5: *Sashimi*
Thinly sliced raw fish served with soy sauce or simple garnishes.

PAGE 96, PANEL 8: *Paulownia*
Also called *kiri* in Japanese, or the "princess tree," since the legend says the name *Paulownia* is in honor of Queen Anna Pavlovna of the Netherlands. Paulownia wood is very effective in keeping out humidity and is therefore often used for clothes chests in Japan.

PAGE 110, PANEL 4: *¥500, ¥300*
Currently the exchange rate is around $1 to ¥90. So ¥500 is about $5.50, and ¥300 is about $3.30.

PAGE 128, PANEL 4: *Jizo*
A bodhisattva often portrayed as a Buddhist monk who carries a staff with six rings. He is also considered a guardian of children and travelers, and his statues are common throughout Japan.

PAGE 149, PANEL 2: *Sweetfish*
Ayu in Japanese. A freshwater fish related to smelt.

PAGE 149, PANEL 2: *Akebi*
A purple fruit that grows on vines. When ripe, the pod splits open to reveal seeds surrounded by sweet white pulp.

VOLUME 4 END NOTES CONTINUED

PAGE 185, PANEL 3: *Bunnies could die*
There is an old wives' tale that rabbits die when they get wet.

PAGE 187, PANEL 8: *Police box*
Called *kôban* in Japanese, these are small neighborhood police stations, usually with a few assigned officers at a time.

PAGE 190, AUTHOR NOTE: *Belly band*
The thin strip of paper often found on Japanese paperbacks, which can be decorative or used for advertising. Called *obi* in Japanese, after the wide strips of fabric used to belt kimono.

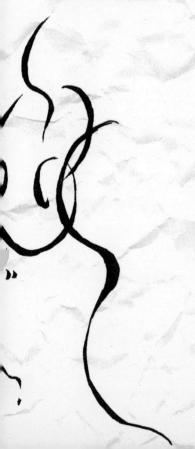

Yuki Midorikawa
is the creator of *Natsume's Book of Friends*, which was nominated for the Manga Taisho (Cartoon Grand Prize). Her other titles published in Japan include *Hotarubi no Mori e* (Into the Forest of Fireflies), *Hiiro no Isu* (The Scarlet Chair) and *Akaku Saku Koe* (The Voice That Blooms Red).

NATSUME'S BOOK OF FRIENDS

Vol. 4
Shojo Beat Edition

STORY AND ART BY Yuki Midorikawa

Translation & Adaptation Lillian Olsen
Touch-up Art & Lettering Sabrina Heep
Design Fawn Lau
Editor Pancha Diaz

Natsume Yujincho by Yuki Midorikawa
© Yuki Midorikawa 2007
All rights reserved.
First published in Japan in 2007 by HAKUSENSHA, Inc., Tokyo.
English language translation rights arranged with HAKUSENSHA, Inc., Tokyo.

Printed in the U.S.A.

Published by VIZ Media, LLC
P.O. Box 77010
San Francisco, CA 94107

10 9 8 7 6 5 4 3 2 1
First printing, October 2010

PARENTAL ADVISORY
NATSUME'S BOOK OF FRIENDS is rated T for Teen
and is recommended for ages 16 and up.
This volume contains fantasy violence.
ratings.viz.com

www.viz.com

www.shojobeat.com

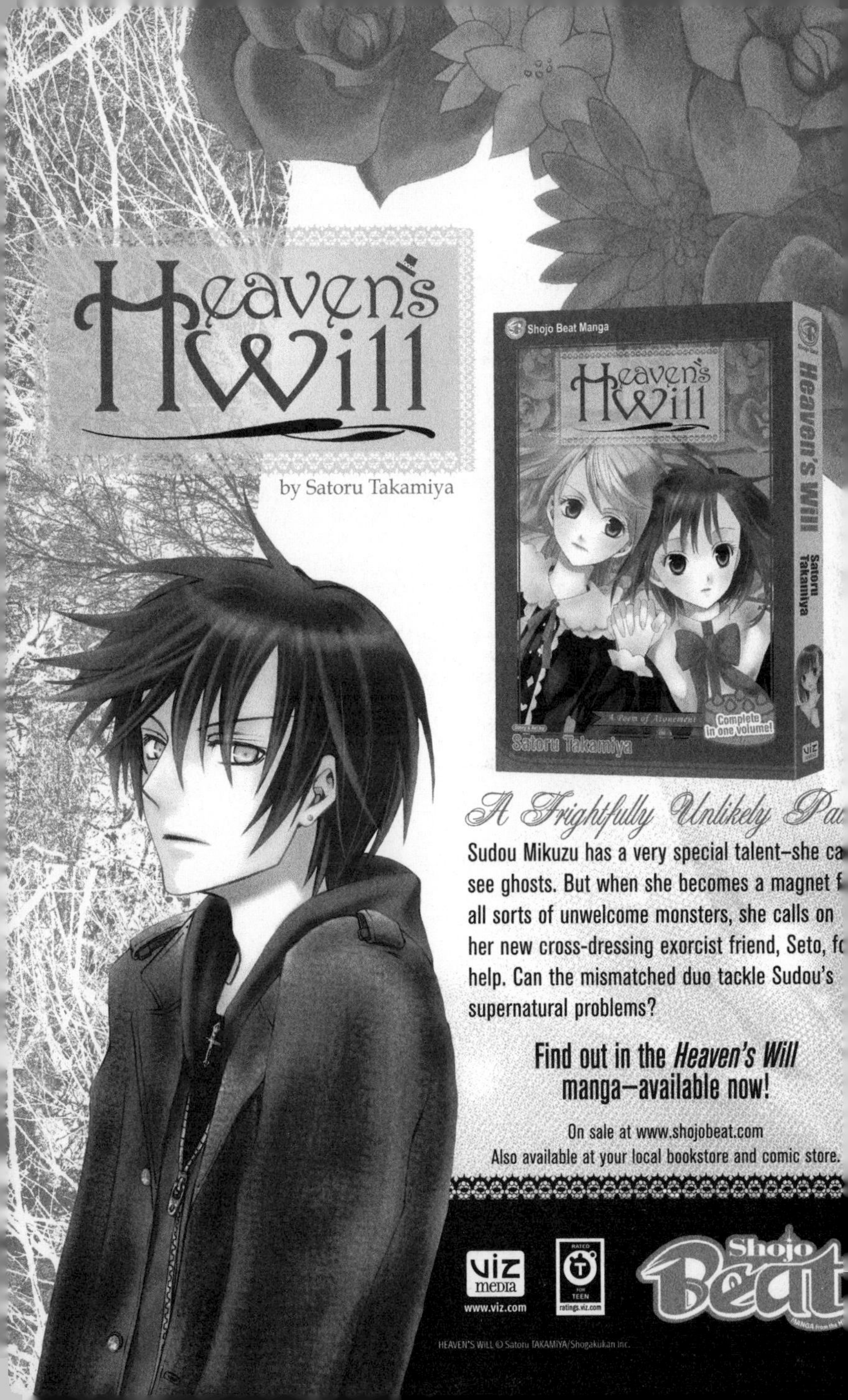
Heaven's Will
by Satoru Takamiya
Shojo Beat Manga
Heaven's Will
Heaven's Will
Satoru Takamiya
A Poem of Atonement
Story & Art by
Satoru Takamiya
Complete in one volume!
A Frightfully Unlikely Pa
Sudou Mikuzu has a very special talent–she ca
see ghosts. But when she becomes a magnet f
all sorts of unwelcome monsters, she calls on
her new cross-dressing exorcist friend, Seto, fo
help. Can the mismatched duo tackle Sudou's
supernatural problems?
Find out in the Heaven's Will manga—available now!
On sale at www.shojobeat.com
Also available at your local bookstore and comic store.
VIZ media
www.viz.com
RATED T FOR TEEN
ratings.viz.com
Shojo Beat
MANGA from the H
HEAVEN'S WILL © Satoru TAKAMIYA/Shogakukan Inc.

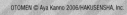